Feminist Theologies

Feminist Theologies

A Companion

Edited by

Kerrie Handasyde
Stephen Burns
and
Katharine Massam

scm press

© Kerrie Handasyde, Stephen Burns and Katharine Massam 2024

Published in 2024 by SCM Press
Editorial office
3rd Floor, Invicta House,
110 Golden Lane,
London EC1Y 0TG, UK
www.scmpress.co.uk

SCM Press is an imprint of Hymns Ancient & Modern Ltd
(a registered charity)

Hymns Ancient & Modern® is a registered trademark of
Hymns Ancient & Modern Ltd
13A Hellesdon Park Road, Norwich,
Norfolk NR6 5DR, UK

All rights reserved. No part of this publication may be reproduced,
stored in a retrieval system, or transmitted,
in any form or by any means, electronic, mechanical,
photocopying or otherwise, without the prior permission of
the publisher, SCM Press.

The editors and contributors have asserted their right under the Copyright,
Designs and Patents Act 1988 to be identified as the Author of this Work

British Library Cataloguing in Publication data
A catalogue record for this book is available
from the British Library

ISBN: 978-0-334-06120-5

Typeset by Regent Typesetting

Contents

Contributors	vii
Introduction: A Special Interest Subject?	xiii
Stephen Burns, Kerrie Handasyde and Katharine Massam	

Part 1 Right of Way

1. Global Christianity and Demographics — 3
   Gina A. Zurlo
2. Latina Feminist Theologies in the United States — 15
   Nancy Elizabeth Bedford
3. Asian Feminist Theologies: A Postcolonial Approach — 30
   Agnes M. Brazal
4. Good Feminist Collaboration — 42
   Cathryn McKinney and Rebekah Pryor

Part 2 Right

5. Poverty, Inequality and their Intersections — 57
   Gale A. Yee
6. Ecofeminism, Theology and the Rise of Alt-Right Christian Nationalism — 70
   Heather Eaton
7. Masculinities: From Feminist Critique to Ensoiled Ecologies — 87
   Al Barrett and Simon Sutcliffe
8. Body/Image — 101
   Hannah Bacon
9. Feminist and Queer Theologies: Friends or Foes? — 113
   Lisa Isherwood
10. Sex and Research: The Twin Loci of Consent — 122
    Karen O'Donnell

| 11 | 'A Solidarity Dance': Feminist Approaches to Abuse
Jane Chevous, Alana Harris and Antonia Sobocki | 135 |

Part 3 Write

12	'O for a thousand tongues': Feminist Theology, Narrative and Storytelling *Tina Beattie*	151
13	Systematic Theology *Janice McRandal*	163
14	Christa/x *Stephen Burns*	175
15	Mariology as Patriarchal Theological Construct: An Ongoing Challenge for Feminist Theology *Cristina Lledo Gomez*	183
16	Post-Christian Feminism *Michael W. Brierley*	197

Part 4 Rite

17	Art and the Theology of Difference *Claire Renkin*	217
18	Feminist Preaching: A Proclamatory Movement to End Patriarchy for Full Humanity *HyeRan Kim-Cragg*	232
19	Vocation: Listening, Persistence and the Hard Work within the Church *Kerrie Handasyde*	245
20	Wording Prayer: Method and Praxis in Feminist Theologies *Gail Ramshaw*	257
21	From a Thursday to a Sunday *Anne Elvey*	270

| *Index of Names and Subjects* | 281 |

Contributors

Hannah Bacon is Professor of Theology at the University of Chester, UK. Her publications include *Feminist Theology and Contemporary Dieting Culture: Sin, Salvation and Women's Weight Loss Narratives* (2019), *Alternative Salvations: Engaging the Secular and the Sacred*, co-edited with Wendy Dossett and Steve Knowles (2015), and *What's Right with the Trinity? Conversations in Feminist Theology* (2009).

Al Barrett is Vicar of Hodge Hill, Birmingham, UK. His publications include *Finding the Treasure: Good News from the Estates: Reflections from the Church of England Estates Theology Project* (editor, 2023), *Interrupting the Church's Flow: A Radically Receptive Political Theology in the Urban Margins* (2020), and *Being Interrupted: Reimagining the Church's Mission from the Outside, In*, co-authored with Ruth Harley (2020).

Tina Beattie is Director of the Catherine of Siena College based at Roehampton University, UK. She was also Professor of Catholic Theology at Roehampton University. Her publications include *Between Two Rivers* (2023), *The Last Supper According to Martha and Mary* (2021), *The Good Priest* (2019), *New Catholic Feminism: Theology, Gender Theory and Dialogue* (2004), and *God's Mother, Eve's Advocate: A Marian Narrative of Women's Salvation* (2002).

Nancy Bedford is Georgia Harkness Professor of Theology at Garrett-Evangelical Theological Seminary in Chicago, Illinois, USA. Her publications include *Nuestra Fe: Una Introducción a la Teología Cristiana*, co-authored with Guillermo Hansen (2023), *Who Was Jesus and What Does it Mean to Follow Him?* (2021), and *Galatians: A Theological Commentary on the Bible* (2016).

Agnes Brazal is Professor of Theology at De La Salle University, Manilla, Philippines. Her publications include *500 Years of Christianity and the*

Global Filipino/a: Postcolonial Perspectives, co-edited with Cristina Lledo Gomez and Ma Marilou Ibita (2024), *A Theology of South East Asia: Liberation-Postcolonial Ethics in the Philippines* (2019), *Intercultural Church: Bridge of Solidarity in the Migration Context*, co-authored with Emmanuel de Guzman (2015), and *Feminist Cyberethics in Asia: Religious Discources on Human Connectivity*, co-edited with Kochurabi Abraham (2014).

Michael W. Brierley is Director of Formation at Ripon College Cuddesdon near Oxford, UK. His publications include *A Way of Putting It: Sermons of Peter Atkinson* (editor, 2023), *Life after Tragedy: Essays on Faith and the First World War Evoked by Geoffrey Studdert Kennedy*, co-edited with Georgina Byrne (2017), and *Public Life and the Place of the Church: Reflections to Honour the Bishop of Oxford* (editor, 2016). He is book reviews editor for *Modern Believing*.

Stephen Burns is Professor of Theology at Pilgrim Theological College, University of Divinity, Melbourne, Australia. His publications include *Anglican Theology: Postcolonial Perspectives*, co-edited with James Tengatenga (2024), Ann Loades' *Explorations in Twentieth Century Theology and Philosophy: People Precoccupied with God* (editor, 2023), *From the Shores of Silence: Conversations in Feminist Practical Theology*, co-edited with Ashley Cocksworth and Rachel Starr (2023), *Twentieth Century Anglican Theologians: From Evelyn Underhill to Esther Mombo*, co-edited with Bryan Cones and James Tengatenga (2021), *Liturgy With a Difference: Beyond Inclusion in Christian Assembly*, co-edited with Bryan Cones (2019) and *Postcolonial Practice of Ministry: Leadership, Liturgy, Interfaith Engagement*, co-edited with Kwok Pui-lan (2016). He edits the *International Journal for the Study of the Christian Church*.

Jane Chevous is Director of Survivors Voices, UK. Her publications include *From Silence to Sanctuary: A Guide to Understanding, Preventing and Responding to Abuse* (2023).

Heather Eaton is Professor of Conflict Studies at St Paul's University, Ottawa, Canada. Her publications include *Earthly Things: Immanence, New Materials, and Planetary Thinking*, co-edited with Karen Bray (2023), *Advancing Nonviolent and Social Transformation: New Perspectives on Nonviolent Themes*, co-edited with Lauren Michelle Levesque (2016), *Introducing Ecofeminist Theologies* (2005), and *Ecofeminism and Globalization: Exploring Culture, Context and Religion*, co-edited with Lois Ann Lorentzen (2003).

CONTRIBUTORS

Anne Elvey is Honorary Research Associate at Pilgrim Theological College, University of Divinity, Melbourne, Australia. Her publications include *Reading with Earth: Contributions of the New Materialism to an Ecological Feminist Hermeneutics* (2022), *Reading the Magnificat in Australia: Unsettling Engagements* (2020), *Ecological Aspects of War: Engagement with Biblical Texts*, co-edited with Keith Dyer (2019), *Ecological Aspects of War: Religious and Theological Perspectives*, co-edited with Deborah Guess and Keith Dyer (2017), and *Climate Change and Culture Change: Religious Responses and Responsibilities*, co-edited with David Gormley-O'Brien (2013).

Cristina Lledo Gomez is Presentation Sisters Lecturer at the Broken Bay Institute, Sydney, Australia. Her publications include *500 Years of Christianity and the Global Filipino/a: Postcolonial Perspectives*, co-edited with Agnes Brazal and Ma Marilou Ibita (2024), and *Church as Woman and Mother: Historical and Theological Foundations* (2016).

Kerrie Handasyde is Associate Professor in the History of Christianity at Pilgrim Theological College, University of Divinity, Melbourne, Australia. Her publications include *Seeing Christ in Australia Since 1850*, co-edited with Sean Winter (2024), *God in the Landscape: Studies in the Literary History of Australian Protestant Dissent* (2021), and *Contemporary Feminist Theologies: Power, Authority, Love*, co-edited with Rebekah Pryor and Cathryn McKinney (2021).

Alana Harris is Reader in Modern British Social, Cultural and Gender History at Kings College, London, UK. Her publications include *Oxford History of British and Irish Catholicism, Volume V: Recapturing the Aspostolate of the Laity, 1914–2021* (editor, 2023), *Rescripting Religion in the City: Migration and Religious Identity in the Modern Metropolis*, co-edited with Jane Garnett (2018), *Faith in the Family: A Lived Religious History of English Catholicism, 1945–82* (2016), and *Redefining Christian Britain: Post 1945 Perspectives*, co-edited with Jane Garnett, Matthew Grimley et al. (2007).

Lisa Isherwood is Professor of Practice at University of Wales, Trinity St David, UK. Her publications include *Queer Ministers' Voices from the Global South: 'A Burning Fire in My Bones'*, co-edited with Hugo Córdova Quero (2023), *Women and Christianity in the Modern Age (1920–Today)*, co-edited with Megan Clay (2022), *The Indecent Theology of Marcella Althaus-Reid: Voices from Asia and Latin America*, co-edited with Hugo Córdova Quero (2020), *Contemporary Theological*

Approaches to Sexuality, co-edited with Dirk von der Horst (2017), *Post-Christian Feminisms: A Critical Approach*, co-edited with Kathleen McPhillips (2013), *Dancing Theology in Fetish Boots: Essays in Honour of Marcella Althaus Reid*, co-edited with Mark Jordon (2010), and *Trans/formations*, co-edited with Marcella Althaus-Reid (2009). She edits the journal *Feminist Theology*.

HyeRan Kim-Cragg is Principal and Timothy Eaton Memorial Church Professor of Preaching at Emmanuel College, University of Toronto, Canada. Her publications include *Conversations about Divine Mystery: Essays in Honor of Gail Ramshaw*, co-edited with Stephen Burns (2023), *Practical Theology Amid Climate Crises*, co-edited with Pamela McCarroll (2023), *Postcolonial Preaching: Creating a Ripple Effect* (2021), *Reading In-between: How Minoritized Communities Interpret the Bible in Canada*, co-edited with Nestor Medina and Alison Hari-Singh (2019), *Religion and Migration: Negotiating Hospitality, Agency and Vulnerability*, co-edited with Andrea Bieler et al. (2019), *Interdependence: A Postcolonial Feminist Practical Theology* (2018), *1–2 Thessalonians: A Wisdom Commentary*, co-authored with Florence Morgan Gillman and Mary Ann Bevis (2016), and *Hebrews: A Wisdom Commentary*, co-authored with Mary Ann Bevis (2015).

Katharine Massam is Professor of History and Chair of the Academic Board of the University of Divinity, Melbourne, Australia. Her publications include *The Promise and the Blessing: Presentation Sisters in Victoria Since Vatican II* (2024), 'Dialogues of Secular and Sacred', a special issue of the *Journal for the Academic Study of Religion*, co-edited with Kerrie Handasyde (2022), *A Bridge Between: Spanish Benedictine Missionary Women in Australia* (2019), and *Sacred Threads: Catholic Spirituality in Australia, 1922–1962* (1996).

Cathryn McKinney is Professional Supervision Program Director at the University of Divinity, Melbourne, Australia. Her publications include *Contemporary Feminist Theologies: Power, Authority, Love*, co-edited with Kerrie Handasyde and Rebekah Pryor (2021).

Janice McRandal is Director of the Cooperative, Brisbane, Australia. Her publications include *Contested Theology: Sport, Bodies, and Motion* (2024), *Sarah Coakley and the Future of Systematic Theology* (editor, 2016), and *Christian Doctrine and the Grammar of Difference: A Contribution to Feminist Systematic Theology* (2015).

CONTRIBUTORS

Karen O'Donnell is Director of Studies and Lecturer in Worship and Human Community at Westcott House, Cambridge, UK. Her publications include *The Dark Womb: Re-conceiving Theology through Reproductive Loss* (2022), *Bearing Witness: Intersectional Perspectives on Trauma Theology*, co-edited with Katie Cross (2022), *Feminist Trauma Theology: Body, Scripture and Church in Critical Perspective*, co-edited with Katie Cross (2020), and *Broken Bodies: The Eucharist, Mary and Body in Trauma Theology* (2018).

Rebekah Pryor is a visual artist and Doctor of Professional Practice Program Director at the University of Divinity, Melbourne, Australia. Her publications include *Feminist Theologies: Interstices and Fractures*, co-edited with Stephen Burns (2023), *Motherly: Reimagining the Maternal Body in Feminist Theology and Contemporary Art* (2022), and *Contemporary Feminist Theologies: Power, Authority, Love*, co-edited with Kerrie Handasyde and Cathryn McKinney (2021).

Gail Ramshaw is a scholar of liturgical language living near Washington DC, USA. She was Professor of Religion at La Salle University, Philadelphia, USA. Her publications include *Blessing and Beseeching: Seventy Prayers Inspired by the Scriptures* (2022), *Word of God, Word of Life: Understanding the Three-Year Lectionaries* (2019), *Saints on Sunday: Voices from the Past Enlivening Our Worship* (2018), *Pray, Praise, and Give Thanks* (2017), *What is Christianity? An Introduction to the Christian Religion* (2013), *Christian Worship: 100,000 Sundays of Symbols and Rituals* (2009), and *Under the Tree of Life: The Religion of a Feminist Christian* (2002).

Claire Renkin is Lecturer in Art History and Spirituality at Yarra Theological Union, University of Divinity, Melbourne, Australia. Her publications include *Re-imagining the Eucharist: Explorations in Feminist Theology and Ethics*, co-edited with Anne Elvy et al. (2012).

Antonia Sobocki is Director of LOUDfence, UK.

Simon Sutcliffe is Learning Development Officer for the North West and Mann, Methodist Church of Great Britain.

Gale A. Yee is Emerita Nancy W. King Professor of Biblical Studies, Episcopal Divinity School, Cambridge, Massachusetts, USA. Her publications include *Psalms: My Psalm, My Context*, co-edited with Athalya

Brenner-Idan (2024), *Towards an Asian American Biblical Hermeneutics: An Intersectional Anthology* (2020), *The Hebrew Bible: Feminist and Intersectional Perspectives* (editor, 2018), *The Fortress Commentary on the Old Testament and Apocrypha*, co-edited with Hugh Page and Matthew Coomber (2014), *Judges and Method: New Approaches to Biblical Studies* (editor, 2007), and *Poor Banished Children of Eve: Women as Evil in the Hebrew Bible* (2003).

Gina Zurlo is Co-Director of the Center for the Study of Global Christianity at Gordon-Conwell Theological Seminary in South Hamilton, Massachusetts, USA. Her publications include *From Nairobi to the World: David B. Barrett and the Re-imagining of World Christianity* (editor, 2023), *Portraits of Global Christianity: Research and Reflections in Honor of Todd M. Johnson* (editor, 2023), *Women in World Christianity: Building and Sustaining a Global Movement* (2023), *Global Christianity: A Guide to the World's Largest Religion* (2022), and *The World Christian Encyclopedia*, co-edited with Todd Johnson (2019).

Introduction:
A Special Interest Subject?

More than 30 years ago Janet Martin Soskice wrote that 'sexism is not something that hurts women's feelings, sexism kills millions and millions of girls and women each year', collating information from the 'eminent Indian economist' Armatya Sen to make this devastating claim (Soskice 1995, p. 55). And as Gina Zurlo reminds us in Chapter 1 of this collection, 'women are not monolith, and their oppression is not the same everywhere'. Western readers of such assertions may be shielded – somewhat – from proximity to the sexist killing of millions, yet are surely well aware of manifestations of their own oppression in working pay gaps, health-care provision and lack and, not least, of the prevalence of abuse at home. Australian research has suggested that at least Anglicans in that country are more likely than the general population to encounter domestic violence (Pepper and Powell 2022). And with whatever awareness or lack of awareness, shielding or otherwise, sexist killing continues somewhere.

Do feminist theologies have resources to engage and contest these situations? It is not obvious that there is wide conviction that we do. Feminist theology – if it is present with any impact at all on university and seminary curricula, or on local Christian assemblies and their liturgical resources – seems often to be a 'special interest subject', annexed from whatever is presented as mainstream (recall 'male-stream' *a la* Mary Daly's 'dicktionary' (Daly 1978)); a particular lens at the tail end of optics. It may also be deemed of limited relevance as opposed to universally interesting. (For example, in the curious arrangement of the 2005 edition of influential British textbook *The Modern Theologians*, feminist theology is 'perspectival' as distinct from 'classic' work of only male European theologians. An earlier 1997 edition of *The Modern Theologians* had placed feminist theology among 'transregional movements' of European theology and within a region of 'theologies of North America' (Ford and Muers 2005; Ford 1997)). Such hardworking categorizations run counter to the view that 'there is no such thing as theology. There is only contextual theology' (Bevans 2002, p. 3). At the same time, links between gender and killing, pay gaps, health and housing lacks, and violence remain peripheral to much of what preoccupies the theological conversation.

This Companion seeks to offer snapshots of the contemporary character of feminist theologies, intentionally and emphatically plural. Our title, using 'feminist' as a qualifier, may also apparently endorse leaving feminism on a perspectival periphery away from the real business at the centre of the discipline. Just one way of starting to contest such marginalization is to assert the place of feminist theology in a deep trajectory of theological endeavour in which second-wave feminist engagement emerged in the 1970s, not least in Britain. That early work often clustered around issues relating to the fight towards the ordination of women in the Church of England, ahead of that milestone in 1992, including for example notable contributions galvanized by Monica Furlong (Furlong 1988; 1991). Jenny Daggers traces particular origins of this movement to 1978 because the Christian Women's Information and Resources Network (CWIRES) was founded in that year (Daggers 2002). Subsequently, the first meetings of the British and Irish Summer School in Feminist Theology in 1989, a university symposium at Lancaster in the late 1990s that asked 'Is there a future for feminist theology?', and the positive responses to the symposium question implied not least by the new journal *Feminist Theology* from 2000, chart an insistent conversation. Lisa Isherwood has been a vital presence among a larger number of persons at the heart of both the journal and various other publishing initiatives. Isherwood's leadership was instrumental in the important series of 'Introductions in Feminist Theology' in collaboration with Sheffield University Press, a shorter-lived collaboration with SCM Press ('Controversies in Contextual Theology', which expired after the death of the other general editor, Marcella Althaus-Reid), and she is also at the helm of a long-standing series with Routledge, 'Gender, Theology and Spirituality'. Isherwood has penned a formidable body of feminist theology within and beyond these series.

Other British publishing in feminist theology through this period included writing by Ann Loades (Loades 1987; 1990), who died in 2022. Her *Feminist Theology: A Reader* (1990) was a milestone, published alongside a companion volume edited by Ursula King that brought voices from 'the Third World' to wider attention (1992), heralding a crucial shift. Additionally, King was productive with other important collections, including with Tina Beattie (e.g. King 1994; King and Beattie 2004), as well as other work in her own hand. Beattie in her turn has produced some of the most

INTRODUCTION

important doctrinal work in feminist mode (Beattie 2002). Also emerging out of the university contexts was the provocative 'post-Christian' stance developed by Daphne Hampson (Hampson 1990; 1992) while from theological colleges work by Elaine Storkey in a series of books beginning with *What's Right with Feminism?* (Storkey 1985; and, for example, 2018, 2000), was particularly influential among evangelicals.

In broad terms, Loades' *Reader* animated the challenge of North Atlantic feminism while King's companion put the task of wider cross-cultural perspectives firmly on the agenda, though they have not always been taken up in Britain – or elsewhere. It is disturbing to note the near or total absence of feminist perspectives in theological education in too many contemporary contexts.

The collaborative nature of some of the feminist theology of the era – notwithstanding very different convictions emerging – is suggested not only by readers and anthologies but by the outstanding and painstaking collaborative work of *Swallowing a Fishbone? Feminist Theologians Debate Christianity*, edited by Daphne Hampson (Hampson 1996). Over time, less positive assessments of the future of feminist theology came to prominence in Sarah Coakley (one of the voices in *Swallowing a Fishbone?*), concerned to differentiate her work from many of her peers (e.g. Coakley 2008; 2013). Nicola Slee, also a participant in *Swallowing a Fishbone* and among the contributors to the Loades reader, published her own introduction to feminist theology in 2004 and, in the same year, a major work of empirical research on women's faith development (Slee 2004b; 2004c). This in turn was instrumental in activating discussion of feminist perspectives in practical theology, a field in which Elaine Graham's work has also been highly significant (e.g. Graham 2018). They each remain among the most vibrant voices in feminist theologies from the 1980s into the 2020s.

The arcs of feminist theological enquiry have subsequently developed much more diffuse foci. A third wave allied closely with queer and 'indecent' approaches has been key in this. It is linked especially with contributions by Marcella Althaus-Reid (e.g. Althaus-Reid 2000; 2001; 2004), and has also been energetically represented and promoted by Isherwood. In the meantime, vibrant 'new' voices have emerged – some of whom are included in this book among a wider international conversation of feminist theologies. Feminist theologies are now concerned about far broader issues than 'hurt' to 'women's feelings'. They carry and commend a comprehensive vision, reflecting an 'enlarged feminism' (Loades 2000, p. 1) which also emerged in response to some of its second-wave manifestations.

This Companion is arranged around categories suggested by Nicola Slee's poem 'Writing the Body' (in Slee 2004a). In that poem, Slee juxtaposes 'write', 'right' and 'rite'. She uses 'write' to speak of things that 'deserve to be heard' about women's lives and bodies, spoken about their experiences and perspectives. She uses 'right' to commend 'throw[ing] off frozen forms' that have 'locked in' women, in search instead of a new 'befriending' of self. And she uses 'rite' to speak about 'singing, dancing' and otherwise occupying 'sacred space'. We have taken inspiration from Slee's evocative ideas and turned them to this book. So here, a skein on 'write' is to do with ways in which theology is written, for example in its disciplines, in the so-called systematic agenda, and its presumed content encompassing Mary and Christ/a/x. Here, 'right' relates to feminist sense about getting things right, making best efforts to think things through in relation to issues such as consent or poverty, while 'rite' considers aspects of feminist expression of spirituality as it touches and wrestles with worship in Christian tradition including prayer and preaching, in a section that ends in an evocative exploration of paschal mystery. To these three skeins we have added a fourth of our own: 'right of way', so as to invite reflection on the diversity of feminist theologies. The book opens with this section, and begins intentionally with 'global Christianity', before moving to discussions arising from particular regions that voice something of the rich wisdoms of *Mujerista*, womanist approaches, and to the dynamics of collaboration as a distinguishing feminist approach. In offering these categories we acknowledge that the distinction we find problematic between 'classic' and 'perspectival' theologies was itself heralded by a caveat that any grouping 'should not have too much read into it' (Ford 1997, p. ix). The same applies to the categories we have chosen, even as we want to encourage active reflection on how feminist theologies from any place might listen widely, test Christian tradition, struggle with Christian community, and do their best in the gaps where more justice and flourishing still awaits.

Welcome to the conversation.

Part 1: Right of Way

We set a large scene at the outset with global Christianity, seeking to decentre traditional flows of feminist theologies. Although our coverage here, and throughout, is partial and indicative, and seeks to invite further discussion, this section invites reflection on the diversity of feminist theologies. Christianity's shift to the global South involves and depends

INTRODUCTION

on women. Women are not simply 'special interest' subjects in this shift but central to it, especially Black women and Women of Colour. Reminding us that there is no genderless experience of the world, religion or the church, Gina Zurlo uses the 2019 United Nations Development report to show that on current trends gender inequality will persist for at least another century, even on the assumption that progress continues, and also allowing for the many organizations, including churches, that assume the situation of women can be understood through collecting data on men, or buildings.

If women have been erased in the statistics and narratives of 'World Christianity', they have carried the Christian story, sustained networks that support conversion and remain vital in the life of faith communities. The contextual theologizing led by women in the global South is generating new questions and giving voice to experience beyond cisgender white theologians, reflecting the far greater participation of women in the life, if not the leadership, of the churches.

Two instances of the development of contextual feminist theologies follow. Nancy Elizabeth Bedford explores the creativity of liminality and hybridity in Latina feminist theologies in the US context. Distinct from but related to the liberation theologies of Latin America, they are written not in Spanish but in an English that 'is flexible, hybrid, de-colonial, and amenable to code-switching and syntactical experimentation'. There is particular good news here in the challenge that the incarnation poses to white assumptions, especially in the reality of pain and suffering for both Mary and Jesus. Multifaceted devotion to Our Lady of Guadalupe, coupled with an emphasis on the daily and mundane, and on 'theologizing together', *teologia en conjunto*, affirm the integration of feminist with religious and spiritual concerns. Then Agnes Brazal traces the move to postcolonial-liberative approaches within Asian feminist theology, demonstrating a hermeneutic of appreciation alongside a hermeneutic of suspicion in reading local, precolonial culture through two themes in particular. The balance of the 'opposites' *lakas–ganda* (strength and beauty) in the Philippines, and Jesus-Sophia as an example of this balance, argues against rigid gender complementarity. The indwelling of the spirit in all things including the cyborg, as in the tools of an Asian craft worker, is the focus of discussion of the anthropology and ecclesiology of the virtual world, and an argument for the incorporation of virtual realities into the body of Christ.

Wider community and theologizing together are congruent with the final chapter in this section where Cathryn McKinney and Rebekah Pryor argue that feminist collaboration involves the dialogue of the self-aware, alert to and respectful of difference, always located in a particular context. Though not a geographical survey, McKinney and Pryor are highly alert to feminist navigations of different sorts. They suggest that feminist theologies engage collaborative processes that are open to the divine. Raising the question of what obstructs good collaboration they point to the need for honest agreement on an intention that does not harm or deceive others in order to maintain the right of way. In the intimate negotiation of power and authority, the hallmark of successful collaboration is liberative change, an enabling of the right of way.

Part 2: Right

Feminist theologies speak to systemic social issues, critiquing and seeking to reconstruct justly so that we might live in right relationship. As Gale Yee notes, systems of economics and power 'interlock' and, in turn, lock women into poverty. Her chapter evaluates methods of research in the cause of liberation, asking how intersectional analysis of poverty and inequality might lead to transformative policy and, with it, the transforming of lives. Seeking social transformation with a whole Earth perspective, Heather Eaton traces the development of ecofeminist theologies and advocates for the kind of 'sturdy analyses and effective actions' that ecofeminist theology might offer a world in crisis. Eaton's own analysis is rigorous in its refusal to settle for greenwashing of religious traditions, in its clear-eyed recognition that women are problematized while the whole ecology in which we live is ignored, and in its insistence on the connections between violence against women and violent disruption to the Earth's systems that manifest in cycles of conflict over resources such as water and arable land, and the 'rise of a political, patriotic and patriarchal Christianity'. Continuing the concern with ecology, Al Barrett and Simon Sutcliffe's chapter on masculinity calls on the work of Donna Haraway, bell hooks and others to critique traditional associations of masculinity as mastery, instead advocating for an earthy 'ensoiled' masculinity that plays, in humility, with the metaphor of humus.

Right as justice and right relationship seeks wholeness not only in the world but within the self, within the body. Hannah Bacon surveys decades of feminist responses to female bodies, both affirming and, problematically, essentializing. With attention to the drivers of the dieting industry, she critiques perfectionism and calls for researchers to listen to the experience of slimming women. In seeking wholeness, incarnational theologies offer profound possibilities for radical engagement with sexuality and, as Lisa Isherwood notes, understandings of sexuality have challenged and expanded the possibilities of incarnation to include queer bodies and queer theology. The quest for 'right' requires the unsettling of dualisms and fundamentalisms, and insists that the 'personal is political': affirmation of sexuality does not end in the privacy of the bedroom but intersects systemically with the whole of society, and the wholeness of divinity.

Concerned with research practice, Karen O'Donnell's chapter on ethical consent in scholarly research challenges policy-makers to look at negotiations around consent in the BDSM community, with its heightened awareness of dominance and submission, and to consider where 'pleasure and satisfaction' is found in the research participant experience. Wherever there is moral risk, feminist research demands attention be directed to power dynamics and the possibilities of abuse, but feminist theology also asks where is the divine, where is God in our midst. Recognizing that faith-based abuse and trauma is only beginning to be researched and confronted within the church, and how theologies and institutions have together had a 'uniquely devastating impact' on women, Jane Chevous, Alana Harris and Antonia Sobocki explore practical and research-based feminist responses. They offer reflections on 'right' and 'rite' praxis that survivor-researchers and survivor-activists employ in healing the body and the body of Christ: in particular, peer support groups following faith-based abuse and LOUDfence activism that might go some way towards righting 'betrayal and moral injury'.

Part 3: Write

Five chapters constitute our section representing the significance of how and what feminist theologians 'write', exploring disciplines, fields, categories and key areas of 'content'. As in other sections, the coverage here is neither comprehensive of the full suite of Christian doctrine nor definitive of feminist positions within it; instead these contributions are indicative and suggestive of the wider conversations that will repay deeper attention.

Tina Beattie opens with Chimamanda Ngozi Adichie to underline 'the danger of a single story' examining the creative rupture when feminist theologies scatter the assumptions of sacred texts. The foundations of this disruption lie in both postliberal theologies and liberal feminist theologies of the 1970s and 80s. Beattie looks for a postliberal feminist theology informed by the intertextuality of Kristeva and others, where the stories women tell contribute to upholding a Christian vision of justice and peace. Towards this, Kochurani Abraham's work on Catholic Syrian women in Kerala is a key example, broadening into reflections on the shaping power of language and how literature ('the stories we tell') can relocate theology.

Decisions about who sets the agenda often determine the work that is done. Janice McRandal's chapter on feminist challenges to systematic theology underlines the significance of where and with whom we theologize, as well as how, where and by whom theological work is made public. The shaping narratives of systematic theology have been hard to shift, as the indebtedness of leading figures like Sarah Coakley and Linn Tonstad to the Anglo-European academy suggests. McRandal calls for tools that will insist 'doctrine matters in tandem to materiality and that theological concepts are only ever alive to the living' in order to dismantle the 'master's house' and shape a new doctrinal dwelling. Solidarity with the community of women to which that dwelling belongs, outside structures that privilege race, gender and academic tradition, is the most powerful instrument for change.

The bright red dress of Emmanuel Garabay's Christ-figure at Emmaus suggests how the Christian community might be reimagined in feminist mode with the help of Christ/a/x. Stephen Burns tracks artists whose images have engaged theologians and the poetic work of theologians themselves, including Rita Nakashima Brock, Sally Douglas, Ivone Gebera and Nicola Slee, to highlight a vision 'more fully inclusive of the rich variety of humanity'. The 'everyday resurrections', and the persistence of sacred activity even through Holy Saturday, combines with and counters the traditions of suffering Christ/a/x to offer the exuberance of Garaby's vision. Similarly, Cristina Lledo Gomez explores the figure of Mary through lenses of dogma, piety and history to argue for a reclaiming of 'empowering motherhood' that counters both binary gender essentialism and male heteronormativity. Her account evokes the complexity of Mary 'as simultaneously a tool of oppression and a tool of survival, even a tool of liberation'. In that complexity, feminist attention to Mary as mother can fruitfully broaden her significance.

Galvanized by a pastoral encounter that interpreted as abusive what had seemed to be a joy-filled parish occasion, Michael Brierley's chapter explores the diversity of post-Christian feminist theologies, from a commitment to explore how and what faith might be reclaimed with integrity from 'an appalling abyss' of patriarchy. He takes the common usage of 'post' as 'after' (rather than the more academic option of 'post' as 'critical') and explores two post-Christian feminists, Mary Daly and Daphne Hampson, especially in relation to their readings of the doctrine of God.

As Beattie names the power of narrative, McRandal the striving for new solidarity, Burns and Gomez the sway of images within devotion, Brierley also holds that symbolic systems influence behaviour, and that 'doctrines need to be wholesomely constructed'. The test of 'wholesomeness' is not the same as intellectual coherence but likely to be a fruit of open dialogue on how symbolic systems and ethical concerns might enter into vibrant conversation.

Part 4: Rite

The final part of this Companion is to do with 'rite', engaging with aspects of Christian spirituality and wrestling with worship in Christian tradition. Five chapters in this section take us from art that confounds tradition, through the need for vigilance to maintain feminist preaching and authentic vocation, before we conclude with an evocative exploration of paschal mystery – an indication on our part that Christian tradition might continue to yield resources to feminist seekers and lovers.

The small ritual presentation of a wooden sculpture of 'Our Lady of the Amazon' to Pope Francis in 2019 provoked an outcry emblematic of the power of art to evade and expand beyond words. Claire Renkin's exploration of the reaction to the pregnant image of Pachamama, and the silencing of the women from the Amazon who identified her as Mary, leads her chapter. Further images of Mary, by Australian painter Jan Hynes, and of Mary Magdalene, famously by Donatello, combine to show how symbols emerge to convey, tease at and make possible new perspectives.

Gail Ramshaw writes of her experience of bringing her feminist convictions into Christian assembly over more than 50 years. Her own words for prayer – always in 'expansive language' – have had as much impact on several churches' liturgical resources as any feminist's work has. Her explorations of the practice of Christian worship have pioneered ways to remain present as a participant in Christian spirituality. As in her theological memoir *Under the Tree of Life* – on 'the religion of a feminist Christian' – she is of the view that 'even feminists need of what Christ might mean and the Spirit give' (Ramshaw 1999, pp. 73–86). In her chapter, she charts ten ways she has seen 'feminist-inspired' changes in worship among some Christians. These changes won't all be present everywhere, but might guide and inspire those willing to struggle for change in Christian institutions, enabling fresh discoveries of the divine 'Thesaurus of mercy' beckoned and addressed in the church's prayer.

HyeRan Kim-Cragg contributes on preaching, situating her own voice in a context of 'urgency' in which feminist concerns receive 'push back' in some churches. She examines an example of a sermon to arise from such push back, deeming it 'dangerous'. Then she proposes how feminist homileticians can preach towards liberation, calling out not only sexist but colonial, classist and racist diminution of human persons in order to proclaim possibilities of a different future. Kerrie Handasyde's chapter on vocation shows the call to preach, like the call to evangelize and to write, has been freighted with gendered assumptions about what is 'natural' and therefore 'decent' for women. Tracking the sidestepping of those assumptions, including through re-purposing maternalism to the racist interests of the settler nation and missionary church, Handasyde argues, with Catherine Keller and Heather Walton in particular, not for a theology of 'being' the heroic self but of 'becoming'. As she warns against complacency about 'progress', notes the reactive hardening of conservative strongholds against women's agency, and rejects self-serving 'training to keep up with the patriarchy', vocation encompasses the hope and courage for embodied, non-coercive engagement with others as 'we move toward God within "the dark"'.

Anne Elvey's meditation on the Triduum, the 'three days' from Maundy Thursday to Easter Day at the heart of the Christian calendar, brings the Companion to an evocative close. It invites to the brink of mystery, in the mode of her poem that stirs up awareness that we 'don't know the whole story', not least given the 'patriarchal denials' with which feminist theologies are concerned and determined to contest. Mysterious movements of words, as poems are, they too are best not 'explained', but safe to say that Elvey invites readers, despite all that can't be known, to assertions of things that she, writing from her colonized context with its violent past, does know, not least: 'there is blood on the ground'. She leaves the reader with an invitation to the thought that not only Jesus – 'one man' – but many persons are 'inside' the days her poem recollects.

Bibliography

Marcella Althaus-Reid, 2000, *Indecent Theology*, London: Routledge.
Marcella Althaus-Reid , 2001, *The Queer God*, London: Routledge.
Marcella Althaus-Reid, 2004, *From Feminist Theology to Indecent Theology*, London: SCM Press.
Tina Beattie, 2002, *God's Mother, Eve's Advocate: A Marian Narrative of Women's Salvation*, London: Continuum.

INTRODUCTION

Steven Bevans, 2002, *Models of Contextual Theology*, Maryknoll, NY: Orbis Books.
Sarah Coakley, 2008, *Powers and Submissions: Spirituality, Philosophy and Gender*, Chichester: John Wiley & Sons.
Sarah Coakley, 2013, *God, Sexuality and the Self: An Essay 'on the Trinity'*, Cambridge: Cambridge University Press.
Jenny Daggers, 2002, *The British Christian Women's Movement: A Rehabilitaion of Eve*, Abingdon: Routledge.
Mary Daly, 1978, *Gyn/Ecology: A Metaethics of Radical Feminism*, Boston, MA: Beacon Press.
David F. Ford (ed.), 1997, *The Modern Theologians: An Introduction to Christian Theology in the Twentieth Century*, 2nd edn, Oxford: Blackwell.
David F. Ford and Rachel Muers (eds), 2005, *The Modern Theologians: An Introduction to Christian Theology in the Twentieth Century*, 3rd edn, Oxford: Blackwell.
Monica Furlong, 1991, *A Dangerous Delight: Women and Power in the Church*, London: SPCK.
Monica Furlong (ed.), 1998, *Mirror to the Church: Reflections on Sexism*, London: SPCK.
Elaine L. Graham, 2018, *Making the Difference: Gender, Personhood and Theology*, London: Bloomsbury Publishing.
Margaret Daphne Hampson, 1990, *Theology and Feminism*, Oxford: Blackwell.
Margaret Daphne Hampson, 1992, *After Christianity*, London: SCM Press.
Margaret Daphne Hampson (ed.), 1996, *Swallowing a Fishbone?: Feminist Theologians Debate Christianity*, London: SPCK.
Ursula King (ed.), 1994, *Religion and Gender*, Oxford: Blackwell.
Ursula King and Tina Beattie (eds), 2004, *Gender, Religion and Diversity: Cross-cultural Perspectives*, London: Continuum.
Ann Loades, 1987, *Searching for Lost Coins: Explorations in Christianity and Feminism*, London: SPCK.
Ann Loades (ed.), 1990, *Feminist Theology: A Reader*, London: SPCK.
Ann Loades, 2000, *Feminist Theology: Voices from the Past*, Oxford: Polity.
Ann Loades and Ursula King (eds), 1992, *Feminist Theology from the Third World: A Reader*, London: SPCK.
Miriam Pepper and Ruth Powell, 2022, 'Domestic and Family Violence: Responses and Approaches across the Australian Churches', *Religions* 13 (3), p. 270, https://doi.org/10.3390/rel13030270 (accessed 27.3.24).
Gail Ramshaw, *Under the Tree of Life: The Religion of a Feminist Christian*, New York: Continuum, 1999.
Nicola Slee, 2004a, *Praying Like a Woman*, London: SPCK.
Nicola Slee, 2004b, *Faith and Feminism: An Introduction to Christian Feminist Theology*, London: Darton, Longman & Todd.
Nicola Slee, 2004c, *Women's Faith Development: Patterns and Processes*, Farnham: Ashgate.
Janet Martin Soskice, 1995, 'Just Women's Problems', in Ann Loades (ed.), *Spiritual Classics from the Late Twentieth Century*, London: Church House Publishing.
Elaine Storkey, 1985, *What's Right with Feminism*, Grand Rapids, MI: Eerdmans.

Elaine Storkey, 2018, *Scars Across Humanity: Understanding and Overcoming Violence against Women*, Downers Grove, IL: InterVarsity Press.

Elaine Storkey, 2020, *Women in a Patriarchal World: Twenty-five Empowering Stories from the Bible*, London: SPCK.

PART I

Right of Way

I

Global Christianity and Demographics

GINA A. ZURLO

One of the most common refrains about World Christianity is that it is shifting to the global South. In 1900, just 18% of all Christians worldwide lived in the global South (defined by the United Nations as Africa, Asia, Latin America and Oceania) and 82% lived in the global North (Europe and North America; see Figure 1). By 2020, 67% of all Christians lived in the global South and only 33% in the North. This shift is continuing, with an anticipated 77% of Christians in the world living in the South by 2050 (Johnson and Zurlo 2023). While Christianity was largely a white faith in 1900, it is now most certainly global. Africa, for example, is 49% Christian and home to 26% of all Christians worldwide, up from 2% in 1900. The shift of Christianity to the global South has inspired a re-evaluation of Christian history, worship, theology, biblical studies, ethics, theological education, mission and nearly every other aspect of the faith.

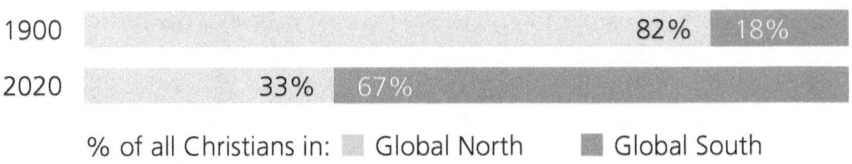

Figure 1: Christianity's North/South Distribution
Source: Johnson and Zurlo 2019, p. 4.

However, perhaps one of the truest but least-recognized aspects of Christianity's shift to the global South is that there would be no such shift without women. Christianity spread throughout the world by Indigenous Bible women who introduced Christianity to their communities and passed the faith on to their children. Church history is full of nuns, martyrs, queens, mystics, pastors' wives, mothers, single and married female missionaries, teachers, nurses, evangelists, and other women who helped Christianity grow, survive and thrive (see Dzubinski and Stasson 2021). Women are central to the faith, not marginal, although they are often treated as special interest subjects in the discipline of World Christianity, not the main historical and contemporary actors in the transmission and preservation of faith. Tradition, culture and the interpretation of scripture often omit the basic reality that life and the church are fundamentally gendered. Quite simply, men and women experience society, the church and ministry differently. However, leaders in these spheres – who are most often men – generally speak, act, preach and teach as if one common 'genderless' Christian experience exists.

Women in the World

Massive gaps exist between men's and women's experiences worldwide. The 2019 United Nations Human Development report (Conceição 2019) made the startling statement that nowhere in the world have women attained complete equality with men. In fact, gender inequality is one of the most persistent inequalities across all countries. Gender equity in health, education and economics has been slowing in recent years as the low-hanging fruit of equality has been achieved, such as women obtaining more primary education and becoming more likely to survive childbirth.

The World Economic Forum's Global Gender Gap Index measures progress between women and men in four dimensions: economic participation and opportunity, educational attainment, health and survival, and political empowerment. It has tracked trends in these areas since 2006; the 2022 report covered 146 countries, making it one of the most global, longitudinal and comprehensive tools available. The report stated that, if current trends continue, it will take 132 years for men and women to reach full gender parity in these four dimensions. While this was a four-year improvement over 2021, not a single country has yet to achieve full gender parity. The political empowerment gap is the most persistent, with an estimated 155 years remaining to close the gap, followed by 151 years to close the economic participation and opportunity gap. The most progress has been made on educational attainment, with just an estimated 22 years to close the gap. Progress has also been made on the health and survival gender gap but stalled due to the Covid-19 pandemic beginning in 2020.

Equality is measured in gaps, not levels, because these indicators are to inform how much more there is to achieve for women and men to reach parity. For example, gaps exist when men substantially hold more leadership roles than women. Of the 19 industries studied by the World

Economic Forum, not even one had a majority of women in leadership. The smallest gap was in non-governmental and membership organizations at 47% women leaders versus 53% men. The largest gap was in infrastructure: 16% women leaders and 84% men (World Economic Forum 2023, p. 38). Women have entered the paid workforce in large numbers, but face tremendous barriers to achieve parity with men, such as societal expectations, employer policies and legal environments that discriminate against them (World Economic Forum 2023, p. 6). A gender gap even exists in stress levels, with women reporting on average 4% more stress than men. Between 1990 and 2019, anxiety and mental disorders increased proportionally higher for women compared to men, and disproportionally among young women aged 15–19. From a geographic perspective, the gender gap is smallest in North America (59 years to close the gap) and widest in South Asia (197 years to close the gap). Perhaps one of the most startling realities related to global gender inequality is that in no country in the world do women have complete physical security (see Figure 2).

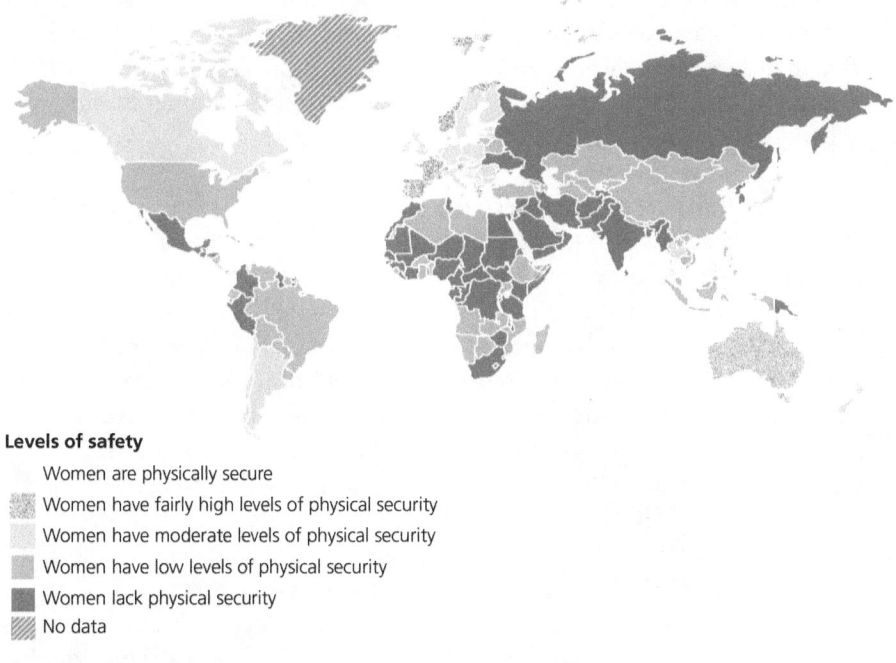

Levels of safety

  Women are physically secure
  Women have fairly high levels of physical security
  Women have moderate levels of physical security
  Women have low levels of physical security
  Women lack physical security
  No data

Figure 2: Physical security of women
Data source: WomenStats Project 2019.

A compounding factor in global gender gaps is missing data. Problems in data collection and availability have in some cases rendered women and girls invisible. Journalist Caroline Criado Perez (2019) investigated the lack of consideration of women in a wide variety of areas, including the order of how snow is cleared off streets, the problems of ill-fitting police uniforms, inequalities in medicine, and crash test requirements for new automobiles. She uncovered numerous areas where research simply failed to account for the unique needs of women's bodies, activities and lives. In some cases, decisions were made that resulted in structures that were merely inconvenient for women, like long lines in public toilets. In other cases, these decisions were downright deadly. For instance, women are 47% more likely than men to be seriously injured in a car crash because they do not sit in the 'standard seating position'; that is, they do not sit the same way as men. In 2018, the Bill and Melinda Gates Foundation released their annual letter reflecting on what surprised them in the previous year. The letter bluntly stated: 'Data can be sexist.' It continued:

> There are huge gaps in the global data about women and girls. For example, we don't know how much income women in developing countries earned last year or how much property they own or how many more hours girls spend on household chores than boys do. Better data will help policymakers take action to improve women's and girls' lives. (Gates and Gates 2018)

One of the most comprehensive efforts to track global statistical trends is the United Nations (UN). Launched in 2015, the UN's Sustainable Development Goals presents 17 initiatives with 169 specific targets that address global poverty, hunger, health, education, gender equality, clean water and sanitation, affordable and clean energy, work and economic growth, industry and infrastructure, reducing inequalities, cities, consumption, climate, sea life, land life, peace and justice, and partnership. Addressing gender inequality is a stand-alone goal, but data are missing to present a complete picture of women's progress towards the goals. Of the 53 gender-specific SDG indicators, only 12 have data regularly produced (23%). Furthermore, six of the 17 goals have no gender-specific indicators at all (65%). As a result, the SDG data have substantial holes that make it even more difficult to close the gap between men's and women's achievement, resource availability, and progress. One explanation for the data gap is simply that countries do not report gender-disaggregated information to the UN. The only way to address inequality is to have disaggregated gender data; that is, data broken down by men and women, and then ideally further broken down by subgroups, such as older women, women with disabilities, and by ethnicity (Emend et al. 2023). Data are needed to ensure that women are visible, counted and empowered.

Women in the Global Church

In 2006, historian Dana Robert asked a poignant question, 'What would the study of Christianity in Africa, Asia, and Latin America look like if scholars put women into the centre of their research?' (Robert 2006, p. 180). The question was precipitated by the observable marginalization of gender in World Christianity studies, where only a minority of scholars were seriously considering the gendered nature of Christian history and current trends. Robert commented that women's participation in Christianity was being buried in the larger narrative of Christianity's shift to the global South. Her two supporting arguments offered a corrective: World Christianity is majority female, and historically there have been gender-based reasons for Christian conversion. On the latter point, she described, among other factors, strong maternal networks, women organizers and female familial spiritual leaders who encouraged women and girls to join churches at higher rates than, or at least earlier than, men and boys. On the former point, besides anecdotal evidence from select churches and regions, there was no comprehensive data that documented the female majority of World Christianity.

The Pew Research Center's 'Gender Gap in Religion Around the World' (2016) study claimed that, indeed, Christian women reported higher rates of church attendance, prayer and religious self-identification than Christian men, supporting the notion that women are more religious than men. More recently, the Women in World Christianity Project (funded by the Louisville Institute and the Religious Research Association from 2019 to 2021) produced a comprehensive literature review, a multilingual survey and a new quantitative dataset on gender in World Christianity down to the denominational level. The project revealed that Christianity, when measured by membership or affiliation, is indeed majority female everywhere in the world, even if by slim margins. On every continent, church affiliation is more female than the general population. Africa, for example, is 50% female, but African Christianity is 52% female; Asia is 49% female, but Asian Christianity is 51% female. Generally, countries with the largest populations of Christians report higher percentage shares of Christian women than the general population. In most of these countries – the United States, Brazil, Mexico, Russia, China, Philippines,

Nigeria, the Democratic Republic of the Congo, Ethiopia, India – women make up one to four per cent more of the churches than of the general population. The Brazilian population, for example, is 51% female, but the Brazilian census reports that Christianity is 52% female. The countries with the highest per cent Christian female are all over the world, with the largest margins in Mongolia, Israel and Estonia (all 63%; see Zurlo 2023 for more detail on quantifying the female majority of World Christianity).

The results from the study, although accurate, were not very interesting. The world's population is 50% female, but World Christianity is 52% female – just two percentage points higher. A significant contribution made by this project was highlighting the chronic lack of data on gender in World Christianity. After years of working to uncover the best sources for the gender make-up of denominations and Christian networks, it became clear that either Christian organizations are not asking questions about gender, or they do ask these questions but do not report the data. This actuality is despite the fact that Christian organizations collect all kinds of information on their members and activities on a regular basis, such as how many people attend services or other ministries, how many people get paid and their salaries, how many buildings they own and how much it costs to keep the lights on, how many Facebook and X followers they have, and all other kinds of variables. Much like the global situation, without good data, it is impossible to have a complete understanding of what gaps exist, how persistent they are, what should be done to overcome them, and what decisions need to be made for the well-being of all its constituents, of all genders.

Membership vs Participation

Nevertheless, all the evidence suggests that World Christianity is indeed a woman's movement, but not only because they make up the majority of congregational members worldwide. Women are also the most active members and are utterly critical for the continuing of Christian faith into the future. Localized, ethnographic and qualitative research reveals a different picture of women's participation in congregational life than the available quantitative data seem to suggest. While a government census might report that Presbyterians in a country are 52% female, reporting from the Presbyterians themselves (where available) is typically much higher, perhaps upwards of 70% female. Consider the following examples from around the world.

Protestant Christianity in late-twentieth-century China was majority female and, in some areas, Protestant communities were comprised of

94% women (Kao 2013, citing Guo 2007). The 2007 Spiritual Life Study of Chinese Residents reported 72% female Protestants and 27% male. On the Catholic Church in Benin, a respondent stated:

> Women are very active in the Church, [she boasted]. For instance, women are the majority in Church attendance everywhere. Women do everything! ... Coming to the Church, you will find out that the population of women is greater. Women could be about 80%, while men would be something like 20% in attendance. (Uchem 2001, pp. 101–2)

In Europe, Christianity is generally more prominent among women, older generations (over 55), people with less education, ethnic minorities and immigrants. Although European women's commitments to religion have dropped substantially, especially since the 1960s, women are still more religious than men on a variety of measures. European Christian women are more likely than men to attend church more regularly, donate to religious institutions, wear religious clothing and symbols, believe in God as described in the Bible, embrace spiritual ideas, pray and have positive views of religion (Pew Research Center 2018). In Latin America, a study of Catholic Charismatics in Haiti reported that women were 90% of church members (Rey 2010). Other groups are entirely female, such as the Sisterhood of Our Lady of the Good Death, an Afro-Catholic group in Bahia, Brazil. In the United States, Black denominations tend to have higher Christian female percentages than white denominations, such as among Pentecostals. Historian Estrelda Alexander stated, 'women not only filled the pews but also established and pastored congregations, served as missionaries and developed the numerous auxiliaries that helped fuel Pentecostalism's phenomenal growth' (Alexander 2011, pp. 293–4). The National Church Life Survey in Australia reports higher rates of women's attendance at Catholic, Anglican and Uniting churches compared to national census figures for membership of these denominations. For example, the Australian census reports the Uniting Church as 56% female, but the NCLS reports that attenders are 63% female (Powell, Pepper and Hancock 2016). More on-the-ground studies like these are needed to uncover women's true contributions to Christianity worldwide.

GINA A. ZURLO

World Christianity, Feminism and Feminist Theology

In the first few centuries of Christianity, women gained new opportunities for leadership and public activity in joining nascent churches, and their contributions helped grow Christianity from a fledgling movement into a world religion (Stark 1996). However, Christianity, Christians, churches and Christian theology have also served as active barriers to women's opportunities.

In the western world, first-wave feminism of the late nineteenth and early twentieth centuries largely addressed legal obstacles to women's rights related to voting and property; that is, it was a movement about political power. Second-wave feminism emerged in the early 1960s with a much broader scope, addressing issues such as sexuality, reproductive rights, domesticity, domestic violence, marital rape and divorce law. It also demanded change in patriarchal structures and cultural practices that deemed women less than men. Concentrated in Europe and North America, both first- and second-wave feminism were largely the initiatives of white, middle-class women, working under the assumption that women everywhere faced similar oppression to them. That is, they assumed all women suffered the same because of patriarchy and sexism. However, this approach ignored intersectional oppression of race, class, ethnicity, religion, colonialism and politics (Herr 2013). In the 1980s and 1990s, women around the world challenged this narrow outlook and argued that their oppression was fundamentally different from that of white western women; women suffer multiple and intersecting oppressions, not some 'common condition' shared by all women worldwide (Herr 2013). The distinction between second-wave feminism and majority world feminist perspectives gave rise to so-called 'third world' feminism (a term now largely out of vogue), transnational feminism (a popular term) and global feminism (or, feminisms); some use these terms interchangeably. Globally, women are not a monolith, their oppression is not the same everywhere (Mohanty 1987), and women's activism is not uniform around the world.

The 1970s–80s is often identified as a turning point for women in the global South, but it should not be read that white western feminism was imported to Africa, Asia, Latin America and the Caribbean, and the Pacific Islands. Much like Black women in the West responding to the colour blindness of second-wave feminism, women in the global South have claimed their agency to identify their own sources of oppression and advocate for their own rights separate from white western women. For example, white female missionaries naively assumed that women's roles abroad should be reshaped according to western gendered norms, and as a result Indigenous women often lost agency and power with the arrival of Christianity, not gained it. Thus, use of the term 'feminism' in the global South is not a reference to white western second-wave feminism, but instead to how women in these places have created their own movements towards equality.

For most of church history, theologizing was done mainly by cisgender white men in Europe and North America. However, over the twentieth century, different kinds of theologizing arose, together referred to as 'contextual' or 'contextualizing' theology. The first wave of these theologies emerged due to the recognition that existing theology did not adequately address Christian experiences and perspectives from ethnic, social, gender, cultural, historical and other contexts outside cisgender white maleness. In addition, the original use of the phrase 'contextual' in relationship to theology was to encourage theological thought to respond to new social, political and cultural conditions – a more incarnated theology (see Kwok and Zurlo 2021).

In response, feminist theology, womanist theology and queer theology worked to highlight the perspectives of white women, Black women and genderqueer people in their fullest societal context. Furthermore, with the shift of Christianity to the global South, the standard white western theologies, again, did not fit the new cultural contexts of the faith. For example, the questions of white European men did not align with the needs of new and quickly growing churches in sub-Saharan Africa. Additional contextual theologies arose such as liberation theology (Latin America), *minjung* theology (South Korea), *Mujerista* theology (Latina theology), *Dalit* theology (India), African *ubuntu* theology, Asian feminist theology, and others. Reading biblical texts differently based on social location, gender, history, language and culture, these theologies approach Christianity as an incarnational faith, finding a home within every language, people and culture in the world. In other words, the work of theology depends not only on the biblical text but the human experiences that engage it; as a result, all Christians can offer unique theological reflections based on their locations and experiences. However, a problem with the term 'contextual theology' is its implication that plain 'theology' (i.e. that of the West) is universal, while everything else is contextual. Because all theology is invariably contextual, the erroneous assumption that western European male theology is universally valid (and not itself contextual) has hindered theological developments in the twentieth and twenty-first centuries, continuing the unsympathetic centring of white male experience above all else. Feminist theology from scholars such as

Kwok Pui-lan, Ada María Isasi-Díaz and Isabel Apawo Phiri have highlighted how the gendered experiences of women in the global South – now the centre of World Christianity – have influenced new kinds of theological thought. Non-male, non-western scholarship should be moving from the periphery to the centre of higher education curricula if schools want to provide more holistic and relevant theological perspectives for their students. Ethnic diversity is an obvious demographic characteristic in World Christianity – when studying Christianity in the global South, one would expect to encounter the stories of Africans, Asians, Latin Americans and Pacific Islanders. However, gender diversity is equally as important, especially since women make up more than half the church. If most of the theological scholarship is done by men and for a male or 'genderless' audience, then over half the church is silenced. If more than half the church is silenced, the entire church is robbed.

Future Study

One of the most common refrains of African Christianity is that the church is majority female. Women were among the first converts to Christianity and, in most places, women are the drivers of church life, whether in official leadership capacities or not. However, it is extremely difficult to obtain exact numbers for the gender make-up of African churches and denominations. Kenyan theologian Philomena Mwaura has drawn attention to this reality, stating that 'the Church in Africa has a feminine face and owes much of its tremendous growth to the agency of women' (Mwaura 2009, p. 114). The Circle of Concerned African Women Theologians, founded by Ghanaian theologian Mercy Amba Oduyoye in 1988, has raised the profile of gender issues in African Christianity by addressing women's leadership, theological education, ordination, women's organizations, gender-based violence, the role of ministers' wives, the exclusion of women from institutions of theological education, polygamy, celibacy of the priesthood, liberation, sexuality, rituals, HIV/AIDS, poverty, generational change, and the climate crisis. The work of the Circle represents the kind of intersectionality, contextual and relevant scholarship that should be emblematic of World Christianity studies. The point of departure in understanding trends in global Christianity should be that women have been the most active Christian participants across time and place. And yet, women's contributions in church and society have often been elided from history. Especially in the global South, women are actively passing the faith to the next generation, engaging in grassroots activism and labouring for the flourishing of their communities often in the face of political, social and environmental turmoil. The gendered discrepancies between congregational membership and participation are real.

Like women's history and feminist theology, engaging in sociological research on women requires new perspectives, methods and sources to identify the deeper level of their commitment to faith and service. While both men and women tend to be *members* of congregations, women report incredibly higher levels of *participation* than men. However, although women make up the majority of church members, they are often excluded from holding official leadership positions, and their ministries are considered secondary to those led by men. Understanding these dynamics in greater detail will help address power imbalances that dictate 'men's roles' and 'women's roles' in churches and shed light on the biases that exist therein. While social norms are extremely difficult to change, in many cases communities lack the information to think or act differently. Having high-quality, relevant data on gender in congregational life, especially from the global South, will help speak to the active barriers that sustain gender inequalities in faith communities. In one sense, the core of World Christianity studies reflects core values of feminism: equality, choice, freedom, peace, solidarity, resistance and sustainability. More fully integrating feminist perspectives in the study and teaching of World Christianity will help centre women's experiences, scholarship and perspectives.

Bibliography

Estrelda Alexander, 2011, *Black Fire: One Hundred Years of African American Pentecostalism*, Downers Grove, IL: IVP Academic.
Pedro Conceição, 2019, *Human Development Report 2019: Beyond Income, Beyond Averages, Beyond Today: Inequalities in Human Development in the 21st Century*, New York: UNDP.
Caroline Criado Perez, 2019, *Invisible Women: Data Bias in a World Designed for Men*, New York: Abrams Press.
Leanne M. Dzubinski and Anneke H. Stasson, 2021, *Women in the Mission of the Church: Their Opportunities and Obstacles throughout Christian History*, Grand Rapids, MI: Baker Academic.
Ramya Emend, Jessamyn Encarnacion, Papa Seck and Rea Jean Tabaco, 2023, Data on Gender: Seeing the True Picture, UN Women, 7 March, https://data.unwomen.org/features/data-gender-seeing-true-picture (accessed 6.4.23).
Bill and Melinda Gates, 2018, Annual Letter 2018, https://www.gatesnotes.com/2018-Annual-Letter (accessed 27.3.24).

Chao Guo, 2007, 'Christianity and Chinese Society: A Religious Vitality Perspective', paper presented at the Biannual Conference of International Society for the Sociology of Religion 29th Conference, Leipzig, Germany, 24 July.

Ranjoo S. Herr, 2013, 'Transnational, Third World, and Global Feminisms', in Patrick L. Mason (ed.), *Encyclopedia of Race and Racism*, 2nd edn, Detroit, MI: Macmillan Reference USA.

Todd M. Johnson and Gina A. Zurlo (eds), 2023, *World Christian Database*, Leiden/Boston: Brill.

Todd M. Johnson and Gina A. Zurlo, 2019, *World Christian Encyclopedia*, 3rd edn, Edinburgh: Edinburgh University Press.

Chen-Yang Kao, 2013, 'Church as "Women's Community": The Feminization of Protestantism in Contemporary China', *Journal of Archaeology and Anthropology* 78, pp. 107–40.

Kwok Pui-lan and Gina A. Zurlo, 2021, 'World Christianity and the Challenge of Interdisciplinarity', in Jehu J. Hanciles (ed.), *World Christianity: History, Methodologies, Horizons*, Maryknoll, NY: Orbis Books, pp. 75–86.

Chandra Mohanty, 1987, 'Feminist Encounters: Locating the Politics of Experience', *Copyright* 1 (Fall), pp. 30–44.

Philomena N. Mwaura, 2009, 'Christianity in Eastern Africa, 1910–2010', in Kenneth R. Ross and Todd M. Johnson (eds), *Atlas of Global Christianity*, Edinburgh: Edinburgh University Press, pp. 114–15.

Pew Research Center, 2016, *Gender Gap in Religion Around the World*, Washington, DC.

Pew Research Center, 2018, *Being Christian in Western Europe*, Washington, DC.

Ruth Powell, Miriam Pepper and Nicole Hancock, 2016, *2011 NCLS Research Collection*, rev. edn, North Sydney: NCLS Research.

Terry Rey, 2010, 'Catholic Pentecostalism in Haiti: Spirit, Politics, and Gender', *Pneuma* 32 (1), pp. 80–106.

Dana L. Robert, 2006, 'World Christianity as a Women's Movement', *International Bulletin of Missionary Research* 30 (4), pp. 180–8.

Rodney Stark, 1996, *The Rise of Christianity: A Sociologist Reconsiders History*, Princeton, NJ: Princeton University Press.

Rose N. Uchem, 2001, 'Overcoming Women's Subordination in the Igbo African Culture and in the Catholic Church: Envisioning an Inclusive Theology with Reference to Women', Doctoral thesis, Indiana: Graduate Theological Foundation.

WomenStats Project, 2019, 'Physical Security of Women', https://www.womanstats.org/substatics/MULTIVAR-SCALE-1-2019-2.png (accessed 6.4.23).

World Economic Forum, 2022, *Global Gender Gap Report*, Insight Report, July.

World Economic Forum, 2023, *Global Gender Gap Report*, Insight Report, June, https://www3.weforum.org/docs/WEF_GGGR_2023.pdf (accessed 9.5.24).

Gina A. Zurlo, 2023, *Women in World Christianity: Building and Sustaining a Global Movement*, Hoboken, NJ: Wiley-Blackwell.

2

Latina Feminist Theologies in the United States

NANCY ELIZABETH BEDFORD

By the early seventeenth century, when the first English colonizers arrived on the shores of the land they named New England, Spaniards had already founded cities and established Roman Catholic missions in what is now the United States (e.g. St Augustine, Florida, est. 1565). Spanish colonial incursions, which mirrored Spain's invasion and occupation of the Caribbean, Mexico and the lands to the south, mark the genesis of Latinx cultures and identities in the United States, born of the intermixture of Indigenous, Spanish and later African peoples. The war against Mexico and the subsequent Treaty of Guadalupe Hidalgo in 1848, whereby the United States annexed a vast expanse of Mexican territory, ensured that territories that had been part of Latin America were added to the continental United States. By 1898, the United States had added Puerto Rico to its possessions beyond the mainland. Beginning in the twentieth century, layered onto this cultural and demographic base, many waves of immigration from Latin America and the Caribbean arrived, often resulting indirectly from US interventionist policies in the region, in a process Juan González has called the 'harvest of empire' (González 2011). By early in the twenty-first century, Latinx peoples were the largest 'minority' in the country.

I use the term Latinx to describe the cultural and ethnographic context out of which Latina feminist theologies emerge. The same matrix is described variously as Hispanic, Latino, Latino-a and Latin@. All these designations attempt to encompass people of Latin American descent who live in the United States and identify themselves as part of a heterogenous yet recognizable demographic.[1] In the case of immigrants, they are not called Latinos or Latinas in their countries of origin, but rather Mexicans, Colombians, Hondurans, Cubans and so on. It is only in the United States, where categorization of people by their ethnicity and race is a cultural imposition, that they discover themselves as Hispanic or

Latinos (Krogstad and Noe-Bustamante 2020).[2] The term *Latinx* (pronounced Latin-ex) avoids grammatical gender, and is explicitly inclusive of 'men, women, agendered, trans, gender-nonconforming, gender-queer, and gender-fluid people' (Peterson and Battle 2018). *Latina* feminist theologies, then, refers to theologies developed by Latinx women or female-identified people, hence the feminine grammatical ending.

In reference to the *mestizaje* or mixing between Spaniards and other Europeans and the Indigenous peoples of the Americas that is part of the heritage of many in the Latinx community, Latinx peoples in the United States are sometimes called 'brown'. This fits in nicely with the dominant racial logic in the country, that of the binary between those who are 'white' and 'black', that is, primarily of European descent and primarily of African descent, respectively. The problem with this nomenclature is that it indirectly reifies black/white binary thinking and simultaneously erases the many people in the Latinx community who consider themselves (or pass for) Black, white, Indigenous or AAPI.[3] To be Latinx is not to belong to a particular 'race' as constructed in the US American imaginary, or even a particular mix of ancestors.[4] Rather, to be Latinx is to be part of a heterogenous conglomeration of people living in the United States who have in common a vital connection to the lands colonized by Iberians. The Spanish language, a Roman Catholic faith heritage, a brown complexion or a Hispanic last name may or may not be a part of that connection. For example, my spouse and I along with our three daughters were all born in Argentina and now live in the United States; we are no less Latinx for being Protestant, light-skinned, and not having Hispanic last names, just as we are not more authentically Latinx for eating rice and beans as a staple or speaking Spanish at home.

References to Spanish continue to be one marker of the Latinx community, but the latter encompasses many who are not fluent in Spanish. Indeed, Latinx theory and theology are written primarily in English. Likewise, Roman Catholic tradition continues as a pervasive influence in Latin American culture and history, but the Latinx community also includes many Protestants, Jews, Muslims, Buddhists and practitioners of Santería and other Afro-Caribbean and Afro-Brazilian religious traditions, as well as many who adhere to no organized religious community. The Pan-Latinx reality includes people of every conceivable heritage: Korean Paraguayans, Japanese Peruvians, Welsh Argentines, Afro-Panamanians, and many other iterations. It is not always possible to guess by looking who is or is not Latinx. And yet, the Latinx community is knit together by many bonds that allow for mutual recognition as inheritors of a common cultural legacy.

Elements of this common heritage are found both as themes in Latinx theologies and as a *Sitz im Leben* for that theology: among them are the place of family and community in the context of an individualistic, competitive dominant culture; the construction of a subjectivity and a particularity woven together from many different influences; the experience of displacement, migration, exile and the search for home; and embodiment as a site of epistemological insight. Another common theme is that of in-betweenness, or not belonging fully here or there, not knowing whether one is authentically Latinx or Latin American or US American, yet creatively negotiating hybridity and the construction of identity in an ever-shifting landscape, and thus seeing oneself as a positive agent for change (Chaney and Clark 2020).

An awareness of commonalities, in a cultural context in which Latinx peoples are minoritized and often caricatured as alien, illegal, foreign, lazy or hot-blooded is important, for it has allowed the emergence of a new belonging, a summative and collective mutual recognition that does not exist in the same way in any of the countries of the Caribbean and Latin America. The Latinx theologies that emerge from this cultural context are likewise different from Latin American theologies. It is therefore important, as a first step, to distinguish Latinx theologies (including Latina feminist theologies) from Latin American theologies. Latin American theologies are appreciated by and incorporated into Latinx theologies but do not answer the questions that emerge out of the Latinx experience. Latinx theologies do drink from the wells of Latin American theologies – especially theologies in the genealogy of liberation – but they also drink from many other sources.

When I was preparing to move from Buenos Aires to Chicago in the early 2000s, I did not at first know how much I had yet to learn about these differences. I assumed that Latina feminist theologies in the United States would be approximately the same thing as the Latin American feminist theologies with and in which I was already engaged. At that time, Latinx theologies were almost unknown to us in Latin America, a pattern that has largely persisted: Latinx intellectual production in general – not just theological production – is too often ignored in Latin American academic circles.[5] In turn, most US American academics (including theologians), unless they are specialists in Latinx studies, at most add Latinx authors in parenthetical ways to a syllabus or a footnote.

As I was soon to discover, Latinx theology has a great deal to contribute. It tends to be theopoetic in its expression, in ways related both to style and to content. It is rooted in the struggles of the community and therefore almost always linked to praxis. It often relies on narrative and biography more than on dogmatic or technical formulations, though the latter also do appear. It requires a hermeneutical capacity to listen to individual stories as well as to theorize about structures. The belief systems and customs of the ancestors are present in various ways in this theology, so that it is intent both on diachronic and synchronic dimensions of reality. It is a theology that emerges by consensus through conversation, in a method that is often called *teología en conjunto* (e.g., Rodríguez and Martell-Otero 1997). It requires epistemological fluidity, imagination, and the ability to think and articulate ideas both analytically and synthetically. Spanish is always present, but the native language of Latinx theologies is English. At its best, such English is flexible, hybrid, de-colonial and amenable to code-switching and syntactical experimentation.

As I was discussing my impending work transition to *el Norte*, I asked María Pilar Aquino for advice, for I knew she had made a similar transition, from Mexico to California. She was one of the most important figures in Latina feminist theology, contributing both to its methodology and its themes; that much I already knew. She told me, 'The first thing that will have to happen is for you to become a Latina.' Since then, I have learned much – and continue to learn – about what her words mean in my own case and that of other Latinas doing theology in the United States. In order to delve into Latina feminist theologies, I will therefore structure this essay in three steps that help unpack that unfolding: (1) Becoming a Latina; (2) Becoming a Latina Feminist; (3) Becoming a Latina Feminist Theologian.

Becoming a Latina

To speak of becoming a Latina reflects the fact that what it means to be a Latina is not static; it constantly shifts and changes. Take, for instance, the insight of Rosario Morales and Aurora Levins Morales (who are mother and daughter) in their 'Ending Poem' (2011). Asserting 'I am what I am', it identifies as child of the Americas, 'light-skinned mestiza of the Caribbean', and offspring of 'many diasporas', birthed in a context 'at a crossroads'. Such assertions, which reflect constant negotiations and rearticulations of identity, permeate the Latinx experience. Thus, being Latina is also always a becoming.

When Latin American women migrate to the United States, they find themselves situated in a new demographic and cultural reality that affects their self-understanding. What once was normal is now coded as exotic;

what once seemed settled and assured is not so at all. As writer Judith Ortiz Cofer recalls, for instance: 'I was born a white girl in Puerto Rico but became a brown girl when I came to live in the United States' (Cofer 2011). Not only migrants, however, but also Latinas born and raised in the United States constantly negotiate the matter of identity, belonging and becoming, constructing their subjectivity and defending their personhood – their right to be who they are as they are – in a society where they tend to be seen as second rate when they are seen at all.

Latinas are pressured to perform *Latinidad* in ways expected and consumed by dominant culture, for example by looking 'brown' and 'curvy' as an imprimatur of their Latina 'authenticity' (Ramirez 2016).[6] This commodification coexists with the regulation and control of Latina bodies, inasmuch as they are to be 'sexy', but not so much as to challenge white normativity or taste (Rojas-Sosa 2020).[7] Latinas are, in sum, expected to keep to impossible, shifting and contradictory standards in ways that often reinscribe the virgin/whore dichotomy.[8] In not a few instances, when they push back against these expectations, they are pathologized. Quotidian acts of resistance (such as talking back or indeed refusing to speak) and other survival strategies of young Latinas in the public school system can be seen as pathological or even criminal (Restrepo 2019).[9] On other occasions, responsibilities at home (such as supervising siblings), or even culturally driven choices such as consulting with one's family before making an important decision (rather than assuming an individualistic posture), are interpreted as signs that young Latinas are not being intellectual or independent enough for success in academia or in the white-collar workforce.

Latinas are often misheard, especially if they are perceived to have an accent. In her poem 'Have you experienced this?' (2010), Myriam Torres evokes common and painful occurrences of being 'heard as Spanish', perceived as being 'sent to help' rather than as meeting as an equal, even 'invisible to some', because never expected to say anything of importance, and all too easily 'tuned out or ignored'. Torres also describes the Latina struggle vividly in her prose:

> Being a Latina woman in the United States is an enduring disadvantage in various ways. The conjunction of gender and Latina ethnicity multiplies vulnerability to discrimination. In addition to many other issues, Latinas, even those who are well educated, are constantly struggling with this given, always attached to their identity. (Torres 2010)

Truly, navigating life as a Latina is not for the faint of heart. On the positive side, however, Latina experiences have led to a vibrant tradition of Latina feminisms, through which Latinas reflect on, articulate and embody the struggle of what it means to live in US society, their resistance to marginalization, and their visions of justice.

Becoming a Latina Feminist

The epistemological flexibility that Latinas need simply to make it through everyday life is reflected in the richness of Latina feminist theory and praxis, including its intercultural ethos. The latter reflects both the cultural complexity of *Latinidad* and the many ways in which Latinas have struggled alongside non-Latinas. Latina feminist theory made its way into academic circles in the United States beginning in the 1970s, often in conversation with Black, Indigenous and Asian American feminisms (e.g. hooks and Mesa-Bains 2006). Many of the early theorists, such as Gloria Anzaldúa, Cherríe Moraga and María Lugones, 'foregrounded the conceptual, affective, and institutional resources within academia that continue to shape scholarly production in Latinx feminist projects today' (Pitts and Medina 2020). Then and now, Latina feminist theories emerge from many different disciplines (such as philosophy, literature, cultural criticism, art, political science and activism); they hold in common a careful attention to the lived experiences of women in the United States who do not fit easily within the bounds of white normativity.

One of the most enduring contributions of Latina feminist theory has been its ability to name and reclaim liminality as a powerful creative space. Building on her own family history on the US–Mexican borderlands, for instance, Gloria Anzaldúa repurposed the Náhuatl word *Nepantla*, which she uses to describe physical or indeed psychic spaces 'caught between worlds'. Such in-between spaces are painful at many levels, but Anzaldúa shows that they are also sites of creativity, where a 'mestiza consciousness' can emerge, one capable of uprooting dualistic modes of thinking with recourse to imaginative retellings of spirituality as well as to analytical modes of thought (Anzaldúa 2012; 2015). I've often observed in my classes just how curative it can be for Latinx – and other – students to discover this language, in order to make sense of their own perplexities and move forward in constructive and creative tasks (Henderson-Espinoza 2019).

Latina feminists acknowledge the problem of androcentrism and patriarchy but deconstruct the racism behind the idea that Latinx *machismo* is somehow harsher than Euro-American sexism. The word 'macho' in Spanish simply means the male of a species; for most Latina feminist theorists, maleness is not a problem, but rather how masculinity is performed. As Anzaldúa puts it:

> Though we 'understand' the root causes of male hatred and fear, and the subsequent wounding of women, we do not excuse, we do not condone, and we will no longer put up with it. From the men of our race, we demand the admission/acknowledgement/ disclosure/testimony that they wound us, violate us, are afraid of us and our power. We need them to say they will begin to eliminate their hurtful put-down ways. But more than words, we demand acts. We say to them: we will develop equal power with you and those who have shamed us. (Anzaldúa 2012, pp. 105–6)

Anzaldúa celebrates the tenderness and the alternative masculinities often exhibited by gay men, who – as she perceives it – challenge dominant models of masculinity and are brave enough to show vulnerability (Anzaldúa 2012). Her desire to deconstruct rigid and reified gendered roles is an example of her non-binary/anti-binary thinking, which is a trait she shares with other Latina feminist theorists, many of whom can also be read as queer theorists (for example, María Lugones, Emma Pérez, Juana María Rodríguez and Mariana Ortega).

A final contribution of Latina feminist theorists that is worth mentioning in this context is the way they have creatively repurposed and reinterpreted many Latin American religious and cultural symbols. The Virgin of Guadalupe, for instance, has been reimagined as an energetic Chicana (Mexican-American woman), most famously in the work of Yolanda M. López, who has painted her mother, a seamstress, as Guadalupe at her sewing machine; she has also imagined Guadalupe as a housekeeper, an Aztec goddess, and a love goddess superimposed on Botticelli's Venus. She has painted herself as Guadalupe, in running shoes, bursting out of the frame (Pérez 2007; López). This aesthetic reframing of symbols – many of them religious – in new and powerful ways allows for the rediscovery of the force of the symbol in a new context. For theology, this work of retrieval and reinterpretation can be very helpful as a hermeneutical paradigm.

Becoming a Latina Feminist Theologian

Many of the traits of Latina feminist theory and praxis re-emerge in Latina feminist theologies. Such theologies might indeed be classified as a subset of Latina feminist theory, though they are usually not very well known in secular settings. Latina feminist theorists have increasingly expressed an interest in spirituality but are as a rule quite suspicious of institutional forms of Christian faith, such as church (Facio and Lara 2014). Latina feminist theologies therefore exist in yet another instance of a borderland, the territory between so-called secular feminist theories and the practices of grass-roots Latinas who, though not as religiously homogenous as they sometimes are depicted in mainstream US cultural production, are indeed often practising Christians.

Two Roman Catholic theologians were especially influential on Latina feminist theology as it began to come into its own in the 1980s and 1990s: María Pilar Aquino (b. 1956) and Ada María Isasi-Díaz (1943–2012). Isasi-Díaz was born in Cuba and migrated to the United States when she was a teenager; she also spent three years in Perú as a Roman Catholic missionary. She coined the term *mujerista* to describe theology developed by Latinas of faith engaged in the struggle for liberation. As is the case with a number of US Black women who espouse womanism and have developed various iterations of womanist theology, Isasi-Díaz held that 'feminism' was too steeped in the efforts and interests of white middle-class women to be truly helpful. Instead, she wrote, '*Mujerista* is the word we have chosen to name devotion to Latinas' liberation', and distanced herself from the noun *mujerismo* which she rightly took to be essentialist (Isasi-Díaz 1996, p. 61; p. 83 n.3).

Her *mujerista* theology was closely linked to an ethnographic approach that centred deep conversation with grass-roots Latinas, women steeped in *mestizaje* and *mulatez* (the *locus theologicus* of *mujerista* theology), that is, racially and culturally mixed people who come up against many obstacles as a result of the way US society is organized to benefit whiteness (Isasi-Díaz 1996, p. 64). Their everyday life, *lo cotidiano*, is the main theological source for her theology and the 'stuff' of its reflection. In other words, for Isasi-Díaz the quotidian experiences of Latinas in the United States have 'descriptive, hermeneutical and epistemological importance' (Isasi-Díaz 1996, p. 68; see also Isasi-Díaz and Tarango 1988). She argues that it is precisely this attention to the actual daily experiences of Latinas that keeps *mujerista* theology from falling into essentialism or romanticizing women's lives (Isasi-Díaz 1996, p. 69). The experiences of Latinas are not the norm of theology or of ethics, but inasmuch as *lo cotidiano* reflects a liberative praxis (the struggle or *la lucha*) it can inform our understanding of reality and indeed what we can know about God (Isasi-Díaz 1996, pp. 70–1). What does it mean, for instance, when a Latina addresses God as *Diosito* in prayer, using an affectionate diminutive for the divine? (Isasi-Díaz 2003). As Isasi-Díaz puts it, she is more interested in 'what we as humans know about God' than in 'academic and churchly attempts to see theology as being about God', for by centring *lo cotidiano*, the fragmentary and provisional nature of theological knowledge comes sharply into focus (Isasi-Díaz 1996, pp. 71–2).

Mujerista theology as deployed by Isasi-Díaz challenges theology to be accountable to the lives of Latinas. Rather than focusing on objectivity and immutability, she calls for theology to be epistemologically vigilant, by which she means aware of its own limitations, able to question its own motivations, and willing to grapple with difference and heterogeneity. Such a theology is inevitably a communal task, willing to centre themes arising from the struggle of Latinas for liberation, such as theological anthropology (particularly identity, ethnicity and agency) and popular religiosity, as a source for understanding God (Isasi-Díaz 1996, pp. 76–9). Her *mujerista* theology never separates theology from ethics: theology is ethical, and ethics is theological. Such a theology always asks: what changes will this way of doing theology bring to the everyday lives of poor and oppressed women (Isasi-Díaz 2004, p. 94)?

Black theologies and Black culture have been very important to Latinx theologies as powerful models of naming and navigating social realities and power structures in the United States. Isasi-Díaz's *mujerista* approach surely owes much of its force to womanism (Isasi-Díaz 2004, p. 21).[10] From the perspective of Latina feminist theologies, however, Black liberation and womanist theologies become troubling when they unwittingly fall into versions of US exceptionalism as a result of their focus on the US Black experience. Thus, Latina feminist theologies not only learn from the model of Womanist/Black feminist theologies rooted in the experience of a US black/white binary, but also challenge them to recognize and dialogue with Black Latinidades, especially since the Latina experience – especially in the case of many Latinas of Cuban, Dominican, Panamanian and Puerto Rican descent – is often also a Black experience. Black Latinas live in another kind of borderland, different from the *Nepantla* of the Mexican–American border, yet equally complicated: the in-between space forged by the crossroads of Latinidad and the Black experience in the United States.[11]

Another challenge emerges when some non-Latinx theologians, desirous of adding a female, Latina perspective to their syllabi or writings, happily latch on to *mujerista* theology as a way of adding and stirring some Latina flavor, without taking seriously Isasi-Díaz's commitment to providing *another way* of doing theology, rather than providing an additional ingredient to a traditional formula (Isasi-Díaz 1996, p. 79). The danger is that the nomenclature *mujerista* is often bandied about in ways that do not live up to the radical possibilities for theology that Isasi-Díaz envisioned in her centring of Latina voices.

Here is where it can be helpful to pay attention to the contribution of another formative figure of Latina feminist theology, María Pilar Aquino. Aquino locates her own work explicitly in the feminist theological tradition as lived out in Latin America, the Caribbean and among Latinas in the United States. As a Mexican formed academically in liberation theology in Mexico and in Spain, she knows both the potential of that trajectory and its limitations; she is also aware of how deep the wells of Latin American and Latina feminist theory and praxis are, and how significant they can be for theology. This insistence on integration of Latin American and Latinx critical resources has been one of the continuing strengths and contributions of Aquino in her theological work (Aquino and Nunes 2007).

Aquino's work pays close attention to the 'pioneers of Latina/Chicana feminism', such as Gloria Anzaldúa, Ana Castillo, Cherríe Moraga and Chela Sandoval, who pushed back forcefully 'against the belief held by many that feminism does not have a Latina/Chicana cradle' (Aquina 2002, p. 135). Such feminism is 'a *mestiza* theory, method, spirituality, and praxis that has egalitarian social relations in everyday life as its principle of coherence, and it seeks to intervene in concrete reality for the historical actualization of social justice' (Aquino 2002, p. 136). It is worth noting here that though Aquino does not call it *cotidianeidad*, she pays careful attention to the 'critically reflective daily life experiences of grassroot, working-class Latina women' as a starting point for *mestiza* feminist theories, transformative practices, and – in the case of critical reflection on faith – theologies (Aquino 2002, p. 136).[12] Aquino also praises Latina theorists for their contributions in the analysis of power and their reappropriation and exercise of the right to be subjects of knowledge, not just objects (Aquino 2002, p. 137).

Latina feminist theology integrates these insights and methodologies as well as those of Latin American liberation theology, to develop a critical language for faith. Its central feature, as Aquino sees it, is precisely this capacity for reflection on faith and for a systematic articulation of faith practices, with a strong emphasis on communal work (*teología en conjunto*), interdisciplinarity and interculturality (Aquino 2002, pp. 148–50).

A careful focus on the day-to-day realities of women and their allies, sustained by a liberating vision of the Christian faith and its practices, leads her to posit four continuing major tasks of Latina feminist theologies: to develop its hermeneutical insights systematically, to claim the right to its own theological constructions, to connect theology and spirituality ever more deeply in feminist terms, and to tease out the effects of the current economic system on the daily lives of grass-roots Latinas (Aquino 2002, pp. 151–4).

The trajectories of Isasi-Díaz and Aquino are not an either–or proposition. As Latina feminist theologies continue to evolve, some of the most exciting theological contributions combine elements from both streams. This is the case of the work of Elizabeth Conde Frasier on Latina spirituality, which pays close attention to the *testimonios* or testimonies of grass-roots women and is equally attentive to the legacies of both the *mujerista* and the Latina feminist approaches (Conde-Frazier, 2008). It is also the case for Nancy Pineda Madrid, who focuses on violence against women, rethinking the meaning of suffering and salvation in Christology from a Latina perspective (Madrid 2011). The number of Latina feminist theologians and Bible scholars, as well as Latina feminist scholars of religion more widely construed, continues to grow and multiply.[13]

In my own work as a Latina feminist systematic/constructive theologian, I try to ponder transversal doctrinal themes, pursuing insights inspired by Latina feminist theologies. Mariology, for example, often appears in Latina feminist theological work, both Protestant and Catholic (for example, in the work of both Nora O. Lozano Díaz and Jeanette Rodríguez). The Mexican Guadalupe/Tonantzin, the Cuban Virgen de la Caridad del Cobre, the Andean Virgin clad in the vestments of the Pachamama, and all the other iterations of Mary who accompany Latina migrants in their journeys to the United States, clamour for theological attention. As I focus Mary and Mariology, working *en conjunto* alongside other Latinas – some of them undocumented and on the run, like the Mary of the flight to Egypt – I have realized with renewed force how important the simple fact is that Mary the mother of Jesus was not a white woman as whiteness is conceived of in the United States. She is a powerful counter-hegemonic force in whom I can re-encounter the liberating, justice-oriented Mary of the Magnificat (Bedford 2018a).

In turn, to pay attention to Mary as the mother of Jesus leads me to revisit the classic theological conviction about how harmful a docetic Christology can be. A ghostly, disincarnate Jesus is harmful to Latinas since he can so easily be manipulated and distorted as a projection of male, ethno-nationalist fantasies, rather than opting for and defending the most vulnerable, as did the Jesus of Nazareth as depicted in the Gospels (Bedford 2018b). I see my own feminist Latina Christology as tasked with pushing back against the apostasy of racist and sexist distortions of Jesus, so common in both liberal and fundamentalist iterations of US Protestantism (Bedford 2020). In turn, to focus on the full humanity of the non-docetic Jesus, confessed as the Christ, leads me to ponder theological anthropology in a society organized for the benefit of those who pass for 'white' (Bedford 2017). Theological anthropology from this perspective touches upon subjects that can be a matter of life and death for Latinas, such as whether their lives and those of their children are worth defending and respecting when they flee violence and seek asylum at the border.

What, then, have I learned in becoming a Latina feminist theologian? I've learned a good bit about embodiment, interculturality, complexity, my own complicities with power and privilege (as an educated, documented, white-passing woman living in the United States), and the joys of doing theology *en conjunto*. I've been reminded of the force of the beautiful in doing theology, alongside the good and the true. I've understood the importance of holding many perspectives, and indeed paradoxes, in tension in the various borderlands and in-between spaces I inhabit. I've realized that my task is to attempt to discern – *en conjunto*, with the help of the Spirit – how to balance these many forces at any given time in view of specific projects and contexts (such as this essay). I am challenged to pay attention to the particularity of bodies, places and spaces, even as I keep in mind that Latina feminist theologies nod towards a horizon of eschatological hope in justice and resurrection life that reminds me that my own theological attempts at construction are always provisional and very limited.

It seems to me that, at the very least, Latina feminist theologies are compelling simply because of the human interest inherent in their close attention to the everyday lives of Latinas and of the way they synthesize feminist concerns with spiritual and religious insights. For those of us who are confessional Christians, Latina feminist theologies challenge us to ponder and rearticulate why we believe that the gospel of Jesus is good news, and how that good news can be expressed concretely and materially in our societies.

Notes

1 Brazilians, Filipinos and Haitians, who share a similar history of colonization to the Spanish-speaking Latin American countries, sometimes include themselves – and sometimes not – in the 'Latinx' collective. Some Latinx are descendants of Spaniards who colonized areas of the United States and therefore are not technically of 'Latin American' descent.

2 It is worth noting that four out of five Latinx are US citizens, and that the percentage of immigrants within the wider Latinx population is on the decline.

3 Asian, Asian American or Pacific Islander.

4 Adding *'mulatez'* to *'mestizaje'* makes visible the heritage of Afro-Latinidad but does not resolve the problem of trying to make Latinidad about 'race' as the concept is constructed in the United States.

5 Some theologians born in Latin America and later active in the United States (such as María Pilar Aquino, Justo González and Luis Rivera Pagán) work in both contexts and serve to some extent as bridges between Latin American and Latinx theologies. I count myself among this group.

6 These pressures are especially strong in visual media and the performing arts, but the stereotypes permeate into private spheres as well.

7 This regulation can be seen in popular women's beauty magazines oriented to the Latina market.

8 Cf. the lyrics of the song 'Double Bind' by Latina rapper Audax the Damsel, https://www.youtube.com/watch?v=7CksBAbyp6k (accessed 27.3.24). She is one of my daughters, all three of whom are important interlocutors for me as I think through Latina feminist issues.

9 Some are diagnosed with Oppositional Defiant Disorder which, in a country in which the prison industrial complex has immense power, can be the first step towards incarceration.

10 Isasi-Díaz mentions the community at Union Theological Seminary in the 1980s and how much she learned from Katie G. Cannon.

11 Two Latina feminist theologians who have worked at this intersection are Teresa Delgado and Michelle González.

12 Aquino (2002, pp. 138–9) explicitly distances herself from the *mujerista* nomenclature because she does not believe that Isasi-Díaz's *mujerista* approach is sufficiently rooted in socio-political movements for change; she also criticizes its lack of exposure to Latina/Chicana and Latin American critical feminist theories.

13 For a snapshot of some recent work by Latina theologians and scholars of religion, cf. the Hispanic Theological Initiative's 'Open Plaza', https://www.htiopenplaza.org/ (accessed 27.3.24).

Bibliography

Gloria Anzaldúa, 2012, *Borderlands – La Frontera: The New Mestiza*, 25th Anniversary 4th edn, San Francisco: Aunt Lute Books.
Gloria Anzaldúa, 2015, *Light in the Dark – Luz en lo Oscuro: Rewriting Identity, Spirituality, Reality*, ed. by Analouise Keating, Durham, NC: Duke University Press.
María Pilar Aquino, 2002, 'Latina Feminist Theology: Central Features', in María Pilar Aquino, Daisy L. Machado and Jeanette Rodríguez (eds), *A Reader in Latina Feminist Theology. Religion and Justice*, Austin, TX: University of Texas Press.
María Pilar Aquino and María José Rosado Nunes (eds), 2007, *Feminist Intercultural Theology: Latina Approaches for a Just World*, Maryknoll, NY: Orbis Books.
Nancy Elizabeth Bedford, 2017, 'Theology, Violence and White Spaces', in Matthew Croasmun, Zoran Grozdanov and Ryan J. McAnnally-Linz (eds), *Envisioning the Good Life*, Eugene, OR: Cascade Books, pp. 149–62.
Nancy Elizabeth Bedford, 2018a, 'The Flight to Egypt: Toward a Protestant Mariology in Migration', in Efraín Agosto and Jacquelyn Hidalgo (eds), *Latinxs, the Bible and Migration*, New York: Palgrave Macmillan, pp. 109–31.
Nancy Elizabeth Bedford, 2018b, 'A Narrow Gate? Proceeding along the Way of Jesus by the Spirit', *Mennonite Quarterly Review* 92, October, pp. 43–55.
Nancy Elizabeth Bedford, 2020, 'The Retrieval of a Liberating Christology', in Elizabeth Soto-Albrecht and Darryl W. Stephens (eds), *Liberating the Politics of Jesus: Renewing Peace Theology through the Wisdom of Women*, New York: T&T Clark, pp. 17–32.
James Chaney and Laura Clark, 2020, 'We're From Here Too: Identity and Belonging among 1.5- and Second-Generation Latinxs in Nashville, Tennessee', *The Latin Americanist* 64, pp. 280–304.
Judith Ortiz Cofer, 2011, 'The Story of My Body', in Ilan Stavans (ed.), *The Norton Anthology of Latino Literature*, New York: Norton, p. 1897.
Elizabeth Conde-Frazier, 2008, 'Testimonios: relato, agencia y la mujer latina', in Jorge E. Maldonado and Juan F. Martínez (eds), *Vivir y servir en el exilio. Lecturas teológicas de la experiencia latina en los Estados Unidos*, Buenos Aires: Kairós, pp. 125–48.
Elisa Facio and Irene Lara (eds), 2014, *Fleshing the Spirit. Spirituality and Activism in Chicagna, Latina, and Indigenous Women's Lives*, Tucson, AZ: The University of Arizona Press.
Juan González, 2011, *Harvest of Empire: A History of Latinos in America*, rev. edn, New York: Penguin.
Robyn Henderson-Espinoza, 2019, *Activist Theology*, Minneapolis, MN: Fortress Press.
bell hooks and Amalia Mesa-Bains, 2006, *Homegrown: Engaged Cultural Criticism*, Cambridge, MA: South End Press.
Ada María Isasi-Díaz, 1996, *Mujerista Theology*, Maryknoll, NY: Orbis Books.
Ada María Isasi-Díaz, 2003, 'Lo cotidiano, elemento intrínseco de la realidad', in Raúl Fornet Betancourt (ed.), *Resistencia y solidaridad. Globalización capitalista y liberación*, Madrid: Trotta, pp. 365–83.

Ada María Isasi-Díaz, 2004, *La Lucha Continues: Mujerista Theology*, Maryknoll, NY: Orbis Books.

Ada María Isasi-Díaz and Yolanda Tarango, 1988, *Hispanic Women: Prophetic Voice in the Church*, New York: HarperCollins.

Jens Manuel Krogstad and Luis Noe-Bustamante, 2020, 'Key Facts about U.S. Latinos for Hispanic Heritage Month', 10 September, Washington, DC: Pew Research Center, https://pewrsr.ch/2oH4TEC (accessed 27.3.24).

'Yolanda López: Artist Provocateur', https://www.lasmaestrascenter.ucsb.edu/yolanda-lopez-1 (accessed 27.3.24).

Nancy Pineda Madrid, 2011, *Suffering and Salvation in Ciudad Juárez*, Minneapolis, MN: Fortress Press.

Rosario Morales and Aurora Levins Morales, 2011, 'Ending Poem', in Ilan Stavans (ed.), *The Norton Anthology of Latino Literature*, New York: Norton, p. 985.

Laura E. Pérez, 2007, *Chicana Art. The Politics of Spiritual and Aesthetic Altarities*, Durham, NC: Duke University Press.

Robert B. Peterson and Juan Battle, 2018, 'Conexión a la Comunidad: Latinx LGBT Feelings of Connectedness', *Women, Gender and Families of Color* 6, pp. 202–25.

Andrea J. Pitts and José Medina, 2020, 'Introduction', in Andrea J. Pitts, Mariana Ortega, and José Medina (eds), *Theories of the Flesh. Latinx and Latin American Feminisms, Transformation, and Resistance*, Oxford: Oxford University Press.

Kimberly Ramírez, 2016, '(un)Learning Curves: Stripping the Myth of the "Real" Woman', *Latin American Theatre Review* 50, pp. 179–90.

Isabella Restrepo, 2019, 'Pathologizing Latinas', *Girlhood Studies* 13, pp. 1–17.

José David Rodríguez and Loida I. Martell-Otero (eds), 1997, *Teología en conjunto. A Collaborative Hispanic Protestant Theology*, Louisville, KY: Westminster John Knox Press.

Deyanira Rojas-Sosa, 2020, '"Should Latinas go blond?" Media representation and the regulation of Latina bodies and Latinas' social and cultural practices in a beauty magazine', *Gender and Language* 14, pp. 49–72.

Myriam Torres, 2010, 'The Constant Struggle of Latinas', *Journal of Latinos & Education* 9, pp. 255–7.

3

Asian Feminist Theologies: A Postcolonial Approach

AGNES M. BRAZAL

The Shift to a Postcolonial Approach

This chapter elaborates on how Asian feminist theologies are increasingly adopting a postcolonial approach, before focusing on my particular contribution to this process (Brazal 2023). Asian feminist theologies started to emerge in the late 1970s amid clarion calls in the relatively new independent countries for churches to contribute to nation-building or national reconstruction. The churches' response to the latter took the form of indigenizing/contextualizing theologies. Active in movements for democracy and national liberation, the first generation of Asian feminist theologians such as the Filipina Mary John Mananzan, Koreans Chung Hyun Kyung and Sun Ai Lee Park, and Hong Kong Chinese Kwok Pui-lan, engaged in liberation-oriented feminist theologizing (Kwok 2000).

By the mid-1980s, global integration, which has become more marked, generated new analytical frameworks. Globalization has intensified the exchange of information, services, goods and capital beyond national borders. Consequently, this led to the decentring of the nation-state, the politicizing of local cultural identities, and the fostering of transnational networks (Giddens 1999, p. 13). This changing context has given rise to new frameworks of analysis, among which is postcolonial theory. Postcolonial criticism aims at decolonizing knowledge by questioning the persistence of colonial/neo-colonial/metropolitan interests in cultural text/artifacts. It is different from decolonization processes that take culture as a homogenous entity. The critique of Orientalism and its concept of hybridity are among postcolonial theory's key ideas. Orientalism is a mode of representing the Orient or the East based on essentialist or stereotypical views, characterized by its dualistic view of the Orient and the Occident, the East and the West, with the effect of further strengthening western domination (Said 1994). Hybridity, on the other hand, refers to the fusion of identities and cultures or the creation of an in-beyond culture, as part of accommodation and resistance, in the context of unequal power relations (Bhabha 1994, p. 54). Orientalism and hybridity are useful analytical tools in the context of an increasingly connected and interdependent world. In the field of theology, the main tasks of postcolonial criticism are deconstruction, reconstruction and interrogation of metropolitan/dominant readings towards resistance and decolonization of knowledge.

By 2000, Asian feminist theologians, in direct conversation with postcolonial theory or via osmosis, have started appropriating a postcolonial lens in their doing of theology. This has resulted in the following shifts that are discernible today: (1) from unicity to multiplicity; (2) from vernacular hermeneutics to vernacular cosmopolitanism; (3) from liberation-feminist to postcolonial biblical reclamations; (4) from decent to indecent/queer theologizing; (5) from theologizing on the concrete to the virtual/cyberspace through the lens of 'unheard' voices.

From Unicity to Multiplicity

Formerly focused solely on women doing theology in Asia in their context of religious and cultural diversity on the one hand, and poverty and oppression on the other, Asian feminists, in the light of the uneven economic development in Asia with the rise of tiger economies, have been challenged to speak of 'multiple Asias' characterized by the juxtaposition of the modern and the traditional, the rich and the poor, the modern and the ancient. The phenomenon of migration, as well as our interconnection through the process of globalization, has also questioned the narrow definition of the Asian woman as 'based in Asia' or 'of Asian blood', and on what can be considered Asian feminist theology (Kwok 2000, p. 13). For Korean Nami Kim who is based in the US, Asian feminist theology encompasses all engagements with the term Asian to produce a feminist theology (Kim 2005). This means that one need not be based in Asia or of Asian descent to do feminist theology from an Asian perspective.

From Vernacular Hermeneutics to Vernacular Cosmopolitanism

Because of accusations that they are simply imitating their western counterparts, Asian feminist theologians recover elements from their indigenous or traditional cultures towards crafting a home-grown brand of feminism. This indigenizing orientation has generated for instance, in the Philippines, a 'national essence' feminism that glorified the precolonial past when it was only women and transgender women or cross-dressing men who could become religious leaders or *babaylans* (Roces 2010, p. 43).

Contemporary attempts at vernacular hermeneutics are more open to expanding the critical interrogation of the local in conversation with the global in what Homi Bhabha calls 'vernacular cosmopolitanism'. While retrieving the wisdom in local traditions/categories, this does not limit its conversation partners to those from the nation but engages as well with experiences and theoretical frameworks outside the country or the continent (Joh 2006). They employ both hermeneutics of appreciation and hermeneutics of suspicion on discourses on local culture as well as those from other contexts.

From Liberation Feminist to Postcolonial Hermeneutics

Asian feminist theologians interpret the Bible, suspicious of its ideological interpretations on the one hand, and foregrounding hidden voices of women in the text on the other, However, they generally assume the scripture text itself is not tainted by ideological contaminations (Gallares 1995; Melanchthon 2012).

Contemporary biblical interpretations critique not only the androcentric interpretations of the text but also ideologies embedded in the scripture texts themselves. In the process, the scripture texts serve as a mirror to engage with current realities. An example is British theologian Eve Rebecca Parker's rereading of Ezekiel 23 in her book *Theologising with the Sacred 'Prostitutes' of South India* (2012). She shows how Ezekiel 23 embeds patriarchal and exclusivist nationalistic ideologies and portrays God as supporting the rape, torture and murder of the sexually immoral. She likened the plight of Oholah and Oholibah in Exekiel 23 to those of the *devadāsīs* or the sacred prostitutes of India and the Dalit women who are likewise considered impure. Rereading this text is important as Dalit Christians establish their identity through sharing the Bible in their communities.

From Decent to Indecent/Queer Theologizing

Asian feminist theologians were more reticent in discussing issues of sexuality since talking about this in public was considered taboo. Thus they initially focused on relatively 'decent' sex-related topics such as prostitution and sexual violence against women (e.g. Mananzan 1998). The anthology *Body and Sexuality*, a compilation of articles by the Ecclesia of

Women in Asia (Brazal and Lizares-Si 2007), started breaking this taboo when it foraged into 'indecent' theology with Joseph Pushpa's article 'Revisioning Eros for Asian Feminist Theologizing', and Sharon Bong's 'Queer Revisions of Christianity', among others. Indecent theology dialogues gender with postcolonial and queer theory (Althaus-Reid 2003, pp. 114, 134), and is also used to refer to any theology that tackles sexuality topics regarded as vulgar, taboo or irreverent.

From Theologizing on the Concrete to the Virtual/Cyberspace

With Asia as a major producer and consumer of cyber-technologies, the Ecclesia of Women in Asia also pioneered Asian theological reflection on cyber-technologies and culture in its anthology *Feminist Cyberethics in Asia: Religious Discourses on Human Connectivity* (Brazal and Abraham 2014). This anthology dealt with how cyber-technologies are shaping gender relations and religious cultures, and examines the ethical, religious and feminist challenges it poses, from voices not usually heard in discussions on cyber-technologies.

My Liberation-Postcolonial Approach[1]

My liberation-postcolonial methodology always starts with a negative contrast experience, an experience of suffering, that demands a rethinking of theology. In engaging in vernacular cosmopolitan and/or constructive theologizing, I have appropriated neo-Marxist and postcolonial theorist Stuart Hall's circuit of culture as a heuristic guide in analysing any cultural or theological category. The circuit of culture consists of steps through which a cultural text/artefact must be analysed: representation, identity, production, consumption and regulation. Representation examines the various ways a cultural 'text' has been represented. Identity looks at the various identities (based on gender, social class, age, nationality, etc.) involved in each of these representations. Production focuses on the socio-economic-political-historical conditions in the development of these discourses. Consumption centres on how these discourses have been received, rejected or negotiated by various groups. Regulation analyses these discourses' ethical impact or how they regulate conduct. The circuit of culture blends philosophico-cultural and structural analysis. My appropriation of the circuit of culture in my method of postcolonial theologizing addresses the critique that postcolonial discourse lacks a structural analysis of power relations, and is the reason why I hyphenate my postcolonial approach with the term 'liberation' (Brazal 2019, pp. xxxi–xxxiii, 31–47).

Employing both a hermeneutics of appreciation and suspicion, I draw on the life-giving discourses related to a theme and engage these with the faith tradition, to construct (a vernacular cosmopolitan) theology. Two themes I have theologized on from a liberation-postcolonial feminist perspective are Balance/Fluidity of Opposites and the Cyborg and Cyberchurch.

Balance/Fluidity of Opposites

A reimagining of what it means to be human (theological anthropology) is called for as an alternative to the rigid gender complementarity in church teaching. Our concept of the human is foundational to how we see the role of women and men in society and in relation to creation. Along this line, one Asian cultural category that promises potential is the belief that power or harmony results from the balance of opposites.

The Javanese in Indonesia view the capacity to hold opposites in balance as a manifestation of power. This is captured in the classic image of the ardhanari statue whose left side is physically female and the right side male. Benedict Anderson describes this as follows: 'The essential characteristic of this combination of opposites is ... their dynamic simultaneous incorporation within a single entity ... He is at once masculine and feminine, containing both conflicting elements within himself and holding them in a tense electric balance' (Anderson 1972, p. 14). In the Philippine context, the same can be said of some discourses on Lakas (strength)-Ganda (beauty).

A popular Philippine creation myth narrates the simultaneous emergence of the first woman and man from bamboo. Possibly in an attempt to impose their complementary and dualistic gender construct on the natives, the Spanish colonizers named the male *Malakas* (strength) and the female *Maganda* (beauty) (Eugenio 1993, pp. 293–6). This however has been ingeniously subverted to represent a more fluid understanding of gender. Powerful women and men are those that can balance or integrate both strength (courage; fortitude) and beauty (gracious goodness). The *babaylans* – the pre-colonial religious leaders consisting mostly of women – are the iconic symbol of female power and leadership. They manifested beauty as friends of the spirits and bringers of peace to the community, and strength in their persistence to resist the colonizers long after the male leaders who stand to benefit from the patriarchal religion have capitulated to the Spanish invaders (Brewer 2001). During the Marcos dictatorship, two female symbols of strength and moral beauty were the militant nun and the political activist. They showed moral beauty as they spoke with or on behalf of the victims of martial rule (Mercado 1994, pp. 88–9).[2]

The beauty–strength dialectic is apparent in popular Catholic beliefs and practices such as the Santacruzan. The Santacruzan, which is the most popular folk religious procession in the country, features physically beautiful women to represent strong female characters in the Bible and in Christian history, such as Esther, Judith and Mary Magdalene, with the focus on Queen Helena who found the cross of Jesus with the young Constantine. Christ has also been imaged by nineteenth-century revolutionaries against imperial Spain as someone whose power (lakas) emanates from his beautiful and attractive *loob* (Ileto 1979, p. 41).

In the light of the Church's notion of complementarity between women and men, which determines a priori their primary role/vocation in the church and in society, the strength–beauty dialectic holds potential for an alternative way of understanding femaleness and maleness as being held in balance within a single entity.

As a way of looking at the human, lakas and ganda here are not opposite and contradictory characteristics that are identified with a specific gender. Beauty and strength are present in each individual. In this Filipin@ theological anthropology, lakas is not considered superior to ganda. Lakas (strength) in fact must be guided by ganda (beauty) while ganda without lakas, on the other hand, is weak. It is best to reimagine lakas-ganda as qualities present in each individual in various degrees. A powerful person or even society is one that can integrate both of these qualities or hold them in balance.

In the article 'Harmonizing Power-Beauty' (2010) I demonstrated how Sophia, in the book of Wisdom, and Jesus manifest lakas (power) guided by ganda (gracious goodness). Spirit-Sophia permeates all things with her creative power (Wisd. 7.23, 25; 8.5–6) and redeems the righteous ones in their travails from the time of Adam to Moses; she led the Israelites out of Egypt and through the desert, because of her boundless mercy (Wisd. 10—11).

Jesus as Sophia made flesh exhibited both lakas (fortitude; courage) and ganda (gracious goodness) in his ministry and in his persistence in preaching the good news of God's reign despite the criticisms from religious authorities. Various expressions of lakas and ganda are likewise evident in migrant mothers and fathers left behind as they navigate their new roles in the family, the mother as breadwinner and the father as caretaker and house manager.

Lakas-ganda is a gender-fluid anthropology primarily in the sense of going beyond the masculine–feminine binary. It examines the dynamics of lakas-ganda within an individual, within a community, or the whole society.

Church as Sacrament of Yin-yang Harmony

One finds a similar discourse in yin and yang. East Asian cultures believe harmony is the fruit of a balance and blending of the fluid dualities of yin and yang. In Daoism/Taoism, yin and yang are the two generative forces in the universe; all beings possess the duality of yin and yang. The imbalance of yin and yang blocks the flow of Qi the 'source of vitality, harmony, creativity, and moral courage' and can lead to chaos or illness (Guiley 1991, p. 627).

Chinese scholar Robin Wang notes that things are not essentially yin nor yang but they are so relative to something (Wang 2005). One may be small compared to a mountain but large compared to an ant. Furthermore, yin and yang forces continuously interact and affect each other in a constant transformation.

The gendering of yin and yang, that is, the association of yin with female and yang with maleness occurred with Dong Zhongshu (179–104 BCE) founder of imperial Confucianism, who merged yinyang theory into Confucianism (Wang 2005, p. 209). This led to the loss of earlier features such as its fluidity since Zhongshu's interpretation favours the superiority of yang over yin.

The earlier interpretation of yin and yang as functions in certain contexts, instead of fixed characteristics, can be fruitful for reimagining man/woman, cleric/lay, and other dualities in the church, as fluid polarities. The ideal person and society is one with a harmonious blending of yin and yang functions. An excess in yang can be addressed by fostering more yin functions, and an excess in yin, by developing more yang functions.

Unlike lakas-ganda, yin and yang are not qualities or characteristics but rather are descriptive of functions (active and passive) relative to certain contexts. Both, however, are not qualities/functions specific to a particular gender but are possessed within an individual/community/society.

In the church as sacrament of yinyang harmony, no one group – male or female, clergy or lay – can be stereotyped as assuming greater yang/'active' or yin/'passive' roles. In their participation in ministries, their yin and yang can be in constant transformation (with some active in certain ministries more than in others).

The Cyborg and the Cyberchurch

The digital revolution challenges us to interrogate its impact on women and theology. Emerging from contemporary cyber cultural discourses, the cyborg is another fruitful image that goes beyond hierarchical dualistic binaries. A cyborg, as Donna Haraway describes it, is a hybrid creature that transgresses the boundaries between animal-human (organism) and machine, male/female, the physical/non-physical, and so on (Haraway 1991). In the cyborg, the machine is no longer just a person's instrument but becomes part of the person's embodiment. In 'A Cyborg Spirituality and its Theo-Anthropological Foundation' (2014), I underscored the similarities between the cyborg – a half-human and half-machine – and East Asian animist beliefs on a tool's possession of the spirit of its owner, as well as how the Spirit in scriptures (ruach, hokmah/Sophia and shekinah) indwells, vivifies and animates not only humans but all of matter and space.

Andrea Vicini and I also explored how the 'body of Christ' metaphor can provide guidelines for evaluating cyber-anthropologies that regard the virtual as bodiless (cybergnosis) (Brazal and Vicini 2015). This notion that the body can be separated from the self in cyberspace has been used to minimize the impact of cyber-violence against women (Brazal 2020). It has also fostered escape from the suffering of human life. By stressing embodiment and sacramentality, the body of Christ metaphor rejects this dualistic cybergnostic anthropology. The Eucharist as the body of Christ highlights the transformation of material elements as an embodiment of the sacred, and thus the potential epiphany of the sacred in the cyborg and the cyborg society. Difference and solidarity in the body of Christ (1 Cor. 12.12–27) call us to recognize the diversity of cyborgs and to avoid replicating exclusionary structures of domination on the Internet.

Based on the above theo-anthropological presuppositions, I outlined the following features of a feminist cyborg spirituality of communication: (1) affirms the presence of God's spirit in all of creation, both in organic and human-made tools or technologies; (2) recognizes the cyborg as a moral agent; (3) respects the plurality and diversity of cyborgs; (4) creates spaces and resists exclusion; (5) networks for social change.

On the ecclesiological front, the pandemic has pushed churches to morph into cyberchurches that do worship, evangelization, Christian formation and community via the Internet. A cyberchurch can either be a fully online church or a hybrid church that is linked to a concrete church. Teresa Camarines and I discovered, in our research on 'Women's Reception of Cyberchurches during the Pandemic' (Brazal and Camarines

2023), that cyberchurches in the National Capital Region in the Philippines have helped sustain women's religious needs during the pandemic.[3] Furthermore, women have played a significant role in maintaining the religious well-being of their household and community. As the study projects an increase in ten online religious activities post-pandemic, this seems to suggest (subject to further validation) that the future of the church is hybrid. A caveat, however, was the significant decrease in Mass attendance of women aged between 30 and 49 years, which corresponds to the age of young mothers who may be finding it difficult to create a sacred space in their homes for online Mass while taking care of young children.

A cyberchurch can likewise help in migrants' integration in the receiving country as well as fortify their links with the home society. The Saint John Neumann Migrant Centre/Facebook page (a virtual extension of the Our Lady of Perpetual Help Shrine in Baclaran, Philippines) has served as a crucial lifeline for Filipina migrants in the Middle East, who experience abuse from their employers (Brazal and Lacsa 2022). It educates the migrants about their rights, rescues migrants in distress, and helps them to start anew. It also responds to their religious needs, especially in contexts where the public worship of Christians is not allowed (Brazal and Odchigue 2015).

An online church can be imagined as an 'altar of remembrance' (Campbell 2005, p. 162). In the Old Testament, at various times in their history, Israel set up an altar of remembrance to mark a space where God performed a miracle or where God rescued Israel or imparted a significant lesson (Gen. 28.10–19; 33.20; 35.1–3; Ex. 17.8–16; 24.4; Josh. 4.1–9). The cyberchurch as an 'altar of remembrance' is a place or a site where, through various activities and rituals, one can relive the moments when one has personally and concretely experienced God's presence and gracious goodness, in situations when it is impossible to meet in person (e.g., during the pandemic, or in countries where public worship is prohibited, etc.). An altar of remembrance, precisely because it serves as a means to remember, implies the need for these memories to be nourished by communal face-to-face encounters whenever possible.

Conclusion

Even without identifying their works as postcolonial, a number of second- and third-generation Asian feminist theologians have manifested a shift towards this approach in their theologizing: (1) from unicity to multiplicity in their concept of Asia, Asian women's identity and Asian feminist theologizing; (2) from vernacular hermeneutics to vernacular cosmopolitanism; (3) from liberation-feminist to postcolonial biblical reclamations; (4) from decent to indecent/queer theologizing; and (5) from theologizing on the concrete to the virtual/cyberspace.

In this chapter, I expounded on my contribution to this process in terms of my liberation-postcolonial approach to doing theology, focused on the themes of balance of opposites and the contemporary cyberculture. The Asian concept of power or harmony in the balance of opposites (lakas-ganda or yin-yang) as well as the more contemporary image of the cyborg, can provide alternative theo-anthropological metaphors that go beyond hierarchical dualisms. My theologizing on the cyberculture has likewise been shaped by a postcolonial approach in its concern with issues of digital exclusion and cyber-violence against women on the one hand, and empowerment of women through cyber-technologies on the other. It reimagines theological anthropology, spirituality and ecclesiology in these contexts.

Notes

1 I consider my engagement with the Ecclesia of Women in Asia as a contribution to Asian Feminist Theologizing in general. As Coordinator of the Ecclesia of Women in Asia in its struggling infancy and Consultant in its first decade of existence, I helped nurture its growth till it attained maturity and stability as an organization. I also served as its Joint Treasurer from 2004 to the present and co-edited three of its biennial publications: *Body and Sexuality* (2007), *Feminist Cyberethics in Asia* (2014), and *Towards Life-giving Communities in a Post-Pandemic World* (2023).

2 In many Philippine languages, the ethically good is referred to as 'beautiful' (*maganda*) while moral evil is called 'ugly' (*pangit*).

3 The Philippines had one of the longest and strictest periods of quarantine so far in the world.

Bibliography

Marcella Althaus-Reid, 2003, *The Queer God*, London: Routledge.
Benedict Anderson, 1972, 'The Idea of Power in Javanese Culture', in Claire Holt (ed.), *Culture and Politics in Indonesia*, Ithaca, NY and London: Cornell University Press.
Homi Bhabha, 1994, *The Location of Culture*, London and New York: Routledge.
Sharon Bong, 2007, 'Queer Revisions of Christianity', in Agnes Brazal and Andrea

Lizares-Si (eds), *Body and Sexuality*, Quezon City: Ateneo de Manila University Press, pp. 234-49.

Agnes Brazal, 2010, 'Harmonizing Power-Beauty: Gender Fluidity in the Migration Context', *Asian Christian Review* 4 (2), pp. 32-46.

Agnes Brazal, 2014, 'A Cyborg Spirituality and its Theo-Anthropological Foundation', in Agnes Brazal and Kochurani Abraham (eds), *Feminist Cyberethics in Asia: Religious Discourses on Human Connectivity*, New York: Palgrave Macmillan, pp. 199-219.

Agnes Brazal, 2019, *A Theology of Southeast Asia: Liberation Post-colonial Ethics in the Philippines*, Maryknoll, NY: Orbis Books.

Agnes Brazal, 2020, 'Recasting Ethics of Face and Hiya (Shame) in the light of Cybersexual Violence Against Women', *International Journal of Practical Theology* 24 (2), pp. 285-302.

Agnes M. Brazal, 2023, 'Asian Feminist Theologies: Shifts and Directions', in Peter Phan (ed.), *Oxford Handbook of Asian Christian Theologies*, Oxford: Oxford University Press.

Agnes Brazal and Kochurani Abraham (eds), 2014, *Feminist Cyberethics in Asia: Religious Discourses on Human Connectivity*, New York: Palgrave Macmillan.

Agnes Brazal and Teresa Camarines, 2023, 'Women's Reception of Cyber Churches during the Pandemic and Indications for the Future', *Acta Theologica* 43 (supp. 35).

Agnes Brazal and Jose Eric Lacsa, 2022, 'Saint John Neumann Migrants Centre/FaceBook Page. A Case Study of a Cyberchurch', *Exchange: Journal of Contemporary Christianities in Context* 51 (1), pp. 3-21.

Agnes Brazal and Andrea Lizares-Si (eds), 2007, *Body and Sexuality: Theological-Pastoral Perspectives of Women in Asia*, Quezon City: Ateneo de Manila University Press.

Agnes Brazal and Randy Odchigue, 2015, 'Cyber-Church and Filipin@ Migrants in the Middle East', in Susanna Snyder, Joshua Ralston and Agnes Brazal (eds), *Church in the Age of Global Migration: A Moving Body*, New York: Palgrave Macmillan, pp. 187-99.

Agnes Brazal and Rasika Pieris (eds), 2023, 'Towards Life-giving Communities in a Post-Pandemic World', *Acta Theologica* 43 (supp. 35).

Agnes Brazal and Andrea Vicini, 2015, 'Longing for Transcendence: Cyborgs, Trans- and Posthumans', *Theological Studies* 76 (1), pp. 148-65.

Carolyn Brewer, 2001, *Holy Confrontation: Religion, Gender and Sexuality in the Philippines, 1521-1685*, Manila: Institute of Women's Studies, St Scholastica's College, pp. 309-50.

Heidi Campbell, 2005, *Exploring Religious Community Online: We are One in the Network*, New York: Peter Lang.

Damiana Eugenio, 1993, *The Myths*, Vol. 2. *Philippine Folk Literature*, Quezon City: University of the Philippines Press, pp. 293-6.

Judette Gallares, 1995, *Images of Courage: Spirituality of Women in the Gospels from an Asian and a Third World Perspective*, Quezon City: Cenacle Philippines and Claretian Publications.

Anthony Giddens, 1999, *Runaway World: How Globalization is Reshaping our Lives*, London: Profile Books.

Rosemary Guiley, 1991, *Harper's Encyclopedia of Mystical and Paranormal Experience*, Edison, NJ: Castle Books.
Donna Haraway, 1991, 'A Cyborg Manifesto: Science, Technology, and Socialist-Feminism in the Late Twentieth Century', in Donna Haraway, *Simians, Cyborgs, and Women: The Reinvention of Nature*, New York: Routledge, pp. 149–81.
Reynaldo Clemeña Ileto, 1979, *Pasyon and Revolution: Popular Movements in the Philippines, 1840–1910*, Quezon City: Ateneo de Manila University Press.
Wonhee Anne Joh, 2006, *Heart of the Cross: A Postcolonial Christology*, Louisville, KY: Westminster John Knox Press.
Nami Kim, 2005, '"My/Our" Comfort Not at the Expense of "Somebody Else's": Toward a Critical Global Feminist Theology', *Journal of Feminist Studies in Religion* 21 (2), pp. 75–94.
Kwok Pui-lan, 2000, *Introducing Asian Feminist Theology*, Sheffield: Sheffield Academic Press.
Mary John Mananzan OSB, 1998, 'Prostitution in the Philippines', in *Challenges to the Inner Room: Selected Essays and Speeches on Women*, Manila: Institute of Women's Studies, St Scholastica's College, pp. 196–208.
Monica Jyotsna Melanchthon, 2012, 'Unleashing the Power Within: The Bible and Dalits', in Roland Boer and Fernando F. Segovia (eds), *The Future of the Biblical Past: Envisioning Biblical Studies on a Global Key*, Atlanta, GA: Society of Biblical Literature, pp. 49–65.
Leonardo Mercado, 1994, *The Filipino Mind: Philippine Philosophical Studies II*, Washington, DC: Council for Research in Values and Philosophy.
Eve Rebecca Parker, 2021, *Theologising with the Sacred 'Prostitutes' of South India*, Currents of Encounter, Leiden: Brill.
Pushpa Joseph FMM, 2007, 'Revisioning Eros for Asian Feminist Theologizing: Some Pointers from Tantric Philosophy', in Agnes Brazal and Andrea Lizares-Si (eds), *Body and Sexuality: Theological-Pastoral Perspectives of Women in Asia*, Quezon City: Ateneo de Manila University Press, pp. 34–57.
Mina Roces, 2010, 'Rethinking the "Filipino Woman": A Century of Women's Activism in the Philippines, 1905–2006', in Mina Roces and Louise Edwards (eds), *Women's Movements in Asia: Feminist and Transnational Activism*, London: Routledge, p. 43.
Edward Said, 1994, *Orientalism*, New York: Vintage Books
Robin R. Wang, 2005, 'Dong Zhongshu's Transformation of Yin-Yang Theory and Contesting of Gender Identity', *Philosophy East and West* 55 (2), pp. 209–31.

4

Good Feminist Collaboration

CATHRYN MCKINNEY AND REBEKAH PRYOR

While we might say that life itself is a collaborative endeavour – a given condition of being – this chapter makes two specific enquiries: What is good collaboration? And, in feminist theological contexts, how do we do it?

Following our feminist theological instincts, we think beyond collaboration as an innate and integral function of human existence to the nature of good collaboration when it pursues a feminist intention and is animated by feminist processes. On the way to proposing methodologies for this way of working, we explore factors such as difference, intimacy, boundaries, power, authority and collusion and critical praxis to understand how they aid or limit good feminist theological collaboration.

What is Collaboration?

Collaboration is when at least two people align to work together to realize a shared intention.[1] To collaborate well is to engage purposefully. Good collaboration requires a degree of unity realized through negotiated intention and processes. Roles emerge out of such negotiation; indeed, successful collaboration is contingent on clarity about specific roles and who they are taken up by.

Etymologically, collaboration is linked to the prefix *com-* ('beside, near, by, with') and the verb *labour* (from the Latin, *laborare* meaning 'to work, endeavour, take pains, exert oneself; produce by toil; suffer, be afflicted; be in distress or difficulty') (see Etymonline), the meanings of which imply the proximity of collaborators to each other and the effort their collaboration inevitably demands of them.

Collaboration's antonyms may best be articulated as resistance, disassociation or neglect – each a consequence of lack or inadequacy of proximity and/or effort – resulting in the erosion and eventual annihilation of all that might have been.

In this chapter, we propose that *intention* is the central feature of collaboration – it is the thing that frames and contains good collaboration. The intention of any good collaboration must be articulated without ambiguity in order for it to enable participation. Clarity of purpose allows possible roles within the collaborative relationship to be identified and considered. Functioning as a container in which the key characteristics of *nature*, *context* and *composition* are contained, intention maintains its own integrity but not without being symbiotically affected by the interplay of the internal features it holds. The nature of any collaboration is determined by the manner in which the collaborators are animated. It is particular: to who is collaborating; what rules of engagement they need to generate in order to achieve their intended objective; practically, how they communicate with each other; and how will they share the work. The nature of collaboration is determined by what approaches collaborators take to ensure their unity of intention, communication, negotiation, critical reflection and reflexive responses. The context of collaboration is also critical to understanding the impact of collaboration. How does the place or setting in which the collaborative relationship arises and operates impact upon its life and potential? What external factors aid or pressure it as the collaborators aim to achieve their shared goal? How might an experience of lack aid in the location of resource in service to the shared goal? The composition of collaboration is also important in understanding its potential outcomes. Determined by the circumstances in which the collaborative intention was devised, the composition of the collaborative relationship is determined by which people or groups are collaborating and what desires, needs, strengths and agendas they bring to the relationship. This, in turn, determines how power and authority will be shared and exercised between them.

Features of Feminist Collaboration

Philosophy has long been concerned with what it means to live a good life, though the popularity of the discipline as an integral part of the everyday has changed over time (Cottingham 1998, pp. 1–4). Nevertheless, like other branches of philosophically informed thought, feminisms remain concerned with the conditions that affect the ability of people to live freely in ways that honour the dignity, autonomy and authority that is innate and proper to their humanity.[2] Feminisms particularly address the patriarchal ideologies, structures and histories that have kept women and others from living full, free lives. While there are as many ways of doing feminist collaboration as there are feminisms, we propose that there are at least four features good feminist approaches share.

Etymological allusions to both the ploughing of fields and the birthing of children already point to the embodied and relational nature of collaboration and its impacts, on certain (labouring) bodies. Compelled by feminist concerns, the first feature of good feminist collaboration is that its intention is *transformation*, achieved via strategies that dissent, deliberately oppose, subvert or otherwise productively counter personal, social and political oppressions brought on by patriarchal ideologies, practices, systems and structures. Whatever the strategies used to achieve it, a feminist intention is developed on the assumption of the autonomy and agency of collaborators and their mutual commitment to an ethical relationship. Far from being naive, these assumptions are grounded in a deep understanding of the distinctions between power and authority, as well as an embodied awareness of the implications of these for the possible liberty, justice and flourishing of women and all others.

The intention, as well as assumptions that inform its development, shape the nature of the collaboration. This leads to a second feature of good feminist collaboration: that its nature is *reflexive*. Guided by an ethics of difference that recognizes the irreducibility and related autonomy of individual collaborators, one with another, feminist collaboration is dialogical and action-oriented. Importantly, it is characterized by postures of movement and pause that help to recognize and, more than that, venerate the irreducibility and related autonomy of each one. Irigaray's 'sensible transcendental' – by which the divine is conjured up 'among us, within us, as resurrection and transfiguration of blood, of flesh, through a language and an ethics that is ours' (Irigary 1993, p. 129) – is helpful in describing what this reflexivity and movement enables. Good feminist collaboration celebrates each collaborator's presence and potential contribution, however small or large, however externally lauded or censured. At its best, a feminist collaborative engagement makes and safeguards the space between collaborators as an ethical space or interval by which their difference is preserved (Irigaray 1993, p. 48). The two (or more) collaborators thus maintain their autonomy, even as they work together to realize their shared intention.

A third feature of good feminist collaboration is that its context is *particular* and acknowledged as the site (or sites) where the lack that potentially limits the collaboration is encountered *and* where the resources on which it depends are located. It is within the collaborative context that anxiety about capacity can emerge. And so, a feminist comprehension of context as complex and plentiful, enables interactions – often discarded as personal – to be distinguished as significant and useful, not least as a resource for working through the emotion, resistance, defence, competition and power 'struggles', all aspects of human experience, that can inevitably arise through the collaboration.

The amalgamation of intention, nature and context affects how any collaborative engagement is composed. Thus, the fourth feature of good feminist collaboration is that its composition is *reflective* of the differences and ongoing differentiation of the collaborators and the multiple enquiries (however aligned) that emerge as they collaborate. Careful, nuanced and expressive use of language is critical as collaborators proceed, not only in articulating their shared intention but in continually communicating their own questions and expectations. This attention to how words are being used can make all the difference to the relationship and its potential for achieving its goals.[3] While there are a whole range of factors that get in the way of good collaboration – and we will elaborate on some on these later – misunderstanding, confrontation and disagreement needn't necessarily be problematic. Indeed, when guided by the good feminist collaboration's reflexive nature, these tensions can be signs of health and, potentially, useful provocations to refine or adjust the collaborators' intention or modes of engagement.

From a feminist perspective, beyond identifying common features such as the four described here, there can be no predetermined formula or recipe for achieving good collaboration. In reality, collaborators must generate processes that are specific only to them and that are developed to suit their particular intention, nature, context and composition. Feminist collaboration can thus look and feel messy, chaotic even. But, as Jeong-Eun Rhee contends, 'Any prototype or ideal of what we yearn for relationship and solidarity may limit what we can do together' (Rhee 2021, p. 82). Feminist collaborative processes therefore are resolutely and necessarily provisional. They always serve the health and success of the collaboration, the collaborators, their context and the shared intention that holds them together.

Relatedly then, while there are no prescriptions or limits regarding duration, collaborations are finite, depending entirely on the achievement of the intention and its objectives. Whether in collaboration or some other kind of relationship of cooperation, companionship or solidarity, as Rhee (with reference to the short-lived collaborative encounter between two different characters in Toni Morrison's 1987 novel, *Beloved*) says, 'We do not have to be bound together for good. Sometimes, these temporary and fleeting connections we can do appropriately and well together can become a name of our future and what can eventually heal and transform us' (Rhee 2021, p. 82).

Feminist Theological Approaches

Feminist theological approaches to collaboration are characterized by theological and spiritual aspects in combination with the specific features of good feminist collaboration outlined above. They are also developed through alignment and engagement with a range of distinct theological areas and ideas.

Through alignment with process theologies, feminist theological approaches draw the apophatic saying and unsaying of certainties about God (who is identified as 'moved and moving' (Keller 2015, p. 122)), which is possible thanks to an assumed posture of reflexivity that helps feminist theological collaborators proceed 'without even an idea' (McRandal 2021, p. 125) or end in sight, that is, without desire or expectation of any teleological arrival. From contextual theologies comes an awareness of proximity to place, especially the people, cultures and ecologies of that place. Such awareness heightens understanding of the collaborative context and composition and helps collaborators refine their shared intention for greatest, most transformative impact. Further, when collaborators come together to work from and within their own contexts, their engagement and the outcomes it can lead to bear particular power and authority and resonance, especially as they 'speak up' and 'speak out' about the impacts of external forces like colonization and of internal challenges like violence against women it and other patriarchal ideologies and structures (including inside the Christian church) incite (Carroll 2021, pp. 16–17).

Through engagement with liberation theologies, feminist theological approaches to collaboration reflect a deep commitment to justice and freedom for all people experiencing extreme vulnerability (particularly through poverty) and oppression. When feminist collaborators purposefully engage with liberation theologies, they effectively 'uncover male supremacy inherent in patriarchal cultures in biblical and contemporary contexts, and discover alternatives that are life-giving and congruent with the Gospel imperative, love plus (+) justice' (Jakobsen and Pillay 2022, p. 339). Heeding the challenges womanist theologians have posed to feminisms throughout their histories, good feminist theological approaches to collaboration centre the experiences, rights and well-being of the person, particularly Black women and People of Colour. When theology 'turns' itself this way, it ensures that the person is not reduced and reproduced as the (imperial) subject (Williams 1991), figured as 'abstract, bloodless, disembodied, deracinated, and distant' (Copeland 2019, p. 768). Rather, 'the *person* is tangible and solid, flesh and blood, material and embodied; rooted in space and time, in culture and relationships. The person is close – so close she or he [or they] can be smelled, heard, touched, seen, even tasted' (Copeland 2019, p. 768).

From ecofeminist theologies comes a certain sense of humanity's connectedness with the Earth and its more-than-human others (Gebara 1999; Elvey 2022). This awareness is carried into good feminist collaboration, with collaborators remaining alert to how their cultural frameworks, theological convictions, collective processes, ideas and actions lead to or away from the flourishing of all of creation.[4] From queer theologies, comes a pattern that rejects grand, homogenizing narratives and seeks 'God' and related spiritual, theological, social and political wisdom in the ordinariness and 'indecency' of everyday life (Althaus-Reid 2000; Isherwood 1999). Feminist approaches that follow this instinct ask related, sometimes-provocative, always-critical questions and proceed with this clear task in mind: 'to find or simply recognize God sitting amongst us, at any time, in any gay bar or in the home of a camp friend who decorates her living room as a chapel and doesn't leave her rosary at home when going to a salsa bar' (Althaus-Reid 2003, p. 4).

Feminist theological approaches to collaboration are bolstered by postcolonial theologies that expose, interrogate and resist hegemonic colonial and empirical histories and myths (including the ways these have essentialized identities). Following this priority, feminist collaborators step into 'critical/radical openness to the cultural hybridity of our time and to have a constant sensitivity to the "other" in various forms, not reducing the "other" to the totality of the "same"' (Kang 2004, p. 117). Good feminist theological approaches to collaboration also lean in to hear the wisdom and challenge of First Nations theologies, learning with respect for their cultural traditions and connections to Country at the same time as remaining 'unsettled' by the colonial histories that have tried to diminish them (Prentis 2020).

Notably, this is not an exhaustive summary. Feminist theological approaches also look for the theologies of women and others in places of life and thought not represented by discourse or literature. They tend to those whose theological instincts and leadership are only ever embodied and visible in their daily rhythms (including of labour) and relationships. They seek out the perspectives and insights of those whose theologies are expressed in oral traditions, ritual practices and domestic gestures of care. Informed as they are by such a breadth of experience and insight, feminist theological approaches thus bring a range of elements to good collaboration. To collaborative intention, they bring divine, fecund, embodied, collective *possibility*, including of revelation. To collaborative nature, they bring a kind of *communion*, cultivated by breath and postures of relationality and connection that bear their own material and ontological implications. To collaborative context: *power* and *authority* informed by *hope* that there are still things about God, the world, ourselves, to be thought and transformed. To collaborative composition: an open *invitation* for others not yet participating in the collaborative relationship to join.

What Gets in the Way of Good Collaboration?

We have started to identify the important factors that make up a congenial environment for good collaboration. But what is the antithesis of this? Feminist collaboration sets out to be good collaboration and, as such, a way of *doing ethics* (Lindemann 2005, p. 4). It seeks to incorporate and align the collaborative features we have defined for the benefit of all parties involved in the collaboration. Given this ambition, the question of what gets in the way of good collaboration is an important enquiry. When a collaborative engagement becomes un-collaborative, we might ask: What *is* in the way? *What is happening here* to cause the collaboration to disintegrate? What is *getting in* the way?

Collaboration can occur with varying degrees of 'success'. We can therefore say that people can collaborate ineffectively, unconstructively and in ways that cause harm. As we have identified, an intention to work purposefully together in service to a mutually agreed upon goal is integral to good collaboration and inseparable from good feminist collaboration. But collaboration can develop into a divisive interaction. The antithesis of collaboration is collusion, disguised sometimes as collaboration but with an entirely different intention. Collusion is an agreement between people to act together secretly or illegally in order to deceive or cheat someone. The intention of a collusive act is deceitful, and whether direct or tacit, to collude is to conspire to harm another person or persons. Collusion is an act of violence.

Why is this a distinction of importance? Good collaboration requires boundaries to be renegotiated in a mutually beneficial way. The sharing of ideas of ownership and revelation, along with the taking up of additional work, are things that can only be done successfully if the collaborators trust one another. Collusion ruptures boundaries, resulting in an environment utterly discordant with good collaboration. Systems theory[5] is helpful here as boundaries need to be identified in order to be crossed and, in the identification process, collaboration is necessary; a reflexive cycle of engagement enabling a growth mindset to be cultivated and good collaborative intention to be nurtured.

When asking what gets in the way of good collaboration, we are moving into an exploration of the nature of being human. Envy, competition and power 'struggles' are present when people engage. To collaborate well, being able to recognize and articulate such dynamics can foster curiosity rather than enabling these animations to eradicate or corrupt an environment where collaboration might be possible. Beyond these things, we identify two other significant factors that 'get in the way' of good collaboration: a lack of capacity to manage intimacy, and a confusion about power and authority.

Intimacy

Etymologically, intimacy is the action of making known or familiar. We can say that to engage intimately in the context of good feminist collaboration is to foster a familiarity with another person or group, to lean towards an idea of belonging in consideration of a good collaborative endeavour. In this sense, good collaborative intention allows for a person to interact authentically in a secure environment. An intimate posture allows for the renegotiation of personal and systemic boundaries to occur and fosters not only an awareness of defensive reactions that might emerge, but a comprehension that nothing is experienced in isolation; a collaborative encounter is always met by a collaborative response.

In addition, an intimate posture allows for collaborators to be alert to the dangers of interactions that become solely fixated on one person or issue. Good feminist collaboration emulates the truth that, while everything is experienced by a person, nothing is ever *just* personal. This is resonant with the age-old feminist conviction that 'the personal is political'; in turn, we contend that the political is never *just* personal. Systemic and contextual influences require people to engage with a degree of intimacy – exploring and wondering together. A lack of capacity to engage with intimacy (Roberts 2006) paradoxically can leave a person feeling isolated within a group and potentially exposed.

Power and Authority

Power and authority are often used interchangeably to explain influence, privilege and capacity. We contend that the difference between power and authority is significant and clarity about this can have a profound impact on how we respond to the inevitable conflicting dynamics that are present within collaborative spaces. Both power and authority, matched in quality and influence, are required if good collaboration is to be undertaken. If one is greater than the other, people can feel dominated and oppressed (where power is exercised without authority), or impotent and frustrated (where there is authority with no power) (Reed and Armstrong 2013, p. 119). Herein lies the issue: if we confuse power and authority then the concept of authority becomes confused with authoritarianism and power can be understood as solely malevolent (McKinney 2021). When power is dominant, the collaborative intention can become corrupted by the control being sought or resisted, hierarchies will emerge and, in this environment, annihilation of mutual capacity is inevitable (Chattopadhyay 1999). Where authority is exercised, there can be space for a person or group to make use of their internal capacity, using judgement and creativity, along with such things as collaborators' existing networks, skills, expertise, cultural, social and historical knowledge, as resources to aid the work. Summarily, good collaboration can exist and flourish when power and authority are understood and activated.

Power is integral to human interactions and can be thought about as an attribute. We can distinguish power as personal (based on skills and experience), instrumental (based on resources available to a person), projected (charisma and appeal), and official (what is put on a person by virtue of a role taken up) (Reed and Armstrong 2013, p 120). In contrast, authority is related to what a person is doing and clarity about roles and intention transforms power into authority, this being manifest as the exercise of being authorized *in a* role, rather than relying on power *over a* role; not power over, but authority in. By definition, authority is contingent on a role within a system: for example, a role within a good collaboration. What is a feminist response to this? Authority needs to be taken up by a person, it cannot be given and so we conclude that good feminist collaborators do not get in the way of one another. To collaborate well is to work mutually, authorized as distinct and unified people engaged in a shared intention. Good feminist collaborators thus give room for each to have their own thoughts and ideas, with full expectation that these two presuppositions are true: thoughts wait for a thinker and ideas wait to be welcomed.

Good Feminist Collaboration as Critical Praxis

We have spoken of good feminist collaboration, but why 'feminist'? Because 'feminism is sensational' (Ahmed 2017, p. 21). Not only does it 'provoke excitement and interest', but it begins 'with a sense of things' (Ahmed 2017, p. 21): a sense of the world, of injustice, of our own bodies and experiences, of personal, social, ecological possibilities and of the symbiogenesis (Haraway 2016) that shapes existence and gives rise to the possibility for transformation. Good feminist collaboration begins with this same sense of things; the presence of intimacy.

Critical praxis is a methodology of presence. It is a cyclical practice of critical reflection and reflexivity that works with what's in the room, so to speak. Good feminist collaboration is effective as critical praxis when, with respect for the particularity and labour of those who collaborate (which we have articulated in terms of *intention*, *nature*, *context* and *composition*), it leads to some kind of change. We know feminist collaboration is good when collaborators recognize and work with the ease and/or limits of their complex relationships; when they anticipate the possibility of surprise in their encounter and of the emergence of previously unimagined outcomes; when they maintain postures of learning from each other as well as those beyond the collaboration. Ultimately, it is change that signals collaborative success: as the liberating experience of collaborating and the transformative outcome that results from good collaboration.

Notes

1 Notably, our focus here is on the nature of human collaboration, specifically when the people or groups who are working together are known or become known to each other through the process of discovering, developing and committing to their shared intention.

2 As Simone de Beauvoir identifies in *The Second Sex* (1949), specifically in her writing on myths and how they are used in western culture to perpetuate the oppression of women, 'it is difficult for women to assume both their status of autonomous individual and their feminine destiny' (p. 283). De Beauvoir anticipates that the achievement of woman's full humanity will only come 'when woman's infinite servitude is broken, when she lives for herself and by herself, man – abominable until now – giving her her freedom' (p. 284).

3 Sara Ahmed (2017, p. 100) illustrates this through her example of the institutional diversity officer, whose small and nuanced shift in language, while an attempt 'to avoid becoming the problem by not naming the problem', inadvertently diminishes the range of relational modes capable of triggering change. As she explains,

'the shift from the language of equality to the language of diversity becomes linked to a shift from a confrontational to a collaborative working model'. In this example, the already-contingent possibility of institutional change is narrowed to a single way of relating: a limited practice of collaboration that avoids confrontation.

4 We refer to definitions of flourishing expressed in terms pertaining to living organisms; to flourish is to grow or develop in a healthy or vigorous way, especially as the result of a particularly congenial environment.

5 Systems theory seeks to make sense of what is present by exploring and developing working hypotheses around dynamics that arise in a complex system context. For example, Wilbur 2000; Lawrence 1979, pp. xiii–xiv.

Bibliography

Sara Ahmed, 2017, *Living a Feminist Life*, Durham, NC and London: Duke University Press.
Marcella Althaus-Reid, 2000, *Indecent Theology: Theological Perversions in Sex, Gender and Politics*, London: Routledge.
Marcella Althaus-Reid, 2003, *The Queer God*, London: Routledge.
Simone de Beauvoir, 1949 (2011 edn), *The Second Sex*, trans. Constance Borde and Sheila Malovany-Chevallier, London: Vintage Books.
Seforosa Carroll, 2021, 'Speaking Up! Speaking Out! Naming the Silences: Women, Power, Authority and Love in the Pacific', in Kerrie Handasyde, Cathryn McKinney and Rebekah Pryor (eds), *Contemporary Feminist Theologies: Power, Authority, Love*, Abingdon: Routledge, pp. 9–20.
Gouranga P. Chattopadhyay, 1999, 'A Fresh Look at Authority and Organisation: Towards a Spiritual Approach for Managing Illusion', in Robert French and Russ Vince (eds), *Group Relations and Organisation*, Oxford: Oxford University Press, pp. 112–26.
M. Shawn Copeland, 2019, 'Turning Theology: A Proposal', *Theological Studies* 80 (4), pp. 753–73.
John Cottingham, 1998, *Philosophy and the Good Life: Reason and the Passions in Greek, Cartesian and Psychoanalytic Ethics*, Cambridge: Cambridge University Press.
Anne Elvey, 2022, *Reading with Earth: Contributions of the New Materialism to an Ecological Feminist Hermeneutics*, London: Bloomsbury T&T Clark.
Etymonline, Online etymology dictionary, https://www.etymonline.com/ (accessed 27.3.24).
Ivone Gebara, 1999, *Longing for Running Water: Ecofeminism and Liberation*, Minneapolis, MN: Fortress Press.
Donna J. Haraway, 2016, *Staying with the Trouble: Making Kin in the Chthulucene*, Durham, NC and London: Duke University Press.
Luce Irigaray, 1993, *An Ethics of Sexual Difference*, New York: Cornell University Press.
Lisa Isherwood, 1999, *Liberating Christ*, Cleveland, OH: Pilgrim Press.
Wilma T. Jakobsen and Miranda N. Pillay, 2022, 'Remembering Tutu's Liberation Theology: Toward Gender Justice from Theoethical Feminist Perspectives', *Anglican Theological Review* 104 (3).

Namsoon Kang, 2004, 'Who/What Is Asian? A Postcolonial Theological Reading of Orientalism and Newo-Orientalism', in Catherine Keller, Michael Nausner and Mayra Rivera (eds), *Postcolonial Theologies: Divinity and Empire*, St Louis, MI: Chalice Press, pp. 100–17.

Catherine Keller, 2015, *Cloud of the Impossible: Negative Theology and Planetary Entanglement*, New York: Columbia University Press.

Gordon Lawrence, 1979, *Exploring Individual and Organizational Boundaries: A Tavistock Open Systems Approach*, London: Tavistock Publications.

Hilde Lindemann (ed.), 2005, *An Invitation to Feminist Ethics*, New York: McGraw-Hill.

Cathryn McKinney, 2021, 'Speaking of Being Heard: Voice and Purpose in Prison', in Kerrie Handasyde, Cathryn McKinney and Rebekah Pryor (eds), *Contemporary Feminist Theologies: Power, Authority, Love*, Abingdon: Routledge, pp. 192–202.

Janice McRandal, 2021, 'Against and without Authority,' in Kerrie Handasyde, Cathryn McKinney and Rebekah Pryor (eds), *Contemporary Feminist Theologies: Power, Authority, Love*, Abingdon: Routledge, pp. 117–29.

Brooke Prentis, 2020, 'Confronting', Common Grace, https://www.commongrace.org.au/daily_disruptions_asylum_confronting (accessed 1.6.23).

Bruce Reed and David Armstrong, 2013, 'Notes on Professional Development', in John Bazalgette (ed.), *Freedom to Make a Difference: The Grubb Reader*, London: unpublished handbook, p. 119.

Jeong-Eun Rhee, 2021, *Decolonial Feminist Research: Haunting, Rememory and Mothers*, Abingdon: Routledge.

Charlotte Roberts, 2006, 'Reinventing Relationships: Leverage for Dissolving Barriers to Collaboration', in Peter Senge (ed.), *The Fifth Discipline: The Art and Practice of the Learning Organization*, London: Random House, pp. 69–72.

Ken Wilbur, 2000, *A Theory of Everything: An Integrated Vision for Business, Politics, Science and Spirituality*, Boulder, CO: Shambhala Publications.

Delores Williams, 1991 (2013 edn), *Sisters in the Wilderness: The Challenge of Womanist God-Talk*, Maryknoll, NY: Orbis Books.

PART 2

Right

5

Poverty, Inequality and their Intersections

GALE A. YEE

In tackling the problem of poverty, especially in its 'feminization' (Pearce 1978), one needs to attend to the different ways in which poverty has been conceptualized. Poverty is usually seen in terms of the income needed for the subsistence survival of members in an 'average' household (Kabeer 2015, p. 191; Henderson and Tickamyer 2009, p. 2). What is considered 'average' is determined by a scientifically devised and ostensibly neutral formula by the state. Poverty is defined as a failure to meet this average income level. It is visualized as a vertical line to be crossed, with men and women above or below this line, women usually situated below men in economic need (Unterhalter 2012, p. 257; Kabeer 2015, p. 190). This gendered hierarchy of the poverty line is layered with ideological and moral judgements stigmatizing those deemed worthy or deserving of economic assistance and those who are not (Pearce 1990, pp. 5–6). When poverty results from an accident of fate to an otherwise responsible and productive person, there is a greater willingness to consign public funds for its abatement. The undeserving are those regarded as lazy, parasitically living off the system (Henderson and Tickamyer 2009, p. 5). The gendered hierarchy of the poverty becomes even more complicated to analyse when one brings in the category of race. Because of racial discrimination, the poverty statistics for racial-ethnic women have historically been bleaker than for white women (Pearce 1990, p. 1).

This vertical conception of poverty, based solely on economic income whose threshold needed to be crossed, is reductive. Poverty is not only marked by economic disadvantage but also by multiple dimensions of deprivation, for example political, cultural, psychological, educational, and medical (Jamir 2015, p. 66). These dimensions are exacerbated by the racial, gendered and classed identities of those suffering poverty. Putting poverty in an economic silo simply cannot deal with the other complex social relations and ideologies that are interlinked with the rising inequality between the rich and the poor in today's neoliberal world.

Poverty and inequality are not the same thing. While poverty focuses on the condition of the poor, inequality focuses on both the rich and the poor. Inequality and poverty are embedded in different power relations, forcing us to confront a question that is often avoided. How can the ways in which the rich obtain their wealth generate poverty? Rather than thinking about poverty as a gendered vertical line to be crossed, other metaphors have emerged that conceive of poverty horizontally as well as vertically (Kabeer 2015, p. 194). Metaphors of poverty as a net (Unterhalter 2009, p. 16; 2012, p. 257), a web (Church Urban Fund 2021), or a matrix of domination (Collins 2009, p. 21) can structurally take into consideration gender, race/ethnicity, class, culture, and other relations of power that contribute to poverty and inequality.

This chapter will take up Kimberly Crenshaw's term 'intersectionality' as a concept to describe this structural convergence of intersecting systems of power that create poverty and inequity (Crenshaw 1989, pp. 139–67). Intersectionality has long been recognized as a productive model of investigation in a number of disciplines such as history, sociology, political science, and feminist, ethnic and queer studies, as well as legal studies where the term was coined (cf. Cho, Crenshaw and McCall 2013; May 2015; Collins and Bilge 2016; Hancock 2016). Intersectionality has also made inroads as a tool for analysis in biblical studies and theology (Yee 2020; Kim and Shaw 2018). This chapter will demonstrate how intersectionality provides a more comprehensive analysis of poverty and inequality that manifests how rich and poor individuals and groups are mutually and relationally embedded within these power systems in interlocking ways.

Even before the term intersectionality became popular, African American feminist theorists had been thinking, analysing, strategizing intersectionally. According to the Combahee River Collective in 1977:

> The most general statement of our politics at the present time would be that we are actively committed to struggling against racial, sexual, heterosexual, and class oppression and see as our particular task the development of integrated analysis and practice based upon the fact that the major systems of oppression are interlocking. (The Combahee River Collective 2017, p. 115; see also, Davis 1981; Lorde 1984; hooks 1984)

What prompted Kimberlé Crenshaw's choice of the term was a legal case involving five Black women who sued the car manufacturer General Motors for racial discrimination. Because they hired Black men and women – albeit *white* women – General Motors claimed that it did not discriminate against these Black women. They saw no need to recognize Black women as a distinct social group. For Crenshaw, this single-axis thinking that paired racism with Black men only and sexism with white women only could not acknowledge the distinctive experiences of women who were not white and Blacks who were not men (Crenshaw 1989, pp. 141–3). The question intersectionality raises for this essay is what distinct social configurations of race, gender, class, etc. have been unrecognized, overlooked or neglected in laws, policies, customs, etc. regarding poverty and inequality?

In the most extensive recent discussion of intersectionality, Patricia Hill Collins elaborates on the core constructs of intersectionality and their guiding premises. I reproduce her helpful grid here (Collins 2019, pp. 44–53):

Core constructs	Guiding premise
Relationality	1 Race, class, gender, and similar systems of power are interdependent and mutually construct one another.
Power Social inequality	2 Intersecting power relations produce complex, interdependent social inequalities of race, class, gender, sexuality, nationality, ethnicity, ability and age.
Social context Complexity	3 The social location of individuals and groups with intersecting power relations shapes their experiences within and perspectives on the social world.
Social justice	4 Solving social problems within a given local, regional, national, or global context requires intersectional analyses.

The core construct of *relationality* is indispensable to intersectionality, underscoring the reality that race, gender, class and other systems of power do not stand alone, but are organized and sustained through their interconnections and interacting processes. Collins describes four interrelated domains of *power* in her 'matrix of domination' through which race, gender and class are organized: the structural (institutional structures of society), the disciplinary (ideas and practices that characterized and sustained hierarchies), the hegemonic (the ideas, symbols and ideologies that shaped consciousness), and the interpersonal (the interactions of people at the macro and micro levels of social organization.

> Each domain serves a particular purpose. The structural domain organizes oppression, whereas the disciplinary domain manages it. The hegemonic domain justifies oppression, and the interpersonal domain influences everyday lived experience and the individual consciousness that ensues. (Collins 2009, pp. 294–307; cf. Hancock 2007, p. 74)

Adding more questions for an intersectional analysis, what are the structural, disciplinary, hegemonic and interpersonal domains of power in which the rich obtain their wealth that create poverty? What are the relations of production in which some individuals and groups become rich or richer while others become or remain poor?

The oppressions of racism, sexism and class exploitation result from the intersections of race, gender and class within these domains of power, creating social formations of complex *social and material inequalities* that generate poverty. Paying attention to power foregrounds the relationship between processes of domination and their role in creating and perpetuating structures of poverty and inequality (Corus et al. 2016, p. 214). Individual persons and groups are *socially located* differently and *complexly* within these intersecting power relations and are thus subject to multiple social advantages of wealth and disadvantages of poverty. These advantages and disadvantages result in differing perspectives and ideologies of one's own and of other's experiences of the social world and its inequalities (Collins 2015, p. 14). Think, for example, of opinions regarding African American female urban poor as welfare queens by the white, rich and privileged. Finally, because the social inequalities of poverty produced by intersecting systems of power are essentially unjust, they must be resisted and combatted. Intersectionality has very deep activist roots with a *social justice* agenda for social analysis and critique (Hancock 2016, pp. 37–72; May 2015, p. 228). Rather than provide value-neutral studies, intersectional research makes value-laden proposals and plans for social change (Gopaldas 2013, p. 93).

The complexity of intersectionality results from its emphasis on the inclusion of all voices, particularly oppressed ones. Consequently, the most difficult part of intersectional research on poverty and inequality is determining the range of a study, figuring out which identity structures to include in the analysis and why (Gopaldas 2013, p. 91). Race, gender, class, etc. can be splintered into ever-increasing sub-categories within the four domains of power, overwhelming and paralysing an ambitious researcher on poverty and inequality (Hancock 2007, p. 66). Complicating the matter, the focus on the categories of identity, such as race, gender and class tends to neglect the analysis of the power of the dominant group in each category, often white privileged males. For example, Crenshaw's analysis of Black men's violence against Black women criticizes white feminists suppressing minority experiences (Crenshaw 1995, p. 1258). However, one must not neglect the role of male racists in the politics of silencing ethnic minority women in issues of domestic violence. Focusing only on disadvantaged people obscures the role of the powerful within sets of unequal social relations. Instead of using concepts such as 'category' for race, gender and class when the focus of analysis are disparities in raced, gendered and classed relations, it is important to specify sets of unequal racial, gendered or class relations when investigating them (Walby, Armstrong and Strid 2012, p. 230). In other words, subjected, impoverished groups need to be investigated with their relations with dominant wealthy groups.

To avoid the single axis approach on the one hand, and an unworkably complex multi-axis study on the other, one can (1) identify social relations of poverty and inequality that have been overlooked or under-theorized in the relevant literature; (2) identify which social relations of poverty and inequality seem most consequential in the chosen context; (3) determine which social relations that participants of the research, in our case the rich and the poor individuals and groups, wish to reveal or conceal (Gopaldas 2013, pp. 91–2). For example, studies of Asian Americans tend to focus on the dominant Asian immigrant groups from China and Japan, whose ostensible social and economic success in assimilation has been stereotyped as the 'model minority' (Wu 2014; Hancock 2007, p. 68). However, there is a large wealth gap among Asian Americans. Twelve per cent of Asian Americans live below the federal poverty line, particularly among the South East Asian American refugees: the Hmong, Burmese, Cambodian, Laotian and Vietnamese. The poverty afflicting these populations was under-theorized within the broader Asian American racial/ethnic grouping.

> As a result of this stereotype, tremendous socioeconomic challenges that affect the SEAA community remain hidden. This stereotype is also reinforced by data policies that lump, or aggregate, all SEAA under the broader Asian American race category. Disaggregated data that allow

us to see how specific ethnic groups are doing within the larger Asian American umbrella are critical to revealing barriers and uplifting necessary solutions to improve socioeconomic outcomes for this community. (The Southeast Asia Resource Action Center (SEARAC), Asian, and Americans Advancing Justice 2020)

After determining the unequal social relations of poverty and inequality in the population one wants to examine, one needs to adopt a methodology for the research. Reviewing the abundance of studies utilizing the concept of intersectionality, McCall identifies three methodological approaches, which can assist in handling the complexity of poverty and inequality in our local and global contexts. The first of these approaches is the intra-categorical approach to complexity, favoured by early Feminists of Colour who initiated the study of intersectionality. The primary subject of analysis was typically a single social group, often ones that have not been examined before. Such a single grouping has tremendous diversities within itself to explore. Of interest were the experiences at 'neglected points of intersection', ones that tended to reflect several subordinate sites as opposed to dominant or mixed locations. At the core of the study were the narratives of an individual whose experiences became the basis for deducing the power arrangements in the individual's broader social location (McCall 2005, pp. 1780–1). For example, Gopaldas cites research on African American consumers living in an urban American ghetto with constricted access to basic goods and services such as food and housing. The study revealed how different political affiliations (Black liberalism vs Black nationalism) produced qualitatively different consumer behaviours (e.g. out-migration vs out-shopping) in this multiply oppressed group (Gopaldas 2013, pp. 91–2). The focus on the single group and its partial perspectives, however, can displace attention to the larger social processes and structures that might be causing the inequalities (Walby, Armstrong and Strid 2012, p. 227); in this case, the racist political and economic policies of red lining by dominant white groups that create food deserts and lack of services and resources.

McCall's second approach to the problem of complexity in intersectional analyses, and the one she favours, is the inter-categorical approach that observes that there are relationships of inequality among already constituted social groups. This approach focuses on the complexity of relationships among multiple social groups within and across analytical sets of unequal relations and not on complexities within single social groups, single unequal relations, or both. The subject here is multigroup, and the method is systematically comparative (McCall 2005, pp. 1784–6). McCall's own research on economic inequality employed the inter-categorical approach analysing the roots of several different dimensions of wage inequality in regional economies in the US. She examined the inequalities between men and women; between the college educated and non-college educated; among Blacks, Asian, Latino/as and whites, and among the intersections of these groups. She synthesized this information into four different configurations of inequality that emerged in the urban areas of St Louis, Miami, Dallas and Detroit. Her key conclusion was that patterns of racial, gender and class inequality were not the same across the configurations:

> For example, heavily unionized blue-collar cities with a recent history of deindustrialization such as Detroit exhibit relatively modest class and racial wage inequality among employed men but elevated gender wage inequality and class inequality among employed women (relative to average levels of wage inequality in the United States as a whole). In contrast, a postindustrial city such as Dallas exhibits the opposite structure of inequality – it is marked more by class and racial inequality than gender inequality. (McCall 2005, pp. 1788–9)

The third of McCall's methodologies, the anti-categorical approach, is based on postmodernist and poststructuralist critiques that deconstruct the validity of modern analytical categories. For example, Feminists of Colour criticized white feminists for not acknowledging the differences among women, assuming that their essentialist categories of *women* and *gender* applied universally to all women. The socially constructed nature of gender and other categories along with the wide range of different experiences, identities and social locations did not fit neatly into any single 'master' category. However, because the categories of race, gender and class were too fluid and unstable in this approach, it made the practical analysis of poverty and inequality difficult (Walby, Armstrong and Strid 2012, p. 227). Instead of analysing multiple inequalities through such categories as race, gender and class, it highlighted the ways, practices and social processes of inequality in which these categories were constructed, such as racism, gender discrimination, geographical segregation, often using historical and longitudinal analyses (Corus et al. 2016, p. 214). For example, a historical analysis of voter registration laws in the early 1900s did not use categories such as ethnicity and/or class but examined the inherent regulatory discrimination within the voting process in light of the unequal social status and literacy skills among white and Black voters. Anti-categorical intersectionality studies the forms of power within the given context and how multiple inequalities and disadvantages are created, reproduced and transformed over time (Corus et al. 2016, p. 214).

Which intersectional methodology to use depends on the goal of the research into the interconnections between poverty and inequality. If the goal of research is the study of one disadvantaged group in depth, then an intra-categorical approach may be useful. For example, Saatcioglu and Corus investigated intersectionally the ways in which the disadvantages experienced by the low-income residents of a trailer park community in the south-east of the US were interconnected and co-constitutive. Mobile homes have become one of the less expensive ways in which transient blue-collar workers and veteran families fulfil the American Dream of home ownership, while struggling to make ends meet. However, the authors did not focus on the categories of the gender or race of the inhabitants, but rather the institutional processes and forms of power that figured in their impoverishment. So, in a sense, their study also involved an anti-categorical methodology. Zoning regulations segregated this trailer park socially and spatially on land of lesser value and economic resources. Studies have documented the disparities in health care between the wealthy and the poor. The health-related disadvantages and disabilities of the trailer park inhabitants overlapped with other disadvantages such as economic deprivation, lack of employment and unjust treatment in the workplace. Being ill or disabled negatively affected their employment opportunities and performance, money for food, family support and education. The financial system marginalized them through predatory lending practices and lack of resources, such as credit and cheque accounts. The welfare system that operated on the demonstrable level of need overlapped with the ideological stigmatization of the residents as 'trailer trash', liars, cheaters and other humiliating and dehumanizing expressions. This typecasting affected student–teacher interactions, in which teachers connected the parents' reliance on public assistance and living in an impoverished trailer park with their students' lack of motivation or intelligence. The social stigmatization exacerbated other deprivations affecting education, such as low literacy and lack of steady employment that might have been achieved through schooling. Structural processes of power, such as the health care, financial, welfare and educational systems, all interacted and overlapped to sustain the marginalization of those living in this trailer park. Vulnerabilities in one domain were dependent on and aggravated vulnerabilities in another domain. Moreover, the cumulative poverty of the park residents was pigeonholed ideologically with demeaning slurs that were perceived as arising from this impoverishment (Saatcioglu and Corus 2014; cf. Castanyer 2019, p. 2).

If the goal of the research is to compare and contrast two or more impoverished social groups or settings, the inter-categorical methodology is the most appropriate. Here, the realities and experiences of more than one oppressed group are investigated through an analysis of the most dominant sets of unequal relations of similarity and difference and multiple inequalities. Inter-categorical analysis involves questions such as, 'What are the divergent experiences across social groups?' and, 'Which diverse groups are connected by common relationships to social and institutional power?' (Corus et al. 2016, pp. 213–14).

Henderson and Tickamyer's intersectional study explores the similarities and differences between impoverished urban African American women and rural white Appalachian women. Although African Americans are over-represented among the poor, they are not the majority or only high-visibility group among the poor. The reality of poverty is much more complex. Whites make up the majority of those below the poverty line with pockets of white, Black, Latinx, Asian and Native American dominating local landscapes. But poverty in the US is largely perceived in a fixed Black/white binary. To deconstruct this binary and the discourses regarding welfare policy in the US, the authors investigate poor white Appalachian women as an entry point through the intersections of race, class, gender, space and culture. 'The purpose is twofold: to expand the multiplicities of poverty identities, locations and control mechanisms; and to show how the existence of this complexity nevertheless reinforces the welfare racism that underlies poverty discourse' (Henderson and Tickamyer 2009, pp. 50–1).

Blackness is the primary racial identity in both academic and popular discourses when examining welfare policies, which rarely refer to other racial, ethnic or cultural groups. The authors argue that poor Appalachian women experience a form of 'welfare culturalism' similar to the welfare racism experienced by poor Black women. They also maintain that the negative stereotypes that control poor white women in Appalachia also undergird a broader system of welfare racism that impinges upon poor racial and ethnic women (Henderson and Tickamyer 2009, p. 51).

Overlooking or neglecting the systemic causes of poverty, the 1960s 'war on poverty' connected urban poverty with the Black cultural experience of broken families, illegitimacy and the intergenerational dependence on welfare. Blaming the welfare recipients for their own poverty was part of a racist discourse that labelled African Americans as lazy welfare cheats, with racial stereotypes that produced controlling images, such as 'the welfare queen'. Even though the majority of welfare recipients are white, the persistent racialized media depictions and racist stereotypes make the cultural face of welfare Black (Henderson and Tickamyer 2009, pp. 53–4). Missing from the discussion is how white poverty fits into the system of welfare racism. The authors argue that lower-class white Appalachian women are doubly exploited by the stereotypical images of welfare recipients. First, they are stigmatized as 'hillbillies' and 'white trash', which affects their economic development in a region already suffering from a dearth of employment opportunities. Second, the whiteness of these Appalachian women becomes the means to argue that the welfare system is bias-free regarding race, gender or any other category (Henderson and Tickamyer 2009, p. 56).

Even though important studies disrupt that Black/white binary by including work on Latinas, Asian Americans, Native Americans, immigrants and other women of various ethnicities and nationalities, the problematic analytic category is whiteness. Whiteness usually denotes the privileged and majority endpoint of racial categorization. However, whiteness does not always result in privilege and power. Race may define whiteness, but distinctions in class and culture determine the boundaries of privilege. When white women are part of the lower classes, a contradiction exists between their alleged racial privilege and their subordinate social location (Henderson and Tickamyer 2009, pp. 57–9). This contradiction exemplifies the shifting locations of different classes of white women within the various domains of power according to Collins' matrix of domination (see p. 59 above). Compared with their African American urban counterparts, Appalachian women living in remote isolated rural communities often deal with the scarcity of resources, such as childcare, transportation, health care and housing. Assessed with those living in urban areas, these women may often suffer more hardship (Henderson and Tickamyer 2009, p. 61). Moreover, human service agencies handling welfare services for Appalachian women are often quick to make use of the derogatory stereotypes of lazy hillbillies who lack ambition for jobs, when evaluating the poverty of the region. The authors maintain that for programmes to deal with poverty successfully, they must be context specific. Welfare programmes that help the urban poor may not be appropriate for the rural impoverished. The hardships and experiences of poverty might be similar, but the causes and solutions need to be evaluated for differences as well as similarities (Henderson and Tickamyer 2009, p. 66).

This chapter argues that a more comprehensive analysis of poverty and inequality must include investigations of the interlocking power relations of race, gender and class beyond the traditional vertical understanding of poverty as an economic line to be crossed. It uses the analytical tool of intersectionality to help researchers and policy-makers recognize and interrogate the invisibility of marginalized populations through its core constructs (relationality, power, social inequality, social context, complexity and social justice) and its guiding premises. Because intersectionality deals with complexity to include all voices, especially the marginalized, this essay describes three methodological approaches to manage this complexity. The intra-categorical approach studies one social group or setting in all its diversities. The inter-categorical approach compares two or more groups in their similarities and differences. The anti-categorical approach eschews categories, preferring to analyse the processes of inequalities in which these categories were constructed, such as racism, sexism, segregation and other institutional forms of power that result in poverty and inequality. This chapter argues throughout that an investigation of the intersections of dominant institutions, policies and powers that create poverty and inequality in the marginalized populations needs to be performed. Finally, the end point of these intersectional analyses is social justice, to provide transformative policy solutions that will have a meaningful impact in mitigating poverty and inequality in our day and age.

Bibliography

Castanyer, Prisca, 2019, 'Notes on Race and Gender in the USA: Poverty and Intersectionality', *Papeles de Europa* 32 (1), pp. 1–12.
Sumi Cho, Kimberlé Williams Crenshaw and Leslie McCall, 2013, 'Toward a Field of Intersectionality Studies: Theory, Applications, and Praxis', *Signs: Journal of Women in Culture & Society* 38 (4), pp. 785–810.
Church Urban Fund, 2021, 'The Web of Poverty', Ending Poverty Together, https://endingpovertytogether.org/the-web-of-poverty/ (accessed 27.3.24).
Patricia Hill Collins, 2009, *Black Feminist Thought: Knowledge, Consciousness, and the Politics of Empowerment*, 2nd edn, New York: Routledge.
Patricia Hill Collins, 2015, 'Intersectionality's Definitional Dilemmas', *Annual Review of Sociology* 41 (1), pp. 1–20.
Patricia Hill Collins, 2019, *Intersectionality as Critical Social Theory*, Durham, NC: Duke University Press.
Patricia Hill Collins and Sirma Bilge, 2016, *Intersectionality: Key Concepts*, Oxford: Polity Press.
The Combahee River Collective, 2017, 'A Black Feminist Statement (1977)', in Carole R. McCann and Seung-Kyung Kim (eds), *Feminist Theory Reader: Local and Global Perspectives*, 4th edn, London: Routledge, pp. 115–21.
Canan Corus, Bige Saatcioglu, Carol Kaufman-Scarborough, Christopher P. Blocker,

Shikha Upadhyaya and Samuelson Appau, 2016, 'Transforming Poverty-Related Policy with Intersectionality', *Journal of Public Policy & Marketing* 35 (2), pp. 211–22.

Kimberlé Crenshaw, 1989, 'Demarginalizing the Intersection of Race and Sex', *The University of Chicago Legal Forum* 40 (1), pp. 139–67.

Kimberlé Williams Crenshaw, 1995, 'Mapping the Margins: Intersectionality, Identity Politics, and Violence Against Women of Color', in Kimberlé Crenshaw, Neil Gotanda, Gary Peller and Kendall Thomas (eds), *Critical Race Theory: The Key Writings that Formed the Movement*, New York: The New Press, pp. 357–83.

Angela Y. Davis, 1981, *Women, Race and Class*, New York: Vintage Books.

Ahir Gopaldas, 2013, 'Intersectionality 101', *Journal of Public Policy & Marketing* 32 (May), pp. 90–4.

Ange-Marie Hancock, 2007, 'When Multiplication Doesn't Equal Quick Addition: Examining Intersectionality as a Research Paradigm', *Perspectives on Politics* 5 (1), pp. 63–79.

Ange-Marie Hancock, 2016, *Intersectionality: An Intellectual History*, New York: Oxford University Press.

Debra Henderson and Ann Tickamyer, 2009, 'The Intersection of Poverty Discourses: Race, Class, Culture, and Gender', in Bonnie Thornton Dill and Ruth E. Zambrana (eds), *Emerging Intersections: Race, Class, and Gender in Theory, Policy, and Practice*, New Brunswick, NJ: Rutgers University Press, pp. 50–72.

bell hooks, 1984, *Feminist Theory: From Margin to Center*, Boston, MA: South End Press.

Arensenla Jamir, 2015, 'Feminization of Poverty in India: A Socio-Ethical Critique', *Bangalore Theological Forum* 47 (1), pp. 65–75.

Naila Kabeer, 2015, 'Gender, Poverty, and Inequality: A Brief History of Feminist Contributions in the Field of International Development', *Gender and Development* 23 (2), pp. 189–205.

Grace Ji-Sun Kim and Susan M. Shaw, 2018, *Intersectional Theology: An Introductory Guide*, Minneapolis, MN: Fortress Press.

Audre Lorde, 1984, *Sister Outsider: Essays and Speeches by Audre Lorde*, Freedom, CA: The Crossing Press.

Vivian M. May, 2015, *Pursuing Intersectionality, Unsettling Dominant Imaginaries*, Contemporary Sociological Perspectives, New York: Routledge.

Leslie McCall, 2005, 'The Complexity of Intersectionality', *Signs* 3, pp. 1771–800.

Diana Pearce, 1978, 'The Feminization of Poverty: Women, Work, and Welfare', *The Urban and Social Change Review*, Winter/Spring, pp. 28–36.

Diana Pearce, 1990, 'The Feminization of Poverty', *Journal for Peace and Justice Studies* 2 (1), pp. 1–20.

Bige Saatcioglu and Canan Corus, 2014, 'Poverty and Intersectionality: A Multidimensional Look into the Lives of the Impoverished', *Journal of Macromarketing* 34 (2), pp. 122–32.

The Southeast Asia Resource Action Center (SEARAC), Asian, and Americans Advancing Justice, 2020, *Southeast Asian American Journeys: A National Snapshot of Our Communities*.

Elaine Unterhalter, 2009, 'Gender and Poverty Reduction: The Challenge of Intersection', *Agenda* 23 (81), pp. 14–24, https://www.tandfonline.com/doi/abs/10.1080/10130950.2009.9676250 (accessed 9.5.24).

Elaine Unterhalter, 2012, 'Poverty, Education, Gender and the Millennium Development Goals: Reflections on Boundaries and Intersectionality', *Theory and Research in Education* 10 (3), pp. 253–74.

Sylvia Walby, Jo Armstrong and Sofia Strid, 2012, 'Intersectionality: Multiple Inequalities in Social Theory', *Sociology* 46 (2), pp. 224–40.

Ellen D. Wu, 2014, *The Color of Success: Asian Americans and the Origins of the Model Minority*, Politics and Society in Twentieth-century America, Princeton, NJ: Princeton University Press.

Gale A. Yee, 2020, 'Thinking Intersectionally: Gender, Race, Class, and the Etceteras of Our Discipline', *Journal of Biblical Literature* 139 (1), pp. 7–26.

6

Ecofeminism, Theology and the Rise of Alt-Right Christian Nationalism

HEATHER EATON

The themes at the intersection of ecofeminisms and theologies are analytically robust and practically useful. They are full of insights, illuminations and pathways forward. Ecofeminism represents many interconnections between ecology and feminism: as analysis, critique, vision and actions. Ecofeminist theologies have made significant contributions to both eco- and feminist theologies. The main concerns within this chapter are to strengthen ecofeminist theologies' responsiveness to a world and Earth community in dire need of sturdy analyses and effective actions.

Yet, recent trends reshaping the world are inhibiting such progress. From Canada, one cannot ignore the rise of a mainly white, usually male, anti-feminist, anti-immigration, anti-intellectual, alt-right 'Christian nationalism/patriotism'. The Canadian Christian Lobby, The Niagara Declaration and The Liberty Coalition, for example, talk about standing guard, defending those who stand, protecting liberties, and putting 'Christian' values and candidates into political systems and structures. This rise of Christian nationalism in Canada mirrors, is influenced by, and at times is funded by, US groups. It is a recent phenomenon, representing a loose 'coalition of populists, racists, conspiracy theorists, anti-science zealots and Christian nationalists' (Coren 2022). These represent, without exception, right-wing cultural agendas, gaining traction and popularity with anti-vaccine and anti-mask mandates. They are a mingling of irrational views and religious vitriol infused with hateful and extreme views on gender identity, immigration and women's reproductive rights.

While Christian nationalism is intensifying in North America, it is also influential in Brazil, Uganda, Central Africa, England, Spain, Poland, Italy, and elsewhere (Saiya 2022). This consortium is aggressively eliminating environmental protections and removing human rights especially for women and the LGBTQIA+ community. In the United States these

'Christians' are banning books, preventing studies on critical race theories, multiculturalism, gender analyses, environmental issues and climate change (see, for example, Vegara 2022; Smeltzer and Buyon 2022; Heyward 2022). They defend these actions with their Christian beliefs.

Studies continue as to why and how this religio-political trend is amplifying. Such social regression and aggression may be connected to myriad insecurities, and economic and ecological decline. The war in Ukraine, the political morass of the United States, and the multiple threats to fair elections and representative institutions are faces of these mounting domestic and international disorders. This includes democratic declines, fascist politics and authoritarian aggression, and a realignment of global geopolitics. The surge of uninformed, conspiracy and anti-intellectual views, and an incessant uncensored media, decrease the ability to distinguish between truth and lies, knowledge and opinion, fact and fiction, or veracity and propaganda. Disenfranchised groups, such as white supremacists, are emboldened and fuelled by pastors, populism, autocratic leaders and some governments. There are countless public spaces to spew bigoted views.

I would prefer to address the effectiveness and importance of ecofeminist theologies. Yet, I am acutely disturbed by these religio-political developments. They are potent and destructive. This deterioration also impedes the mechanisms through which liberal government policies are developed, funded and actualized. Academic endeavours, including ecofeminist or other progressive theological work, that ignore these developments may become culturally irrelevant. A robust rebuttal to such trends is crucial.

This chapter is a juxtaposition of above-mentioned realities with ecofeminist efforts and theology. My views are influenced by decades of involvement in the fields of feminism, religion and ecology. My penchant has always been threefold: the deep beauty and suffering of Earth's life communities, the nature of religions and religious experiences, and the relevance and capacity of theology to respond to these realities. Hence, the ecological decline of the Earth is unbearable. The lack of human rights is reprehensible. These, together with the political and intellectual deterioration, at least in some parts of the world, are most worrisome.

The first section offers an overview of ecofeminism. The second examines crossroads between ecofeminism and theology. The third considers topics of pluralities, epistemologies and theological constrictions, including a few comments on the rise and influence of alt-right Christian nationalism. A final section suggests some contributions and caveats within ecofeminist theologies, followed by a brief conclusion.

Ecofeminist Overview and Trends

Ecofeminism, short for ecological-feminism, represents multiple connections between ecological and feminist analyses and actions. It includes myriad efforts that expose a women/nature nexus and connect feminism(s) with ecology. Ecofeminism can be seen as a junction, similar to a roundabout, with multiple entry and exit options, and many facets and varieties (Eaton 2005).

Ecofeminism came on the scene in the 1970s predominantly in North America, although the expression was coined by French feminist Françoise d'Eaubonne in *Le Féminisme ou la Mort* (1974). She encouraged women to incite an ecological revolution. In 1975, theologian Rosemary Radford Ruether wrote an influential book entitled *New Woman, New Earth*. She claimed:

> Women must see that there can be no liberation for them and no solution to the ecological crisis within a society whose fundamental model of relationships continues to be one of domination. They must unite the demands of the women's movement with those of the ecological movement to envision a radical reshaping of the basic socioeconomic relations and the underlying values of this society. (Ruether 1975, p. 204)

This insight remains the foundational premise of all versions of ecofeminism.

The core realization is that the oppressions of women and the disdain for the natural world are built into the way both are ideologically represented, historically and currently. Central to early ecofeminist theories is that the women/nature nexus is embedded in Euro-western world view, values and actions. This engenders and justifies a sexual division of labour, limits women's lives, and disregards ecological degradation.

Development of a lucid body of theories and appreciation of ecofeminism as a specific subject, or new wave of feminism, began to take shape. Ecofeminism became an umbrella term for historical, ideological and practical associations between women and nature, and feminism and ecology. Illuminating and robust inquiries progressed to reveal and assess interconnections and layers of associations. Ecofeminism includes a large range of topics: historical excavation of the women/nature nexus; in depth understanding of patriarchal social structures and world views; exposing hierarchical dualism; studies of and resistance to domination as a mode of inter-human and human–earth relations; social movements that see the oppression of women and the domination of the natural world as interconnected. Ecofeminism exemplifies the plurality within feminist analyses and the diversity within environmental studies.

Ecofeminist theorists reflect differently on the relationships between women and the natural world, and misogyny and the ecological crisis. Activists and academics can have distinct priorities. Ecofeminists are rarely conservative, and may be liberal, socialists, cultural, radical, postmodernist, postcolonialist or ecowomanist, or other distinctions. For some, religion is a central element and there are Buddhist, Native American, Goddess, Hindu, Muslim, Christian and Jewish ecofeminists. For others, religion and spirituality are inherently problematic. The ecological emphases differ: resource management; deep or social ecology; anthropocentric or Earth/centric; or, cosmological frameworks.

The connections made sense to many, including activists, academics and those working in international development and gender. Ecofeminism expanded, exposing these complex and interrelated historical, ideological and practical associations at the women/nature and feminism/ecology nexus. For example, it became evident that the issues and analyses among race/ethnicity, class, gender, poverty, social inequalities, economic policies and practices, militarism and environmental degradation share similarities. Patterns and ideologies of domination and intersectionality became and remain a focus for ecofeminism.

From the beginning, those who agreed that ecology is a feminist issue and that solutions to ecological problems must include feminist analyses, disagreed as to the nature of these connections, and what the best solutions could be. Ecofeminist philosopher Karen Warren wrote:

> The varieties of ecofeminism reflect not only the differences in the analysis of the woman/nature connection, but also differences on such fundamental matters as the nature of and the solutions to women's oppression, the theory of human nature, and the conceptions of freedom, equality, epistemology on which various feminist theories depend. (Warren 1987, p. 4)

There has been much written about the emergence and elaboration of ecofeminisms (e.g. Fakier et al. 2020; Sikka 2019; Vakoch and Mickey 2017; Gaard 2017; Philips and Rumens 2016). There have been extensive internal debates about topics such as gender essentialism, the relevance of spirituality, white myopia, ignorance of or inattention to affluence and poverty disparities, social inequalities, cross-cultural applicability, representation, or absence of intersectional analyses. Furthermore, ecofeminist frameworks are not useful in all contexts. Case studies revealed that the women/nature nexus and ecofeminist evaluations are not ideologically constructed, experienced or lived out in identical ways in distinct cultures (Eaton and Lorentzen, 2003).

Ecofeminist analyses gained considerable interest and traction from 1980 to 2000. Then it went in and out of favour. Much of the early ecofeminist endeavours emerged in North America, although recent work is from a variety of countries, many in the global South, and with specific regional, ethnic and cultural concerns. Ecofeminism is now a global, multifaceted, multidisciplinary discourse. There are countless books, articles, workshops, conferences, retreats, rituals, art, activism and politics. There are publications covering ecofeminist philosophy, spirituality and religion, science, psychology, sociology, political thought and activism, economics, animal rights and climate change (e.g., Isla 2019; MacGregor 2017; Nagle 2016; Adams and Gruen 2014). There are academics, authors and activists contributing to ecofeminist enterprises now, noting that no one covers all the topics, or equally well.

Crossroads Between Ecofeminism and Theology

Ecofeminism had a robust and early history in Christian theology. Influential thinkers such as Ivone Gebara, Rosemary Radford Ruether, Ursula King, Sallie McFague, Mary Grey, Anne Primavesi, Mary Ress, Aruna Gnanadason and others de- and re-constructed aspects of Christian theologies. Critiques of patriarchy, anthropocentrism, misogyny, hierarchical dualisms, salvation claims, other-worldly redemption, and anti-science stances were forceful, bringing stinging rebukes to classical theologies. As with the broader ecofeminist contributions, ecofeminist theologies surged in the 1990s, went quiet for a while, and over the past ten years have been active around the world. Ecofeminist theologies are explored in distinct traditions, countries and contexts, and in fields such as liturgy and rituals, spiritualities, systematics, social justice and multi-religious efforts, to name only a few.

The most obvious alignment between ecofeminism and theology is with efforts to critique injustices and promote justice and equality. Numerous and interconnected injustices are ideologically, socially and economically structured within many cultures. The subsequent crippling of lives continues to be confronted. Liberation and resistance movements, feminist theologies, gender and queer justice, anti-racist efforts, and eco and climate justice provide incisive analyses, and constructive life-changing impacts (Eaton 2021). The contributions of these denouncing and announcing activities are immense. This sustained engagement between theology and justice is the most relevant alignment with ecofeminism. Contemporary and robust analyses of injustices must address gender and ecological degradation, and the associated social patterns of domination, intersectionality and gender identity challenges. Here ecofeminism and theology are allies.

Enter Global Pluralities, Epistemologies and Theological Constrictions

It must be noted that to use the terms theology and ecofeminism in the singular is incorrect. Both represent multiplicities. The range of theological diversities and pluralities within and between Christian traditions is immeasurable. Theological studies are also vast – histories, doctrines, methods, hermeneutics, interests, inquiries – all entangled within heterogenous Christian conventions, doctrines, churches, biblical studies, and truth and authority regulators. Rituals, practices and beliefs are wildly divergent. Cultural and contextual distinctions are immeasurable. Recent decades have expanded, exponentially, awareness and understanding of the broad and deep pluralities and diversities that are, and have always been, the norm.

As countries and cultures extricate themselves from colonial rule, world views and ideologies, and as individuals and communities add their views on countless issues, it is indisputable that heterogeneity infuses all realms of societies. This has opened large spaces for multiplicities of voices, viewpoints and values. Cultural agendas of diversity, equity and inclusion (DEI) reinforce the importance of pluralities. The DEI country index reports on how over 190 countries perform on issues of gender, race, ethnicity, social engagement, opportunities, disability and more. Ecofeminism embraces and encourages these pluralities, the DEI agenda, and welcomes distinct and multiple perspectives. Ecofeminism does not seek uniformity. The advantages of such inclusion and diversity are abundant and do not need to be enumerated here.

Reworking theological frameworks to incorporate pluralities can, at times, create epistemic dilemmas. Those that focus on theological ethics and responses to the social, political and ecological realities are malleable to this revision. However, classical theology was ideologically rooted in modernism, with notions of universality, absolutism and immutable truth claims. Intellectual positions were derived from assumed static beliefs about God, the world, nature, sin and salvation, *sola scriptura* and biblical inerrancies, and teleology. A homogenous perspective seemed essential, although individuals and groups consistently broke off due to irreconcilable differences in interpretations. Each continued to proclaim supreme truth.

The shift from philosophy to social sciences as the main theological interlocutors and, more recently, to evolutionary and other Earth sciences also induces numerous epistemic challenges. For example, the interface between creation stories and evolutionary evidence has required considerable reconceptualizing and interpretation. The extreme responses are to denounce evolution in favour of various creationist positions, or to replace religious narratives with scientific accounts. Those that integrate Earth sciences and theology, such as ecofeminist theologians and others, expand their epistemic frameworks and develop intellectual acuity and suppleness. They are outside classical or conventional theological approaches and have multiple interlocutors. Traditions based in variations of biblical inerrancy, doctrine/dogma and Christian imperialism are less supple. This renders theology a difficult, if not impossible, dialogue partner with religious studies, humanities, social and Earth sciences and ecofeminism.

Postmodernist probing has exposed and dismantled hegemonic, homogenous world views, beliefs and ethics, and confronted constricted epistemologies. The impact and importance of postmodern critiques have shaken conventional theological foundations, or should have. The softening of absolutist and universal stances, of revising methodologies and evaluating notions of truth are occurring, more or less. Theology, like many religions, has had to face the limitations and errors of epistemological methods, certitudes and truth-claims in the light of postmodern epistemologies and the radical plurality of the world's peoples and traditions.

This is a large topic for discussion. However, it is central to this chapter's juxtaposition of the rise of alt-right Christian nationalism and the relevance of progressive ecofeminist theologies. My general observations are that the more conservative, insular and uniform a Christian tradition presents itself, the less interested, or able, it is to respond to pluralities, diversities and postmodern epistemologies. The oft-times indifference to science, to other religions, and to critical theories of religions – in theological training or churches – remains troublesome. The anti-intellectual elements in some theological studies and church traditions are alarming. Together these fuel alt-right Christian nationalism.

The worry of falling into relativism and meaninglessness can be acute. While there are more complex epistemic possibilities, they require intellectual effort and elasticity. Many working from a perspective of cosmology,

Earth sciences or evolution see these as the context out of which religious sensibilities evolved. Specific religions come and go, while religious sensibility endures. What is noteworthy here is that, in response to these challenges, one move is to reinforce Christian ramparts by buttressing creationism, Christian supremacy, static revelation, and biblical and dogmatic certitudes. The resistance to evolution makes the case clearly. Another move is to delve into studies of religious experiences, symbolic thinking, social imaginaries and world-view processes, and other discerning disciplines. A third move is to begin with cosmogenesis, evolution and the primacy of the Earth for all human development. While these are ongoing, the latter two are becoming marginalized in public discourses, and could be obscured by the alt-right narrow Christian agenda.

Living in North America, one sees the rise of far-right Christian views, activism and nationalism, which are, simply put, intellectually vacuous. Numerous white evangelical elements promote positions that are restricting women's rights, and are anti-LGBTQIA+, anti-evolution, anti-intellectual, climate change denying, pro-guns and often overtly pro white supremacy (Berry 2021). They actively denounce multiple and diverse viewpoints and analyses, and claim God or Jesus is directing them (see Willingham 2023 for Christian lobby groups and funding of alt-right causes). These 'Christian' philistines are now de facto governing in the United States. They are woefully unaware of other religions, cultures, viewpoints, and more. They are aggressively changing legislation on human rights, women's rights and freedoms, are banning books and loosening gun restrictions. Slogans saturate the United States: 'Jesus, Guns and Babies'; 'God's word in one hand, a gun in the other – glory follows'; 'God, Guns, and Trump'; 'God, guns, and guts made America'; 'Faith, firepower, and freedom'. This Christian-backed gun idolatry is becoming a weaponized political movement. Christians join with the National Rifle Association to promote greater access to guns where there are already more guns than people in the United States and children as young as six years of age handle weapons (*Daily Mail* 2023). The US has no ability to discuss gun control in spite of weekly mass shootings and an average of 327 people shot each day (Brady key statistics; Gun Violence Archive). The broader implications are another topic for another time, but worth noting here as these views prevent any meaningful exchange with ecofeminist or any progressive theologies.

Even away from such extremism, it is my enduring position that, in general, theology has never sufficiently probed, not to mention proven, its epistemological frameworks. In what manner are theological claims 'true'? Are they empirical, metaphoric, figurative, symbolic, subjective?

When beliefs or doctrines masquerade as empirical knowledge, myopia increases. It leans towards dogmatism or Gnosticism. While there are, and always have been, robust academic theological studies, contemporary theology is frequently explained in a tautology of beliefs, truth claims and biblical or doctrinal proof-texting. The focus on normative doctrines, revelations and conventional beliefs fosters a fundamentalism ubiquitous across Christian theologies, leaving them intellectually frail. Furthermore, this diminishes a profound reflection on the nature and meaning of religious and Christian insights. I suggest this frailty is also why the Christian alt-right can gain such traction and such cultural and political influence. It feeds the intellectually vacuous but politically powerful alt-right Christian nationalism. This is a very serious indictment.

Religions, Relevance and the Alt-Right

Religions are highly symbolic languages. They are symbols and imagery that express profound interiority. They strengthen the impulses to understand, appreciate and orientate oneself in a living universe and an Earth community with complex life exigencies. They correspond to the mysteries, beauty, elegance and indeed numinous dimensions of the universe, embedded in and lived throughout the Earth community. These symbolic languages are codified and ritualized. They express, and can provide, personal and social coherence, ethics, interpretations of grief and gratitude, and an overall orientation to life. They are symbols representing, even eliciting, deep existential realities, and are not to be taken literally. Needless to say, not all religions manifest their best insights. All have ethical lacuna. For classical religions, patriarchy and the domination of women are pervasive, even foundational. Nonetheless, the power of religious, symbolic languages is undeniable.

The rise of alt-right Christian nationalism is harnessing this symbolic power. It is infusing it with a slew of narrow, rigid and hate-filled meanings. It emboldens religious identities that justify the swelling of public bigotry. The violence that emerges from these cultural forces is acute. The riots at the United States capital building, the truckers' convoy in Canada that occupied Ottawa in February 2022 (Public Safety Canada 2022), and the increasing hate-motivated crimes (Brady factsheet) are the consequences of this religious transformation. Of course, the bigotry is already part of the cultural dynamics. However, when encased in Christian rhetoric, it is symbolized, amplified, justified and entrenched. How long it will endure, and with what costs, is undetermined.

The frenetic, hysterical opposition to trans rights is a case in point. In North America, the anti-trans actions are at a ridiculous point of mania and hate; banning education, care, discussions, medical treatment, bathroom access, athletics, etc. Then there are the protests at drag queen story times at libraries, schools or community centres. These are expanding into parents' rights groups, at least in Canada and the United States, to control (i.e. limit) any discussion, books, supports and care surrounding gender identities, same-sex couples and parenting, and reproductive education for women. This is an emerging cultural force, presented within Christian packaging.

This is a new theological reality (albeit with historical antecedents to the rise of this form of Christian nationalism). In ecotheologies, much has been debated about problematic Christian orientations and the embedded anthropocentrism and patriarchal claims. Historically, the beliefs of post-Enlightenment Christian cultures were to dominate the natural world and be 'lifted up' and saved from the conditions of life. However, I worry that the debates between classical and progressive theologies, feminist analyses, and the expanding ecological crises are being sidelined with the rise of a political, patriotic and patriarchal Christianity.

While this may seem harsh, it is imperative we strengthen Christianity to address global political, social and ecological crises. Of course, the work in ecotheology is significant. The revisions, reformations and revitalizations it has spawned are outstanding, and from all over the world. Those working in the fields of ecofeminism, ecotheologies and religions and ecology have argued for decades that religions cannot afford to be anti-science, climate deniers or ignore the massive social and ecological degradation. I would add that religions, Christian theologies, ecofeminist or otherwise, cannot afford to ignore the ideologies, strategies and actions of Christian nationalism.

Ecofeminist Theologies: Contributions and Caveats

How do these issues relate to ecofeminist theologies? While considerable ecotheology has developed within mainstream theologies, this cannot be said of ecofeminist theologies. They remain fringe in many traditions, cultures and contexts. While feminist theologies are acknowledged worldwide as relevant, for some it means including women, more or less, in the current system. Others require substantial changes. Ecofeminist theologies also range from mild to wild. The more zealous versions of ecofeminist theologies incorporate evolution and cosmology as the orienting and primary framework. Others see human rights and social/gender justice as predominant. Intersectionality is a customary analysis. Eco- and climate justice concerns are central for a viable human future. Here is where ecofeminist theologies overlap more with the broad ecofeminist analyses and proposals, and with theological ethics, and less with theological mainstreams. Ecofeminism remains a marginalized aspect of theological and church endeavours. I am suggesting this is due to the issues mentioned above: inability to embrace plurality and diversity; flawed epistemologies; Christian supremacy; anti-intellectual stances; and alliance with populist, socially regressive movements.

Ecofeminist theologies are constructive, with an overall aim to orientate Christianity towards an ecological transformation of the tradition and the society. Ecofeminist theologies actively confront and condemn the oppression of women, oppose ecological ruin, and expose the multiple connections between the two. Nonetheless, there are several caveats within ecofeminist religious efforts that also hamper their effectiveness.

Ecofeminist insights and analyses are part of most religious and spiritual traditions today. There are numerous publications on ecofeminism and Jewish, Hindu, Muslim, Christian, Buddhist, Wiccan, Goddess, Indigenous, and more, traditions. There are ecofeminist themes and resources in each tradition. Nonetheless, there are caveats to mention, in order to bolster ecofeminist approaches.

The first is a tendency, at times, to elucidate religious texts and teachings that support women and ecological sustainability, while sidestepping the more problematic elements. The same can be said of some religious efforts that 'greenwash' their tradition. All patriarchal religions have misogynist and other-worldly facets, which need to be exposed and denounced, noting that the balance between denouncing and announcing can be difficult to attain.

A second caveat is that, in the large field of women and religions, ecofeminism is not a key topic. Much has been explored, excavated, reviled and reassessed, with the key themes being *women and* – religious texts, imagery, ritual, leadership, and a host of ethical concerns and injustices. Intersectional analyses are the norm. *Women* and *gender* are the contested categories to be problematized, diversified and celebrated. The same cannot be said of the categories of *religion* or *ecology*. Critical studies in religions have barely touched the broad field of women and religions. It is startling how often, and in innumerable publications, *women* are scrutinized persistently, and *religion* is undefined consistently. Furthermore, while ecological issues are increasingly addressed, they have not made a significant impact and are overall anthropocentric.

A third caveat is about overt connections between ideological and lived realities. Ecofeminist religious claims are, foremost, a liberatory project seeking social transformations. Yet, it is facile to say how the world should be, and call for justice, equality and peace. It is far more arduous to understand why, for example, the domination of women and the subjugation of the natural world are occurring, and what ways forward are possible. Gender-based violence remains acute, with the oppression of women being the most pervasive human rights abuse, according to the World Health Organization (WHO 2021). The spectrum of gender-based violence is staggering and occurs daily in religiously influenced cultures (UN Women 2023). Afghanistan should serve as an extreme warning that women's rights are more tentative and less secure than assumed. Afghan women have lost virtually all their rights, in less than a year. Women in Iran, Iraq, Pakistan, China, United States and Poland must fight for basic rights. For some, imprisonment and death are the costs. These may be extreme examples in a globally complex world. Yet we must be attentive to the precariousness of women's rights. In March 2023, Amnesty International wrote a piece on the Global Backlash Against Women's Rights:

> In multiple countries, rights have been rolled back in recent years with anti-feminist rhetoric and policies. According to UN Women, gender disparities are worsening. They believe it could take another 286 years to close the global gender gaps in legal protections for women and girls. (Human Rights Watch 2023)

As an aside, it is deplorable how easy it is to find money, power and political will for military arms and activities, such as the war in Ukraine, and not for women's rights. The trillions spent on the war machine could be spent on human rights, strengthening democratic institutions, reducing climate change and so much more. Furthermore, the ecological and social costs of armed conflicts are reprehensible.

While there is positive global momentum, overall, on gender rights, there are counter moves. The elimination of hard-earned women's reproductive rights in the United States sends a chilling message about the fragility of women's autonomy in democratic countries. The increased withdrawing of gender-affirming care, the criminalizing of LGBTQIA+ identities, and the threat of a death penalty for homosexual acts in Muslim- and Christian-influenced countries are appalling. If ecofeminist religious claims are detached from these cultural and lived realities, they may be insightful, offering prescriptive, even graceful, views, but with little or no political awareness, emancipatory potential or social responsibility.

The fourth caveat is that the topic of *ecology*, even in ecofeminism, is often left undeveloped. Anthropocentrism is common in ecofeminism. Classical religious traditions, and Christianity in particular, decreed a women/nature nexus and used this to subvert both. Exposing this is often a focus. Yet, where, precisely, is the ecological side of ecofeminist theologies? Early ecofeminist theologians looked at the cosmological arc and evolution to include the natural world and its processes within a theological horizon. Recent work focuses on specific contexts and issues. Some consider climate justice, food insecurities, water shortages, and other stressful realities for women and communities (see, for example, Becci and Grandjean 2022; Eaton 2021; Kitch 2023; Mwale 2023; Spratt 2022; Valmiki 2021; Walker-Jones 2020; Zuhriddin 2022). These are serious issues.

Yet to focus only on the impact of ecological issues on humans re-inscribes an anthropocentric bias. Planetary systems are destabilizing: weakening ocean currents, biodiversity loss, species extinction, deforestation, soil depletion, and pollutions and toxins in all life-ways. The Cenozoic era is deteriorating, if not ending. Few in ecofeminism or ecotheology seem to fathom the depth and breadth of the 'ecological crisis'. To mention climate change, without stating more than weather disruptions, reveals a lack of ecological literacy. We must acknowledge that ecological policies are still contrasted with economic profit in most countries, ignoring long-term ecological deterioration. Meanwhile, right-wing political agendas continue to dismantle environmental protections. How can ecofeminism respond more effectively?

Although we are in the sixth great extinction, with unfathomable consequences, animal and Earth rights are often considered to be extraneous to human rights and justice issues. Animal rights are disparaged as a pursuit of the privileged. To give rivers, mountains and animals rights, when humans are suffering, is interpreted by some to be callous. Too many times this critique has been levied in ecofeminist multi-cultural contexts where privilege and poverty, humans and other animals, are contrasted. Yet, animal versus human rights is not an appropriate juxtaposition. Animals, especially large mammals, are suffering greatly and their prospects are dire. They have habitat, food and water shortages too, and can be hunted and killed for sport with impunity. Is this, or is this not, an Earth community that needs to thrive for all to be well? If not, then animals will become extinct, and large animals within a few years. If so, then we need to change the conversation. Ecofeminist theologians can promote a view that all of creation, all life, is an integral part of a divine milieu.

The fifth caveat is an unpopular topic that provokes disagreement and derision; human overpopulation. Most feminists have little tolerance for this subject. Those who do are seen as unenlightened Malthusians. And yet, it must be discussed. There are too many people, in addition to too many consumers with huge ecological footprints, for the planet's carrying capacities. It is undeniable. Yet feminists, and poverty, social justice and reproductive rights activists become apoplectic when the topic is broached. Donna Haraway felt the brunt of this wrath when she addressed human overpopulation (Haraway 2018). It sparked considerable backlash, which has been tracked in academic articles, blogs and discussions (Mattheis 2022). It seems easy to fall prey to fundamentalisms, dogmatism and intransigent assessments and reflections, even for ecofeminists. While surely uncomfortable, and difficult to settle, human overpopulation is a necessary conversation.

The last caveat is not a criticism. A main theme of this chapter is that anyone working in the field of Christian theologies must attend to the rise of Christian nationalism. Their influence should not be considered fringe. In Canada alone, as of 2021, there were 6,660 right-wing extremist channels, pages, groups and accounts operating (Luna KC 2021). The 2019 Global Terrorism Index identified that acts of terrorism committed by far-right groups have increased around the globe by 320%, many of which are religiously motivated (Luna KC 2021). In North America, this is a new face of Christianity. Where are the 'other' Christians who do not espouse, or tolerate, such views and social presence? Can ecofeminism be part of the resistance? Can ecofeminism inspire alternative cultural directions?

Conclusion

This chapter has presented various intersections of ecofeminism, theology and the rise of Christian nationalism. The impetus is to assist ecofeminist theologies to be more robust and relevant to the world. Politically, there are alarming threats and sustained acts of violence, on large and small scales. What has happened to commitments to peace, non-violence, social equity and ecological stability? The dismantling of women's and gender rights is dreadful. The planetary situation is very serious. There will not be a recovery of life abundance. Survival is at stake in many places. How do communities respond to these looming threats?

Yet, we cannot be in alarm mode all the time. How can we nurture and sustain ourselves to be engaged, relevant and influential people on these roads ahead? I find myself, after over 30 years on these issues, needing both wonder and justice, beauty and moral outrage, contemplation and engagement, diversity and common ground. I need a cosmological horizon and daily actions for peace and ecological restoration. And I need to face, and grieve, the losses and the violence, for hope to resurface.

While religions can be readily critiqued, they are also the language of profound insights, compelling visions, and ethics. They are the language of resilience, resistance, revolutions and revisionings. They can illuminate beneficial pathways forward. Perhaps these can provide sufficient opposition to the alt-right movements, as well as inspire genuine alternative analyses, visions and actions.

Bibliography

Carol J. Adams and Lori Gruen (eds), 2014, *Ecofeminism: Feminist Intersections with Other Animals and the Earth*, New York: Bloomsbury Academic.

Irene Becci and Alexandre Grandjean, 2022, 'Is Sacred Nature Gendered or Queer? Insights from a Study on Eco-Spiritual Activism in Switzerland', *Religions* 13 (1), pp. 2–15.

Damon T. Berry, 2021, *Christianity and the Alt-Right: Exploring the Relationship*, London: Routledge.

Brady United Campaign to Prevent Gun Violence, factsheet, https://www.bradyunited.org/resources/issues (accessed 9.5.24).

Brady United Campaign to Prevent Gun Violence, key statistics, https://www.bradyunited.org/key-statistics (accessed 27.3.24).

Michael Coren, 2022, 'Canadian Christian nationalism not Christian, it's not Canadian, or patriotic either', *The Toronto Star*, 17 August.

Daily Mail, 2023, 'Kids young as six handle real firearms', 17 April, https://www.dailymail.co.uk/news/article-11980735/Kids-young-six-handle-real-firearms-NRA-convention.html (accessed 26.6.23).

DEI Country Index, https://www.denominator.one/dei-country-index/ (accessed 26.6.23).

Heather Eaton, 2005, *Introducing Ecofeminist Theologies*, London: T&T Clark International.

Heather Eaton, 2021, 'Ecofeminist Theologies in the Age of Climate Crisis', *Feminist Theology* 29 (3), pp. 209–19.

Heather Eaton and Lois Ann Lorentzen, 2003, *Ecofeminism and Globalization: Exploring Culture, Context and Religion*, Lexington: Rowman and Littlefield.

Kyayaat Fakier, Diana Mulinari and Nora Räthzel, 2020, *Marxist-Feminist Theories and Struggles Today: Essential Writings on Intersectionality, Labour and Ecofeminism*, London: Zed Books.

Greta Gaard, 2017, *Critical Ecofeminism*, Lanham, MD: Lexington Books.

Gun Violence Archive, https://www.gunviolencearchive.org (accessed 26.6.23).

Donna Haraway, 2018, 'Making Kin in the Chthulucene: Reproducing Multispecies

Justice', in A. E. Clarke and Donna Haraway (eds), *Making Kin Not Population*, Chicago, IL: Prickly Paradigm Press.

Carter Heyward, 2022, *The Seven Deadly Sins of White Christian Nationalism: A Call to Action*, Lanham, MD: Rowman and Littlefield.

Human Rights Watch, 2023, 'Global Backlash Against Women's Rights', https://www.hrw.org/news/2023/03/07/global-backlash-against-womens-rights (accessed 27.3.24).

Ana Isla, 2019, *Climate Chaos: Ecofeminism and the Land Question*, Toronto: Inanna Publications.

Sally L. Kitch, 2023, 'Reproductive Rights and Ecofeminism', *Humanities* 12 (2), pp. 1–19.

Luna KC with Jackie Neapole and Miriam Edelson, 2021, 'The Rise of the Alt-Right in Canada: A feminist analysis', Canadian Research Institute for the Advancement of Women, https://www.criaw-icref.ca/publications/the-rise-of-the-alt-right-in-canada-a-feminist-analysis/ (accessed 27.3.24).

Sherilyn MacGregor (ed.), 2017, *Routledge Handbook of Gender and Environment*, London: Routledge.

Nikolas Mattheis, 2022, '"Making Kin, not Babies"? Towards Childist Kinship in the "Anthropocene"', *Childhood* 29 (4), pp. 512–28.

Nelly Mwale, 2023, 'Earth, Gender and Food Security: Maria Zaloumis' Journey of Feminising Agric-Business in Zambia', *Hervormde Teologiese Studies* 79 (3), pp. 1–8.

Joane Nagel, 2016, *Gender and Climate Change*, New York: Routledge.

Mary Phillips and N. Rumens (eds), 2016, *Contemporary Perspectives on Ecofeminism*, London: Routledge.

Public Safety Canada, Government of Canada, 'Parliamentary Committee Notes, Overview, Freedom Convoy 2022', https://www.publicsafety.gc.ca/cnt/trnsprnc/brfng-mtrls/prlmntry-bndrs/20221013/03-en.aspx (accessed 26.6.23).

Rosemary Radford Ruether, 1975, *New Woman, New Earth: Sexist Ideologies and Human Liberation*, New York: Seabury Press.

Nilay Saiya, 2022, *The Global Politics of Jesus: A Christian Case for Church–State Separation*, Oxford: Oxford University Press.

Tina Sikka, 2019, *Climate Technology, Gender, and Justice: The Standpoint of the Vulnerable*, Cham, Switzerland: Springer.

Mike Smeltzer and Noah Buyon, 2022, 'From Democratic Decline to Authoritarian Aggression', Freedom House, https://freedomhouse.org/report/nations-transit/2022/from-democratic-decline-to-authoritarian-aggression (accessed 26.6.23).

Rachel O. Spratt, 2022, *Queer Phenomenological Framework of Gender and Sexuality for the Discourses of Environmental Religion and Ecofeminism*, ProQuest Dissertations Publishing.

UN Women, 2023, Ending Violence Against Women, https://www.unwomen.org/en/what-we-do/ending-violence-against-women (accessed 26.6.23).

Douglas Vakoch and Sam Mickey, 2017, *Ecofeminism in Dialogue*, Lanham, MD: Rowman and Littlefield.

Douglas A. Vakoch and Sam Mickey, 2018, *Literature and Ecofeminism: Intersectional and International Voices*, Abingdon: Taylor and Francis.

Amita Valmiki, 2021, 'Ecofeminism and Social Ecology in Indian Context: Exploration in Customs, Cultures, and Religions', *Future Human Image* 16, pp. 102–9.

Camila Vegara, 2022, 'How Christian Nationalism is Taking Root Across the World', *Politico*, 27 October, https://www.politico.com/news/magazine/2022/10/27/global-far-right-christian-nationalists-00063400 (accessed 26.6.23).

Arthur W. Walker-Jones, 2020, 'Ecofeminist Biblical Hermeneutics for Cyborgs and the Story of Jezebel', in Susanne Scholz (ed.), *The Oxford Handbook of Feminist Approaches to the Hebrew Bible*, Oxford: Oxford University Press.

Karen J. Warren, 1987, 'Feminism and Ecology: Making Connections', *Environmental Ethics* 9 (1), pp. 3–20.

A. J. Willingham, 2023, 'The truth behind the "He Gets Us" ads for Jesus airing during the Super Bowl', CNN, 13 February, https://edition.cnn.com/2023/02/11/us/he-gets-us-super-bowl-commercials-cec/index.html (accessed 26.6.23).

World Health Organization (WHO), 2021, 'Violence Against Women: Key Facts', https://www.who.int/news-room/fact-sheets/detail/violence-against-women (accessed 26.6.23).

Juraev Zuhriddin, 2022, 'Ecofeminism Topics: Water Scarcity in Remote District of Uzbekistan', *Ecofeminism and Climate Change* 3 (2), pp. 104–11.

7

Masculinities: From Feminist Critique to Ensoiled Ecologies

AL BARRETT AND SIMON SUTCLIFFE

Rooting Our Masculinities

Our first (foot)step is to locate ourselves – our bodies, our stories, our writing – in 'specific dirt'. 'Each person exists inside a different landscape ... Our greatest spiritual teacher does not need to be bought or sought ... It is the specific dirt between our toes' (Strand 2022a, p. 17). Even this is to perform a(n) (un)certain kind of masculinity. We – Simon and Al – are both cis-gendered men. As such we are 'invited outsiders' here. Wanting to resist 'mansplaining', we seek to 'read between the lines' of the feminist theological conversation, to better understand our own place(s) in relation to it (Barrett 2023, p. 175).

We are both straight-ish, non-disabled-ish, and racialized as white. We are both ordained ministers in white majority 'mainstream' Christian denominations in England, with academic theological 'credentials', and professional roles that include enabling others to engage and reflect theologically. We are rooted in different 'classed' backgrounds and geographies, and our experiences of masculinities (both received and performed) are very different. We write out of these particular 'landscapes', which offer us specific, significant and yet limited experiences and knowledge, and also many 'obliviousnesses' (of which, by definition, we are only at best semi-aware).

We both choose, intentionally, to engage in ongoing, receptive relationships with a multitude of different 'others' (human and more-than-human), in our social, professional, academic and spiritual lives – including in the writing of this chapter, which has emerged in conversations both between us and far beyond us – a process we will describe as one of mutual 'decomposition' and 'sympoiesis'. This, too, is an intentional performance of a(n) (un)certain kind of masculinity.

Feminist Theologies: Exposing Mastery

Mary Daly's maxim – 'if God is male, then the male is God' (Daly 1985, p. 19) – famously sums up the patriarchal, androcentric entanglement of *theological* imagination with *social* imaginings, performances, relationships and structures of domination and oppression. Feminist theologians have come to know these entanglements as not just sexed and gendered, but to also include race, class, nationality, sexuality, disability, and relationships between human and more-than-human life – all relationships deformed by domination and submission that we might more generally name '*mastery*' (Singh 2018). Mastery polarizes all of life into stark, hierarchical *dualisms*: male/female, rational/emotional, powerful/weak, speaking/silent, active/passive, autonomous/dependent, mind/body, spirit/flesh, heaven/earth, culture/nature, civilized/wild, light/darkness, straight/queer, certainty/uncertainty, and so on. The first term in each dualism is imagined to be both *superior* and the *norm* from which the binary opposite is 'deviant' (Totton 2021, p. 14).

It is primarily from a combination of these normative characteristics (the exact mix varying over time and across different patriarchal cultures) that a culturally hegemonic ideal of '*masculinity*' is constructed, 'a Voice, *the* Voice which knows no ambiguity or diversity', which claims both authority and universality: 'incontrovertible, unaccountable, impenetrable' (Pryce 1996, p. 35). Concealing the actual, infinitely varied performances of being male, this homogenous ideal of masculinity-as-mastery, 'predicated on the domination of others', is then 'backed by institutional and systemic power that rewards ... those closest to the norm' and penalizes all those deviating from it (Mutua 2006, pp. 12, 17). The 'gaze' of this mastery – all-seeing but defended against scrutiny – surveys its 'others' in the interests of possession and consumption, categorization and control (Mulvey 1975). Furthermore, this patriarchal-god-like mastery has found a *globalized* form in the violent expansions and extractions of 'modernity/coloniality', itself manifesting a 'deeper, older violence' rooted in an imagined *separability* between human beings 'and the dynamic living land-metabolism that is the planet' (de Oliviera 2021, pp. 19–20).

Entangled Life: From Feminist Critique to Ecofeminist Ontologies

To this swirling nexus of powerful imaginings, feminist theologies have consistently brought challenge in at least three dimensions. First, the profoundly embodied challenge of *ethics* and *justice*: *mastery isn't just unfair – it's deadly.* It kills women, men and other human and more-than-human life.[1] Second, the *epistemological* challenge: *what if we see the world differently?* Attending to women's experience, and centring women's voices – long before 'feminist theology' named itself – have always brought to the surface ways of knowing and describing the world radically different to those articulated through the gaze of mastery. Which leads to the, third, *ontological* challenge: *what if reality is, actually, not like that?* What if the world described by mastery is *just not true?* What if, feminist theologians have long been asking, 'fluidity and interpermeability, long associated with the monstrous and feminine, show themselves to be the character of every being: every entity in the universe can be described as a process of interconnection with every other being' (Keller 1986, p. 5)?

Recent discoveries in quantum physics and evolutionary biology (disciplines emerging, ironically, from a western science of mastery) confirm that much earlier feminist insight: that separability – the 'self-sufficient man' – is a lie, and we human beings are inescapably *entangled* with all the more-than-human matter in the universe (e.g. Keller and Rubenstein 2017). This shift in our understanding requires, as multispecies feminist theorist Donna Haraway (2016) repeatedly highlights, a radically different *ethical 'onto-epistemology'*: new forms of language and concepts to enable us both to perceive and inhabit the world differently, in the process involving ourselves in changing that world. The term indicates the 'undoing' of 'the divisions between being and knowing – ontology and epistemology': 'knowledge practice is a practice of worlding; the world and "us" with it, are continuously performed; that is, continuously coming into being' (Juelskjaer et al. 2020, p. 14). No boundaries are impermeable, it turns out, and even the 'human body' is better conceived as a 'microbiome', 'holobiont' or 'holoent': a 'symbiotic assemblage' (which includes more 'non-human' micro-organisms than 'human' cells) that should be imagined less like a bounded entity and more like a 'knot of diverse intra-active relatings in [multiple] dynamic, complex systems' (Haraway 2016, p. 58). This means, further, that 'agency' itself is complexified: individual 'autonomy' and 'intentionality' are inadequate concepts. The patriarchal fantasy of *autopoiesis* (the 'self-made man') is replaced by *sympoiesis*: who 'I am', and what 'I do' are always more-than-human, relational, collective and ongoing processes (Taylor and Pacini-Ketchabaw 2019, p. 2).

Re-routing/Rooting Our Masculinities

Our – Simon's and Al's – routes towards Haraway's work, and the decomposition that follows, are different but converging. For Al as an Anglican parish priest, a rootedness in place (neighbourhood) has developed into a practised 'radical receptivity', at local church level, to the gifts and challenges of our non-Christian neighbours, as a counter-movement to colonial and 'penetrative' ideas of mission entangled with class, whiteness and masculinity-as-mastery. The ideas of personal and structural 'decomposition' and 'resurrection from the compost heap' began to emerge in his co-writing amid the collective trauma of the Covid-19 pandemic (Barrett and Harley 2020, pp. 204–9), alongside some intense trauma and therapeutic work in Al's personal life. Over recent years, repeatedly finding a 'groundedness' in – and receptivity to – the more-than-human world has, for Al, become increasingly a matter of survival, healing and flourishing.

For Simon, an 'at-homeness' in the more-than-human world has been with him for many years (from wild camping to growing stuff on his allotment), as has his desire to find creative ways of supporting Christians to reflect more deeply on their faith and theology (the focus of his current paid role). During his recent DProf research on the latter, Simon stumbled upon Haraway's work, and found these two worlds coming suddenly and surprisingly together in a new understanding of the 'entangled', 'sympoietic' nature of life, and the unavoidability, and generativity, of decomposition within that picture.

Decomposing Mastery (1): From Domination to Partnership

Mastery and hegemonic masculinity, then, are not just deadly and partial in their description of the world. They are also less *accurate* and less *interesting* than the world that feminist theologians (and many others) have long known. Alongside other subaltern disciplines, feminist theologies not only reject mastery in all its forms, resisting its power and seeking its demise. They also turn their attention *elsewhere*, dethroning and decentring masculinity-as-mastery and seeking to describe *the-world-as-it-is* – one of inescapable entanglement – and *the-world-as-it-could-be* – oriented towards the life and flourishing of all, rooted in the life-giving flows of God through all creation (Moe-Lobeda 2013, pp. 301–2).

Because feminist thinkers are committed to doing this describing primarily through the eyes and voices of *women*, bell hooks is relatively rare in actively seeking to 'reclaim feminism for men, showing why feminist thinking and practice are the only way we can truly address the crisis of masculinity today' (hooks, 2004a, p. xvii). It is not *men* as such but 'imperialist white-supremacist capitalist patriarchy' (p. 17), she argues, that is 'the enemy' of both women *and* men, and of more-than-human life too. hooks believes there could be 'a creative, life-sustaining, life-enhancing place' for forms of masculinity (p. 115), but only if the 'underlying [patriarchal] ideology ... [of] our culture' is fundamentally dismantled and changed (p. 116): 'the dominator model' (of selfhood) must be replaced with 'a partnership model that sees interbeing and interdependency as the organic relationship of all living beings', that 'defines strength as one's capacity to be responsible for self and others' (p. 117), and discovers beyond narrowly penetrative heterosexual sex a much more holistic, life-affirming 'eroticism' that deepens and widens connections (pp. 181–3). The end of masculinity-as-mastery is not, ultimately, a *loss* for men (as mastery's zero-sum games suggest), but a call out of 'exile' into 'the communion of all creatures' (p. 138).

Decomposing Mastery (2): From Homo to Humus

'Human as humus has potential, if we could chop and shred human as Homo, the detumescing project of a self-making and planet-destroying CEO' (Haraway 2016, pp. 58). Where hooks longs for change in 'the underlying ... culture', we hear earthy echoes of Haraway's invitation to the decomposition of 'Homo' to 'humus', in ways that we believe helpfully further hooks' agenda for change, both theoretically and, crucially, practically. If a man's disobedience to masculinity-as-mastery requires him to understand 'that to save himself means not grasping the patriarchy closer, but letting it die – even the part of it that resides within himself' (Carlin 1992, p. 124), we want to locate that dying in the compost heap. So, what might 'decomposing mastery' look like (Ewell 2019, pp. 201–2, 239; Abrahamsson and Bertoni 2014, pp. 125–48)?

First, decomposition goes beyond 'dismantling' in recognizing that there is 'no such thing as "away"' (Leonard 2010, p. 207) for us to discard what we dismantle: we must contend with *what remains*. Composting attributes enduring value to what we often regard as 'waste', even as it gradually breaks it down. While the structural evil of mastery is anything but 'good' (the Hebrew *tov* of Genesis 1), the created stuff and beings that have constituted those structures nevertheless *have* been named 'good', *tov*, 'life-furthering' (Moe-Lobeda 2013, p. 55) – and have the potential to become so again, as decomposition releases them into the humus.

Second, composting has no use for homogeneity, but rather requires an ongoing assemblage of *diverse* matter (balancing 'browns and greens', 'wet and dry'), in an intimate 'thrown-togetherness' (Doreen Massey in Taylor and Pacini-Ketchabaw 2019, p. 17). It is, as Sophie Strand describes it, a process more of 'addition' than 'subtraction' or removal. Patriarchal culture 'is a very complicated piece of shit,' she explains: 'it needs to be broken down, but the way I'm going to break it down is by adding it to a pile with a load of other stuff, and seeing if in that complicated interplay something new can sprout from the old' (Strand 2022b).

Third, then, composting refuses mastery's imaginings of hierarchical 'food chains' and solitary activities (human or otherwise). It is, rather, 'a precarious composition of different, yet potentially converging, activities and processes', involving a '*decomposer community*' that includes a myriad of different agents (including worms and other invertebrates, fungi and bacteria, of which we may often be disgusted, fearful or simply oblivious). Where humans *are* occasionally involved (as partners with worms in vermicomposting, for example), a slow, delicate dance of 'practical tinkering' and 'letting be' is needed, requiring 'provisional and makeshift adjustments' based on careful attention, 'educated guesses, lucky strikes, and failures' in a 'co-constructed, mutual, ongoing ... effort to attune your caring with the activities of the worms' (Abrahamson and Bertoni 2014, pp. 129, 133–4).

Beyond the persistent exposure and rejection of mastery by feminist theorists and theologians, and beyond hooks' call to men and women together to take responsibility for mastery's dismantling and replacement, composting demands a further broadening and complexifying of agency, beyond the human. For Haraway, 'communities of compost' are *multi-species sites* for 'be[ing] truly present' to one another as 'oddkin', 'cultivating ways to render each other capable' of response (becoming 'response-able' together), resisting delusions of savourism and 'techno-fixes', but rather practising 'staying with the trouble', learning 'to live and die well with each other in a thick present' (Haraway 2016, pp. 1, 8, 34–5).

Finding Our Place in a Biodiversity of Masculinities

In the complex processes of decomposition, new 'compositions' are always forming. Decomposing mastery refuses the 'masculine/feminine' dualism where dominant, normative 'masculinity' is defined in terms of its submissive 'feminine' other(s). Feminisms seek to liberate women from the toxic, restrictive, patriarchal imaginings of 'femininity'; but the decomposition of mastery also potentially releases the concept of 'masculinity' not just from the fiction of homogeneity but also from being something only available to men (Halberstam 1998, pp. 1, 13, 29). What place is there, though, for ongoing talk of 'masculinities' at all?

Acknowledging that the structures of 'the master's house' (Lorde 1984, pp. 110–14) are far from broken down in our world, we suggest that there is a need for an 'in-the-mean-time resource', particularly (but not exclusively) for men, to be able to perform masculinities in ways that refuse, and fail at, mastery. Such 'defective', 'fugitive', *'anti-mastery masculinities'* contribute, with a multitude of other agents, to the ongoing decomposition of mastery. They emerge as a plurality, a 'biodiversity of masculinities' (Strand 2022a, pp. 98–9). And they are already numerous. Naming themselves as 'female', 'queer' and 'crip' masculinities (Halberstam 2019; Barounis 2019), '(progressive) black masculinities' (Mutua), 'postcolonial' and 'indigenous masculinities' (Kabesh 2013; Innes and Anderson 2015), among many others, they insistently spring up among those whom straight, non-disabled, white, western masculinity-as-mastery has always pushed down, pushed out, discarded and destroyed. Consistently, at their best these diverse anti-mastery masculinities refuse domination, and seek not just their own dignity and flourishing but also that of their wider kin.

To survey and summarize (let alone evaluate) this glorious biodiversity would be neither possible nor desirable (yet another trace of mastery's colonizing tendency towards knowledge-as-possession-and-control). We – as co-authors – want not to consume them but to be decomposed and nourished *by* them. What we offer in our final section, then, is a humble addition to that biodiversity, some paths towards anti-mastery masculinities composed from the particular 'landscapes' in which we find ourselves, and the receptive wanderings of our own root systems. In brief, we want to gesture towards a case for 'ensoiled masculinities' both *theoretical* and much more profoundly *embodied*, suggesting that the practical liberation of men (especially those whose identities have been formed within modernity/coloniality) from the domination of mastery might be enriched with a new-old (re)rooting in the earth and a being-opened-up to/by the decomposing and life-generating *sympoiesis* of our chthonic (i.e. soil-dwelling) creature-kin (Haraway 2016, p. 2).

Ensoiled Masculinities: Feeling Our Way in/to the Contact Zones

Before we conclude with some wanderings/wonderings towards 'ensoiled masculinities', we briefly distinguish our position from two others with some family resemblances.

Responding to the perceived 'softening' of western masculinity, the 'mythopoetic men's movement' (originating in 1980s North America) sends men into the depths of the woods and their own psyches, to discover and embrace their inner 'Wild Man', with his capacities for grief, spontaneity, risk-taking and 'resolve' (Bly 1990). While seemingly a call to connection, the movement has been critiqued for focusing on individualized personal development, avoiding the political, instrumentalizing the more-than-human world, and 'hardening' a hegemonic, homogenous (white, straight) masculinity-as-mastery against critique and change (Hultman and Pulé 2019, pp. 83–4; Gelfer 2009, p. 44).

A more recent proposal for 'ecological masculinities' draws on 'deep ecology', eco-feminisms and feminist care theory to outline 'a practical pathway' towards a 'new kind of Adam' in the face of the global destruction being wrought by 'toxic/extreme masculinities'. 'Ecologized' (i.e., earth-caring) masculinities, the authors argue, need to be 'proactive, productive and reach across the widest possible gendered and political spectrum', and thus need to be framed in ways that 'will slip between malestream armouring to facilitate change' (Hultman and Pulé 2019, pp. 231, 155, 227). While seeking to hold together the personal and the political, however, their pragmatism tends again to slide towards an emphasis on individual, self-reflexive behavioural change, detached from community, with a lingering one-way, 'heroic' sense of agency (albeit expressed as 'care' and 'service').

What other moves, then, might be possible, imaginable? While these concluding thoughts certainly have roots (and references in footnotes!), we deliberately frame them as open-ended 'wonderings', further 'scraps' to add to the compost heap, invitations to explorations and conversations beyond this short chapter.

Ensoiling Our Bodies

We wonder towards a somatics of male bodies. Becoming more aware of the locations, intensities and changes-over-time in our bodies of our energies, wounds and wisdom. Learning to 'think-feel' through our bodies, rather than the supposedly disembodied mind. Renouncing the knowing-as-mastery of the 'enlightened', 'overseeing' male gaze, for other forms of sensing, especially the darker and more elusive, localized, momentary knowing of touch. Re-grounding our bodies (traumatized and disconnected by mastery's violent disconnections) in the earth beneath our feet, between our fingers, not as 'virgin territory' to be penetrated, 'resource' to be extracted, or 'property' to be possessed and controlled, but as our common substance: *humus*, '*adamah*' (Hebrew). We wonder towards learning to know-with-the-earth – 'ensoulment as ensoilment' – and tentatively 'sensing life' in and through that earth (Strand 2022a, pp. 15–17, 128).

Composting as Breaking Down

We wonder towards the 'down' of 'breaking down'. Humbled, but without humiliation or annihilation. A *'katabasis'* (= journey of descent, Greek), surrendering the illusory rigidities, separations and superiorities of mastery to find ourselves brought 'down to earth' (Akomolafe 2020). A dying and burial in the earth – as for the grain of wheat – as a necessary prior step to opening to life. Getting lost in the 'dark night of the soil' (Wirzba 2022, p. 112), a 'sacred disintegration' (Kidd 1996, p. 88) that begins when we – individually, collectively – encounter obstacles, limits, impasse. When we come into contact with the apparently unmovable, that which is not ours, or too hard for us, to enter, understand, 'process' or 'fix' – and the 'monsters' of the compost heap that want to decompose us. And all we can 'do' is wait in the stuckness and bewilderment and broken-heartedness, hallow our own limits and the boundaries of others (remembering obstacles, too, are vibrant matter) (Akomolafe 2017, pp. 102–3), and '*stay* with the trouble' (Haraway 2016), as we allow ourselves to be softened, broken down, un-done.

Rooting as Opening Out

We wonder towards the 'breaking open' of the germinating seed, the 'reaching out' of root systems and mycelial networks. Rooting as embracing and furthering the permeability of our boundaries, and our inescapable interconnectedness, interdependence, entanglement within the ever-changing web of life. Deepening our attentiveness. Allowing our gates of perception and imagination to be opened wider as we seek to *love* that which we can't *grasp*. Learning a 'con-sensuality', a feeling-with that, through ongoing dialogue, invites and responds to invitation, refuses to over-reach our limits or abuse our power (Crooks 2021, pp. 252–7). Learning to 'correspond' with our creature-kin, letting them 'be' and attuning ourselves to their movements, their communications, their desiring-through-us (Coles 2017, pp. 95–100). Letting ourselves gravitate towards them, be affected (be moved, disconcerted, enlivened and changed) by them, wonder at – and through – their mysterious otherness (Bennett 2017, pp. 92–3).

Up-rising (Rooted)

We wonder what difference the differences encrusted in mastery make to ensoiled masculinities. What a call 'to go deep into the soil' means for those who have already been ground down in it, or who have long made it their home. For those for whom ongoing struggles – *against* domination and *for* survival, dignity and well-being – demand an individual and collective up-rising: a resurrection that nevertheless remains deeply rooted, in the social life of the subterranean 'undercommons' that eludes mastery's surveillance (Moten and Harney 2013). We wonder also at the seasonality of vegetal up-rising and falling, sprouting and decay, and the unpredictable, uncontrollable up-rising and falling of phallic energy and softness in the male genitalia (Nelson 1988, pp. 89–100). We wonder towards the 'emotional discernment(-with-others)' required to know when to be fierce and when to be tender (hooks, 2004a, p. 120). We wonder if Christianity really is 'fixated on ascension', returning an up-rooted body to the sky-god (Strand 2022a, p. 124). We find ourselves wondering towards an African-rooted god-story of a man, disloyal to the culture of mastery, who is slaughtered and his body dismembered, then later sought out and re-membered by the one(s) who loved him, and venerated in an annual cycle of compost-making, ensoiled again to nurture new life (see the myth of Osiris and Isis in hooks, 2004b, pp. 160–2).

Tending Holy Grounds

We wonder at the sheer scale and staying-power of the structures and cultures of mastery in our world, the inescapability of toxicities, and the unavoidable 'impurity' of our ethics (Shotwell 2016). And yet we wonder too at compost heaps as 'contact zones', places of encounter, of leaning-on-one-another, of mutual vulnerability, accountability and transformation: 'communities of compost'. We wonder at small *'refugia'* which survive and shelter diverse life through dramatic ecological crises (Rienstra 2022). We wonder, again, at those subterranean networks of in-touch-ness, communication, mutual nourishment and solidarity. We wonder towards the nurture and 'partial recuperation' of small, local patches of earth and trans-local subcultures, and the possibility of the gradual turning of common worlds towards common goods (Taylor and Pacini-Ketchabaw 2019). We wonder where in all of these we hear specific invitations to us, as men, as humans, as creature-kin. We wonder what it might mean to pay humble, bare-footed attention to a bush, ablaze with divine life, reminding us that the common ground we share is holy ground.

Offering to be Eaten

We wonder at the mutual metabolizing in the compost heap. We wonder at a god-story of a man-become-grain-become-bread, a vine-man, who decomposes the food-chain of domination in a eucharistic eating-and-offering-to-be-eaten, which he calls his friends to re-member and repeat (Bruteau 2005, pp. 58–62). We wonder at the playful en-trustment observed between children and animals, a back-and-forth of movement and communication that deepens connections and kinship (Taylor and Pacini-Ketchabaw 2019, pp. 42–5). We wonder at the necessity of *pausing* within such playful encounters, awaiting a response, embracing unfinishedness, enduring uncertainty, noticing what difference our differences might be making (Goto 2016, pp. 15–21, 104–7). We wonder what feminist theologians, other men, and other readers might make of the (un)certain kind of masculinity we playfully offer here … (Barrett and Sutcliffe). '[A]s we make compost, we also make love. Love as dirt. Love as vegetation' (Strand 2022a, p. 124).

Note

1 'Other human life' here recognizes that the male/female binary itself is a fundamental aspect of mastery that needs decomposing.

References

Sebastian Abrahamsson and Filippo Bertoni, 2014, 'Compost Politics: Experimenting with Togetherness in Vermicomposting', *Environmental Humanities* 4, pp. 125–48.
Bayo Akomolafe, 2017, *These Wilds Beyond Our Fences: Letters to My Daughter on Humanity's Search for Home*, Berkeley, CA: North Atlantic Books.
Bayo Akomolafe, 2020, 'Dr Bayo Akomolafe on Unlearning Mastery', *Humans & Earth* podcast, 26 September 2020, https://humansandearth.com/bayo-akomolafe-on-unlearning-mastery/ (accessed 27.3.24).
Cynthia Barounis, 2019, *Vulnerable Constitutions: Queerness, Disability, and the Remaking of American Manhood*, Philadelphia, PA: Temple University Press.
Al Barrett, 2023, 'Praying Like a White, Straight Man: Reading Nicola Slee "Between the Lines"', in Ashley Cocksworth, Rachel Starr and Stephen Burns (eds), *From the Shores of Silence: Conversations in Feminist Practical Theology*, London: SCM Press, pp. 173–92.
Al Barrett and Ruth Harley, 2020, *Being Interrupted: Re-imagining the Church's Mission from the Outside, In*, London: SCM Press.
Jane Bennett, 2017, 'Vegetal Life and Onto-Sympathy', in Catherine Keller and Mary-Jane Rubenstein (eds), *Entangled Worlds: Religion, Science, and New Materialisms*, New York: Fordham University Press, pp. 89–110.
Robert Bly, 1990, *Iron John: A Book About Men*, Reading, MA: Addison-Wesley.
Beatrice Bruteau, 2005, *The Holy Thursday Revolution*, Maryknoll, NY: Orbis Books.
Kathleen Carlin, 1992, 'The Men's Movement of Choice', in Kay Leigh Hagan (ed.), *Women Respond to the Men's Movement*, San Francisco, CA: Pandora, pp. 119–26.
Romand Coles, 2017, *Visionary Pragmatism: Radical and Ecological Democracy in Neoliberal Times*, Durham, NC: Duke University Press.
Gabriel Crooks, 2021, 'Under Control: Theology, Mastery, and the Autopoiesis of Masculine Identities', unpublished PhD thesis, Madison, NJL Drew University.
Mary Daly, 1985, *Beyond God the Father: Towards a Philosophy of Women's Liberation*, 2nd edn, London: The Women's Press.
Samuel E. Ewell, 2019, *Faith Seeking Conviviality: Reflections on Ivan Illich, Christian Mission, and the Promise of Life Together*, Eugene, OR: Cascade.
Joseph Gelfer, 2009, *Numen, Old Men: Contemporary Masculine Spiritualities and the Problem of Patriarchy*, London: Equinox.
Courtney Goto, 2016, *The Grace of Playing: Pedagogies for Leaning into God's New Creation*, Eugene, OR: Pickwick.
Jack Halberstam, 2019, *Female Masculinity*, Durham, NC: Duke University Press.
Judith Halberstam, 1998, *Female Masculinity*, Durham, NC: Duke University Press.
Donna Haraway, 2016, *Staying with the Trouble: Making Kin in the Cthuhlucene*, Durham, NC: Duke University Press.
bell hooks, 2004a, *The Will to Change: Men, Masculinity, and Love*, New York: Washington Square Press.
bell hooks, 2004b, *We Real Cool: Black Men and Masculinities*, London: Routledge.

Martin Hultman and Paul M. Pulé, 2019, *Ecological Masculinities: Theoretical Foundations and Practical Guidance*, London: Routledge.
Robert Alexander Innes and Kim Anderson (eds), 2015, *Indigenous Men and Masculinities: Legacies, Identities, Regeneration*, Winnipeg, MN: University of Manitoba Press.
Malou Juelskjær, Helle Plauborg and Stine W. Adrian, 2020, *Dialogues on Agential Realism: Engaging in Worldings through Research Practice*, Milton Keynes: Taylor & Francis Group.
Amal Treacher Kabesh, 2013, *Postcolonial Masculinities: Emotions, Histories and Ethics*, London: Routledge.
Catherine Keller, 1986, *From a Broken Web: Separation, Sexism, and Self*, Boston, MA: Beacon Press.
Catherine Keller and Mary-Jane Rubenstein, 2017, 'Introduction: Tangled Matters', in Catherine Keller and Mary-Jane Rubenstein (eds), *Entangled Worlds: Religion, Science, and New Materialisms*, New York: Fordham University Press, pp. 1–20.
Sue Monk Kidd, 1996, *The Dance of the Dissident Daughter: A Woman's Journey from Christian Tradition to the Sacred Feminine*, New York: HarperCollins.
Annie Leonard, 2010, *The Story of Stuff*, New York: Free Press.
Audre Lorde, 1984, *Sister Outsider: Essays and Speeches*, Berkeley, CA: Crossing Press.
Cynthia Moe-Lobeda, 2013, *Resisting Structural Evil: Love as Ecological-Economic Vocation*, Minneapolis, MN: Fortress Press.
Fred Moten and Stefano Harney, 2013, *The Undercommons: Fugitive Planning and Black Study*, Wivenhoe: Minor Compositions.
Laura Mulvey, 1975, 'Visual Pleasure and Narrative Cinema', *Screen* 16 (3), pp. 6–18.
Athena D. Mutua, 2006, 'Theorizing Progressive Black Masculinites', in Athena D. Mutua (ed.), *Progressive Black Masculinities*, London: Routledge, pp. 3–42.
James B. Nelson, 1988, *The Intimate Connection: Male Sexuality, Masculine Spirituality*, Philadelphia, PA: Westminster Press.
Vanessa Machado de Oliveira, 2021, *Hospicing Modernity: Facing Humanity's Wrongs and the Implications for Social Activism*, Berkeley, CA: North Atlantic Books.
Mark Pryce, 1996, *Finding a Voice: Men, Women and the Community of the Church*, London: SCM Press.
Debra Rienstra, 2022, *Refugia Faith: Seeking Hidden Shelters, Ordinary Wonders, and the Healing of the Earth*, Minneapolis, MN: Fortress Press.
Elisabeth Schüssler Fiorenza, 1994, *Jesus: Miriam's Child, Sophia's Prophet – Critical Issues in Feminist Christology*, New York: Continuum.
Alexis Shotwell, 2016, *Against Purity: Living Ethically in Compromised Times*, Minneapolis, MN: University of Minnesota Press.
Julietta Singh, 2018, *Unthinking Mastery: Dehumanism and Decolonial Entanglements*, Durham, NC: Duke University Press.
Sophie Strand, 2022a, *The Flowering Wand: Rewilding the Sacred Masculine*, Rochester, Vermont: Inner Traditions.
Sophie Strand, 2022b, 'On mycelium, compost, and animate sensibilities', *Embodiment Matters* podcast, 21 April, https://embodimentmatters.com/on-mycelium-compost-and-animate-sensibilities-a-conversation-with-sophie-strand/ (accessed 27.3.24).

Affrica Taylor and Veronica Pacini-Ketchabaw, 2019, *The Common Worlds of Children and Animals: Relational Ethics for Entangled Lives*, London: Routledge.

Nick Totton, 2021, *Wild Therapy: Rewilding Our Inner and Outer Worlds*, 2nd edn, Monmouth: PCCS Books.

Norman Wirzba, 2022, *Agrarian Spirit: Cultivating Faith, Community, and the Land*, Notre Dame, IN: University of Notre Dame Press.

8

Body/Image

HANNAH BACON

Introduction

According to feminist liberation theologian Marcella Althaus-Reid, if there is one thing that feminist theologies can claim in common it is that 'the body always takes charge: our armpits come first', more specifically our 'bushy' armpits (Althaus-Reid 2004, pp. 157–8). No doubt the choice of armpits here is deliberate by Althaus-Reid given the way this part of women's bodies has been disparagingly associated with feminism and with the western feminist project of resisting restrictive beauty standards. To begin feminist theologies with women's 'bushy armpits' is to begin with a confidence in women's flesh and with a preparedness to confront and transgress social and religious norms that contain women's bodies and mark them as disgusting. This chapter explores the ways in which Christian feminist theologies[1] have approached the body, paying particular attention to feminist theological discussion around body image, especially concerning beauty, fatness and thinness. It first considers how feminist theologies have exposed, challenged and reclaimed aspects of Christian body theology before considering how feminist theologians have explored body image and women's struggles for bodily integrity.

Critiquing Christian Theological Approaches to the Female Body

It is no secret that Christianity has approached embodiment with ambivalence. In Christian thought, the body has been approached both as something to celebrate and lament. While Christianity has always been an embodied religion, rooted in creation, incarnation, resurrection and sacrament, it has also been suspicious of the body's desires and passions. The body has been affirmed as a site of revelation and redemption, seen in Mary's agreement to bear a special child, in Jesus' ministry which is a very physical ministry, and in his body which is a site of 'profound and subversive hospitality' (Isherwood and Stuart 1998, p. 58). It is seen too in Paul's theology in the New Testament where the body emerges as a key theme. But the body has also been seen as a source of decay in need of escape or tight control (Isherwood and Stuart, pp. 11, 65). Inheriting from Greek philosophy the 'deadly weapon of dualism' (Althaus-Reid and Isherwood 2008, p. 2) where women were considered to be analogous to the inferior realm of matter, passivity, temporality and death, and men connected to the superior realm of mind, activity, reason, spirit and divinity, classical Christian theologies often encouraged a type of 'split thinking' (Isherwood 2004, p. 141) or 'dismemberment' (Althaus-Reid and Isherwood 2008, p. 2), seeing the body as separate from the soul and women as in need of tight control by the male transcendent mind (Ruether 1992, pp. 26–39).

Such views have impacted ordinary Christian women's ability to embrace their bodies with positivity. Writer Jo Ind, for example, observes how growing up in the UK as a Protestant evangelical, her desire to be a 'good Christian' caused her to see her body as 'a ravenous and obsessive beast' and as 'gross and base'. The body was 'acceptable only inasmuch as it was directed by the higher forces of the mind', she believed, and holiness was achieved by refusing to give in to her body's desires (Ind 1993, pp. 76–7). Such an approach to embodiment, she reflects, fuelled her own body hatred and compulsive eating.

Dualism, though, does not just devalue women's bodies. Because the feminine side of dualism has been considered 'dark', 'inferior' and 'less gifted' (Gebara 2002, p. 73), and has been linked to disorder, a lack of self-control, sin and the sensible realm of feeling and sexuality, dualism resources numerous intersecting hierarchies related to race, class, dis/ability, sexuality, size, culture and ethnicity. Feminist disability theologian Nancy Eiesland, for example, maintains that dualism renders disabled bodies defective and casts them as tragic through association with sin, (virtuous) suffering and charitable action (Eisland 1994, pp. 95–6). Speaking about the racist roots of fat phobia in America, sociologist Sabrina Strings (2019) argues that common connections between fat, sin, lust and gluttony have racial underpinnings, linked to the transatlantic slave trade where racial distinctions were not only made on the basis of skin colour but on the basis of body size. As slavery became established in the US, fatness came to be identified with barbarism and blackness, and thinness with whiteness and civility.[2] Such examples show how dualism supports a network of hierarchies ensuring that certain bodies are established as especially dangerous and excremental.

Of course, one of the most important ways in which Christian thought has vilified women's corporeality is by blaming Eve for the Fall. Seen as luring Adam away from perfection, Eve has been depicted as the 'the devil's gateway' and blamed for sabotaging God's holy order (Tertullian II.1.1). These views have been challenged by Christian feminists like Brazilian liberation theologian, Ivone Gebara, who insists that such views identify women with evil 'as if women incarnate evil' (2002, p. 4). Mary Daly has called this reading of 'woman' the 'myth of feminine evil'; for Daly, such misogyny aids the non-being of women and justifies male hatred of women, and women's hatred of themselves ([1973] 1986, p. 48). Many have argued that it must be resisted and itself named as 'sin' if women are to affirm their flesh as good (Bacon 2019; Isherwood 2007). Some feminists draw attention to the ongoing currency of such toxic depictions of women in the western media and advertising (Edwards 2012), while others see the legacy played out in the 'epidemic' of contemporary 'eating problems' (Lelwica 1999, p. 16)[3] and in obsessions with thinness, including rising patterns of body-discontent among non-white women in westernized, post-colonial societies (Lelwica 1999; Lelwica, Hoglund and McNallie 2009, p. 20). For Althaus-Reid, it is reflected too in practices like cosmetic surgery, which restate the need for women to cut away the flawed parts of their flesh in order to remake their bodies in the name of 'improvement' (2008, p. 73). For such feminist theologians, the myth of the Fall has shaped a culture of guilt and shame around women's bodies, feeding women's low self-esteem and confirming their bodies as deficient and in need of confession and repair.

The Good News of the Body!

One of the most important ways in which feminist theologians have responded to the defamation of women's bodies is by foregrounding the theological idea of incarnation. According to Elizabeth Johnson, the incarnation 'sounds a ringing affirmation of the cherished feminist value of bodiliness' (Johnson 1992, p. 168). For her, the principle that God assumes human flesh can only mean that the body is good and that women's bodies are to be celebrated. Others, like womanist theologian Shawn Copeland insist that incarnation reveals a queer Christ who is throbbing with passionate love. The queer Christ, she explains, 'embraces *all* our bodies passionately, revalorizes them as embodied mystery, and reorients sexual desire toward God's desire for us in and through our sexuality' (Copeland 2010, p. 80). Such views challenge the demonization of women, sexuality, passion and desire that Christian dualism has helped cement and begin to heal the traditional split between God and embodiment. Indeed, for Latina theologian Mayra Rivera, the incarnation points towards the inseparability of divinity and embodiment and reinforces spirit as integral to the flesh. The spirit is found in other non-human elements on which life depends – the water, the wind – revealing the way non-human elements shape our corporeality, exposing all spirit-flesh as interconnected, and affirming the epistemic importance of materiality (Rivera 2012, pp. 222–4).

The notion of relationality has become a central theme in many feminist theologies and in Christian feminist appraisals of incarnation. A number of feminist 'body theologies' have emerged over the last 40 years that deliberately proceed from an incarnational *'YES! to the flesh'* and that identify incarnation with forms of mutual relation. These have reclaimed the language of 'eros' to establish human sexuality as sacred and as expressive of divine passion and connection. 'God is our relational power,' says American lesbian feminist theologian, Carter Heyward, 'our power in mutual relation' (1989, p. 23). For her, God becomes through our right relating so when we join together in the midst of brokenness, 'hands joined and bodies leaning into one another' (p. 26), we incarnate God and embrace our relational or 'erotic' power. God is erotic power and to respect as holy and sacred the power of our embodied yearnings and those of others is to make God present or 'to god' (p. 140).[4] God thus is made flesh in and through our erotic particularities. For her, to be human is to claim our *dunamis*, our raw, divine relational power. Asian American feminist theologian Rita Nakashima Brock (1988) agrees, arguing that erotic power is a 'sensuous, transformative whole-making wisdom' (p. 26), a power that drives us all towards connection and relationship, integrating the sensual, rational, spiritual and political. It is a power that resides in community, in what she terms 'Christa/community', and not in any one body or individual (p. 52).

Such a celebration of the body, senses and sensuality has positioned embodiment centrally in feminist theologies but risks, at times, presenting the body, and women's bodies in particular, in essentialist ways. Daly and Carol Christ, for example, call for a return to women's immanent spirituality grounded in their bodily experience (Daly [1973] 1986; Christ 1997); Heyward, Brock and Rosemary Radford Ruether insist that bodies find their 'natural' place in community with others and experience an innate yearning for connection or relatedness. Such views might suggest that women are naturally more relational because of their bodies and might imply some kind of 'natural' relational self lurking behind cultural scripts. But the meaning of bodies is not self-evident. Indeed, feminist theologians like Isherwood and Althaus-Reid, informed by Judith Butler's theory of gender performativity, remind readers that the body is never a given since it is always entangled in systems of meaning and power (Butler 1993; 2004; 2007). The gendered body is produced through the 'stylized repetition of acts' (Butler 2007, p. 191) and can be a site of resistance, radical subversion and experimentation. Bodies are also lived in specific historical and economic contexts and this insight has been especially stressed by women from the global South concerned to draw attention to the ways in which colonialism, migration, ethnicity, sexuality, class and economic disparities shape women's diverse bodily experiences (Chung 1990; Oduyoye 2001, pp. 11–15).[5] Such appraisals of the body from across contexts affirm that 'the body is no mere object – *already-out-there-now* – with which we are confronted [but] ... is with us, inseparable from us, *is* us' (Copeland 2010, p. 7; see also Moltmann-Wendel 1994, p. 86). They locate women's bodies within complex economic, political, religious and cultural contexts and often trouble the assumption that gender is universal, natural or fixed.

Of course, if gender is permeable and up for negotiation then this also resists the 'tyranny of the gender binary', bringing to the fore the fluidity and transience of our gendered and embodied selves (Cornwall 2022, p. 601). This has especial significance for transgender theologies as Susannah Cornwall has argued. Restating the goodness of bodies as created by God, she suggests that transgender and gender-variant persons reveal a feature of humanity that many still dare not embrace, namely that we are transformative and transient creatures who, despite receiving cultural scripts, have the capacity to curate our own identities and body stories (Cornwall 2022; 2010). We can maintain an attachment to the body in the doing of theology while embracing the fluidity of embodiment, she claims, and we do this by celebrating our human creative ability to shape and transform our flesh. Transgender bodies, after all, she argues, are like all bodies, on a 'journey towards perfection' (2022, p. 610).

Feminist Theologies and Body Image: Critiquing the Pursuit of Perfection

Of course, the journey towards perfection is not without its problems. It is often fuelled by the hetero-patriarchal system of normalization and commodified by neoliberal capitalism. This is why Althaus-Reid sees cosmetic surgery as an act of 'mutilation': because it is, in her view, a technique intent on perfecting women's bodies in compliance with the demands of heteronormative capitalist patriarchy. For her, religion is no impartial bystander because cosmetic surgery continues the legacy of Christian tradition in its offer to restore women's bodies to their original form, promising to remove the tarnished impurities that threaten to soil them (Althaus-Reid 2008, p. 72).

Fear and hatred of women's flesh and the related assumption that women's bodies are in especial need of correction informs the western culture of self-improvement marketed at women and regularly transported across the globe (Lelwica, Hoglund and McNallie 2009). Feminist theorists have long since argued that the western feminine ideal of thinness is established on the premise that there is something wrong with women taking up space, viewing the western obsession with thinness as a 'backlash' against women's power (e.g., Faludi 1993; Orbach 1978; Chernin 1981; Wolf 1991; Hartley 2001, p. 66). Surprisingly, however, discussion of the pursuit of perfection and its relationship to women's body image remains sparse in feminist theologies. This is alarming given that the idealization of thinness through the media, heightened pressure to attain thinness, and the internalization of the thin ideal have all been named as environmental risk factors linked with the development of so-called eating 'disorders', especially among women and girls (Culbert et al. 2015). They have also been linked to increased levels of depression, low self-esteem and body dissatisfaction (NEDA 2022b). This is not just the case for white middle-class women. Cross-cultural studies suggest that disturbed eating among girls is also evident in non-industrialized societies heavily influenced by western norms and institutions (Lelwica 1999, p. 20), and that low socio-economic status and non-whiteness do not protect women from the thin ideal (NEDA 2022a).[6]

Concerned about this ongoing picture, Lelwica suggests there is a pressing need for people in Euro-American culture to step off the 'commercially sponsored "better body" treadmill' to allow for an appreciation of the body, including the limitations, unpredictability and fragility of embodiment, and a radical acceptance of ourselves. She asks, 'Why are so many of us deeply dissatisfied with our bodies? Why are we convinced we need to improve them?' (Lelwica 2017, p. 10). In response, she probes the religious dimensions of the culture of physical improvement, attending to the ways in which patriarchal religion informs cultural discourses about age, weight, illness, pain and disability. The language of conquest plays a key role, she claims, since age is to be 'defied', fat to be 'blasted', cancer to be 'fought', and disability to be 'overcome' (2017, p. 3). But the patriarchal norms of Christianity have been especially influential in generating a quasi-religious salvation myth of physical improvement that fills the gap left by the demise of traditional religion in the West. This quasi-religion of thinness meets women's desire for meaning and purpose but borrows from patriarchal religion a number of religious ideas and forms. Here, the female body serves as a secular 'icon' and magazines as 'sacred texts', helping to communicate Euro-American 'civilizing' values and norms (Lelwica 1999, p. 40). But what is striking about this 'new' religion, says Lelwica, is that it is not new at all! It is resourced by features of historical religion that have helped to encourage distrust of the body. Lelwica thus concludes that body shame is a religiously informed and culturally conditioned response to the commercial fantasy of physical perfection. Weight loss organizations are guilty of fuelling the myth of thinness by enticing women with the (false) promise of hope, friendship and community, and they are not good for women. They encourage conformity and competition between women and profit from women's desire for a sense of belonging.

In response, Lelwica calls her readers to decolonize their imaginations and 'liberate them from the norms that keep us fixated on fixing our bodies' (2017, p. 94). One way to do this is found in the Christian notions of incarnation and grace which, when taken together, affirm the presence of the divine in the body and God's unconditional acceptance of all bodies. Such a theology provides a different vantage point on disability, age, illness and fat, she argues, and recognizes the shame often associated with such bodies as a fear of corporeality influenced by culture and by Christian religion. She promotes 'spirituality' as an alternative to the religion of thinness and cultural criticism and mindfulness as two spiritual practices that can facilitate greater awareness of our thoughts, behaviours and attitudes. These can assist with thinking differently about food and bodies, and with recognizing and resisting the seductive myth of thinness.

Lelwica is not alone in identifying the religious dimensions of the contemporary obsession with thinness. Foundational works by feminists such as Kim Chernin, Naomi Wolf and Shelley Bovey map some aspects of the role religion plays in feeding women's contemporary body concerns in the West, but none of these thinkers are theologians and religion does not figure prominently in their overall discussions. Lisa Isherwood has provided one of the most important feminist theological discussions of weight to date and has addressed how contemporary hatred of fat exposes a hatred of women who refuse to be contained. Worried about the increasing number of deaths from anorexia and mounting anti-fat feeling in the West, she sees in this disturbing pattern the hallmarks of Christian dualism. Within this symbolic, God is viewed as the 'hard upright male' who, in his absolute separation from the world, has no need of anyone or anything. This God makes a reappearance in the lucrative industry of Christian dieting on the rise among Protestant evangelical Christianity in the US, where the risks of eating are managed by giving God total control and cutting off the self from feeling.

Isherwood is rightly critical of this business that fails to care about food waste or those who are starving, or about the toxic economic system of consumer capitalism that sustains poverty. She is though, confident that there are resources in Christian thought that radically challenge this suspicion of desire, among them the celebration of sexual love, food and women's oral stimulation in the Song of Songs. But it is the counter-cultural tradition of incarnation that provides the most radical challenge to the body- and desire-denying features of contemporary thin-centric culture, she argues, transgressing all the boundaries we commonly associate with embodied reality. Fat bodies reveal the truth of incarnation, she suggests, by occupying space 'in a way that violates the rules of sexual politics and of body movement'; by refusing to be contained (Isherwood 2007, p. 103). Following the likes of Heyward and Brock, she presents the notion of an erotic Christ who encourages us to claim our desire. This is a sensual Christ, a Christ connected to the flesh and a Jesus who calls us to connect with our *dunamis*, our divine-human natures. This Jesus calls us to passionately celebrate God's abundance by caring about food and the need for everyone on the planet to have access to it. This Jesus is a *Fat* Jesus who proclaims the kingdom of God through eating and who calls Christians to connect eating to their own erotic/sensual lives. The Fat Jesus embraces the flesh with riotous passion and calls us to do the same.

Lelwica and Isherwood have provided incredibly important contributions to feminist theological discussion on body image with Isherwood providing an especially important challenge to the ways in which capitalist economics shore up gender and socio-economic inequalities. However, neither provides sustained engagement with the lived experiences of slimming women. My work on body image addresses this by drawing on ethnography inside a secular commercial slimming group in the UK. It exposes how weight-loss culture recycles body-affirming as well as body-denying traditions in Christianity and identifies religion as both a positive and negative influence on women's body culture. I show how Christian ideas about sin and salvation are recycled in women's weight-loss narratives in ways that confirm fat as fault(y) while also partly mirroring forms of historic asceticism where body policing techniques assist women with the projects of self-possession and self-care. In the weight-loss group, women develop real friendships and are not simply tricked by the promise of a thinner self as Lelwica and others assume. This does not negate the fact that slimming compels women towards the hegemony of the thin ideal. 'Sizeism', the 'victimization of food' and the 'divided self' are three forms of sin that speak meaningfully about some of the distortions worn on women's bodies (Bacon 2019, pp. 189–221). These sins can be resisted, however, through the 'meaningful work' of salvation, specifically through the alimentary practice of 'sensible eating', an approach to food that refuses to take leave of the senses, and through a living out of a 'Sabbath sensibility' that dares to rest from the frenetic sacrificial work of burning fat.

'Sensible eating' is theologically rooted in the celebration of food and appetite lauded by Qohelet in the book of Ecclesiastes, and by the generosity and inclusive practice of Jesus' ministry of food. It calls for a hearty celebration of passion and desire, while attending to an ethics of taste and touch that remembers eating as a communal political activity inseparable from the doing of inclusion and justice. As a living out of a Sabbath repose, salvation is a practice of delight in fat embodiment. To enter the Sabbath rest is to notice the presence of God in all bodies, in fat bodies, and to rest in the face of fat with peace and joy. This offers a challenge to sizeism because it encourages thankfulness rather than hatred or regret for our current bodies and calls us to face our fat rather than rush to de-face it. Sabbath calls us into a space where we can allow our fat to be, to exist before our eyes and in God's face. Salvation as sensible eating and as a Sabbath repose thus emerges as an embodied performance through which women can resist the current hegemony of fat hatred and food victimization and emerge from the tomb of fat shame with pride.

Conclusion: From Good News to Good Food!

Feminist theologians have been concerned to speak back to the harmful religious discourses and practices that support 'body fascism', a form of violence, where bodies that fail to conform to hegemonic norms are controlled and punished (Quero 2008, pp. 83, 96). The quest for body satisfaction has been embraced by feminist theologians as an invitation to embrace the revolting body as a site of transgression and revolution, but there is more work to do when it comes to shaping feminist theologies that emerge from the real lived experiences of diverse women, especially diverse fat women. Feminist theologies of fat which take fat women's lived experiences seriously stand to nourish the lives and bodies of women dehumanized because of their size and will thus serve as good food, and not just good news in a world where fears about food and fat show no sign of abating.

Notes

1 Following Helene Tallon Russell, I am using 'feminist theologies' in this chapter as an inclusive umbrella term that refers to any theologies that are for or by women seeking liberation from patriarchal and phallocentric norms (Russell 2011, p. 4).

2 Strings argues that because Europeans were seen as the most rational and self-disciplined racial group, and Black people, and Black women more particularly, seen as stupid, gluttonous and more sexual, fatness came to be identified with blackness and thinness with whiteness.

3 Lelwica prefers this terminology to 'eating disorders' because it avoids pathologizing certain approaches to food and setting up a dichotomy between 'disordered' and 'normal' eating.

4 Heyward maintains that 'to god' is to love God in the act of loving humanity.

5 Chung argues that Asian women's bodies have been desecrated by foreign domination, state oppression, militarism and capitalism, and calls for an 'epistemology from the broken body', a way of knowing and thinking about God that emerges out of Asian women's concrete experiences of violence, humiliation and poverty. Oduyoye, describes the particular 'place' of African women's theologies as a place overshadowed by economic exploitation, political instability and militarism. This is a place where women in Africa engage in the 'cultural hermeneutics' of critiquing African culture, including the colonial Christianization of Africa, and in promoting those aspects of African culture they experience as life affirming.

6 Soh, Touyz and Surgenor (2006) also claim that '[t]he treasured ideal of slimness has percolated through all levels of society via the media', lending increasing support to the view that eating pathology is no longer restricted to the wealthy (p. 59).

Bibliography

Marcella Althaus-Reid, 2004, '"Pussy, Queen of Pirates": Acker, Isherwood and the Debate on the Body in Feminist Theology', *Feminist Theology* 12 (2), pp. 157–67.

Marcella Althaus-Reid, 2008, 'Mutilations and Restorations. Cosmetic Surgery in Christianity', in Marcella Althaus-Reid and Lisa Isherwood (eds), *Controversies in Body Theology*, London: SCM Press, pp. 70–9.

Marcella Althaus-Reid and Lisa Isherwood, 2008, 'Introduction. Slicing Women's Bodies: Christianity and the Cut, Mutilated and Cosmetically Altered Believers', in Marcella Althaus-Reid and Lisa Isherwood (eds), *Controversies in Body Theology*, London: SCM Press, pp. 1–6.

Hannah Bacon, 2019, *Feminist Theology and Contemporary Dieting Culture. Sin, Salvation and Women's Weight Loss Narratives*, London and New York: T&T Clark.

Susan Bordo, 1993, *Unbearable Weight. Feminism, Western Culture, and the Body*, Los Angeles, CA: University of California Press.
Shelley Bovey, 1989, *The Forbidden Body: Why Being Fat is Not a Sin*, London: Pandora.
Rita Nakashima Brock, 1988, *Journeys by Heart: A Christology of Erotic Power*, Eugene, OR: Wipf & Stock.
Judith Butler, 1993, *Bodies that Matter: On the Discursive Limits of 'Sex'*, New York: Routledge.
Judith Butler, 2004, *Undoing Gender*, New York: Routledge.
Judith Butler, 2007, *Gender Trouble: Feminism and the Subversion of Identity*, London: Routledge.
Kim Chernin, 1981, *The Obsession: Reflections on the Tyranny of Slenderness*, New York: HarperCollins.
Carol Christ, 1997, *Rebirth of the Goddess: Finding Meaning in Feminist Spirituality*, New York: Routledge.
Chung Hyun Kyung, 1990, *Struggle to Be the Sun Again: Introducing Asian Women's Theology*, Maryknoll, NY: Orbis Books
Shawn Copeland, 2010, *Enfleshing Freedom: Body, Race and Being*, Minneapolis, MN: Fortress Press.
Susannah Cornwall, 2010, *Sex and Uncertainty in the Body of Christ: Intersex Conditions and Christian Theology*, London: Equinox.
Susannah Cornwall, 2022, 'Transformative Creatures: Theology, Gender Diversity and Human Identity', *Zygon* 57 (3), pp. 599–615.
Kristen M. Culbert, Sarah E. Racine and Kelly L. Klump, 2015, 'Research Review: What We have Learned about the Causes of Eating Disorders: A Synthesis of Sociocultural, Psychological, and Biological Research', *Journal of Child Psychology and Psychiatry* 56 (11), pp. 1141–64.
Mary Daly, [1973] 1986, *Beyond God the Father: Toward a Philosophy of Women's Liberation*, 2nd edn, London: Women's Press.
Katie Edwards, 2012, *Admen and Eve: The Bible in Contemporary Advertising*, Sheffield: Sheffield Phoenix Press.
Nancy Eiesland, 1994, *The Disabled God: Toward a Liberatory Theology of Disability*, Nashville, TN: Abingdon Press.
Susan Faludi, 1993, *Backlash: The Undeclared War Against Women*, London: Vintage.
Ivone Gebara, 2002, *Out of the Depths: Women's Experience of Evil and Salvation*, Minneapolis, MN: Fortress Press.
Naomi R. Goldenberg, 1993, *Resurrecting the Body: Feminism, Religion and Psychoanalysis*, New York: Crossroad.
Cecilia Hartley, 2001, 'Letting Ourselves Go: Making Room for the Fat Body in Feminist Scholarship', in J. E. Braziel and K. LeBesco (eds), *Bodies Out of Bounds: Fatness and Transgression*, Los Angeles, CA: University of California Press, pp. 60–73.
Carter Heyward, 1989, *Touching Our Strength: The Erotic as Power and the Love of God*, New York: Harper San Francisco.
Jo Ind, 1993, *Fat is a Spiritual Issue: My Journey*, New York: Mowbray.
Lisa Isherwood, 2004, 'The Embodiment of Feminist Liberation Theology: The Spiralling of Incarnation', in Beverley Clack (ed.), *Embodying Feminist Liberation Theologies*, London: T&T Clark, pp. 140–56.

Lisa Isherwood, 2007, *The Fat Jesus: Feminist Explorations in Boundaries and Transgressions*, London: Darton, Longman and Todd.
Lisa Isherwood and Elizabeth Stuart, 1998, *Introducing Body Theology*, Sheffield: Sheffield Academic Press.
Elizabeth A. Johnson, 1992, *She Who Is: The Mystery of God in Feminist Theological Discourse*, New York: The Crossroad Publishing Company.
Michelle Lelwica, 1999, *Starving for Salvation: The Spiritual Dimensions of Eating Problems Among American Girls and Women*, Oxford: Oxford University Press.
Michelle Lelwica, 2017, *Shameful Bodies: Religion and the Culture of Physical Improvement*, London: Bloomsbury.
Michelle Lelwica, E. Hoglund and J. McNallie, 2009, 'Spreading the Religion of Thinness from California to Calcutta', *Journal of Feminist Studies in Religion* 25 (1), pp. 19–41.
Elisabeth Moltmann-Wendel, 1994, *I Am My Body: New Ways of Embodiment*, London: SCM Press.
NEDA, National Eating Disorders Association, 2022a, 'Culturally Diverse Communities and Eating Disorders', https://www.nationaleatingdisorders.org/grace-holland-cozine-resource-center-culturally-diverse-communities/ (accessed 9.5.24).
NEDA, National Eating Disorders Association, 2022b, 'Statistics and Research on Eating Disorders', https://www.nationaleatingdisorders.org/statistics-research-eating-disorders, (accessed 27.3.24).
Mercy Amba Oduyoye, 2001, *Introducing African Women's Theology*, Sheffield: Sheffield Academic Press.
Susie Orbach, 1978, *Fat is a Feminist Issue*, London: Arrow Books.
Hugo Córdova Quero, 2008, 'This Body Trans/Forming Me: Indecencies in Transgender/Intersex Bodies, Body Fascism and the Doctrine of Incarnation', in Marcella Althaus-Reid and Lisa Isherwood (eds), *Controversies in Body Theology*, London: SCM Press, pp. 80–128.
Mayra Rivera, 2012, 'Thinking Bodies: The Spirit of a Latina Incarnational Imagination', in Ada María Isasi-Díaz and Eduardo Mendieta (eds), *Decolonizing Epistemologies: Latina/o Theology and Philosophy*, New York: Fordham University Press, pp. 207–25.
Rosemary Radford Ruether, 1983, *Sexism and God-Talk: Toward a Feminist Theology*, Boston, MA: Beacon Press.
Rosemary Radford Ruether, 1992, 'Dualism and the Nature of Evil in Feminist Theology', *Studies in Christian Ethics* 5 (1), pp. 26–39.
Helene Tallon Russell, 2011, 'Introduction to Feminist Theology', in Monica Coleman, Nancy R. Howell and Helene Tallon Russell (eds), *Creating Women's Theology: A Movement Engaging Process Thought*, Eugene, OR: Pickwick Publications.
N. L. Soh, S. W. Touyz and L. J. Surgenor, 2006, 'Eating and Body Image Disturbances Across Cultures: A Review', *European Eating Disorders Review* 14 (1), pp. 54–6.
Sabrina Strings, 2019, *Fearing the Black Body: The Racial Origins of Fat Phobia*, New York: New York University Press.
Tertullian, 1995, 'On the Apparel of Women', in Alexander Roberts and James Donaldson (eds), *Ante-Nicene Fathers*, Vol. 4, Peabody, MA: Hendrickson.
Naomi Wolf, 1991, *The Beauty Myth: How Images of Beauty are Used Against Women*, New York: Doubleday.

9

Feminist and Queer Theologies: Friends or Foes?

LISA ISHERWOOD

The twentieth and early twenty-first centuries witnessed the development of feminist theologies and the emergence of queer theologies. Feminist theologies emerged from the liberation movements in the global South which sadly did not always appreciate that the position of women, even poor women, was different from that of men. Many early feminist theologians such as Rosemary Radford Ruether and Carter Heyward were involved in the civil rights movement in the US, in many cases putting their lives on the line. These experiences made them acutely aware on returning to their churches and institutions that women too were less than equal in both settings. They and many others set about examining the Bible, the Christian tradition and ethics through feminist eyes and declaring that it was no surprise that theology made by men over centuries was patriarchal at heart. It is this hierarchical, patriarchal scheme at the core of theology that feminists then and now expose and dismantle. Mary Daly took on the language about God, declaring that if it is male language then God is male too (Daly 1973, p. 19). She said the task was to castrate the male God and address the maleness of Jesus, and argued that it was this double male divinity that dictated secular roles too. Her line of questioning was taken up by Ruether (1983) who asked how a male saviour could save women since Christian doctrine declared Jesus saved what he experienced, hence the need for incarnation.

Feminist theologians argue that the construction of gender, sexuality and the construction of religion work hand in hand. They argue that there are hetero-patriarchal assumptions underpinning the construction of religion and sexuality/gender which result in narrow and hierarchically driven narratives about both. With its emphasis on experience, feminist theology has allowed a new relationship between sexuality and religion to emerge, with the body gaining a voice and certain legitimacy within a hitherto dualistic and spiritually dominated set of doctrines and practices. This piece will examine the ways in which incarnation theology has provided the theological possibility for a radical new engagement with sexuality and how, in turn, this engagement has challenged and expanded the possibilities of incarnation.

Christianity declares itself to be a religion with incarnation at its heart – the entering into flesh of the divine, and the transformation and salvation of the world through such an event. Unfortunately, the religion that sprang from such an understanding has never to date managed to find the courage to take that declaration seriously and has operated from its earliest days within a split world. The initial split of material and spiritual led to further splits within the material world itself: between men and women, animal and human, Black and white, and so on. In most cases, oppression and exploitation have been the order of the day with those at the head of the hierarchies benefiting often in financial terms.

The split between man and woman has had devastating consequences for women who have also had to carry the weight of patriarchal disapproval in matters of sexuality, having been believed to be the more material of the two genders and therefore more prone to sexual immorality than the more spiritual man. Indeed, the early church Fathers often warned against intercourse as the spiritual man would be literally trapped in the material women who, allegedly, would have enticed him through her lisping speech and devilish flesh. Then, danger always accompanied women, and so salvation and redemption did not tend to include women 'as they are', in rhetoric or even in possibility until relatively late (Ruether 1998).

It is not surprising then that Christianity has been historically blind to questions of gender, believing that 'mankind' includes the experiences of women and men and encompasses all that makes us human. This assumption works in many ways; to a certain extent it becomes self-fulfilling in that women begin to understand themselves through the male lens and, in so many respects, begin to see themselves as defective, insufficient or as simply experientially deluded. As de Beauvoir realized, all those years ago, a woman is not born, she is made – and her making is in order to support the male-dominated status quo. She is made into what is useful for men. As de Beauvoir also so movingly noted, women apprehend their own bodies not as 'instruments of her transcendence but as an object destined for another' (Bartky 1990, p. 38). This destination is usually the physical male but can also be the great Phallus in the sky, the patriarchal father who invades all manner of relationships. Having once invaded the 'intimate recesses of the personality ... it may maim and cripple the spirit for ever' (Bartky 1990, p. 58).

Although God plays no part in our secular society, it has to be acknowledged that this making of women has its roots in theology, since the way in which men and women are meant to be supposedly reflects God's design for the universe. For example, the inequality between the sexes has been and still is attributed to the notion of complementarity, which can be derived from a patriarchal reading of the Genesis myth. In this reading, Eve is taken from the side of Adam thereby signalling that the two halves need to be made whole once more. Woman, being a derivative of man, can thus never expect to possess the original, holy qualities to the same extent as a man. This is not just a view that can be lifted from the Hebrew scriptures. Some scholars also argue that it is there in what seems, at first, a very positive statement for women: the Pauline injunction regarding equality in Christ (Gal. 3.28).

On closer inspection, it is argued that what is actually assumed in Genesis is that woman disappears – the rib slots neatly back into place and the male image of God is left as he was first placed on this earth. In Christ, the breach that occurred in Genesis is healed and man once again shines in unitary glory (Borresen 1995, p. 62). Presumably, it is not beyond the bounds of speculation to assume that at the eschaton woman will cease to exist, but until that time she will be judged against an androcentric norm. Borresen argues that Christ had to be incarnate as a male if he was to represent perfect humanity, such is the weight of patriarchal ideology (Borresen 1995, p. 190).

If feminists ever believed that opening up the sacredness of female sexuality would be an easy path, then time has proved otherwise. As we may have expected, there has been a great deal of backlash from the churches, but the path has also not been smooth within the discipline itself. While many have welcomed this development, there have been others who have seen it as another way of reinforcing the relationship between the nature of women and sexuality in a less than positive way.

In addition, concern was voiced through the Good Sex project that western values were once again to the forefront when the reality of many women's lives, particularly in the East, was that sex was far from a blessing let alone a place of sacred meaning. Those who are in the sex trade that serves western consumerism were felt to have no voice in this discourse, while those from religions such as Buddhism felt that this was a Christian dialogue that took little account of other ideas of the body. At the time of the project, it was also felt that little if any attention had been paid to the notion of celibacy. Although I was not the first to do so, we can now reply that it has been addressed (Isherwood 2006b), and with some seriousness but as a sexual stance. Further, there has always been a keen awareness that women are situated differently and that this contextuality hugely affects all matters to do with the divine through the lived reality of women. Exploitation is always a reality and one that feminist theology is keen to oppose – and it does highlight that feminist theologians need to tread carefully when they open areas for discussion.

While some feel that the feminist theological interventions in the area of sexuality may have broken open the narrow boundaries too wide, there are others, such as Marcella Althaus-Reid (2001), who call feminist liberation theologies to task for not having the honesty to face the full reality of women's lives. She claims that much liberation theology, of which the feminist sexual theology was a part, can only deal with 'decent women', that is to say, with those who are seen as suffering and sexually pure. The married mother who is the victim of domestic abuse is within the remit, but the poor woman who likes sex, all kinds of transgressive and beyond-the-pale sex, is a test for feminist liberation theology. Althaus-Reid points out that the experiences of many women are not included in the activity of feminist sexual theology and she urges a new look and a move beyond. The drag queens of her home town, Buenos Aires, are brought into the theological conversation and no longer held at the edges in a morally disapproving cage. Rather, their lived experience and what they signal about sex and gender is in the centre of theological considerations.

In Althaus-Reid's theology, backstreet prostitutes become images of Christ as they give their bodies for the lives of others, normally their children, and the child prostitute becomes Christ since her suffering calls us to redemptive action; that is, to deep and transforming action within ourselves and the systems that create such suffering. If we are declaring the sacredness of female sexuality, it is counterproductive to place a ring around the good sex and the bad sex. Feminist theologians have to get far more comfortable with sex, all kinds of sex, and not run and hide behind the gender discourse. Althaus-Reid did not name herself as a queer theologian but rather as an indecent theologian but many of her insights are useful for feminist and queer theology.

Here Come the Queers

Gay and lesbian theologies had developed as part of the theology of experience helped by feminist liberation methodology. For the most part, in their early days they argued for equality and looked to the Bible to consent with this assertion. The arguments tended to be around the full humanity of gay and lesbian people and their acceptance in the churches as full participants. This, while needed, tended to lend itself to much repetition. Some gay and lesbian theologians felt something else was needed (Goss 1993; Stuart 2003), and it began to emerge in the mid-twentieth century.

The word queer comes from Indo European roots meaning across, to transverse, to move to; and queering is a method by which we expose and engage with the untidy edges, the bits that do not fit a neat system. Through trespassing and transgressing, through mining submerged knowledges, queering attempts to change the way we see and act. It is a refusal to be normalized into oblivion through the deadening systems of a binary opposite world; it is a contradiction and a fluid revolution. Queer should, then, no longer be understood as a noun that marks an identity that we have been taught to despise but, rather, as a verb that destabilizes any claim to identity. It has come to symbolize the moving around or crossing of boundaries in order to get another eye on the tradition. The straight mind is one that is divided within itself since it has to cut out so much that is real in order to maintain the illusion of unity – a unity ironically based in dualism, the hetero of the straight mind. The queer mind lives with the opposites and indeed embraces the contradictions as a way of moving more deeply into an understanding of what may be real. It is then an extremely useful hermeneutical device with which to subvert the rigid doctrinal discourses of Christianity and to release people from their worst excesses.

An example of how this works can be found in Marcella Althaus-Reid's Bi-Christ which, in theory, overcomes mono-relations in sexuality and beyond (2001). A Bi-Christ, a figure who is not bi in the sense of sexual preference but rather in terms of thought and life, is a challenge to the way in which western theology and society is constructed. Althaus-Reid sees this Christ as fluid and full of contradictions, a gospel-based picture in fact. She argues that the Gospels present us with the Prince of Peace and the one who whips the traders from the temple, the one who talked to the woman at the well and could not change the impurity laws regarding menstruation. When we take these stories as starting points for Christology, we go in contradictory directions but, far from wishing to harmonize these points of tension, Althaus-Reid wants us to embrace them as the fluid movements of Christology.

Althaus-Reid gives examples of how the mono-relational pattern, that she rejects, actually works. The hetero-Christ even defines sexual relations that are not heterosexual: the gay man is seen as effeminate and the lesbian as either butch or femme. These are heteronormative categories that prohibit naming the diverse range of sexual identities that are actually operational within people's lives. Heteronormativity stabilizes categories and colonizes experience in order to keep some control. Althaus-Reid points out that the relationship under one (mono) heavenly Father could never be equal; that father was not flexible enough. The exclusion of 'otherness' meant that needs and desires of the other do not enter the equation.

She argues that the Bi-Christ dismantles the mono-relations of naming, organizing, exploiting and owning that underpin economic, racial and sexual exclusions and the worlds that this leads to. Bi-Christ allows other ways to think and to be, other ways to build the world and other ways to understand the sacred. This destabilizing of the mono-God, which Althaus-Reid enables with a reading of the Bi-Christ, has enormous political implications. There is no longer One reality that is seen as legitimate and best; the mono begins to dissolve and other voices and bodies step into the picture as places of revelation and the shining through of the sacred. This sends shock waves through theology.

A further lived reality that challenges the mono reality in a more subtle way is that of the lived experience of transpeople, those who are either transgendered, transsexual or transvestite. They are not tied to what Daniel Maguire calls 'pelvic orthodoxy' and therefore move beyond many accepted gender orthodoxies (Maguire 2008). This could be questioned in relation to transsexuals who may feel compelled to change sex in order to fit a gender identity. Virginia Mollenkott (2001) suggests that the challenge offered to gender orthodoxy by transpeople is needed not only to remind religious congregations of human diversity but also to remind that all of us in all our diversity are made in the image of one dazzlingly diverse Spirit. Here is a radical challenge to religious fundamentalism – just the mention that such sexual outsiders may offer anything to churches or hold within them anything of the nature of God. This form of human diversity is outside the remit of fundamentalist religion, which understands God to have created genders as well as sex that are fixed and distinct, and are thus able to feed into unequal power relations anchored in a narrow reading of the Genesis stories.

B. K. Hipsher argues that because a transgender image of God is so unsettling to people, we are compelled to argue for it because it gives fullness to the idea of ongoing incarnation. She says:

> We need a trans-God ... one that transgresses all our ideas about who and what God is and can be, one that transports us to new possibilities for how God can incarnate in the multiplicity of human embodiments, one that transfigures our mental images from limitations, one that transforms our ideas about our fellow humans and ourselves, one

that transcends all we know or think we know about God and about humanity as the imago Dei. (Hipsher 2009, p. 99)

There is no doubt that queer theory/theology has impacted feminist theology and vice versa. This postmodern agenda makes it imperative that we look with new eyes at the old questions and, especially in the light of rethinking what it is that women may be, that we do not come to easy and safe answers. Feminist theology asks that we be bold in order to fully explore the depths of our human-divine nature. If Heyward (1989) is right, then it is in the depth of our relationality, a relationality that is tested, stretched and enabled through skin-on-skin engagement, that we find the depth of the divine. While embracing much that queer theology has offered, there is concern in some feminist circles that we are being blind to some of the old ways creeping in under another and seemingly more inclusive name: queer.

Although Sheila Jeffreys is not a theologian, she is an activist with a keen eye for the pitfalls lurking in sexuality and gender. She is concerned that, in considering gender as a performance, we are still stuck within binary opposites when looking for ways to perform and that, in perhaps being afraid to question such things as butch/femme relationships and transsexual surgery, we are reinforcing all that we say we have stood against for years: that is, the binary opposition of male and female and the unequal power structure that it enables. She is concerned that a number of older butches are opting for sex-change surgery as their bodies soften and look more female. She believes that both womanhood and lesbianism are being undermined here in an attempt to opt into male power and privilege (Jeffreys 2003, p. 130). She is also aware that when sexuality is spoken of in academic language it becomes difficult to criticize without being labelled as out of touch or prejudiced.

She ventures to suggest that much butch/femme role-playing popularizes a watered-down form of S/M in which dominance and submission are embraced as delights and not political problems (Jeffreys 2003, p. 127). Of course, as many feminist theologians have pointed out, S/M may be a very enabling and empowering practice for women and so original feminist concerns may have to be revisited and thought through from a different starting point. However, questions such as S/M and pornography, which do not cause much concern in queer theology, do highlight some of the tensions felt in feminist theology. Nonetheless, feminist theology still declares embodied eros is a place to begin the creation of theology and the revelation of the divine. But, at what point, if any, do we declare actions to be outside the unfolding of the divine? The narrow boundaries may have shifted, but does this mean there are no longer any boundaries at all?

More fundamental is the question of 'what is a woman?', which many feminist theologies believe to be central to the continued fight for equality and justice. Despite many years across many continents, it cannot be claimed that women are understood as fully human and equal. This remains a fight and one that requires women to be identifiable. This is not to exclude transwomen but it may be to suggest that, for these fights, there needs to be a female body from birth or from post-op.

For queer theologians there is the question of how queer can one be. They argue that queer theology has, to some degree, sanitized the representation of queer lives for the sake of acceptability. I hope this is just a temporary aspect of queer theology and that, in due course, all aspects of all lives will be allowed to challenge theology.

In the area of sexuality, it does seem that there is tension in feminist theology particularly over whether the discipline can carry forward the harder questions as already mentioned. There is a more disturbing notion in secular queer groups, that sexuality is once again a private matter, one that is concerned with integrated, happy people doing whatever gives them pleasure. Feminist theology has helped to make sexuality a broader playing field and contributed to both the political move for more rights and the social movement for more acceptance regarding a range of sexual preferences. It is therefore alarming, since the political goes much deeper than more diverse pleasures and performances being accepted across a greater range of society.

In my opinion, it would benefit us to keep the words of Heyward in front of us: 'When I say I love you, let the revolution begin.' This is no statement of simple self-acceptance and contentment; it is a fundamental declaration of the personal as political and a commitment to embodied justice-seeking between two people and far beyond into the whole social order. It is the kind of revolution that is spoken of in the Song of Songs where the lovers challenge all convention, race, class, economics, and place their sex – there is very little mention of love and certainly no marriage envisaged – within the widest possible context, that of the cosmos itself, as an act of revolution (Isherwood 2006a).

Feminist theology has always been concerned with freeing people from the narrow confines of patriarchally constructed discourses but it has also seen links between many of those discourses. In this way, free expression in the body should also be linked with social change. We have come a long way from the dualism of early and much contemporary Christian doctrine with its negative impact on sex and gender. We no longer have to see both as aspects of ourselves that are fixed in the material realm and so in need of transcending if we are to fulfil our spiritual natures. We have indeed come far, but there is much further to go. Now, due to the opening up of theology by feminist and queer methodologies, we may go there in the arms of lusty lovers in order to speak more moistly of the passionate God who draws us on.

Bibliography

Marcella Althaus-Reid, 2001, *Indecent Theology: Theological Perversions in Sex, Gender and Politics*, London: Routledge.
Sandra Bartky, 1990, *Femininity and Domination*, New York: Routledge.
Karen Borresen, 1995, *The Image of God*, Minneapolis, MN: Fortress Press.
Judith Butler, 2004, *Undoing Gender*, London: Routledge.
Mary Daly, 1973, *Beyond God the Father: Toward a Philosophy of Women's Liberation*, 2nd edn (1986), London: Women's Press.
Robert Goss, 1993, *Jesus Acted Up: A Gay and Lesbian Manifesto*, San Francisco, CA: HarperCollins.
Carter Heyward, 1989, *Touching Our Strength: The Erotic as Power and the Love of God*, San Francisco, CA: HarperCollins.
B. K. Hipsher, 2009, 'Love is a Many Gendered Thing: An Apophatic Journey to Pastoral Diversity', in Lisa Isherwood and Marcella Althaus Reid (eds), *Trans/Formations*, London: SCM Press, pp. 92–104.
Lisa Isherwood, 2006a, 'Eat, Friends, Drink. Be Drunk with Love' (Song of Songs 5.2): A Reflection', in Lisa Isherwood (ed.), *Patriarchs, Prophets and Other Villains*, London: Equinox.
Lisa Isherwood, 2006b, *The Power of Erotic Celibacy*, London: T&T Clark.
Sheila Jeffreys, 2003, *Unpacking Queer Politics*, Cambridge: Polity Press.
Daniel Maguire, 2008, *Whose Church? A Concise Guide to Progressive Catholicism*, Ann Arbor, MI: University of Michigan.
Virginia Mollenkott, 2001, *Omnigender: A Trans-religious Approach*, Cleveland, OH: Pilgrim Press.
Rosemary Radford Ruether, 1983, *Sexism and God-Talk: Toward a Feminist Theology*, London: SCM Press.
Rosemary Radford Ruether, 1998, *Women and Redemption: A Theological History*, London: SCM Press.
Elizabeth Stuart, 2003, *Gay and Lesbian Theologies: Repetitions with Critical Difference*, London: Routledge.

10

Sex and Research: The Twin Loci of Consent

KAREN O'DONNELL

As a feminist theologian, the two contexts in which I find myself thinking about consent are in discussions about sex and in conversations about the ethics of research, most frequently with students who are taking their first steps into empirical theological research. In my context as a theologian interested in trauma, the discussions around sexual consent are often wrapped up with distressing accounts of rape and sexual abuse where consent was not sought, not given, or not meant if it was given. However, in the context of theological research, discussions about consent are often quite perfunctory as students consider the ethical questions around consent to be a hoop to jump through as they get their projects approved by the ethics committee. I find it fascinating that these two discussions of consent are so different; in one, consent is paramount and there is much discussion around the insufficiency of consent as a category for good, ethical sex. In the other, consent is often the signature on a piece of paper before the researcher can get going with their agenda.

In this chapter, I consider what it might mean to bring discussion about sexual consent into the context of theological empirical research. To bring the concerns around the in/sufficiency of consent for good, ethical, sex into dialogue with theological empirical research and consider the ways in which such research would benefit from a richer, more nuanced feminist theological ethic of consent. I begin by outlining the ways in which we can consider theology, particularly the theological empirical research interview, as a sexual act. I then draw on current discourses of consent in order to construct a feminist theological ethic of consent that requires the theologian to perform the *imago Dei* in the context of their empirical research. Finally, I consider what empirical theological research might look like if it constructed its discourse of consent from the feminist theological ethic of consent. Such research would seek to disrupt power dynamics, enabling relational negotiation of research 'scenes', requiring attunement to and empathy with our research participants, and demanding a shift towards concepts of invitation and gratitude in addition to that of consent alone.

Theology is a Sexual Act

It is not new, radical or revolutionary for me to claim that theology is a sexual act, either in the literal or the metaphorical understanding of the phrase. Indeed, theology (words about God) has been tangled up with desire, sex and penetration for centuries. Knowing God – the foundation of theology – for the mystics at least, is very often equated with a sexual act. Bernard McGinn notes:

> Christian mysticism, like Jewish and Islamic mysticism, has always implied the transformation of the sexual energy of *erōs* as a way of attaining God ... If God is erotic in a transcendental sense (as the mysterious fifth-century writer Dionysius, the creator of Mystical Theology, insisted) then the power of *erōs* is necessary in order to attain him. (McGinn 1993, p. 49)

This erotic aspect of knowing God manifests itself at various intervals in the Christian tradition. We see it in Hadewijch's account of the Eucharist when she equates receiving the Eucharist (and Christ himself) with being penetrated by Christ and abiding with Christ 'mouth in mouth, heart in heart, body in body, soul in soul' (Hadewijch 1980, p. 66). Similarly, Teresa of Avila describes her *transverberation* as that of an angel thrusting his spear into her repeatedly, causing her to moan with the sweetness of the pain and setting her on fire with love for God (Teresa of Avila 1991, p. 164). Knowing God is an (not even quasi!) orgasmic experience. Or consider the experience of Angela of Foligno on Easter Sunday in 1294 in which she finds herself kissing and snuggling up to the dead body of Christ in the sepulchre (Angela of Foligno 1993, p. 182). Space does not permit us to unpack the centuries of interpretation of texts such as the Song of Songs, nor the writings of Gregory of Nyssa, Bernard of Clairvaux or John of the Cross. Suffice to say that the relationship between theology and sex is grounded in the Christian tradition.

Of course, it is in the work of the late Marcella Althaus-Reid that we find the explicit recognition that 'theology is a sexual act' (Althaus-Reid 2000, p. 87). She writes:

> Theology is a sexual ideology performed in a sacralizing pattern: it is the sexual divinised orthodoxy (right sexual dogma) and orthopraxy (right sexual behaviour); theology is a sexual action. Theologians, therefore, are nothing else but sexual performers ... (2000, p. 87)

Theologians are sexual performers partly because all people are sexual performers, but also because theology itself is a sexual ideology that is obsessed with guarding right sexual belief and right sexual activity. Althaus-Reid highlights that the fundamental symbols of Christianity (Father and Son, holy family, male Jesus, Virgin Mary) are all inherently sexual symbols. To these sexual symbols, she adds the recognition that 'all concepts of sin and grace seem to be unendingly tangled around the theologian's gaze at other people's beds, bathrooms, or sofas' (Althaus-Reid 2000, p. 88). Theology is tangled up with and obsessed with sex. But more than that, the doing of theology is a sexual act and the theologian is a sexual actor.

Althaus-Reid is, of course, the primary theologian to engage with if one wants to explore the concept of theology as a sexual act. I have no doubt that she does an excellent job of demonstrating that theology is tangled up with and obsessed with sex. She also does an excellent job of situating the theologian as a sexual person, with a sexual context. Where I think she comes up short is in demonstrating *how* theology is a sexual act. She certainly believes it is. But I am less convinced that she demonstrates the ways in which it is. That is not to say I think she is wrong. On the contrary, I think she is right (and I want to demonstrate the ways in which I develop her discourse in this direction). But in any engagement with Althaus-Reid's work we must heed the warning of Kwok Pui-lan who reminds us not to appropriate the sexual theology aspects of Althaus-Reid's work without also taking in her liberationist concerns (Kwok 2003, p. 156). This is a sexual political theology in which power dynamics, ideologies and patterns of domination play integral parts.

It is this intersection of power, ideologies, bodies and theology that I want to pick up as we consider theology as a sexual act. I suggest that when it comes to empirical theological research, particularly qualitative theological research, theology is a sexual act. Namely, theological research of this nature is an act of BDSM.[1] There are many different kinds of acts that come under the title of BDSM. Some of these acts are much more explicitly sexual than others. Some are much more explicit (full stop) than others. But I specifically want to draw a parallel to a BDSM scene between a dominant and a submissive. In BDSM, the dominant is often referred to as a 'top' and the submissive as a 'bottom'. Prior to engaging in a scene, the two (the top and the bottom) will negotiate the nature and limits of the scene, setting a safeword and ensuring consent to what is about to happen. During the scene, the dominant will lead the scene, perhaps inflicting pain or humiliation on the bottom, perhaps teasing and tormenting them for hours at a time, or a hundred and one other things.

Central to many experiences of BDSM is the concept of power or, more precisely, an unequable distribution of power between those engaged in the act. But this power is fluid, dynamic and difficult to pinpoint. Of course, as we might imagine, the person in the dominant role holds plenty of power. The other person literally submits to them as the submissive. However, as Gary Taylor and Jane Ussher note in their work with BDSM participants, the dominant role is not the only place where power lies. The bottom often has plenty of power too (Taylor and Ussher 2001, p. 299) One of their research participants says: 'I'm the one who decides what will happen ... how it will happen ... how far it will go. I call him master but it's my needs that are being met' (p. 299).

So what has this to do with empirical theological research? Imagine the theological research interview as a BDSM scene. Here theology is the dominant discourse and the theologian is the dominant. They are in charge of the scene. The dominant/theologian sets the parameters of the scene/interview. They have a significant amount of power within the scene (and likely away from it too). The submissive/research participant has to trust that the dominant/theologian will do what they have said they will do and will not stray from the previously proscribed limits. The dominant/theologian engages in the scene to get their (research) needs met.

This scene could be broadly true of many disciplines within arts, humanities and social sciences. What is it specifically about theology that lends itself to the association with the sexual act? Here I think is where Althaus-Reid's analysis bears fruit. In this BDSM/theological research interview, the discourse that drives both the need for the scene and the dialogue within the scene is one that is shot through with sexual imagery, sexual obsession, sexual language of bodies, desire and intimacy. It is a discourse that has, more than any other, been used to dominate and to subject in terms of race, gender, sexualities and class. In this respect, the theological discourse, as engaged in the BDSM scene, is one uniquely situated within dominance, sexuality and bodies.

In his research on the life stories of non-normative Christians, Chris Greenough includes one life narrative with a Christian BDSM practitioner. In this chapter, Greenough explores the life story of Cath Artic (her BDSM name) in dialogue with her faith. Through his interviews with Cath, Greenough concludes that there is value in drawing BDSM into dialogue with theology, particularly as he highlights that 'the BDSM space allows for encounters with the divine through alternative spiritual practices, resulting in an emerging theology of BDSM' (Greenough 2018, p. 157). Few theologians have made any substantial comment specifically on BDSM and Greenough's work is, therefore, significant in this field. However, Greenough is (un)doing theology through his research with a BDSM practitioner. I propose, as I have outlined above, something quite different both methodologically and theologically.

In the last section of this chapter, I will return to my theological BDSM scene to problematize some of what I have outlined here and to analyse the ways in which the BDSM theological research scene might offer some creative ways forward in thinking about how feminist theological research can develop evocations of consent. Before turning our attention to feminist theological ethics of consent, I want to finish this section by briefly considering some of the risks of thinking of theology as a sexual act.

I am aware that, in turning this chapter to a discussion of BDSM scenes, I have likely already alienated some of my readers. This is the primary risk of thinking about theology as a sexual act. While the sexual turn is generative and creative it is also distancing and potentially alienating to those who find such sexual acts distasteful or even sinful. While this is undeniably true, theology cannot distance itself from things that some find distasteful or else it runs the risk of irrelevance and false pride in its perceived 'purity'.

Such a turn towards the sexual also runs the risk of tangling theology up with the incredibly problematic Christian sexual discourse. Even the paragraph above hints at the destructive nature of purity culture! To consider theology as a sexual act is, for me, a creative and liberative turn. But it does draw theology into close association with negative Christian discourses on issues like abortion, homosexuality and transgender people. It is, however, arguable that theology is *already* tangled up with these things, whether people like it or not. Drawing a closer connection between the sexual nature of theology might allow further creative space to consider these issues more positively (as well as more imaginatively!).

Towards a Feminist Theological Ethic of Sexual Consent

Having established ways in which we might begin to think about theology and theological research as a sexual act, let us turn our attention then towards the ethics of sexual consent and specifically to a consideration of a feminist theological ethic of sexual consent. Before we begin constructing such an ethic, it is important to recognize the powerful work that has been undertaken to problematize any simple understandings and valuing of consent. Consent, despite the ways in which it is promoted on college campuses, in schools and across the Internet, has significant limitations.

Consent, in the ways in which it is usually understood, is based on neoliberal formulations of the individual in which the proprietary concept of selfhood is derived from social contract theory. Such a foundation results in a concept of the human as one who 'owns' their body and can sign that body away through a statement of consent. This account of consent is problematic. Primarily, as philosopher Ellie Anderson notes, this account of consent

> presumes a level of self-knowledge that individuals often lack. Many of us are ignorant of our own desires, so suggesting that we can know what we want the moment we are asked overlooks historically coded forms of behaviour, the effects of past experiences, and the relative power of differing social locations. (Anderson 2019)

From a feminist perspective, there is a tendency for discussions about consent to polarize into two camps. On the one hand, some feminists take an agential feminist position in which everyone is regarded as free and autonomous and able to consent as an expression of their own will. On the other hand, the radical feminist position considers the freedom to consent impossible under the conditions of patriarchy and kyriarchy (Barker 2013, p. 905). Drawing on developing discussions around consent within the BDSM community, I offer a feminist theological position on consent that goes some way in mitigating these very real limitations of consent, while also drawing these dialogues about consent into conversation with theological perspectives.

I argue, therefore, for three shifts in our thinking about consent. First, in a rejection of neoliberal individualism, I argue that consent is a relational dialogue. Second, I argue that consent should be considered on the felt register drawing on etymological unpicking of the word 'consent'. Finally, I argue that consent should be better equated with invitation in which gratitude is reciprocal and hospitality essential.

In the BDSM community, the ethical model of BDSM participation has long been a topic of discussion. Over the decades, this module has moved from promoting 'safe, sane, and consensual' participation, to 'risk-aware consensual kink', to the 4Cs, 'caring, communication, consent and caution' (Williams et al. 2014, pp. 1–10). The only shared concept across these three ethical models is that of 'consent'. Joseph Fischel notes that '[A]mong BDSM practitioners and advocates, consent is of primary, nearly summary ethical import' (Fischel 2019, p. 37). What better place could there be, therefore, to begin our consideration of consent?

Within the BDSM community, the giving of consent is largely understood to be not simply a one-off thing but rather something that is negotiated before an activity takes place and an ongoing, relational dialogue. Good dominants – often sought after for the kinds of experiences they can provide – are understood to be those who find the balance between respecting the consented limits agreed within a scene and pushing the submissive to the edge of those limits. Good dominants know how to read submissives well. The use of safewords to slow down (in the case of a traffic light system) or to completely end a scene (in the case of a hard safeword or 'red' on the traffic light system) represents this ongoing relational dialogue of consent. Not something given at the beginning of an activity and then never discussed again, but rather an ongoing conversation that respects all parties and draws on the wisdom of all those involved. We might term this shifting of consent something like 'attunement'. As attunement, consent draws participants into an 'embodied, reciprocal interaction that requires nonverbal, and often verbal, negotiations as individuals interpret and invent their desires' (Anderson 2019). This attunement to the needs of the other is foundational to relational dialogue in the context of consent.

Attunement as embodied, reciprocal interaction unsettles some of our more legalistic understandings of consent as a contract. But perhaps this is not so surprising. Etymologically, the word 'consent' derives from the latin *consentire*, which means to feel together (from the Latin *com*, 'with, together', and *sentire*, meaning 'to feel'). Consent, therefore, is something that happens in the felt register. Again, this disrupts our usual legalistic understanding of the term 'consent' by shifting it closer to the body. Consent, therefore, requires attention be paid not only to our own bodies but also to the bodies of those we are interacting with, and it values the body – encompassing the thinking and feeling parts of ourselves – as the basis for consent.

This feeling together draws consent into discourses of empathy. As empathy, feeling together requires reflection on and experience of a consciousness different from one's own. It requires you to put yourself in the other's position and care about what that person's experience feels like. Empathy and valuing of the body are distinctly feminist theological characteristics, recognizing and valuing the experience of both the self and the other.

However, I wonder if our discussion about consent requires more than just agreeing to (or rejecting) particular activities or even empathetic attunement to the needs of the other. Perhaps it requires a linguistic shift as well. Rebecca Kukla (2019) argues that 'an invitation is more typical and more conducive to good, flourishing sex than a request.' I argue that a feminist theological ethics of consent is one that is grounded in invitation and hospitality. This grounding develops the ongoing, relational negotiated aspect of consent as it draws on Christian practices of hospitality as the invitation creates a hospitable space for the invitee to enter. Jayme Reaves, in her discourse on protective hospitality, reminds us that love of God is demonstrated in the ways in which the other is loved. This love is expressed in terms of hospitality – the welcome and care for the other (Reaves 2017, p. 90). This hospitality – welcome and care for the other as an expression of the love of God – underpins a feminist theological ethic of consent.

Kukla develops her pursuit of the invitation as a grounding of ethical sex:

> Notice that if I *invite* you, appropriately, to have sex with me, then *consent* and *refusal* are not even the right categories of speech acts when it comes to your uptake. It is not felicitous to consent to an invitation; rather, one accepts it or turns it down. So the consent module distorts our understanding of how a great deal of sex is initiated, including in particular pleasurable, ethical sex. (Kukla 2019)

The addition of the hospitable invitation to the notion of consent (note, invitation is not replacing consent) shifts our conversation about ethical sex further into the relational mode. Such a shift better respects the dignity of each person and begins to disrupt some of the power dynamics of sexual acts. Consent is a response to a request and puts the requester in the active position and the one who consents in a passive position. The invitation, however, calls for gratitude from both parties (I thank you for inviting me to dinner, you thank me for coming). Such a shift begins to create a greater sense of equilibrium between the participants, disrupting power dynamics and patterns of domination and submission.

Much of this feminist ethic of consent would be agreeable to feminists from a range of disciplines, so what is it that makes it theological? In part, it is directed towards the particular dynamic of domination and submission made possible by theology that has long been entwined with misogyny, sexism, colonialism and racism. But in a more positive strand, it is an ethic of consent based on a particular theological anthropology that places an incarnational value on the dignity of the body and concern for the other. In this context, the *imago Dei* is a performative act rather than a taxonomic definition. To be in the *imago Dei* is to perform the image of God in concrete circumstances in order to promote the full flourishing of people.[2] This approach to consent is one that requires the performance of the *imago Dei* in the context of sexual activity in order to ensure the full flourishing of all those involved in the sexual activity.

This feminist theological ethic of consent that I have briefly constructed here is one in which consent is understood as an ongoing relational dialogue and negotiation rather than a one-off act of agreement, after which all things are consented to. It is an ethic of consent grounded on feminist principles of valuing the body and bodily experience. It attempts to honour what bodies can say to us, experiencing in the felt register both attunement to and empathy for the other. This ethic of consent requires a shift into language of invitation and hospitality as love of God is expressed in love for the other, disrupting damaging power dynamics.

A Feminist Theological Ethic of Consent and Empirical Theological Research

Feminist theologians, as well as scholars from a wide range of disciplines, have dedicated considerable time and scholarship to the consideration of the ethics of consent as it pertains to sexual encounters and sexual acts. But far less attention has been paid to the questions of consent in terms of the empirical theological research act – a similarly sexual encounter, couched in hierarchies and domination, and reliant upon intimacy and disclosure for its success. Let us consider, then, the extent to which this feminist theological ethic of consent can be applied to the empirical theological research act.

Let us return, first, to the exploration of the empirical theological research act as a manifestation of a BDSM scene. As I outlined above, this scene places the theologian in the dominant (or top) position and the research participant in the submissive (or bottom) position. But let's bring our theological BDSM scene into dialogue with the consent discourses that characterize the BDSM community. Here we might renegotiate the space somewhat. Imagine a theological research interview in which the researcher and participant negotiated what the scene would look like beforehand; where the limits of the research interview were agreed and a safeword put in place to guard those limits.

Imagine a BDSM/theological research interview where the power of the submissive/research participant, as the one who holds the answers the dominant/theologian wants, is recognized. What might it mean to recognize the power of the submissive/research participant to shape, allow and restrict the direction of the research interview?

Imagine a BDSM/theological research interview where the primary concern of the dominant/theologian was not the meeting of her research needs but the pleasure and satisfaction of the submissive/research participant. What would such a research interview look like? What would it mean to put the pleasure and satisfaction of the research participant first, even before the gathering of research data? What might it mean to ensure that there even was pleasure for the submissive/research participant in the course of theological empirical research?

The best dominants are the ones who not only read their submissives (both verbally and non-verbally) exceptionally well and know when to push and when to pull back, they are also the ones who know that their responsibility as a dominant does not end with the last dominant act in a scene. A crucial part of the dominant role is the provision of aftercare to the submissive, recognizing the intense sensations and emotions the submissive has experienced and the ways in which they need to be cared for in the immediate aftermath of a scene. What would such aftercare look like in the context of a theological empirical research scene that has potentially stripped the submissive/research participant bare and exposed them intimately to the dominant/theologian? Imagine building aftercare into such a research scene.

Perhaps this seems incongruous to you. Perhaps the lines I have drawn from the BDSM scene to the empirical theological research scene are lines that make no logical sense for you. However, we would be naive to think that dynamics of domination and submission do not occur in society all around us – the BDSM community is a primary example of a group trying to negotiate these dynamics in a mutually orientated way. I am not the first to suggest that the considerations we make in terms of consent and the sexual act should be applied beyond the confines of sex itself. For example, the non-consensual cultures of dominance and submission that operate in the corporate world have been previously highlighted by scholars in various disciplines (Chancer 1992). Similarly, the hierarchical nature of academic culture encourages non-consensual dominance and submission undercurrents (Williams 2002). Barker acknowledges, 'cultures of consent toxicity are thus commonplace across romantic relationships, everyday social interaction, and the operation of corporate and public institutions' (2004, p. 97). As feminist theologians (among many others) work hard to reshape our understanding of sexual consent so that it is fit for purpose in twenty-first-century life, so we must apply these principles of good and useful consent to all those areas in which 'consent toxicity' is present, recognizing that dynamics of dominance and submission are not relegated to the bedroom.

The feminist theological ethic of consent I outlined above requires the dominant/theologian to develop a praxis of consent in the midst of their theological research. Developing principles from the theological BDSM scene I considered above, the dominant/theologian can begin by recognizing the power dynamics at play in this kind of scene and approach the empirical research with an aim of relational dialogue and negotiation in which the 'scene' is discussed beforehand, limits are set, and safewords (or a traffic light system) are put in place. Only once they fully understand what is taking place can a submissive/research participant consent to their participation.[3]

This praxis of consent requires hard work on the part of the dominant/theologian to develop their attunement and empathy to the verbal and non-verbal cues of the submissive/research participant. This praxis of consent requires a shift into the language and attitude of invitation and hospitality in which the needs and pleasure of the other are dominant, driving forces such that in the aftermath, gratitude might flow in both directions. I use the term 'praxis' as a reminder of Paolo Friere's definition of the term as 'reflection and action directed at the structures to be transformed' (Friere 1970, p. 126). It is the structures of power, dominance and hierarchy that must be transformed if consent, in any context and any capacity, is to have any meaning and significance at all. Our praxis of consent is aimed, in this case, at dismantling these structures of power, dominance and hierarchy as a liberative practice of justice.

Evoking Consent

This contribution to this volume was designed to explore feminist approaches to the ways in which consent is evoked in the context of feminist theological methodologies and research. Most of the feminist theologians and religious studies researchers I know take the evocation of consent in empirical research very seriously and work exceptionally hard to ensure that they are not taking advantage of their research participants. They seek to ensure that their research participants give informed consent to their participation and that they are cared for and supported throughout their involvement. Nothing in this chapter is meant to critique the many examples of good practice already evident in so much feminist theological work. My intention in this chapter has been to ground this approach to consent in a wider ethical framework, taking the rich and varied discussion of the possibilities and conditions for sexual consent as a starting point.

Theology is a sexual act and empirical theological research is a sexual act rife with dynamics of domination and submission that must be recognized and mitigated if our research participants are to give informed consent. There is much that can be learned from the approach that the BDSM community has taken towards both consent and good practice in scenes that play with these dynamics of domination and submission. Disrupting and dismantling some of these dynamics enables us, as feminist theological researchers, to stretch the concept of consent further still into modes of invitation and gratitude. It allows us to reimagine what participation in our research might look like. It encourages us to develop both attunement to and empathy with our research participants to see their experience in our research from their perspective. Recognizing theology as a sexual act must encourage us to ask, when we seek consent from our participants, where is the pleasure and satisfaction in this experience for them?

Notes

1 BDSM is an acronym for bondage, domination, sado-masochism and refers to a sub-culture in which BDSM is the dominant (pardon the pun) driving force.

2 For a fuller account of this perspective on theological anthropology, see Alistair McFadyen 2016; Karen O'Donnell 2018.

3 For an excellent articulation of this kind of consent see Dawn Llewellyn 2015, Appendix A.

Bibliography

Marcella Althaus-Reid, 2000, *Indecent Theology: Theological Perversions in Sex, Gender and Politics*, Abingdon and New York: Routledge.

Ellie Anderson, 'Women in Philosophy: The Limits of Consent in Sexual Ethics', blog of the APA, https://blog.apaonline.org/2019/04/24/women-in-philosophy-the-limits-of-consent-in-sexual-ethics/ (accessed 27.3.24).

Angela of Foligno, 1993, *Complete Works*, trans. Paul Lachance, New York: Paulist Press.
Meg Barker, 2013, 'Consent is a Gray Area?', *Sexualities* 16 (8), pp. 896–914.
L. Chancer, 1992, *Sadomasochism in Everyday Life*, New Brunswick, NJ: Rutgers University Press.
Joseph J. Fischel, 2019, *Screw Consent: A Better Politics of Sexual Justice*, Oakland, CA: University of California Press.
Paulo Freire, 1970, *Pedagogy of the Oppressed*, New York: Bloomsbury Academic.
Chris Greenough, 2018, *Undoing Theology: Life Stories from Non-Normative Christians*, London: SCM Press.
Hadewijch, 1980, *The Complete Works*, trans. Columba Hart, Classics of Western Spirituality, New York: Paulist Press.
Rebecca Kukla, 2019, 'Sex Talks', *Aeon Essays*, https://aeon.co/essays/consent-and-refusal-are-not-the-only-talking-points-in-sex (accessed 27.3.24).
Kwok Pui-lan, 2003, 'Theology as a Sexual Act', *Feminist Theology* 11 (2), pp. 149–56.
Dawn Llewellyn, 2015, *Reading, Feminism, and Spirituality: Troubling the Waves*, London: Palgrave Macmillan.
Alistair McFadyen, 2016, 'Redeeming the Image', *International Journal for the Study of the Christian Church* 16 (2), pp. 108–25, https://doi.org/10.1080/1474225X.2016.1196539 (accessed 27.3.24).
Bernard McGinn, 1993, 'Mysticism and Sexuality', *The Way Supplement* 77, pp. 46–54.
Karen O'Donnell, 2018, 'Performing the Imago Dei: Human Enhancement, Artificial Intelligence, and Optative Image-Bearing', *International Journal for the Study of the Christian Church* 18 (1), pp. 4–15.
Jayme Reaves, 2017, *Safeguarding the Stranger: An Abrahamic Theology and Ethic of Protective Hospitality*, Cambridge: The Lutterworth Press.
Gary W. Taylor and Jane M. Ussher, 2001, 'Making Sense of S&M: A Discourse Analytic Account', *Sexualities* 4 (3), pp. 293–314.
Teresa of Avila, 1991, *The Life of Teresa of Jesus: The Autobiography of Teresa of Avila*, ed. and trans. E. Allison Peers, New York: Doubleday.
C. L. Williams, 2002, 'Sexual Harassment and Sadomasochism', *Hypatia* 17 (2), pp. 99–117.
D. Williams, Jeremy Thomas, Emily Prior and M. Candace Christensen, 2014, 'From "SSC" and "RACK" to the "4Cs": Introducing a New Framework for Negotiating BDSM Participation', *Electronic Journal of Human Sexuality*, 17 August, pp. 1–10.

11

'A Solidarity Dance': Feminist Approaches to Abuse

JANE CHEVOUS, ALANA HARRIS AND ANTONIA SOBOCKI

Setting the Scene

Abuse and trauma are 'slippery' phenomena (Bond and Craps 2020); hard to define and difficult to measure. Definitions are not universally agreed (Matthews and Collin-Vézina 2019, p. 131); for example, traditional understandings of abuse and violence are often expressed as traumatic actions or episodes within defined frameworks (Walby et al. 2017), while survivors talk about incomprehensible, distressing or frightening experiences and a continuous happening with a cumulative, harmful impact (Myhill and Kelly 2019). Abuse may be understood as mistreatment or neglect of another person that causes harm (WTSC 2018), and may be physical, sexual, emotional or spiritual. Whereas trauma is often defined as the long-lasting damage to someone's mental, physical, social, emotional or spiritual well-being, resulting from adverse or life-threatening experiences (SAMHSA 2014). Within faith settings, trauma might also be vicarious, sacramental, ecclesial and intergenerational, magnified by a recognition of the church as an especially charged site of authority and vulnerability (Oakley and Humphreys 2019).

Challenges in quantifying and 'measuring' abuse (Gilbert et al. 2012) mean that while the World Health Organization (2021) estimates indicate that one in three women experience gender-based violence, and over half of all children experience emotional, physical or sexual abuse each year (Hillis et al. 2016), this is likely to be a significant underestimate (Stoltenborgh et al. 2011). As #ChurchToo followed #MeToo, we see increasing revelations and interrogations of faith and church-based abuse, although it is also under-reported and remains under-researched (Witt et al. 2019). While more studies of church-based child abuse (contact and non-contact) are emerging, most clergy sexual abuse victims are *adult* females (Reisinger 2022) and the church is a particularly dangerous place for women and girls (Flynn 2008). Nearly 13% of clergy in a key but dated study admitted to having sexual intercourse with a member of the congregation (Fortune and Poling 1994), and some experts suggest that as many as 8% of priests may be paedophiles (SNAP 2023), with cases in their thousands leading to survivors filing a complaint with the International Criminal Court as a crime against humanity (CCR 2023).

Abuse by clergy and others in faith settings has a uniquely devastating impact, arising from the pentagonal dynamic between victim, abuser, faith leaders, faith community and God (Fogler et al. 2008b). Survivors have described the trauma as 'annihilation of the soul' (Clites 2019b, p. 269) or a 'daily crucifixion' (Chevous 2004, p. 29) which is almost impossible to report because God (through his male representative on earth) has silenced them (Fogler et al. 2008a). Church responses to disclosure have been characterized by denial, disbelief, theological deflection (through recourse to 'sin' or 'forgiveness'), institutional damage limitation or protectionism and a lack of care or compassion for victims (IICSA 2017).

We recognize that the root causes of the global endemic in gender-based violence are gender inequality and misogynistic beliefs that normalize violence against women, such as sexual purity and family honour, and ideologies of male sexual entitlement, coupled with weak legal sanctions for sexual violence and abuse (WHO 2021). Feminist theologians have helped us to recognize and challenge the 'texts of terror' (Trible 2002) and abusive theologies that make the church a place where silence, secrecy and bystander complicity have flourished (Cashwell and Swindle 2018; Mulvihill et al. 2022). The emergence of trauma theology, which has established itself as a vibrant field of research (O'Donnell and Gross 2022), directs attention to the construction of reimagined theologies that are attentive to the voices and embodied experiences of survivors. In the remainder of this chapter, we will explore specific feminist methodologies and 'right' or 'rite' praxis, offering examples that foreground the activities of survivor-researchers and survivor-activists who want to speak (as catalysts for change) and seek to craft their own strategies for turning 'pain into power' (SV Charter 2018).

Allyship, Active Listening and Embodied Accompaniment

As feminist psychiatrist Judith Herman (1997, p. 175) powerfully argued some time ago, to heal we need to recognize ourselves as *wounded storytellers*, and through reconstruction 'transform the traumatic memory so that it can be integrated into a survivor's life story'. For allies working with survivors in the co-production of research and remedial action that is relational and reciprocal (Clites 2019a), there is the opportunity to collaborate together to forge transformed theological insights into key concepts such as suffering, justice, patient waiting and resurrection (Sords 2019). This requires, as feminist methodologies in allied fields have also identified, an orientation towards 'active' or 'deep' listening (Stetz 2001) and reverent attention to the 'speaking wound' (Caruth 1996, p. 9). In order to 'listen to hear' (Lagan 2017) – following the biblical injunctions in Isaiah and Matthew that we should have 'eyes to see and ears to hear' – we must be open to *metanoia* and recognize a collective need for lamentation and repentance (Francis 2019). We all, as members of the body of Christ, will be changed through this process of compassionately sitting with and grieving through the pain, while together, prophetically, we play our part in seeking truth, bringing hope and finding healing (CBCEW 2022; Jones et al. 2024).

This receptivity may also take us beyond words and narratives that are inadequate for what is fragmented or renders us inarticulate, towards an embrace of metaphor (Westin 2022), imagery (Traumascapes 2023) and embodied ways of knowing and healing (Rothchild 2000). Inevitably this might also encourage us to move beyond traditional communication modes such as judicial reports, academic articles or media exposés: as creative, arts-based approaches encourage different expressive forms and affective connections (Malchiodi 2020) (Figure 1). These have the power to break down barriers to engagement, hierarchical imbalances and status around certain forms of knowledge that undergird and sustain certain ways of telling a narrative as necessary for 'legibility', 'credibility' and acknowledged agency (Leavy 2020).

Such relational, radical, vulnerable solidarity between survivors and their allies moves beyond more formal and static theological processes of 'accompaniment' (Doughtry and Green 2020) and needs to be orientated, fundamentally, to what survivors want and to what works. Rendering this trauma-informed discipleship through a biblical register might require us to adopt the stance and the strategies, at different times or for different audiences, of 'Mary' and 'Martha' in seeking to follow the Lord (Wyant 2019, pp. 1–32). The active and the contemplative, speaking and

Figure 1: Infographic summarizing conversations at a workshop with survivor-researchers and their allies, 9 November 2022. Used with permission JennyLeonardArt.com

doing, righteous anger and prayerful supplication are in a creative, trinitarian perichoresis when finding strategies to respond, and heal from, church-based abuse.

This relational, creative response is essential to recovery; the rupture of abuse requires relationship, trust and reconnection to repair (Grosh-Miller 2021). Abuse cannot be fully articulated through verbal narratives, as trauma disrupts our ability to translate feelings into words (Rothschild 2000; Nemeroff 2004; Levine 2015; Van der Kolk 2015). Art, symbols and liturgy offer a rich expressive register beyond words (Gantt and Tinnin, 2009; Morrissey 2013) (Figure 2). Ritual, religious memory and spiritual practice may offer an alternative mode to speak through or past 'silence', through scripted actions and affective gestures, which open out spaces for peace and healing (Miller 2021). Engaging people in accessible discourses through an artistic or meditative imagination can evoke empathy, insight and transformative action (Abramson and Abramson 2019; 2020). Creative peer support groups and the LOUDfence activism are two examples of such transformative praxis.

*Figure 2: Chair at Birmingham Cathedral, May 2023
(photo courtesy of Jane Chevous)*

Peer Support Groups: Speaking, Listening, Sustaining

Survivors Voices and Little Ro's survivor-led peer support groups bring creativity and solidarity to repairing the betrayal and moral injury (Griffin et al. 2019) of faith-based abuse. As a Black and People of Colour, and LGBTQIA+ inclusive group, Mix Up/Talk, Heal, Seal (Little Ro 2023) recognizes the intersectionality of trauma with multiple oppressions (O'Donnell and Cross 2022). These groups offer a safe haven and an experience of creative healing for people subjected to the additional trauma of Afriphobia, structural and interpersonal racism.

The group #Healing&Recovery is for any survivors abused in a faith setting, or for whom faith plays a significant part of their journey (SV Support 2023). These peer-led groups hold compassionate space to hear each other's hurt and pain and explore together what brings healing and justice (Herman 2023). Our open letter to churches, published in May 2023, called on people to 'walk with us in a Solidarity Gospel, living the Beatitudes with a bias for the poor, the captives, the oppressed' (SV Faith

2023). These initiatives invite the entire church to recognize the potential for survivors to bring restoration to the wider faith community: 'When you focus on survivors' strengths and gifts, instead of treating us as fragile, flawed and damaged goods, you'll find the treasure we bring. We're transforming our own trauma, and together we can transform yours too' (SV Open Letter 2023). While highlighting these peer support groups as an example of feminist theological praxis, the most powerful testimonies to their power and efficacy are from members, some of whom agreed to attribution:

- It provides 'solidarity and engaged listening with unconditional support'.
- 'Survivor Voices has been in my awareness for a long time but as a [psychiatric] practitioner I had forgotten myself as a survivor for so long because I've never been good at self-disclosure … I again was offering to support Jane and others to keep my skills tuned in, yet I was the one needing support.'
- 'First time I met the facilitators I was bowled over because on that day one of my family abusers had died and my head was everywhere. The custom in SV is to check out how we are all feeling before planning. I blurted this news out quite dissociated and nonchalant, and I was surprised when one of the group said that if I needed to talk I could have the whole time for me. I've never forgotten that … what I value most is how free I can be and even though I'm facilitating when I'm well I can still talk about me. I think I still carry the Catholic messages drummed into me at home in school and in the convent that one doesn't talk about self as its selfish … a sin … attention seeking and the rest …'
- 'It took a while because trust is still [a] huge [issue] but that's because the hierarchical Church keeps fucking up, so while I'm paid by the Church I can't avoid their hypocrisy and abuse daily in blatant and very subtle ways even though I'm now surrounded by people who want change and to be progressive Church.'
- 'Survivor Voices means I'm not on my own … I love the gentleness … the permission giving … the real care in each other in SV even when we meet [initially] we are strangers. SV is balanced with humour, sadness, messing things up … none of us experts or there to control anyone and definitely no pressure.' (Col, Liverpool)
- 'At 61 years of age after countless attempts to get help with the mental health problems I suffer as a result of abuse by a Church of England vicar, peer support has proved to be the only route to feeling fully accepted and understood, no explanation necessary, and without the

necessity for a formal diagnosis. The sense of relief that the shared space of survivors has brought me is invaluable. I just wish that the powers in the various Churches, the NHS and the courts, would come to realize that the route to curtailing years of unnecessary suffering lies in hearing OUR voices and acting upon what we say.' (Julia Szajdzicka)

Opening out safe spaces and private platforms for survivors to speak and listen to each other, and as secondary product creating a collective for sharing the burden of speaking, disclosing (or not) and public truth telling, is an integral part of the healing process (Jeong and Cha 2019). Studies of those who are engaged in healing from childhood sexual abuse have stressed the importance of reframing traumatic experiences and developing agency over disclosure (Patterson, Justice and Rapsey 2022). Alongside this intimate supporting and sharing, for those willing and able to open out a public conversation about abuse – and for allies who want to add their own voices in solidarity, amplification and 'righteous clamour' – the symbolic 'speech acts' of an arts-intervention like LOUDfence offer another mode for giving voice and taking action.

LOUDfence UK: its Genesis and Growth

The LOUDfence was an experiment that started on my (Antonia's) kitchen table in 2020. I designed LOUDfence to be a response to a local crisis in the Anglican Church in Cumbria to help a friend, the act of one friend comforting another who was crying because she wouldn't be permitted to bring her grandchildren to church any more. The LOUDfence was designed to give her and everyone in the church, survivors and their allies, a voice. I did not know if anyone would want to speak. They did and they have not stopped speaking.

The LOUDfence in its original form started in Ballarat in Victoria, Australia (Bell 2019). During the Australian Royal Commission Maureen Hatcher decided to tie ribbons to the railings of the municipal buildings where victims were giving their testimony as an act of solidarity with survivors and as a way of protesting against abuse within the church (McDonald 2023). Using ribbons to publicly recognize loss is an ancient and transcultural practice.

I wanted to use the LOUDfence for something different. Instead of using ribbons as markers of protest within a landscape of pronounced cultural trauma, I wanted to use the same mechanism to give a voice to all in the Catholic church, my home. We all needed to collaborate for culture change. My logic was if it is possible to use ribbons to send a message to an organization, it is possible for an organization to use ribbons to send a message to the wider world, almost like semaphore flags. Traditionally bishops and cardinals have always spoken for the church but LOUDfence is different because every single person in the church has the opportunity personally to contribute and say something with a ribbon or a message.

When the church is hurting because of safeguarding failures, it is very common for the laity to feel deeply grieved about the harm that has occurred. This is all too often compounded by a sense of powerlessness and inability to do anything to effect change. The silence that follows revelations coming into the public domain is interpreted as indifference, but many parishioners have told me they want to be able to tell survivors they are sorry and they care, but feel they have no means to do so. How do you tell someone you care about their injuries if you don't know who they are? How do you begin those conversations even if you do know who they are? Survivors of abuse also hear the silence and understandably interpret this as indifference or lack of care directed at them. Survivors need to hear what the church has to say to them, and the rest of the church needs to be able to show their care and compassion for those who have been harmed. Without the capacity to do this, the body of Christ is being forced to walk by on the other side of the road and in doing so is denying its very essence as a beatitudinal church.

The first LOUDfence I ever organized was held in a little rural parish church in Cumbria (Coleman 2021) – prompted by the actions of the Bishop of Carlisle (BBC 2021) and fuelled by IICSA's final report on child sexual abuse within the Church of England (IICSA 2020). The UK LOUDfence movement was born in the flames and, like its Australian counterpart, has spread as a visual, symbolic expression of pain, anger, support and solidarity over social media to reach people across the globe.

One such person, who called me from Canada on the referral of a journalist, was a woman in her eighties. She had been evacuated to Kirkbampton during the Second World War as a child, and sexually assaulted by the parish vicar as a six-year-old. She told me she had never told a single person. She described how her childhood abuse had impacted her whole life and her relationship with her husband and children. She telephoned me to ask if I thought it would be OK to tell her daughters, as she didn't want to take her secret to the grave. I assured her it would be absolutely the right thing to do, and I know that she has now contacted her family doctor for ongoing support.

The method, now a movement, has spread from these beginnings. The Anglican Rochester and Carlisle cathedrals were first adopters,

'A SOLIDARITY DANCE'

key institutional pioneers for the LOUDfence. The Canon Chancellor of Rochester Cathedral, Dr Gordon Giles, and the Canon Warden of Carlisle Cathedral, Dr Benjamin Carter, did something really brave and contrary to all accepted wisdom. They went first. They, like us, decided that something must be done because the crisis in care for all those who have been affected by safeguarding failures in the church could not continue. The LOUDfences held at both cathedrals were successful. They opened dialogue, they challenged myths concerning abuse in faith-based settings and the taboo around the discussion of such a sensitive subject. The public installations caught the attention of diocesan safeguarding officers in the Catholic Church, which prompted LOUDfences to be held in Northampton, Plymouth and Birmingham (Arch)dioceses (Figure 3) and at the pilgrimage site of Lourdes in France.

Since then, more LOUDfences have been held at various cathedrals, often ecumenically by Catholic and Anglican bishops working together, in Cardiff, Southwark, Carlisle, Rochester, Newcastle, Liverpool, Truro, and Wheeling in West Virginia, USA. In September 2023 I was also invited to address the Pontifical Commission for the Protection of Minors, and unexpectedly on that visit I was offered the profound privilege of an audience with Pope Francis. He read the dozens of messages penned by CSA survivors and their supporters I had brought to Rome with me and offered his imprimatur and blessing to the lay volunteers in Britain (and increasingly beyond) who seek to expand this penitential and reparative work.

Throughout we have always stressed that there can be no hierarchy of pain. The LOUDfence is there to support all who have been subjected to abuse in any setting and all of those people who have been upset and angered by safeguarding failures but feel unable to speak about it. It has given a voice to all those people who have stepped back from the practice of their faith in church and also to all those people who still have a reciprocal relationship with God in the church but feel unable to speak openly about their concerns. I have been shocked by the number of ordained priests and religious (men and women) who have also found in the LOUDfence an opportunity to speak for the first time about their own sexual abuse by clergy – in seminaries, convents or other religious settings in which power imbalances evade safeguarding and collude to prevent disclosure. There is no problem that is best served with silence. Churches that 'talk together, stay together', so the LOUDfence has prompted many conversations that have enabled the start of a long and gradual process of some healing and repair.

The LOUDfence is not a 'silver bullet'. It will not undo the failures of

Figure 3: LOUDfence at Birmingham Cathedral, 7–13 May 2023 (photo courtesy of Jane Chevous)

the past, but just because we cannot repair everything does not mean we cannot repair anything. As a survivor of abuse myself, I can only describe it as being a form of trauma that attacks our being at its very core. It can drive you to believe you are your injuries and since the harm from abuse seeps into every facet of your life, it is very easy to succumb to this lie. It certainly feels like it's true, but it isn't. We are not our abuse. It is possible to do more than just survive. It is possible, with time and healing, to thrive. From my personal experience I found tying a ribbon to acknowledge pain was the first step in addressing it. I have throughout my life tried to ignore, bury and suppress the sexual abuse I suffered as a seven-year-old, but acknowledging it and simply setting it down in front of God really helps. It gives relief.

Despite the apologies and speeches from high-ranking clergy over the years, I don't think the church has really 'let it in'. The church has acknowledged the facts but not the feelings. I think this is the key to culture change. We will be, as a church, not just what we tolerate but what we are afraid to face. Just as I have had to gaze upon my abuse in all its horror and confront all the injury it has caused, my church must do this too. The LOUDfence is the mirror the church must look into and bravely face. As a church we long to heal from this persistent wound. The LOUDfence has revealed itself to be a way to begin the healing process.

Bibliography

Tanya L. Abramson and Paul R. Abramson, 2019, 'Charting New Territory: The Aesthetic Value of Artistic Visions that Emanate in the Aftermath of Severe Trauma', *Contemporary Aesthetics* 17 (8).
Paul R. Abramson and Tanya L. Abramson, 2020, 'Should Art about Child Abuse be Exhibited in Corridors of Health Professional Schools?' *AMA Journal of Ethics* 22 (6), pp. 525–34.
BBC, 2021, 'Bishop of Carlisle informally rebuked for "significant errors of judgment"', 16 March 2021, www.bbc.co.uk/news/uk-england-cumbria-56412568 (accessed 19.6.23).
S. J. Bell, 2019, 'Loud Fence ribbons in show of solidarity for sexual abuse survivors in Ballarat cut down', https://www.abc.net.au/news/2019-12-29/loud-fence-ribbons-in-show-of-solidarity-for-sexual-abuse-cut/11830160 (accessed 19.5.23).
Lucy Bond and Stef Craps, 2020, *Trauma*, London: Routledge.
Cathy Caruth, 1996, *Unclaimed Experience Trauma, Narrative and History*, Baltimore, MD: John Hopkins University Press.
Craig S. Cashwell and Paula J. Swindle, 2018, 'When Religion Hurts: Surviving Cases of Religious Abuse', *The Clinical Supervisor* 37 (1), pp. 182–203.
CBCEW, 2022, 'The Isaiah Journey', https://www.cbcew.org.uk/the-isaiah-journey/ (accessed 21.6.23).
Center for Constitutional Rights (CCR), SNAP Fact Sheet, http://nationbuilder.s3.amazonaws.com/snap/pages/795/attachments/original/SNAPFactSheet_9_11_11_FINAL.pdf?1315879320 (accessed 20.6.23).
Jane Chevous, 2004, *From Silence to Sanctuary: A Guide to Understanding, Preventing and Responding to Abuse*, London: SPCK.
Brian J. Clites, 2019a, 'Our Accountability to Survivors', *American Catholic Studies* 130 (2), pp. 4–7.
Brian J. Clites, 2019b, 'Soul Murder: Sketches of Survivor Imaginaries', *Exchange* 48, pp. 268–79.
P. Coleman, 2021, 'Pioneering Carlisle "Loudfence" campaign to beat clerical abuse looks set to go national', https://www.newsandstar.co.uk/news/19683333.pioneering-loudfence-campaign-beat-clerical-abuse-looks-set-go-national/ (accessed 20.6.23).
Phil Doughtry and Maxine Green, 2020, *The Art of Accompanying*, Hackham West: Immortalise.
Massimo Faggioli and Alana Harris, 2024, 'Pursuing the Long Shadow over the "Domestic Church": Toward a Global History of Abuse in Catholic Settings', *Catholic Historical Review* 110 (1), pp. 55–84.
Kathryn A. Flynn, 2008, 'In Their Own Voices: Women Who Were Sexually Abused by Members of the Clergy', *Journal of Child Sexual Abuse* 17 (3–4), pp. 216–37.
J. M. Fogler, et al., 2008a, 'The Impact of Clergy-Perpetrated Sexual Abuse: The

Role of Gender, Development, and Posttraumatic Stress', *Journal of Child Sexual Abuse*, 17 (3–4), pp. 329–58.

J. M. Fogler, et al., 2008b, 'A Theoretical Foundation for Understanding Clergy-Perpetrated Sexual Abuse', *Journal of Child Sexual Abuse* 17 (3–4), pp. 301–28.

Marie M. Fortune and James N. Poling, 1994, *Sexual Abuse by Clergy: A Crisis for the Church*, Decatur, GA: Journal of Pastoral Care Publications.

Francis, 2019, 'Vos Etis Lux Mundi', https://www.vatican.va/content/francesco/en/motu_proprio/documents/papa-francesco-motu-proprio-20190507_vos-estis-lux-mundi.html (accessed 22.6.23).

Linda Gantt and Louis W. Tinnin, 2009, 'Support for a Neurobiological View of Trauma with Implications for Art Therapy', *The Arts in Psychotherapy* 36 (3), pp. 148–53.

R. Gilbert, et al., 2012, 'Child Maltreatment: Variation in Trends and Policies in Six Developed Countries', *The Lancet* 379 (9817), pp. 758–72.

Katie Graham, Tess Patterson, Tonya Justice and Charlene Rapsey, 2022, '"It's not a Great Boulder, It's Just a Piece of Baggage": Older Women's Reflections on Healing from Childhood Sexual Abuse', *Journal of Interpersonal Violence* 37 (1–2), pp. 705–25.

B. J. Griffin, et al., 2019, 'Moral Injury: An Integrative Review', *Journal of Trauma Stress* 32 (3), pp. 350–62.

Carla A. Grosch-Miller, 2021, *Trauma and Pastoral Care: A Ministry Handbook*, London: Canterbury Press.

Health Development Agency (HDA), 2000, *Art for Health: A review of good practice in community-based arts projects and initiatives which impact on health and wellbeing*, London: NHS HDA, https://www.england.nhs.uk/wp-content/uploads/2021/05/Art_for_Health.pdf (accessed 20.6.23).

Judith Herman, 1997, *Trauma and Recovery: The Aftermath of Violence – from Domestic Abuse to Political Terror*, London: Basic Books.

Judith Herman, 2023, *Truth and Repair: How Trauma Survivors Envision Justice*, London: Basic Books.

Susan Hillis et al., 2016, 'Global Prevalence of Past-year Violence Against Children: A Systematic Review and Minimum Estimates', *Pediatrics* 137 (3): e20154079. doi:10.1542/peds.2015-4079 (accessed 20.5.23).

IICSA, 2017, *Child Sexual Abuse within the Catholic and Anglican Churches: A Rapid Evidence Assessment*, London: IICSA, https://webarchive.nationalarchives.gov.uk/ukgwa/20211201193545/ (accessed 27.3.24); https://www.iicsa.org.uk/key-documents/3361/view/iicsa-rea-child-sexual-abuse-anglican-catholic-churches-nov-2017-.pdf (accessed 20.6.23).

IICSA, 2020, *The Church of England Investigation Report*, https://www.iicsa.org.uk/reports-recommendations/publications/investigation/anglican-church (accessed 20.6.23).

Sookyung Jeong and Chiyoung Cha, 2019, 'Healing from Childhood Sexual Abuse: A Meta-Synthesis of Qualitative Studies', *Journal of Child Sex Abuse* 28 (4), pp. 383–99.

Pat Jones, Marcus Pound and Catherine Sexton, 2024, *The Cross of the Moment: A Report from the Boundary Breaking Project*, Centre for Catholic Studies, University of Durham.

Hugh Lagan, 2017, 'Listening to Hear', *The Furrow* 68 (7–8), pp. 387–400.

Patricia Leavy, 2020, *Method Meets Art: Arts-Based Research Practice*, 3rd edn, New York: Guildford Press.

Peter A. Levine, 2015, *Trauma and Memory: Brain and Body in a Search for the Living Past*, Berkeley, CA: North Atlantic Books

Little Ro, 'Black and BIPOC Support', https://www.littlero.org/black_bipoc_support/ (accessed 20.6.23).

Cathy A. Malchiodi, 2020, *Trauma and Expressive Arts Therapy: Brain, Body and Imagination in the Healing Process*, New York: Guildford Press.

Ben Matthews and Delphine Collin-Vézina, 2019, 'Child Sexual Abuse: Toward a Conceptual Model and Definition', *Trauma, Violence, and Abuse* 20 (2), pp. 131–48.

Dave McDonald, 2023, 'The Work of Acknowledgment: "Loud Fence" as Community-Level Response to Institutional Child Sexual Abuse Testimony', *Social and Legal Studies* 33 (2), pp. 213–35.

Lisa Miller, 2021, *The Awakened Brain: The Psychology of Spirituality*, London: Penguin.

Patrick J. Morrissey, 2013, 'Trauma and Expression through Art Therapy', *Health Progress*, 94 (3), pp. 44–7.

Natasha Mulvihill et al., 2022, 'UK Victim-Survivor Experiences of Intimate Partner Spiritual Abuse and Religious Coercive Control and Implications for Practice', *Criminology and Criminal Justice*, https://doi.org/10.1177/17488958221112057 (accessed 27.3.24).

Andy Myhill and Liz Kelly, 2019, 'Counting with Understanding? What is at Stake in Debates on Researching Domestic Violence', *Criminology & Criminal Justice* 21 (3), pp. 280–96.

Charles B. Nemeroff, 2004, 'Neurobiological Consequences of Childhood Trauma', *Journal of Clinical Psychiatry* 65, pp. 18–28.

Lisa Oakley and Justin Humphreys, 2019, *Escaping the Maze of Spiritual Abuse: Creating Healthy Christian Cultures*, London: SPCK.

Karen O'Donnell and Katie Cross, 2022, *Bearing Witness: Intersectional Perspectives on Trauma Theology*, London: SCM Press.

Doris Reisinger, 2022, 'Reproductive Abuse in the Context of Clergy Sexual Abuse in the Catholic Church', *Religions* 13 (3), https://doi.org/10.3390/rel13030198 (accessed 27.3.24).

Babette Rothschild, 2000, *The Body Remembers: The Psychophysiology of Trauma and Trauma Treatment*, New York: W.W. Norton.

SAMHSA, 2014, *SAMHSA's Concept of Trauma and Guidance for a Trauma-Informed Approach*, Rockville, MD: HHS Publication https://ncsacw.acf.hhs.gov/userfiles/files/SAMHSA_Trauma.pdf (accessed 20.6.23).

SNAP, 2023, 'Q&A About SNAP', https://www.snapnetwork.org/q_a_about_snap (accessed 20.6.23).

Charles V. Sords, 2019, 'When a Stone is Not a Stone: Memories of Sexual Abuse', *Dignity* 4 (2) https://doi.org/10.23860/dignity.2019.04.02.06 (accessed 27.3.24).

Margaret D. Stetz, 2001, 'Listening "With Serious Intent": Feminist Pedagogical Practice and Social Transformation', *Transformations: The Journal of Inclusive Scholarship and Pedagogy* 12 (1), pp. 7–27

Marije Stoltenborgh et al., 2011, 'A Global Perspective on Child Sexual Abuse:

Meta-analysis of Prevalence around the World'. *Child Maltreatment* 16 (2), pp. 79–101.

Survivors Voices (SV) Charter, 2018, https://survivorsvoices.org/charter/ (accessed 20.6.23).

Survivors Voices (SV) Faith, 2023, https://survivorsvoices.org/faith-and-abuse/ (accessed 20.6.23).

Survivors Voices (SV) Open Letter, 2023, https://survivorsvoices.org/wp-content/uploads/2023/05/SurvivorsPodCollectiveResponse-Final.pdf (accessed 20.6.23).

Survivors Voices (SV) Support, 2023, https://survivorsvoices.org/support/ (accessed 20.6.23).

Traumascapes, 2023, 'T.R.A.U.M.A. Card Deck', https://www.traumascapes.org/trauma-cards (accessed 23.6.23).

Phyllis Trible, 2002, *Texts of Terror: Literary-Feminist Readings of Biblical Narratives*, London: SCM Press.

Bessel Van Der Kolk, 2015, *The Body Keeps the Score: Mind, Brain, and Body in the Transformation of Trauma*, 3rd edn, London: Penguin.

Sylvia Walby, Jude Towers, Susan Balderston et al., 2017, *The Concept and Measurement of Violence Against Women and Men*, Bristol: Policy Press.

Anna Westin, 2022, *Embodied Trauma and Healing: Critical Conversations on the Concept of Health*, London: Routledge.

A. Witt, E. Brähler, P. L. Plener and J. M. Fegert, 2022, 'Different Contexts of Sexual Abuse with a Special Focus on the Context of Christian Institutions: Results from the General Population in Germany', *Journal of Interpersonal Violence* 37 (5–6), pp. 3130–51.

Working Together to Safeguard Children, 2018, *A Guide to Inter-agency Working to Safeguard and Promote the Welfare of Children*, London: Department for Education.

World Health Organization, 2021, 'Violence Against Women: Key Facts', https://www.who.int/news-room/fact-sheets/detail/violence-against-women (accessed 19.6.23).

Jennifer S. Wyant, 2019, *Beyond Mary or Martha: Reclaiming Ancient Models of Discipleship*, Atlanta, GA: SBL Press.

PART 3
Write

12

'O for a thousand tongues':[1] Feminist Theology, Narrative and Storytelling

TINA BEATTIE

In a widely quoted TED talk, Nigerian writer Chimamanda Ngozi Adichie cautions against 'the danger of the single story'. She tells of how, as a child in Nigeria, she started writing on the basis of the stories she was reading:

> All my characters were white and blue-eyed. They played in the snow. They ate apples. And they talked a lot about the weather, how lovely it was that the sun had come out. Now, this despite the fact that I lived in Nigeria. I had never been outside Nigeria. We didn't have snow. We ate mangoes. And we never talked about the weather, because there was no need to.

Having grown up in sub-Saharan Africa, I relate to much of that – though I could at least identify with the white characters. Adichie describes how, through discovering African authors, she changed her perception of what kind of characters could occupy a story: 'I realized that people like me, girls with skin the colour of chocolate, whose kinky hair could not form ponytails, could also exist in literature. I started to write about things I recognized' (Adichie 2009).

In this essay, I consider the role played by narrative and storytelling in feminist theological writings. How might feminist thinkers exploit the creative tensions that arise when literary texts rupture the boundaries of biblical and theological scholarship? This question could be applied to many religious contexts, but my own theological perspective is shaped by a Catholic sacramental understanding of a graced material world.

I trace the origins of this postmodern narrative approach back to a paradigmatic shift involving two scholarly movements that emerged during the 1970s and 1980s – postliberal theologies, and liberal feminist theologies. Though they acknowledged little mutual influence, and indeed were in some sense antithetical to each other, both were concerned with questions of objectivity and interpretation in the study of Christian texts and sought to draw attention to the ways in which communal contexts shape how theology is written and received.

Postliberal Theology

Postliberal theology associated with scholars such as Hans Frei and George Lindbeck marks a methodological shift away from liberal approaches to the study of Christianity with their objectifying modes of interpretation and analysis. Postliberal theologians argue for the return of Christian studies to communal contexts of interpretation informed by historical traditions and confessional practices. William C. Placher summarizes this as 'Respect the local, mistrust the universal' (Placher 1993, p. 16). Referring to Lindbeck's influential *The Nature of Doctrine*, Placher describes his approach as

> a 'cultural-linguistic' way of interpreting religious doctrines, one in which their meaning was their use as rules in the life of a religious community. The biblical narratives 'absorb the world' by providing and illustrating the language within which it is possible to live as a Christian. The way the Christian community uses them in that way, then, is their normative meaning. (Placher 1993, p. 17)

This positioning of theology within the overlapping spheres of church and academy opened the way to a wide range of contextual and narrative approaches, but it brought with it challenging questions to do with the privileging of certain perspectives over others, the struggle between the universality and authority of doctrinal claims and the diversity of interpretative cultures, and the locus of legitimate academic study.

From a feminist perspective, postliberal theologies have tended to reinforce the hegemonic influence of white western male theologians, who occlude the hermeneutical influence of their own cultural and subjective positioning. While claiming to be located within the practices and traditions of the Christian community, this is a homogenized and to some extent idealized community that floats free of the inter- and intra-cultural differences, conflicts and tensions that constitute Christian communities in time and space, while ignoring the ways in which questions of gender, race and class destabilize authoritative interpretations.

Liberal Feminist Theologies

Postliberal theologies construct their narratives as counter-cultural, reading against the grain of western liberalism to re-establish the authority of ecclesial traditions, but pioneering feminist theologians of the 1970s and early 1980s made the opposite move. They criticized theological and biblical narratives, doctrines and rules of engagement from a perspective influenced by liberal feminism and progressive/liberationist politics. Like postliberal and narrative theologies, this theological trend emphasized the importance of context for theological hermeneutics, but it privileged women's experience as the vantage point from which theological claims must be evaluated.

Early feminist theologians unmasked the androcentric bias of theological claims to normativity, but they soon fell prey to similar criticisms, being accused of making universal claims that failed to acknowledge their own academic positioning as middle-class, predominantly white western women. As in the case of postliberal theologies, questions arise as to inclusion and exclusion, legitimation and obliteration, in the selection of some texts and experiences over others. In both contexts, the dynamics of power are masked by those who claim the right of interpretation.

Mary McClintock Fulkerson points out that, while feminist theological texts use the rhetoric of pluralism, inclusivity, liberation and solidarity with the oppressed, such texts are produced within an exclusive and elitist academic environment. The validation of experience by liberal academics takes place without sufficient acknowledgement that 'real authorizing power is located' in institutions that have 'the capacity to host the discussion and provide chairs at the table – or to shut down the building altogether, so to speak' (Fulkerson 1994, p. 16). She writes of the need for feminist theology to recognize the complexity of issues of 'gender, language, social location, and feminist theological resources for respecting difference', but also to see that feminist theologies must focus on 'meeting women whose struggles are for physical survival rather than on the feminist transformation of the academy' (Fulkerson 1994, p. vii).

Fulkerson was writing at a time when the linguistic turn signalled a paradigm shift affecting many academic disciplines, including feminist theology. The progressive, politicized movements of the 1970s and 1980s yielded to a focus on discourse, influenced by poststructuralist, psychoanalytic, Marxist and cultural linguistic methods of analysis. In recognition of the need to incorporate diversity with regard to class, race, sexual orientation, culture, religion, ability and disability, etc. – what, in recent years, has become known as intersectionality – feminist theology became an ever-expanding discourse, until feminism itself was absorbed by a shift to the terminology of gender.

In many ways, this is the pivotal point upon which feminism balances today, challenged as it is by two conflicting demands. On the one hand, the language of gender introduces a rhetorical inclusivity that dissolves the material realities of women's lives into a more generalized and conflicted discourse of gendered identities and rights. On the other hand, claims that focus on female identities and subjectivities risk universalizing the idea of woman in ways that fail to respect the vast and perhaps irreconcilable diversity of women's lives and cultures.

Postliberal Feminist Theology

Theologians such as Fulkerson position themselves in critical but constructive engagement with both feminist and postliberal theologies, addressing questions of power, normativity and context from perspectives informed by deconstructive and theoretical approaches to language.

Fulkerson argues that liberal feminism privileges women's experience with insufficient regard for the ways in which that is filtered through and shaped by textual traditions, while postliberal theology privileges fixed textual meanings with no acknowledgement of the experiential significance of material contexts of interpretation and enactment. She proposes Julia Kristeva's concept of intertextuality as a way of navigating between 'the ostensible *extratextualism* of liberal theology or the *intratextualism* of so-called postliberalism' (Fulkerson 1994, p. 156). This entails respecting the communicative and communal significance of embodied practices of interpretation as well as written texts, so that 'the notion of textuality serves as a metaphor for cultural and social realities as well as written texts' (Fulkerson 1994, p. 165). All experience is linguistically/textually interpreted and mediated, but intertextuality respects the processes of 'ordinary semiosis' (Fulkerson 1994, p. 159), by way of which scripture and doctrine are creatively interpreted and enacted in diverse communities that cannot be subsumed under a single authoritative reading of a textual tradition. Fulkerson identifies three themes in postmodern feminist thought that can contribute to feminist theology: '(1) the instability of the subject, (2) the force of the "unsayable, the unrepresentable as it constitutes and ruptures all that is said," as one theological student of postmodernism puts it, and (3) the liberative implications of these ideas when applied to the category of gender' (Fulkerson 2003, pp. 110–11).

This is the background against which I ask how a narrative approach might contribute to the feminist production and interpretation of theological texts. Can the stories women tell contribute to a feminist theological vision that respects the diversity of women's lives, while upholding key Christian principles of justice, peace and the integrity of creation, nurtured in faithful communities of prayer and worship?

Women's Stories, Women's Struggles

Kochurani Abraham's study of the lives of women in the Catholic Syrian Church in Kerala, *Persisting Patriarchy: Intersectionalities, Negotiations, Subversions*, is a fine example of a narrative approach that pays close attention to the ways in which religion and culture conspire to maintain sexual hierarchies of domination and subjugation. Her 'critical feminist theorizing of patriarchy' is a 'multipronged approach' (Abraham 2020, p. 56), informed by interwoven concepts of power, space and consciousness, and attentive to the intersectional influences of factors such as class, race, ethnicity and religion. This analysis of the positioning of women within a particular social, domestic and religious environment exposes the many structural and psychological factors that subjugate women through the internalization of gendered hierarchies of authority and subservience. It explores how the dynamics of power and domination insinuate themselves through pervasive religious and cultural influences, while revealing the subtle subversions and compromises by way of which women negotiate small spaces of freedom within larger structures of subjugation.

Abraham is a scholarly activist who has spent many years immersed in the lives of the women she writes about. Some of these women describe how they have achieved spaces of autonomy and equality within the domestic sphere by 'tactical bargains' (p. 173). Their economic dependence on their husbands limits their capacity for deviance, while 'Compliance brings them gains, both material and symbolic' (p. 172). For others, the burden is too great, and they 'continue to be like "bread that is broken" so that others in the family may have life' (p. 118). Abraham observes that 'The pain and anguish conveyed through these stories interrogate the cultural paradigm that prescribes suffering as an "unavoidable companion" of women and romanticizes women's capacity to suffer' (p. 120).

These women are expressing what Abraham describes as 'the dialectic tension between tradition and modernity ... a pull between gendered consciousness and the desire for a liberative breakthrough' (p. 169). Women who achieve some level of autonomy and self-esteem have resisted the denial of their dignity and have worked towards a more liberating consciousness, even while recognizing that, in the words of interviewee Siji, 'a woman's life is a constant bargain' (Abraham 2020, p. 186).

Abraham's study exposes how the intricately woven mesh of religious, cultural and economic influences in different spatial and social contexts calls into question the grandiloquent rhetoric of liberation. To discern the ways in which universal human experiences of suffering and joy, fear and freedom, play out in the lives of women, it is necessary to ask of each and every neighbour in need, what are you suffering? – the question that, according to some versions of the Arthurian legend, is the secret of the Holy Grail. To slightly modify the words of William Blake, 'Labour well the Minute Particulars: attend to the Little Ones ... [S]he who would do good to another must do it in Minute Particulars. General Good is the plea of the scoundrel, hypocrite, and flatterer' (Blake 2019, p. 283).

At what point is it possible for a feminist scholar to draw together the particularities of women's lives which proliferate before the attentive gaze, to communicate across differences of culture and context? Scholars like Abraham provide one example, by drawing on a wide range of academic methods in order to interpret the stories women tell about their lives through a theological and theoretical lens. But what happens if we turn to literature and literary theory rather than experience for feminist insights into the human condition and its gendered sufferings? How far can fictitious characters become bearers of meaning that well up from the pregnant silences of unrecorded lives and untold stories?

The Stories We Tell

The opening up of theological language to literary and poetic forms of expression entails a shift away from propositional and dialectical approaches to knowledge, towards more affective, fluid and dialogical styles. Luce Irigaray's mimetic feminization of philosophical language, Kristeva's attentiveness to the gendered psychological dynamics of self and other that rupture the linguistic subject through the seepage of turbulent bodily undercurrents of love and abjection, and Hélène Cixous's quest for an *écriture féminine* through the invocation of bodily metaphors of desire and suffering, mortality and vulnerability, all invite attentiveness to the ways in which style and substance interact. Our lives are shaped by the contours of language – we inhabit the house of language (Heidegger) – but our bodies also pulverize language by their unruly and uncontainable drives and instincts. Whereas Irigaray understands sexual difference in the context of linguistically constructed social hierarchies and occlusions, Kristeva internalizes sexual difference as the split psyche of the modern subject dirempted between masculinized identity and feminized otherness. Each of these thinkers invites attention to the gendering of language as the medium through which hierarchies of inclusion and exclusion, authority and subjection, are maintained through the veiled play of sexual difference.

In *A Poetics of Church*, Jennifer Reek tracks her existential scholarly quest through a labyrinthine collection of theological and literary texts, as she explores possibilities for reimagining church as 'poetic sacred space' (Reek 2018, p. 11). She cites Richard Kearney's description of poetics as 'in the broad sense of the term – an exploration of the human powers to make (*poiesis*) a world in which we may poetically dwell' (Reek 2018, p. 10, quoting Kearney 1998, p. 8). For Reek, inspired by Cixous, to read is to plunge into transformative encounters with difference and otherness, so that 'being read, I write. My readings are relational, encounters, conversations in which reading is a careful listening to texts and writing is what arises out of that listening' (Reek 2018, p. 5).

Like Reek, Heather Walton draws on Cixous and other literary theorists to explore the relationship between theology and literature. Walton's work seeks to stage a creative encounter between theology and literature, and she suggests that this lends itself to a gendered analysis of the ways in which these different forms of writing are understood:

> It becomes apparent that literature and theology are ... commonly located on opposite sides of a binary schema through which meaning is generated in Western culture. Theology is placed on the side of spirit, reason, light, truth, order, God. Literature is associated with the body, desire, darkness, mystery, humanity. Theology is the place where God and 'man' meet. Literature ... endlessly seduces and gives birth. (Walton 2007a, p. 35)

This idea of literature as giving birth is key to Cixous's understanding of what it means to write as a woman:

> A woman who writes is a woman who dreams about children. Our dream children are innumerable ... The unconscious tells us a book is a scene of childbirth, delivery, abortion, breast-feeding. The whole

chronicle of childbearing is in play within the unconscious during the writing period. (Cixous 1993, p. 74)

Walton points out that 'for Cixous the body is never a natural presocial given'. Rather, she is committed to exploring 'The idea that women can practise a different form of writing if they explore their bodies as material systems of knowledge' (Walton 2007b, p. 148).

The symbolic association between language and the maternal body is characteristic of Lacanian psychoanalysis, and it also informs the writings of Kristeva and Irigaray. The maternal body is a rich treasure house of metaphors and capacities that transcend but also incorporate the female body and its differences. To speak of giving birth to texts invites a feminist reclamation of a rich seam of mystical and devotional language sculpted around maternal metaphors in premodern Christian writings which has been neglected and overlaid by an excessively rational approach in modern theology.

Cixous may not be writing in an explicitly theological register, but by delving deep into the relationship between language, death and desire she has much to contribute to feminist theology. She describes writing as a process of being led towards

> [w]hat I call *the truth*, toward what calls me, attracts me magnetically, irresistibly. Of course, I circle 'the truth' with all kinds of signs, quotation marks, and brackets, to protect it from any form of fixation or conceptualization, since it is one of those words that constantly crosses our universe in a dazzling wake, but is also pursued by suspicion. I will talk about truth again, without which (without the word *truth*, without the mystery *truth*) there would be no writing. It is what writing *wants*. (Cixous 1993, p. 6)

This could serve as a summary of what it means to read and write theology against the grain, persevering in the quest for truth but mindful of the suspicion that pursues it – what feminist theologians call a hermeneutics of suspicion.

Walton draws attention to the ways in which Cixous's later work 'takes up the theological question ... how can literature become for us the bearer of our pain in the face of God?' (Walton 2007b, p. 146). She describes Cixous's work as 'a precious resource to those of us who are seeking an encounter with literature that deepens our sense of wonder and strangeness and pain – rather than one that confirms us in our convictions and comforts us in our sorrows' (Walton 2007b, p. 146).

These literary approaches relocate theology, not by banishing its disciplinary sources and boundaries but by breaching them through the intrusion of strange and unsettling poetic voices. Nevertheless, questions arise as to their relevance for a theological approach that seeks to transform the material realities of women's lives through activism rooted in communal strategies of resistance and solidarity. Is this literary perspective just another esoteric western dalliance with ideas that are remote from the contexts within which women endure daily struggles against the powers of misogyny, oppression and violence? Does the quest for truth evaporate in a plethora of literary and poetic voices engaging in language games that celebrate fluidity, paradox and plurivocality while silencing the cries of those who speak in the unadorned language of pain and sorrow that emanate from the body in distress?

This is a valid caution, and it requires a discerning engagement with literature as well as theology. Do we read and write stories as imaginative acts of transformation, or as escapist fantasies? Do we understand fiction as a distraction from the realities of life, or as an invitation to broaden our horizons and attend to silenced and marginalized voices that, lacking authority and authorship, nevertheless assume fictitious identities through authors whose characters become bearers of untold stories and negated lives?

These questions become particularly important given that so many discursive strategies of de(con)struction engage in a nihilistic violation of all truth claims, values and traditional ways of knowing and believing, in the name of a freedom that is little more than the loquacious narcissism of intellectual elites. As Clara A. B. Joseph and Gaye Williams Ortiz observe:

> Highly influential academics have found it quite convenient to move into a game of deconstruction (a word that not for no reason rings of destruction). If the author, reader, text, and the world are text, then the chief function of academics in the arts and the humanities is to engage in a game of indiscriminate undermining, be it parables or child pornography. The aim is to lay bare the contradictions and then sit back and watch the structure shatter – deconstruct. (Joseph and Ortiz 2006, p. 2)

The approaches I have been exploring in this essay are mutually informative and supportive of one another, in ways that I hope avoid the risks identified by Joseph and Ortiz. All are concerned to locate the voices of academic theologians within communities in which Christian institutions, doctrines and beliefs have a profound impact on women's daily lives, often in ways that conspire with culture to suffocate Christianity's fragile promise of liberation and redemption. All such approaches have weaknesses as well as strengths, for in the end there is no vantage point free from the entanglements of historical conditioning and personal fallibility and finitude.

To craft language in ways that express our bewilderment and our wonder before the vast mystery that enfolds us is to embark upon a process of encounter with lives interpreted and made meaningful through the stories we tell. This invites a theological anthropology that recognizes the human as a storytelling creature yearning for the creator. It requires language that breaks under the weight of meaning, knowing that what it seeks to express is for ever beyond the grasp of human understanding. A literary approach that can encompass vulnerability and fallibility, sorrow and insatiable yearning, is more able to express the complex worlds of women's lives than the politicized rhetoric of liberation with its utopian claims.

Conclusion

Let me draw towards an open-ended conclusion with a personal story. I publish novels alongside my academic writing. Some readers have expressed surprise that these are not feminist theological novels, but to write fiction truthfully is to allow our imaginations to break free of all our ideas about how the world should be, in order to let the world answer back from its fractured, prismatic realms of possibility. This means allowing voices of unsettling otherness to emerge in the form of characters who break free of our authorial intentions, so that we become their scribes rather than their creators. Of course, these characters come out of an author's deepest and often unformed desires, intuitions, memories and fears, but to probe too deeply into those sources would be to stifle the fearful freedom of creativity.

In one of my novels set in pre-independence Zimbabwe (then Rhodesia), a Shona maid called Beatrice disappears (Beattie 2022). I was nervous about writing her, because I was not sure that, as a postcolonial white woman, I had the insight needed to honour the authenticity of her life. Yet she was the character who attracted the most interest, to such an extent that many readers have asked me what happened to her. The answer is, I don't know. There is no sequel to Beatrice's story. She disappeared into a hinterland of magic and folklore, ancestral worlds and spirit traditions that I do not understand. That is the world I grew up in without insight or curiosity. Beatrice withheld such knowledge from me and I had to let her go. Writing her was perhaps an act of atonement for all those unexplored lives of my childhood years, when we white colonials never asked that vital question, what are you suffering? I dare to hope that Beatrice gives voice to what Johann Baptist Metz calls 'the dangerous memories' of the forgotten ones of history, possibly as the fictionalized voice of my own conscience.

Mary Oliver describes the discipline needed to acquire the skills of writing poetry as 'a kind of possible love affair between something like the heart (that courageous but also shy factory of emotion) and the learned skills of the conscious mind'. She describes the patient, attentive practice that is needed if writing poetry is to give expression to 'that wild, silky part of ourselves without which no poem can live' (Oliver 1994, p. 8). This is a beautiful way to describe how a theologian might become a poet of the incarnate soul, observing the disciplined practices of her faith tradition but adopting a creative and imaginative hermeneutics that allows the hauntings of desire and otherness to breathe through her voice. That means the language we use must perch on the very edge of meaning, for it must seek meaning in those vast mysteries that draw us towards the far horizons of existence – God, love and sorrow. What else is there in life?

Note

1 Charles Wesley's hymn of this name was first published by his brother John Wesley in *A Collection of Hymns for the Use of the People Called Methodists* in 1780.

Bibliography

Kochurani Abraham, 2020, *Persisting Patriarchy: Intersectionalities, Negotiations, Subversions* in *New Approaches to Religion and Power* series, Cham, Switzerland: Palgrave Macmillan.
Chimamanda Ngozi Adichie, 2009, 'The danger of a single story', TEDGlobal, at https://www.ted.com/talks/chimamanda_ngozi_adichie_the_danger_of_a_single_story/c (accessed 26.4.23).
Tina Beattie, 2022, *Between Two Rivers*, Harare, Zimbabwe: Weaver Press.
William Blake, 2019, *Selected Poems*, ed. Nicholas Shrimpton, Oxford: Oxford University Press.
Hélène Cixous, 1993, *Three Steps on the Ladder of Writing*, New York: Columbia Press.
Mary McClintock Fulkerson, 1994, *Changing the Subject: Women's Discourses and Feminist Theology*, Minneapolis, MN: Fortress Press.

Mary McClintock Fulkerson, 2003, 'Feminist Theology', in K. Vanhoozer (ed.), *The Cambridge Companion to Postmodern Theology*, Cambridge: Cambridge University Press.

Clara A. B. Joseph and Gaye Williams Ortiz, 2006, 'Reader Responsibility: An Introduction', in Gaye Williams Ortiz and Clara A. B. Joseph (eds), *Theology and Literature: Rethinking Reader Responsibility*, New York: Palgrave Macmillan.

Richard Kearney, 1998, *Poetics of Imagining: Modern to Post-Modern*, 2nd edn, New York: Fordham University Press.

Mary Oliver, 1994, *A Poetry Handbook: A Prose Guide to Understanding and Writing Poetry*, Boston, MA and New York: Mariner Books.

William C. Placher, 1993, 'Introduction', in George Hunsinger and William C. Placher (eds), *Theology and Narrative, Selected Essays: Hans W. Frei*, Oxford: Oxford University Press.

Jennifer Reek, 2018, *A Poetics of Church: Reading and Writing Sacred Spaces of Poetic Dwelling*, London: Routledge.

Heather Walton, 2007a, *Imagining Theology: Women, Writing and God*, London and New York: T&T Clark International.

Heather Walton, 2007b, *Literature, Theology and Feminism*, Manchester and New York: Manchester University Press.

John Wesley, (1780), 1830, *A Collection of Hymns for the Use of the People Called Methodists*, London: Wesleyan Conference.

Further Reading

Tina Beattie, 2006, *New Catholic Feminism: Theology and Theory*, London: Routledge

Luce Irigaray, 1985, *This Sex Which Is Not One*, trans. Catherine Porter with Carolyn Burke, Ithaca NY: Cornell University Press.

Maggie C. W. Kim, Susan St Ville and Susan M. Simonaitis (eds), 1993, *Transfigurations: Theology and the French Feminists*, Minneapolis, MN: Fortress Press.

Julia Kristeva, 1986, 'Word, Dialogue and Novel', in Toril Moi (ed.), *The Kristeva Reader*, New York: Columbia University Press.

George Lindbeck, 1984, *The Nature of Doctrine: Religion and Theology in a Postliberal Age*, Louisville, KY: Westminster John Knox Press.

13

Systematic Theology

JANICE McRANDAL

Many conversations on the possibility of a feminist systemic theology circle around this famous declaration of Audre Lorde:

> For the master's tools will never dismantle the master's house. They may allow us to temporarily beat him at his own game, but they will never enable us to bring about genuine change. And this fact is only threatening to those women who still define the master's house as their whole source of support. (Lorde 1983, p. 99)

There is no small irony in the way this quote, abstracted entirely from the event of Lorde's utterance, has become a conceptual challenge for those feminists engaged in systematic theology. Within such communities, systematic approaches are up to the task of feminism only if and when they can respond to the critical feminist theoretical issues of one's age. One can easily turn to recent attempts within systematic theology to mine doctrine for explanatory and liberatory theories related to contemporary ideological concerns such as ableism, queerphobia or ecological catastrophe. However, the occasion and content of Lorde's comments regarding the master's house were orientated towards the academic, domestic, structural *practices* that reproduce the dominant conditions of theoretical work; specifically, the conditions that produce space for white middle-class women at the expense of Black women and Women of Colour.

Lorde's analysis and critique remain vital, especially if and when Christian theology is questioning the practice of systematic theology, a field that continues to be centred within theological curriculum and esteem. To reduce the *tools* of the master to the realm of metaphysics is to entirely misunderstand, even ignore, the basis of Lorde's critique. As Lorde argued on that now infamous day in 1979, 'What does it mean when the tools of a racist patriarchy are used to examine the fruits of that same patriarchy? It means that only the most narrow perimeters of change are possible and allowable' (Lorde 1983, p. 98). Consequently, it can only be considered a further extension of the master's tools that these conversations nearly always ignore the experience of life and the troubling question of what it means to etch out a career or vocation as a feminist within or attached to practices of systematic theology. In this chapter, I will attempt to survey the field and methodologies without succumbing to the temptation of a view from nowhere, without ignoring the structural practices and patterns that emerge as the mode of systematic theology.

Second- to Third-Wave Dogmatic Traditions and Constructive Theology

Second- to third-wave feminist theologies emerged in a variety of complex modes that are often cited as demonstrative of a large-scale and universal rejection of systematic theology. Systematic theology, with its hegemonic, phallocentric metaphysics, was abandoned by feminists for greener pastures. This claim is especially emphasized when narrating the birth of disciplines such as constructive theology. For example, the appointment of feminist theologian Sallie McFague as Dean of Vanderbilt Divinity School in 1975 is said to be the catalyst for the first meeting of what became the Workgroup on Constructive Theology (Wyman 2017). As McFague had argued a year before this appointment, 'If theology becomes overly abstract, conceptual, and *systematic*, it separates thought and life, beliefs and practice, words and their embodiment' (McFague 1974, p. 630). Instead, McFague argued for a theological practice of contingency and imaginative interdisciplinary work that eschewed unitary or final readings of any theological matter. Such insistence is markedly present in the Workgroup's second publication, *Reconstructing Christian Theology*, in which the majority of contributors were indeed feminist theologians. Notably, it is here that Elisabeth Schüssler Fiorenza spells out most simply her classic fourfold method of feminist biblical interpretation: a hermeneutics of suspicion, remembrance and reconstruction, proclamation, and creative imagination and ritualization (Schüssler Fiorenza 1994, pp. 90–1). In a separate chapter, Catherine Keller begins a project of combining feminist theology with eschatology and ecological theory and ethics that eventually led to numerous books and many more essays (Keller 1994). However, as Jason A. Wyman has argued across numerous publications, *Reconstructing Christian Theology*, like most of the Workgroup's subsequent publications, was entirely structured around dominant Christian doctrine, with each chapter attending to classical doctrine in a structure basically indistinguishable from typical textbooks of systematic theology. As Wyman shows:

> Despite its discomfort with the traditional nature of doctrine and its echo of 'orthodox' or conservative types of theology, constructive theology has nevertheless remained moored to doctrines as, at the very least, a convenient entry point into engaging with the traditions it seeks to reconstruct. (Wyman 2020, p. 25)

Furthermore, while constructive theology has been marked by a significantly high contribution of (white) feminist theologians, its history bears a strained relationship with and resistance to incorporate and include the broad scope of liberationist theologies. Dorothy Soelle critiqued the all-white group for being 'too standoffish about liberation theology' in its earliest days and ultimately left, leaving McFague as the only other woman member (Wyman 2020, p. 25). All of which suggests that the story of birthing constructive theology as a discipline reveals an ambivalence towards systematic theology, and the development of practices – centring doctrine and the voices of middle-class white academia – that by no means represented a radical new approach to theology.

At the same time, many, often Catholic, feminist theologians were engaged in and constructing what could easily be described as feminist systematic theologies. Such scholars were undoubtedly energized by earlier critiques and expositions of patriarchy within Christian theology. Mary Daly, for example, had taken a traditional systematic route, completing a doctorate in sacred theologies and then in philosophy. *Beyond God the Father* (1973) has been consistently treated as a work of systematic theology, and by the time she abandoned Christian faith and published *Gyn/Ecology* (1978), Daly's practice continued to systematically attend to doctrine within the corpus of doctrine as a whole: in this instance, the doctrine of the Trinity. Of course, none of this is presented in a tone or as an argument that resembles typical systematic theology, with Daly describing the divine processions within the godhead as:

> The most sensational one-act play of the centuries, the official Love Story, performed by the Supreme All Male Cast ... the epitome of male bonding ... It is 'sublime' (and therefore disguised) erotic male homosexual mythos, the perfect all-male marriage, the ideal all-male family, the best boys' club. (Daly 1978, p. 290)

Yet even as a stinging critique, Daly's publications comfortably sat as, or at least adjacent to, systematic theology. Two salient points emerge here. First, it's telling that *Gyn/Ecology* occasioned a public response from Audre Lorde, who critiqued Daly's reading, writing and collegial practices, adding, 'To me, this feels like another instance of the knowledge, crone-ology and work of women of Color being ghettoized by a white woman dealing only out of a patriarchal western european frame of reference' (Lorde 1983, p. 68). And second, it is unsurprising that a generation of white feminist theologians who followed would begin to reimagine and systematically reconstruct the same doctrinal ideas, but now as feminist theology. Having already famously asked, 'Can a male saviour save women' (Ruether 1981), Rosemary Radford Ruether tackled Christology in *Sexism and God-Talk* (1983). Virginia Ramey Mollenkott took on biblical theology and images of God in *The Divine Feminine* (1983), and in two immensely influential texts, the Trinity was systematically rebuilt from a feminist perspective. First, with Catherine LaCugna's *God for Us* (1991) and then, only a year later, Elizabeth A. Johnson's *She Who Is*. As Johnson writes, while her feminist theology had an agreed commitment to foregrounding analysis of sexism and deconstructing traditional ideas, the ultimate goal was 'to transform the system' (Johnson 1992, p. 32). Certainly, other forms of feminist theology were being positioned as explicitly post-Christian, as in the work of Daphne Hampson, or they advocated for the Goddess, such as Carol P. Christ's use of the concept 'Thealogy' (e.g. Christ 1987). But a consistent commitment to the themes and practices of systematic theology remained as feminist theology moved from a second to third wave. This included gaining tenured faculty positions as systematicians within the university and teaching across some of the world's best-known institutes of learning, which were often sites of contestation and struggle – not least of all for Daly, during her tumultuous later years at Boston College.

Throughout these years, feminist theology became increasingly marked as a signifier of white middle-class feminism. This is despite some feminist theologians seeking to expand their engagement beyond Anglo and European sources, in the development of Womanist, Mujerista, Asian and postcolonialism feminisms, which resulted in all sorts of differences and antagonisms in both methodology and theological content. For example, even a cursory comparison between LaCugna's *God For Us* and Delores Williams' *Sisters in the Wilderness*, both enormously influential books published in 1991, shows a dramatic and telling difference in form and argument. And while all sorts of radical non-confessional forms of feminist theology emerged during these years, feminist theology also became the placeholder for some of Christianity's most traditional ideas and practices. Jacqueline Grant's *White Women's Christ and Black Women's Jesus* (1989) exemplifies the situation, where she writes:

> It would be inaccurate to assert that because feminist theology is White, it is also racist. To be White does not necessarily mean to be racist, though the behaviour of Whites makes the distinction difficult. Nevertheless, my claim that feminist theology is racist is best supported by a definition of racism. (Grant 1989, p. 199)

While there is no straightforward way to historicize the relationship between feminist theology and systematics during the second and third wave of feminism, it is clear that significant portions of feminist theology developed during these years were far more closely aligned to the mores of systematic theology than many would perhaps like, or have since suggested.

Recent Feminist and Systematic Theologies

After the turn of the century, a variety of feminist theologians began to argue explicitly for a systematic approach. For some, this was the result of a waning hope in liberation theology. As Susan Frank Parsons argued, the central dogmatic claims of Christian feminism had unravelled and failed to emancipate Christian woman. Indeed, for Parsons, feminist theology had created a 'hierarchy of victimhood' while inspiring no *telos*, no eschatological hope (Parsons 2002, p. 121). For others, there was genuine concern around disciplinary and discursive identity, such that Tina Beattie suggested, 'If Christianity uncritically conforms itself to secular discourse, including feminism, it risks losing its identity and becoming the poor relation of secular theory' (Beattie 1999, p. 125). In a postliberal gesture that tracked with currents across systemic theology in general, these feminist theologians who began to look within the Christian tradition for resources for their feminism and hermeneutics of suspicion were turned towards critical and philosophical theory. A well-known advocate for such feminist systematic theology, Sarah Coakley exemplified this confidence in the sources of Christian tradition, arguing that in fact it is *only* systematic theology that can 'adequately and effectively respond to the rightful critiques that gender studies and political and liberation theology have laid at its door' (Coakley 2009, p. 2). While Coakley represents much that is typified in systematic theology – a doctorate from Oxford that focused on a German scholar, followed by long stints teaching at Harvard and Cambridge – she differs from normative systematic theology by insisting that contextual and identity issues such as gender, race and class are integral to a properly systemic approach. And as she published the first of a planned four-volume systematic theology (again, an essay on the Trinity), she rather unusually insisted on centring the topic of sexuality and privileging the practice of contemplation. As she concludes, 'contemplation as an ascetical discipline, a regular and repeated act, must attend to the insights of any feminist theology' (Coakley 2013, p. 340). Coakley has had enormous influence within systematic theology. She is widely cited in systematic theology texts and is a sought-after speaker at both academic and ecclesial conferences. And yet it is precisely her handling of gender and sexuality that has been the occasion of sustained critique from other feminists, especially in relation to uncritical claims about 'God' and academic theology. As Brandy Daniels puts it, Coakley 'inadvertently reifies mastery and identity through other means ... [re-performing] mastery the very practices that are meant to produce un-mastery' (Daniels 2016, p. 68).

Proposing an alternative way into feminism and systematic theology, Linn Marie Tonstad instead argues that doctrine such as the Trinity should not be put to such work when it comes to sexuality and gender. Tonstad's 2016 *God and Difference* sets up a kind of rendezvous between queer theory and systematic theology. To be sure, for Tonstad, like Coakley, engaging systematic theology largely means attending to the theories of Anglo and European men. But unlike Coakley, Tonstad argues against practices that seek to secure selfhood or personhood in relation to God. For Tonstad, the Spirit works in an entirely opposite and gratuitous way and provides insight into how we should view the godhead in general. She writes, 'the way the Holy Spirit is often treated gives us a model for how the other two should be "neglected" as well' (Tonstad 2016, p. 227). Tonstad pushes typical systematic theology further than ever before, with *God and Difference* (2016) ultimately calling for the abortion of the church. However, a recent essay restages the same critical question of systematic theology and its relation to the master's house.

Tonstad begins her essay '(Un)wise Theologians: Systematic Theology in the University', with this statement of intent:

In reflecting on the nature and task of systematic theology in this article, I argue that theology needs to pay more attention to the setting and context within which theology is typically pursued today, that its setting affects systematic theology in ways theology often has difficulty accounting for, and that some influential strategies that do take theology's context into account end up frustrating rather than advancing the very aims they believe theology ought to seek. (Tonstad 2020, p. 494)

Reminiscent of Coakley, Tonstad then proceeds to argue for a systematic theology within the university that eschews the pursuits of mastery and recognition. The paper is published in the *International Journal of Systematic Theology* (*IJST*), the world's most esteemed journal for systematic theology. So perhaps it is un-ironic that a weird and curious repetition emerges in this 'setting and context within which theology is typically pursued today'. In a paper in which Tonstad notes how John Webster cites only one woman theologian in his dogmatics, *Confessing God*, Tonstad does just the same, in this essay engaging only men save a minor nod towards a single woman's translation (i.e., Alexandra R. Brown's translation of 1 Cor. 1.28 – Tonstad 2020, p. 511, n. 50). On the one hand, this is certainly surprising from a feminist, queer scholar, and yet, on the other, entirely predictable of the conversations that take place within the journal.

In the first half of 2020 *IJST* put out two issues. After excluding women on the editorial board, the first volume (Vol. 22, Issue 1) had seven essays, all written by men, and five book reviews, all five books written by men, and all five reviewers being men. The second volume (Vol. 22, Issue 2) had four articles, all written by men, and nine book reviews, all nine books written by men, and eight of the nine book reviews written by men. Late in 2020, *IJST* was challenged on its race and gender representation and its leadership. Immediate commitments to improve and editorial shifts were made in response, with the next two editors both being non-white women. And yet the editorial board, listed on the website, continues in exactly the same pattern as previous years: class of 2022 being all men and one white woman, class of 2024 being all men, class of 2026 being all men and one white woman, and class of 2028 being all men and one white woman. The dynamic is such: systematic theology, within its most esteemed location, continues to be a practice through which a nearly exclusively white group of men discuss each other's speculative work and the men who came before them. The data for such a claim is most obvious in the footnotes. But the data is also easily located in the class reading lists, in the monograph studies of great men, the theological societies, and the endless array of panels and theology conferences with all white men line-ups.

The Australian context where I work is more of the same. A basic 2021 survey into the full-time systematic theology faculty positions held within the three largest theological college consortiums in Australia – Sydney College of Divinity, Australian College of Theology and the University of Divinity – showed that there were 62 positions in total: 58 positions were held by men. Or in other terms, around 94%.[1] The master's house is doing just fine.

Future Practice in Feminist Systematic Theology

Of course, claiming that systematic theology remains the master's house is not solely a statement regarding representation, but an entire linguistic ordering that founds the discourse. From this vantage point, it is clear to see that the great critiques of the twentieth century remain unanswered – whether it be the phallocentricsm unravelled by French feminists, such as Luce Irigaray or Julia Kristeva, the naming of sanctioned ignorance by Spivak, or the heteronormative performativity described by Judith Butler. The patterns of rhetoric, style, form, logic and *wissenschaft* performed and re-performed in the essays and books and presentations of systematic theology are exemplars of the mode of discourse each of these critiques exposed. After more than 50 years of academic feminist theology, clearly, we can conclude that systematic theology continues to produce a culture in which journals and papers and events and reading and writing is entirely orientated around men and metaphysics, and by and large cares little for the material and contextual concerns feminists continue to raise. This is not because it is unaware of these critiques, but because it does not care.

It is a situation that Mary Daly foresaw 50 years ago, writing in *Beyond God the Father*:

> I have already indicated that it would be unrealistic to dismiss the fact that the symbolic and linguistic instruments for communication – which include essentially the whole theological tradition in world religions – have been formulated by males under patriarchy. It is therefore inherent in these symbolic and linguistic structures that they serve the purposes of patriarchal social arrangements. Even the usual and accepted means of theological dissent have been resisted in such a way that only some questions have been allowed to arise. Many questions that are of burning importance to women now simply have not occurred in the past (and to a large extent in the present) to those with 'credentials' to do theology. Others would have been voiced timidly but quickly squelched as stupid, irrelevant, or naïve. Therefore, attempts

by women theologians now merely to 'up-date' or to reform theology within acceptable patterns of question asking are not likely to get very far. (Daly 1973, p. 22)

However, it would likewise be simplistic to suggest or demand feminists entirely retreat from these spaces. Part of the demand of systematic theology, on women of faith especially, is the way it continues to shape both the theological discourse and the practice of Christian communities. Arguments for or against a feminist systematic theology are as facile as those arguments that either demand women leave all major religions, on the one hand, or condemn all women who do leave as lacking courage, on the other. If second- to third-wave feminist theology engaged systematic theology in inexplicit and obviously ambivalent terms while it fought to become an academic discourse, and post-twentieth-century feminist theology sought in some ways to become self-consciously 'systematic' as it fought to maintain a theological tradition, a future feminist systematic theology must become attuned to the critical questions of practice and location that move beyond the theological and beyond the academy. How might a feminist politics and direct action move in tandem with systematic theology today?

Certainly, this would mean that feminist theologians in systematic theology will finally *organize*. It continues to be an oddity that feminist theology is not first and foremost a practice of community organizing. Early feminist activist participation was already waning across theoretical feminism by the early 1990s, such that Charlotte Bunch declared:

> I definitely see myself as a practitioner. In the 70s I saw myself as a practitioner and feminist theorist. Today I don't think I am qualified to teach 'Feminist theory' because I don't know what it has become. It depresses me. (Bunch, quoted in Hartman et al. 1996, p. 923)

A failure to organize ensures that the kind of publishing, teaching, administrative and reading practices that uphold systematic theology continue to support patriarchal structures. Systematic approaches that consider theoretical issues of sexism or phallocentrism, for example, are not enough for robust feminist systematic theology, just as one middle-class white woman on every board will never be enough.

But feminist systematic theology will also need to broaden the scope yet again for what counts as systematic. The inclusion of simple demographic data (as offered in this chapter) provides a basic sample of the kind of information overlooked and kept at a distance when scholarship maintains rigid boundaries of speculative input. And how well this serves the master! Future feminist systematic theology will employ quantitative and qualitative research methods, insisting that doctrine matters in tandem to materiality and that theological concepts are only ever alive to the living.

And finally, feminist systematic theology will return to the challenge of Lorde, to the very specific challenge of its racism and indifference to the community of women to which it belongs. A future feminist systematic theology must be rooted in the different but connected struggles of women who are not in the master's house. Today that continues to be Black women, Women of Colour and the Indigenous, queer and trans women, poor women, women of the global South, disabled women, women towards whom academia and normative theology usually only glance. This will slow down and radically change the nature of the academic work, inexorably. As Lorde says, 'Difference must not be merely tolerated, but seen as a fund of necessary polarities between which our creativity can spark like a dialectic. Only then does the necessity of interdependency become unthreatening' (Lorde 1983, p. 99).

Nothing in the formation of the systematic theologian prepares a scholar for such a political and activist position. Sadly, the same can often be said of the feminist formation within the university. However, in the world of Christian studies, and in Christian adjacent feminist theology, systematic theology remains a bastion, a symbolic master's house that has managed the demands of feminism with little material change to its structures. Yet many of us continue to hope that feminism, at its best, can provide the tools of dismantling. But these tools are to be found on the outside, with the community of women to whom we belong. To give Lorde the final word, 'I urge each one of us here to reach down into that deep place of knowledge inside herself and touch the deep place of terror and loathing of any difference that lives there. See whose face wears it. Then the personal as the political can begin to illuminate all our choices' (Lorde 1983, p. 101).

Note

1 This data was accurate at 18 March 2021, and was presented at a 19 March ANZATS Symposium, 'Theology and the Uuniversity: Queen of the Sciences?', https://brisbaneanzats.org/2021/03/12/seminar-on-theology-and-the-university-next-friday-19-march-with-brisbane-branch-of-the-association-of-theological-studies-anzats/ (accessed 27.3.24).

Bibliography

Tina Beattie, 1999, 'Global Sisterhood or Wicked Stepsister: Why Don't Girls with God-mothers Get Invited to the Ball?', in Deborah Sawyer and Diane M. Collier (eds), *Is there a Future for Feminist Theology?*, Sheffield: Sheffield Academic Press, pp. 115–25.

Carol P. Christ, 1987, *Laughter of Aphrodite: Reflections on a Journey to the Goddess*, San Francisco, CA: Harper and Row.

Sarah Coakley, 2009, 'Is there a Future for Gender and Theology? On Gender, Contemplation and the Systematic Task', *Criterion* 47 (1), pp. 2–11.

Sarah Coakley, 2013, *God, Sexuality and the Self: An Essay 'On the Trinity'*, Cambridge: Cambridge University Press.

Mary Daly, 1973, *Beyond God the Father: Toward a Philosophy of Women's Liberation*, 2nd edn (1986), London: Women's Press.

Mary Daly, 1978, *Gyn/Ecology: The Metaethics of Radical Feminism*, London: The Women's Press.

Brandy R. Daniels, 2016, 'Getting Lost at Sea? Apophasis, Antisociality, and the (In-)Stability of Academic Theology', in Janice McRandal (ed.), *Sarah Coakley and the Future of Systematic Theology*, Minneapolis, MI: Fortress Press, pp. 50–66.

Jacqueline Grant, 1989, *White Women's Christ and Black Women's Jesus: Feminist Christology and Womanist Response*, Atlanta, GA: Scholars Press.

Heidi Hartmann, Ellen Bravo, Charlotte Bunch, Nancy Hartsock, Roberta Spalter-Roth, Linda Williams and Maria Blanco, 1996, 'Bringing Together Feminist Theory and Practice: A Collective Interview', *Signs* 21 (4), pp. 917–51.

Elizabeth A. Johnson, 1992, *She Who Is: The Mystery of God in Feminist Theological Discourse*, New York: Crossroad.

Catherine Keller, 1994, 'Eschatology, Ecology, and a Green Ecumenacy' and 'Christian Redemption between Colonialism and Pluralism', in Rebecca S. Chopp and Mark Lewis Taylor, *Reconstructing Christian Theology*, Minneapolis, MN: Fortress Press, pp. 79–95.

Catherine Mowry LaCugna, 1991, *God for Us: The Trinity and Christian Life*, New York: HarperCollins.

Audre Lorde, 1983, 'The Master's Tools Will Never Dismantle the Master's House', in Cherríe Moraga and Gloria Anzaldua (eds), *This Bridge Called My Back: Writing by Radical Woman of Color*, New York: Kitchen Table/Women of Color Press, pp. 94–101. Originally presented at 'The Personal and the Political' panel of the Second Sex Conference, 29 October 1979.

Sallie McFague Teselle, 1974, 'Parable, Metaphor, and Theology', *Journal of the American Academy of Religion* 42 (4), pp. 630–45.

Virginia Ramey Mollenkott, 1983, *The Divine Feminine: The Biblical Imagery of God as Female*, New York: Crossroad.

Susan Frank Parsons, 2002, 'Feminist Theology as Dogmatic Theology', in Susan Frank Parsons (ed.), *Cambridge Companion to Feminist Theology*, Cambridge: Cambridge University Press, pp. 114–32.

Rosemary Radford Ruether, 1981, *To Change the World: Christology and Cultural Criticism*, New York: Crossroad.

Rosemary Radford Ruether, 1983, *Sexism and God-Talk: Toward a Feminist Theology*, Boston, MA: Beacon Press.

Elisabeth Schüssler Fiorenza, 1994, 'Christian Redemption between Colonialism and Pluralism', in Rebecca S. Chopp and Mark Lewis Taylor, *Reconstructing Christian Theology*, Minneapolis, MN: Fortress Press, pp. 79–95.

Linn Marie Tonstad, 2016, *God and Difference: The Trinity, Sexuality and the Transformation of Finitude*, New York: Routledge.

Linn Tonstad, 2020, '(Un)wise Theologians: Systematic Theology in the University', *International Journal of Systematic Theology* 22 (4), pp. 494–511.

Delores Williams, 1991, *Sisters in the Wilderness: The Challenge of Womanist God Talk*, Maryknoll, NY: Orbis Books.

Jason A. Wyman, 2017, 'Interpreting the History of the Workgroup on Constructive Theology', *Theology Today* 73 (4), pp. 312–24.

Jason A. Wyman, 2020, 'Constructive Theology: History, Movement, Method', in M. Grau and J. Wyman (eds), *What is Constructive Theology?: Histories, Methodologies, and Perspectives*, London: T&T Clark, pp. 9–30.

14

Christa/x

STEPHEN BURNS

Contending with the figure of Christ Jesus has involved a range of feminist suggestions, with considerable weight given to an argument that Sophia, lady/woman-wisdom, is ripe for revival because eminent in scripture. In her biblical and patristic studies, Sally Douglas unambiguously connects this figure from both Hebrew scripture and the apocrypha to Jesus, concluding that 'it is Jesus-Woman Wisdom who is the giver of the feast, and who lives and dies and is raised in radiance, and it is the paradoxical face of Jesus-Woman Wisdom who can both challenge *and* comfort, with a fresh yet ancient, expression of christology'. Wisdom 6.12; 7.26–27, 29; 8.17–18; John 1.15; 2 Corinthians 4.4–6; and *1 Clement* 36.2 are just some of Douglas's clues (Douglas 2016, p. 169; 2023).

Sophia has now been key to several major feminist works in christologies – the best known no doubt being Elisabeth Schüssler Fiorenza's *Jesus* (1995) – and is one point of access towards a further development in exploration of a figure, 'Christa', more recently also dubbed 'Christx'. At the outset it should be noted that this figure has not been used in feminist theologies to depict some sort of de-historized Jesus of Nazareth, but she/they is being brought to bear on several aspects of Christian doctrine. One starting place for exploration of this/these figure/s might be from recognition that '[w]ell-crafted prose can minimize masculine pronouns even in narratives about Jesus and avoid masculine language altogether when texts focus on Christ's divine nature' (Ramshaw 1995, p. 31; 2022, p. 22), then that naming towards God might also avoid masculine language. A next step taken by some feminist theologians has been to foster the symbol of Christa/x to work in the space between and around such convictions.

In the first place, Christa if not Christx – Christ in female form if not imaged as trans – came to some prominence in Christian theology in the 1970s. This was much to do with the work of artists who may or may not have themselves been Christian, but their impetus allowed for the symbol to be made an intentional part of thinking by some second-wave feminist theologians such as Rita Nakashima Brock and Carter Heyward. Later aficionados of the symbol such as Nicola Slee have, however, suggested a much longer pedigree for Christa – and this is also hinted by Douglas as cited above. For her part, Slee proposes that 'the idea of a female Christ is nothing new, but a very ancient idea rooted in Scripture, tradition and Christian practice down the centuries' (Slee 2011, p. 4).

Christa Making Visible Women's Suffering

In early contemporary re/discovery of Christa, 1970s on, Christa did not so much function as a way to speak of the divine nature of Christ but of a more fully inclusive humanity of God claimed to be incarnate, and also as code for Christian community, at least in some idealized form. It was the artists who emphasized the humanity of the symbol, vividly in the case of perhaps the most famous example, *Christa*, by Edwina Sandys, an image of a crucified woman produced in 1974 in relation to the United Nations Decade for Women: Equality, Development and Peace (1976–1985). Sandys' *Christa* started out in galleries but in 1984 made its way to an exhibition in New York's Episcopal (Anglican Communion) Cathedral of St John the Divine, where it met with a mixed reception, but in 2016 it was eventually installed as a reredos behind a holy table. Identified by the 'non-religious' artist as a 'compassionate' image, she evidently intended it to speak of the 'suffering' of women (Reynolds 2015). Also in New York, and coterminously, the Union Theological Seminary chapel hosted *Christine on the Cross* by James Murphy, a person with dual roles as both United Church of Christ minister and psychiatrist. This spreadeagled crucified woman, intended by its maker to speak of both 'the world's hatred' of women and the church's teachings about sex and guilt, was used in some liturgy relating to the then newly published *Texts of Terror* (1984) by Phylis Trible (see also Trible 2023, pp. ix–xii). But ahead of both of these quite well-known appearances of Christa, in a central Toronto United Church of Canada building, *Crucified Woman* by Almuth Lutkenhaus-Lackey had been used in a Good Friday service about 'battered women' back in 1979. Lutkenhaus-Lackey's art later became associated with a mass killing in a Canadian university, in which a failed male student gunned down female colleagues. The statue now stands in the grounds of Emmanuel College, University of Toronto, as some kind of memorial that speaks across the education sector.

Christa as a Cipher for Community

When, each independently of the other, Brock and Heyward took hold of the Christa symbol in their writings in the 1980s, it was not so much in continuity with artistic expressions of women's experience of suffering. Rather, it was part of their searching for ways of conceiving Christian community in feminist mode. In her work at this, Carter Heyward put space between Jesus and Christ, for while Jesus was 'a Jewish male with a particular relationship to his "abba"', Christ 'may be for Christians the salvific implications of the Jesus story' (Slee 2011, p. 8). Hence Heyward employed language of 'the christic' in order to speak of 'God taking shape among us' (Heyward 2017, p. 80), with 'Christa' a kind of shorthand for that. Christa then sat within Heyward's sense that 'God's incarnations are as many and varied as the persons who are driven by the power in relation to touch and be touched by sisters and brothers' (Heyward 1989, p. 164). In Heyward's wider thinking, Christa plays an important part in what Heyward names as the 'unholy trinity of injustice' – that is, gender, race and class. Christa stands squarely within her depiction of a different realm (Heyward 2017, p. 29).

For Rita Nakashima Brock, too, Christa is a way of reimaging community – at least at its best, in certain ways – in a move she intended not only to 'point ... away from sole identification of Christ with Jesus' but to 'shift the focus away from heroic individuals, male or female' (Slee 2011, p. 9).

With these germinal ideas in print, numerous feminist and liberation theologians have subsequently suggested – albeit largely in brief and fleeting forms – developments and deviations on the Christa symbol. Among them are persons as diverse as Choi Man Ja, Chung Hyun Kyung, Kelly Brown Douglas, Aruna Gnanadason, Kwok Pui-lan, Park Soon Kyung and Choan-Seng Song (Burns 2023, pp. 69–84).

Christa's 'risen forms'

Lisa Isherwood paid attention from the UK, drawing attention to Brock's reserve about 'heroic individuals' to make the point that identification between Christa and any individual may 'not seem far enough removed from Christ to avoid lapses into old bad habits' (Burns 2010, pp. 9–19); lack of feminist reflection on eucharistic presidency is just one obvious area where 'old bad habits' abound. Nonetheless, Isherwood could add that Christa may be the means for some to find a 'stepping-stone to totally new ways of imaging the divine' (Isherwood 1999, p. 103).

That imaging has been most sustained by British feminist practical theologian Nicola Slee, whose work emphasizing the 'risen forms' of Christa is itself a fresh accent against the background of images of women suffering crucifixion (Cocksworth, Starr and Burns 2023). The very first words of the first chapter of Nicola Slee's *Seeking the Risen Christa* are a question that suggests the focus she wants to broaden: 'Why is the Christa always suffering, broken, dying?' – which she immediately follows up with another question, 'Where is the risen Christa?' (Slee 2011, p. 1, cf. p. 24). Again art is key, not only in Slee's poetic mode of theology but in that she finds clues to her emphasis on Christa's 'risenness' in painted contestations to ways in which 'almost all of the theological interest in the Christa ... [has] centred on a *crucified* woman' (Slee 2011, p. 121; 2012, pp. 71–90, original emphasis). The contestations include Jill Ansell's reworking of Grünewald's Isenheim altarpiece, and above all Emmanuel Garibay's *Emmaus*, a woman in a red dress, with stigmata visible in her hands, sitting drinking in a tavern, happy with her friends. Slee's own quest for 'symbols of the feminine divine which can speak to and of women's risenness, strength, power, vitality and liveliness, our quest for life in all its fullness' (2011, p. 24), goes on to invoke Mary Daly's castigation of 'necrophiliac' religion (e.g. Slee 2011, p. 114), which lead her in turn to an exploration of 'biophiliac' alternatives stressing natality and flourishing.

Essential in Nicola Slee's thinking in *Seeking the Risen Christa* is her employment of Ivone Gebara's idea of 'everyday resurrections', which Gebara elaborates as a way of speaking about 'a process of salvation ... of recovering life and hope and justice', even as experience of justice and hope may be 'frail and fleeting'. Gebara suggests that everyday resurrections may include 'a moment of peace and tenderness in the midst of daily violence, beautiful music that calms our spirit, a novel that keeps us company, a glass of beer or a cup of coffee shared', 'a sentiment, a kiss, a piece of bread, a happy old woman' (Slee 2011, p. 25). At least some of these images are resonant with the way in which Rosemary Radford Ruether closes her book on redemption in feminist perspective, citing a 'women's creed' prepared for a conference in Beijing in 1995:

> Bread. A clean sky. Active peace. A woman's voice singing somewhere. The army disbanded. The harvest abundant. The wound healed. The child wanted. The prisoner freed. The body's integrity honoured. The lover returned ... No hand raised in any gesture but greeting. Secure intentions – of heart, home and land ... (Ruether 1998, p. 120)

In its own particular appropriation of these 'everyday' hopes, *Seeking the Risen Christa* (2011) depicts risen forms of Christa bathing in spas, dancing, laughing, running across the grass, pouring Pimms and Tequilas, cooking up extra food for unexpected guests. Christa is 'in some bar ... a little drunk', hitch-hiking across borders, listening to those who cannot speak or are usually ignored, embracing anxious bodies, reaching across 'intolerable pain' (pp. 124, 122, 121, 137, 128, 138, 122, 118, 144, 120, 131). In the later trajectory of this work, Slee herself expresses some 'hesitation' about too much emphasis on resurrection, favouring instead a focus on 'the middle space of Holy Saturday' rather than Easter, so celebrating persons who, as she evocatively puts it, 'survive, who remain, who will not leave, who cannot forget; and God in them remains, remembers, retrieves and refuses to give up' (Slee 2020, p. 165). As Slee's thought develops, it is Christa in the depths of Holy Saturday who might best embody convictions about divine desire for justice and one person's manifestation of profoundly compassionate presence to another. So this turn is not a return to the centrality of crucifixion in earlier theologies of Christa but to celebration of embodied and fierce persistence, day in, day out.

Christa Facing Questions? Christx

Christa, then, has had a lively brief history since the 1970s in which 'she' has been found to speak of suffering, and of strength, of joy and resilience, with reference to women. At least some of this may have been occluded without elaboration of the Christa symbol, as witnessed in testimony about some of that art from the 1970s, to which some women responded that it allowed them to perceive themselves as never before as 'close to Christ' (Clague 2005, p. 89).

However, with theological appropriation of third-wave feminism Christa faces some challenges, quite apart from whatever reticence she may be met with among Christians who have never entertained her. The third-wave challenge is that Christa may redefine a gender binary rather than subvert it, whatever else she may unsettle. The figure of Christx is yet to emerge in much theological reflection, but likely has a role to play in inviting respect and value of transpersons. Arguably, Christx may also invite appreciation of quite queer orthodox convictions that in their own ways defy boundaries, not least the human and divine nature of Christ, which may be part of what Lisa Isherwood and Marcella Althaus-Reid had in mind when they wrote about a '"trans" core to this incarnational religion' (Isherwood and Althaus-Reid 2007). That in turn may relate to Susannah Cornwall's contention that 'the counter-cultural importance of Christianity's focus on being human, rather than male or female', could prove to be more 'traditional' than some Christians yet imagine, given the connection Cornwall makes between 'the "kenotic hymn" of Philippians 2:5–11 [which] counsels that humans emulate Jesus, who did not consider equality with God something to be grasped' and the view that 'to exploit, to cling, or to grasp at equality with God is what is happening when humans decide that single reading of gender tells the whole story of God' (Cornwall 2008, p. 189). In any case, transgender experience now unsettles second-wave feminist work over several decades, insofar as shunting into more inclusive modes had previously involved preoccupation with decentring 'man', 'he', 'him' and male-gendered metaphors. Now female-gendered alternatives, where they have emerged at all, also stand in question, and binary terms such as 'men and women', 'he or she', naming towards God as 'mother and father', and so on, may still fail to see the diversity of a Christian assembly, quite apart from other mixed groups of human persons. In the light of lessons learned with transgendered siblings, then, feminist work needs to be rethought. What had been considered gains perhaps now need to be let go. What has come forward is need for new searching for language and ritual forms more fully humanly inclusive.

Notably, Nicola Slee's poetry about Christa sits amid numerous prayers – for example, a prayer opening, 'Christa, our sister/come spread your table in our midst', asks that Christa would break the bread of freedom, pour the wine of jouissance, dance and delight, 'banquet among us/at the tables of the poor' (Slee 2011, p. 149). Were these or likekind (expanded to Christx?) able to be incorporated into liturgical resources, they would be first of a kind, but as yet Christa/x does not seem to have turned up in many churches – at least in official texts for prayer, though she is doubtless present in pews, incarnate in the diversity of worshipping communities. And one place in which glimpses of her presence are possible is in the body of the eucharistic presider, who may among other possibilities be a menstruating woman (Jagger 2023, pp. 144–60). So a liturgical theology of Christa/x is called for, whatever may also be said in other theological disciplines. Future challenges in liturgy include not only naming her/them in prayer but gestures and etiquette that manifest her/them in ceremonial scenes and ritual pictures, the presider's and anyone else's. So Christa/x's future may be bright, like that red dress on the way to Emmaus.

Bibliography

Stephen Burns, 2010, '"Four in a Vestment"? Feminist Gestures for Christian Assembly', in Nicola Slee and Stephen Burns (eds), *Presiding Like a Woman*, London: SPCK, pp. 9–19.

Stephen Burns, 2023, 'Celebrant: Sheezus Christa', in Bryan Cones with Sharon R. Fennema, Scott Haldeman and Stephen Burns (eds), *Queering Christian Worship: Reconstructing Liturgical Theology*, New York: Seabury Press, pp. 69–84.

Julie Clague, 2005, 'The Christa: Symbolizing My Humanity and My Pain', *Feminist Theology* 14, pp. 83–108.

Ashley Cocksworth, Rachel Starr and Stephen Burns (eds), 2023, *From the Shores of Silence: Conversations in Feminist Practical Theology*, a Festschrift for Nicola Slee, London: SCM Press.

Susannah Cornwall, 2008, 'The *Kenosis* of Unambiguous Sex in the Body of Christ: Intersex, Theology and Existing "for the Other"', *Theology and Sexuality* 14, pp. 181–99.

Sally Douglas, 2016, *Early Christian Understandings of Jesus as Female: The Scandal of the 'Scandal of Particularity'*, London: Continuum.

Sally Douglas, 2023, *Jesus Sophia: Returning to Woman Wisdom in the Bible, Practice, and Prayer*, Eugene, OR: Wipf & Stock.

Carter Heyward, 1989, *The Redemption of God: A Theology of Mutual Relation*, Lanham, MD: University of America Press.

Carter Heyward, 2017, *She Flies On: A White Southern Debutante Wakes Up*, New York: Church Publishing.

Lisa Isherwood, 1999, *Introducing Feminist Christologies*, Sheffield: Sheffield Academic Press.

Lisa Isherwood and Marcella Althaus-Reid, 2007, *Trans/formations*, London: SCM Press.

Sharon Jagger, 2023, 'Presiding Like a Woman: Menstruating at the Altar', in Ashley Cocksworth, Rachel Starr and Stephen Burns (eds), *From the Shores of Silence: Conversations in Feminist Practical Theology*, a Festschrift for Nicola Slee, London: SCM Press, pp. 144–60.

Gail Ramshaw, 1995, *God Beyond Gender: Feminist Christian God-language*, Minneapolis, MN: Fortress Press.

Gail Ramshaw, 2022, *Blessing and Beseeching: Seventy Prayers Inspired by the Scriptures*, Minneapolis, MN: Fortress Press.

Nettie Reynolds, 2015, 'Christa Interview with Edwina Sandys', *Feminism and Religion*, https://feminismandreligion.com/2015/10/06/christa-interview-with-edwina-sandys-by-nettie-reynolds/ (accessed 27.3.24).

Rosemary Radford Ruether, 1998, *Introducing Redemption in Christian Feminism*, Sheffield: Sheffield Academic Press.

Elisabeth Schüssler Fiorenza, 1995, *Jesus:Miriam's Child, Sophia's Prophet*, London: SCM Press.

Nicola Slee, 2011, *Seeking the Risen Christa*, London: SPCK.

Nicola Slee, 2012, 'Visualizing, Conceptualizing, Imagining and Praying the Christa: In Search of Her Risen Forms', *Feminist Theology* 21, pp. 71–90.

Nicola Slee, 2020, *Fragments for Fractured Times: What Feminist Practical Theology Brings to the Table*, London: SCM Press.

Phylis Trible, 1984, *Texts of Terror*, London: SCM Press.
Phylis Trible, 2023, 'Foreword', in Monica Jyotsna Melanchthon and Robyn Whitaker (eds), *Terror in the Bible: Rhetoric, Gender, and Violence*, Atlanta, GA: SBL Press.

15

Mariology as Patriarchal Theological Construct: An Ongoing Challenge for Feminist Theology

CRISTINA LLEDO GOMEZ

Feminist theology is well known for its critique of Mariology – the use of Mary as a tool of oppression, to promote a certain type of ideal which keeps women oppressed – sometimes to the point that women have internalized this oppression and perpetuate it among themselves. But what are the actual teachings on Mary and thus the basis for this critique? And even if she is a tool of oppression, has she not been a help to many thousands of people who endure suffering because of their belief in her? Further, if the Mary of history cannot be recovered, how can feminist theologians suggest an alternative to the Mary of patriarchal construct? This chapter will seek to address these questions by exploring three facets of Mary for the understanding and more nuanced critique of the feminist theologian: the Mary of dogma, the Mary of piety, and the Mary of history. It aims to assist in the understanding of Mary as simultaneously a tool of oppression and a tool of survival, even a tool of liberation for some – a nuance that any Mariological critique must have if it is to be incisive and forceful. The chapter ends with the acknowledgement that instead of placing all feminist theological discourse on arguments against this patriarchal Mariology, feminist theologians have sought to expand Mariology such that it is empowering for women of their time and that maternal philosophy may be a helpful tool in its expansion.

The Mary of Dogma

Whenever Mary appears in conversation, almost always people recall the peculiar Christian teaching of Mary's simultaneous virginity and motherhood. They recall this for its inconceivability according to common understanding of human biology, specifically its anomaly with reproductive and birthing processes. But what does the Catholic Church specifically teach about Mary?

Of the many Catholic teachings that lie at the heart of the Christian faith, four of these are about Mary. They are her: (1) divine motherhood; (2) perpetual virginity; (3) immaculate conception; and (4) bodily assumption; and the first of the four forms the basis for the other three. The first dogma, Mary's divine motherhood, was proclaimed at the Council of Ephesus in 431. It describes Mary's role as the Mother of God, the 'theotokos' or the 'God-bearer'. Mary's divine motherhood ensures both the humanity and divinity of Jesus – born from a human mother but 'begotten not made' by the first Person of the Trinity, the Father/Source of all Being, given that the Son/Word/Logos/Second Person of the Trinity existed before all time and continues to exist, and therefore is not created. In a time when paternity was often in question because of limited scientific knowledge, remaining a virgin at least before birth (*ante partu*) assured Jesus' divine nature.

But the early church fathers also argued for Mary's perpetual virginity. That is, that Mary remained a virgin during (*in partu*) and after birth (*post partu*). Hence, the second teaching on Mary, her perpetual virginity. In a time when asceticism was seen as the divine path in contrast to carnality, carnal motherhood could not be imagined for a woman who would give birth to the divine; she had to be pure and worthy. In the ancient world, it was perceived that asceticism, celibacy and, moreover, virginity was the closest a human being could reach the divine.

Marian proponents might also argue that Mary had to be ever virginal (also known as Mary's perpetual virginity). Otherwise, her motherhood would be reduced to functionalism – giving birth to the divine and protecting his paternity by being a virgin but having no use after his birth. Thus, later, Mary would eventually be named Mother of the Church, *Mater ecclesia*, its spiritual mother; that is, her motherhood would not only be towards Jesus but also towards the entire church. Consequently, her perpetual virginity enabled her to become mother to all believers, not just Jesus.

In contrast, Nestorius (386–450 CE) believed Mary gave birth only to the human Jesus. God the Father provided Jesus' divine nature and person. In Nestorius' theory Jesus would exist with two natures and two persons, which contradicts the teaching on hypostatic union – two full natures in the one person. Nestorius thus preferred to call Mary *Christokos* (Christ-bearer), rather than *Theotokos* (God-bearer). But Nestorius would later be condemned at the Council of Ephesus. Mary's perpetual virginity would be affirmed at the Lateran Council in 649.

In 2018, Pope Francis would reiterate the belief in Mary as Mother Church and inscribe it as a devotion and an annual feast day in the Roman Catholic liturgical calendar. The feast was introduced by the Pope to 'encourage the growth of the maternal sense of the Church in the pastors, religious and faithful, as well as a growth of genuine Marian piety' (Congregation for Divine Worship 2018). Further, the celebration would 'help us to remember that growth in the Christian life must be anchored to the Mystery of the Cross, to the oblation of Christ in the Eucharistic Banquet and to the Mother of the Redeemer and Mother of the Redeemed, the Virgin who makes her offering to God'. Clearly this Mariology, formed from the days of the early church fathers and early church councils is about Jesus and the church – one centred on the cross and the Eucharist and not at all about Mary as the term 'Mariology' (the study of Mary) would suggest.

An interesting perspective on the insistence on Mary's perpetual virginity is that it raises the question of the validity of her marriage to Joseph, according to canon law, given one of the conditions for a valid marriage is consummation (the other is ratification, see canon 1141). If Mary and Joseph were Catholics, they would have had grounds for divorce: 'Antecedent and perpetual impotence to have intercourse, whether on the part of the man or the woman, whether absolute or relative, nullifies marriage by its very nature' (Code of Canon Law, 1084 §1). But the teaching on Mary's perpetual virginity was not created to support teachings on Catholic marriage. Rather, like the other three Catholic Marian dogmas or teachings, they were more about supporting Christological dogmas that were being questioned in the early church, saying less about the real Mary, and more about Jesus, her son (Gomez 2018). More specifically, presenting Mary as both virgin and mother supported the belief of Jesus as truly the Son of God and Mary, and thus affirmed that Jesus was both fully divine and fully human.

The remaining two doctrines, Mary's immaculate conception (declared in 1854 by Pope Pius IX) and bodily assumption into heaven (declared in 1950 by Pope Pius XII), also exist to convey something more about Jesus and the church than about Mary in her humanness. Her immaculate conception (the doctrine that Mary was born without sin, *not* that Mary miraculously 'conceived' the Son of God in her womb) was declared to enable the possibility of imagining the God-human, Jesus, to be born without sin. Meanwhile, the teaching on Mary's bodily assumption (that is, being raised to heaven in both body and soul and not just the soul) was created in a context in which there was a great disregard for human lives and bodies, as men and women died by the thousands in various wars, particularly through the First and Second World Wars. Mary's assumption would foretaste the rising of our own bodies and souls to heaven when Jesus returns and at the end of time. Mary would thus be the first human to experience this privilege. Of the four Marian dogmas, the last two have been proclaimed infallible, or *ex cathedra*, dogmas of the Catholic Church. It does not make them above other dogmas. Rather, their infallible character underlines the state in which the declaration was made – there was no error in declaring these beliefs; no culture, time or scientific discoveries could change these beliefs.

To the readers of today, the Marian dogmas do not only create a dissonance with women's everyday lives but are also unfathomable. Yet, viewed as teachings about Jesus rather than on motherhood, virginity or even female experience, one can see that Mary's motherhood and virginity are theoretical notions for the purpose of affirming Catholicism's central teachings about Jesus and the church. Note here that it is a concept of 'woman' that is utilized to justify the position of a man, no less the mother for her son.

For the early church fathers, it was important to affirm Jesus/the Word's incarnation since it enabled the belief that humanity shared in the divine life. As Gregory of Nazianzus taught, 'what is not assumed cannot be saved'. The divine Word's/Jesus' integration of full humanity with divinity enables the 'hypostatic union' or the dual natures of Jesus. The incarnation, together with the hypostatic union, enables the possibility of transformation, salvation and the divinization of all humanity. In other words, Jesus made it possible for humans to become more divine and the more they become divine, the more they can become fully human (understood as *theosis* in the Eastern Church). The Eucharist especially enables this divinization of the living.

Given that Mary's virgin motherhood sends a different message about sex and marriage, specifically, a contrary model of Catholic marriage with Mary's perpetual virginity, this shows that the Marian dogmas can be understood for what they are – as primarily concerned with asserting a theological point, in this case a christological point, rather than recording a historical-scientific account or upholding sexless marriages as an ethical ideal or primarily concerned with the diminishment of women. This does not take away the truth that there was a Mary of history who gave birth to a son who would minister to people and be cruelly put to death. It does not also remove the possibility of God's miraculous intervention making a virgin pregnant according to God's own whims, or that indeed Joseph and Mary never had sex throughout their marriage. We will not be able to verify these as historical truth and that is why they are asserted as 'theological truths' according to scripture and the early church fathers who themselves were predominantly concerned with theological truth.

Unfortunately, just as the Bible is often read in the contemporary world in a literal-historical way, this image of the virgin-mother has also been read and promoted in a literal-historical sense throughout the ages. This highlights the reality that this Marian image of the virgin-mother has been instrumental in the oppression of and the discrimination against women for centuries. As oppression, this Marian image presented to women an impossible ideal that they could never achieve for themselves. As discrimination, women's ultimate vocation was tied to her biological reproductive potentiality. That is, since women have wombs and men do not, the woman's ultimate role is to be a mother, to populate the world, even if she acts as a spiritual mother to others (as in the case of women who choose celibacy and enter the religious life). Meanwhile, men, because they do not have wombs, have the responsibility to rule the world – to rule those that are birthed by women.

Mary would later be inscribed in the Catholic imagination as not only the Mother of God and Mother of the Church, but also Mother Church herself. While the beginnings of Christianity had a church imaged as a mother, whose martyrs, virgins, celibate or ascetic clergy, as well as the entire congregation, enabled faith conversions and thus the 'birthing' and 'nurturing' of new Christians, eventually this maternal title would be designated solely to Mary, such that she was called its archetype (Gomez 2018). While Mother Church began as a designation for the faith community called to spiritually grow, birth and nurture other Christian believers, this designation turned solely towards Mary. Elsewhere, I argue that this encouraged and continues to encourage passivity and infantilization of the people of God, the entire Church community (Gomez 2015).

Collapsing the image of the church as a virgin-mother and Mary as the virgin-mother had the double-effect of elevating Mary's status (as virgin-mother) while reducing community agency, in which they see themselves as called to mature into adults in Christ and to mother others into that maturity. At the Second Vatican Council (1962–65), the church fathers debated over whether or not Mariology would be treated in a separate document to the church: the result was a margin of 40 votes between those in favour (1,074) and those against (1,114). This meant Mary would be placed within the context of a theology of the church (ecclesiology), consequently discouraging a Marian faith which was disconnected from the church community and the sacraments. That is, one could not have a genuine Marian faith if people only turned to their Marian devotions but did not connect them with the trinitarian God, the church, and the sacraments, particularly the Eucharist. This move to place Mariology within ecclesiology would also recognize Mary as part of the communion of saints rather than encourage tendencies towards the making of Mary as the feminine divine, which is argued belongs to God alone who is, as God-self, both the feminine and masculine divine but also beyond gender. Yet the way Mary was placed into Vatican II's Constitution on the Church, *Lumen Gentium* (chapter 8), was in such a way that the church community was called to place themselves under her maternal care and, as already mentioned above, with the effect of infantilizing the church.

The topic of Mariology under the hands of men, patriarchs to be exact, would understandably make of Mary a patriarchal construct to serve the needs of men, who at the time were concerned with clarifying the identities of Jesus and the church in the hope of staying true to the gospel handed on from Jesus himself and his apostles. But this patriarchal construct would depend upon presenting Mary as a particular type of woman and mother – an eternal and mystical figure, but also the 'ideal woman'. This figure, of course, has nothing to do with the Mary of history who becomes a single Jewish mother at about 12 years of age and must deal with the shame, taboo and marginalization that comes with such a situation. The patriarchal portrayal of Mary is neither interested in the bodily and messy picture of Mary nor is it interested in the messy and complex picture of mothering (including moments in which a mother can wish she was not a mother and only live for herself, because she might have had a series of days without sleep and has not been able to attend to her basic needs such as showering and enjoying an uninterrupted meal) or a messy and complex womanhood. As Marcella Althaus-Reid describes the conception of Jesus in Mary, she has become 'the myth of a woman without a vagina'. A woman without a vagina will also be a woman without the concerns of menstruation, menopause, messy and/or complicated births, messy conception experiences, illnesses and debilitating pains connected with the womb such as endometriosis or polycystic ovaries. A Marian image without a vagina is unconcerned with the real and detrimental impacts upon women in the presentation of this patriarchal construct. Moreover, since Christian teaching states Mary's birthing of Jesus was painless, in its efforts to contrast the obedient Mary (because she said yes to the incarnation) with the disobedient Eve whose punishment was to experience birth pangs (Gen. 3.16) (because she ate the fruit from the forbidden tree), the virgin birth serves as an indictment against women who do give birth and will experience suffering in birth. When we contrast Mary's bodilessness and painlessness (or absence of any mention of pain) in birth and Jesus' very physical pain in death portrayed in Christian teaching and the Gospels (placing aside the necessity of Jesus' physicality to show his full humanness), we are left with the question of how much women, women's bodies and their real pains actually have a place in a male-centred faith in which God chooses to incarnate as the male Jesus. (Although, thanks to queer theologies, at least we can begin to move from the singular idea of a solely male incarnation and, of course, the Word, the second person of the Trinity, is beyond gender.)

The patriarchal portrayal of Mary is rather interested in how this Mary as a particular woman and mother can serve the needs of men of the church, whether it is to define aspects of the faith or to address their own needs to make room for the feminine divine. That is, one who mothers men but does not overpower them or seduce celibate male priests (making Mary a suitable figure who is not Mother-God, who is less than the male powerful Father-God, but powerful enough to be the ever-present comforting, non-sexual mother and woman). The irony of this picture is that to be a mother, one must engage in sexual intercourse. Moreover, mothers can and do have pleasure during sexual intercourse. But to the man who needs to be mothered (assured of care in this world) but remain celibate, it is unimaginable that a mother can also be a sexual being because she is meant to be one or the other: the pure eternal carer (the all-giving, all-sacrificial mother) or the sexually desired (the impure whore), but not both. Elsewhere, I have discussed how the 'Good Mother' myth is perpetuated through Mary and thus perpetuates an oppressive figure for women (Gomez, forthcoming). The difficulty for the church is that many of its metaphors that explain its dogmas are tied to this virgin-mother image so that the removal and the replacement of this image will not be anywhere near an overnight task.

The Mary of Piety

But it is not the Mary of dogma whom Christian believers have more often connected with through centuries. Rather, it has been the Mary with whom one prayed to, with or requested for intercessions and protection on one's behalf. This devotion to Mary is especially heightened during the periods, and thereafter, of her apparitions, during which she appeared to little children and called for more praying and fasting, traditions themselves that are not new and are rather deeply embedded in Christian historical practice. Mary has appeared in various manifestations all over the world, often with this message of turning to peace through these Christian tools of praying and fasting. These manifestations include: Mary as the undoer of knots (c. 1700), popular with the current pope, Francis, and said to untie any complex problem; Mary of Perpetual Help (or Our Lady of Perpetual Succour, 1453), the Lady known for her numerous miracles, cures and graces, granted to her devotees who saw her miraculous picture; Our Lady of Guadalupe (1531), who appeared to an Aztec Indian of Mexico and enabled the conversion of 8 million Indigenous Mexicans to Christianity after their resistance to conversion by the Spanish clergy (in Mary, the Indigenous people recognized the maternal-divine figure, the virgin mother of god whom they had already worshipped through Tonantzin (Mong 2018)); and, the controversial Mary the co-redemptrix, who is said to work with Jesus for the salvation of all God's people. As co-redemptrix, the mother and son partnership is elevated and seen as the means with which to engage with the trinitarian God of the Christian faith who would otherwise seem unreachable, for both the Father and Spirit are non-human. Meanwhile, Mary as mother was not only a human with whom one can engage, but a mother (everyone comes from a mother!) and is consistently presented as tenderness and love exemplified. Yet Jesus is the sole mediator to the divine and thus Mary as co-redemptrix was and would never be approved by the hierarchical church, despite the popularity of this devotion.

Some may view the Mary of piety as the mother constructed in the minds of believers who project on to Mary their maternal ideals and needs. Others are simply captured by her apparitions and the resulting cures (physical, emotional and spiritual) or at least the promise of those cures that enables one to push through the difficulties of life. Whether imagined or not, these ideals often do have a basis in both scripture and tradition. At the same time, they can move beyond reality and history to become myths constrained only by the stretch of the imagination. An example of such maternal idealism assigned to Mary is seen in Pope Francis' explanation of why the current church must become more 'feminine', specifically more 'bridal', and more 'maternal' like Mary:

> The Church is feminine, because it is 'church' and 'bride' [both grammatically feminine]: it is feminine. And she is mother; she gives life. Bride and Mother. And the Fathers go further and say that even your soul is the bride of Christ and mother. And it is with this attitude that comes from Mary, who is Mother of the Church, with this attitude we can understand this feminine dimension of the Church, which, when it is not there, the Church loses its identity and becomes a charitable organization or a football team, or whatever, but not the Church. (Francis 2018)

Further, Francis explains specifically how the church is a mother:

> A Church that is a mother goes along the path of tenderness. It knows the language of such wisdom of caresses, of silence, of the gaze that knows compassion, that knows silent [sic]. It is, too, a soul, a person who lives out this way of being a member of the Church, knowing that he or she is [like] a mother [and] must go along the same path: a person [who is] gentle, tender, smiling, full of love. (Francis 2018)

The church as a woman is said to be found in Revelation 12.1, as a bride or spouse in Ephesians 5.25 and Revelation 19.7, and a mother in Galatians 4.26 and Revelation 21.9–10. Except for the Ephesians text, in each case the term 'church' is never explicitly mentioned but rather implied based on the understanding of Christ as the 'Lamb' who is 'Spouse' to the church, sometimes imaged as the 'New Jerusalem'. Mary as mother (of God) is found especially in the Gospel of Luke at the annunciation. But there are no scriptural texts that refer to Mary as either bride or spouse to Jesus, her son. However, some might argue she is the spouse of God the Father or the Spirit, given that through them she became miraculously pregnant as seen in Luke 1. Given the trinitarian nature of God, in this roundabout way, it is argued that Mary is thus spouse to God the Son, who is her own son as the incarnation! Meanwhile, there are no scriptural bases for the church or Mary as compassionate, tender, gentle, smiling, silent or full of love (though one might argue that when Mary 'pondered' all these things 'in her heart' (Luke 2.19), she was exemplifying these characteristics – an example of exercising the stretch of the Christian imagination).

In terms of tradition, the church as woman, mother and bride has been in use since the early church (Gomez 2018). The early church fathers described Mary as a mother but never as a bride or spouse to Christ, despite contrary arguments by Von Balthasar, Ratzinger, Lubac and Congar alike, who reason that since Mary is designated as archetype of the maternal and virginal church (in both tradition and Vatican II's Constitution on the Church, *Lumen Gentium*), she thus becomes spouse to Christ who is more than just her human son but is the Word/*Logos*/second Person of the trinitarian God incarnate.

It is not only the incestuous and oedipal relationship suggested and unquestioned by a hierarchical church that is troubling (and part of the reason why many women and men have long had difficulties with Mariology). Rather, it is the way in which Mary, a woman, has been utilized for the needs of men to express their theological meaning-making. Mary here represents women in both Christian and secular traditions whose voices are not heard. We barely hear from Mary in the scriptures, only at the annunciation, the visitation, and at the finding of Jesus in the temple. The magisterium barely, if ever, emphasizes Mary's non-passivity or empowered female image, even if her very name, 'Miriam', means 'rebellion' and she exemplifies this rebellion in the Magnificat (Luke 1.46–55). Mary also represents women whose messy and complex realities are not taken seriously and suffer the consequences of the constant projection and perpetuation of the mythical woman, mother and wife.

Further, sexuality contained by the simultaneously permissible and contained relationship between the virgin mother and her son makes exploration of sexuality, of what it means to be a sexual adult (the son redefining his relationship with his mother as an adult rather than as infant or child) and Mary and Christ as sexual beings, as outside the Christian imagination. If the Christian community wishes to take seriously its tradition that affirms being an integral human includes being a sexual adult in its messiness and complexity, then Christian teaching, tradition, liturgy, iconography and representation must enable the imagination that Mary and Christ were sexual beings too, and the community must take seriously what this implies about being fully human. Further, if the church truly desires to protect children and vulnerable adults from sexual abuse, then sexuality, sex and associated and necessary topics of discussion such as consent, boundaries, mutuality, intimacy, power dynamics and healthy relationships must be the responsibility of the community to each other. To limit teaching to the insistence that people should simply not have sex except inside marriage and only for the purpose of procreation does not equip vulnerable persons, young and old, as they encounter different people. It does not help those who are unaware of the dynamics of grooming and normalization of sexual abuse and violence, or of the cycle of abuse in relationships, or that how sex is expressed and experienced is representative of a healthy or unhealthy relationship.

When Pope Francis describes the church as maternal and proclaims its need to become even more so, he reasons that the current Catholic Church is masculine, 'a church of old bachelors' (Francis 2018). They 'live in this isolation' and are 'incapable of love, incapable of fruitfulness'. Francis explains that 'without the woman, the Church does not advance – because she is a woman. And this attitude of woman comes from Mary, because Jesus willed it so.' For Francis, 'tenderness' is 'the main virtue that distinguishes a woman and said the Church must learn from mothers' examples of meekness and humility'. Turning to Mary as model of mothering, and as mother of all the baptized who can help them become more maternal (that is, to become more 'tender', 'meek' and 'humble'), Francis reminds his audience of the three women who are called mothers in church tradition – Mary, the church and our soul (see chapters on Augustine and Ambrose in Gomez 2018). While Augustine and Ambrose spoke of the soul as necessarily becoming more maternal, it is neither meekness, tenderness, humility nor passivity in general which characterized their call to maternity for the baptized. Rather, these early church fathers called for the church to become spiritual adults and to spiritually mother others, remembering that they themselves were once newly baptized and were spiritual infants. Thus, there is a contrast between Francis' encouragement of the church to become more tender and Ambrose's and Augustine's call for the church to 'grow up' and to help others to 'grow up'. Again, as I have argued above, encouraging the church to place themselves under the maternal care of Mary can be infantilizing and can make it difficult for the church itself to 'grow up', to participate as church fully, actively and consciously, in their baptismal call to be priestly, prophetic and servant leaders (Gomez 2015).

Yet, there are women who claim that this Mary of piety is anything but an oppressive figure. Rather, she is a woman who understands a woman's suffering in a man's world. She is both sister (a fellow woman who understands) and mother (a figure who cares and protects the individual when there is no one else to turn to) to the abandoned, orphaned, forgotten, continually discriminated and marginalized woman. Women (and men) who live lives in which they are unable to escape their situations of oppression look to Mary as the singular person who walks with them in their suffering, understands their suffering (having experienced suffering herself), and gives them reason to continue living even while they suffer because a divine maternal figure loves and cares for them. This is a reality that feminist theological critique of Mariology must grapple with. That is, feminist theology must ask how one might challenge Marian piety given its ability to help women in their oppression but also keep them in their oppression. As an oppressive tool (whether intentional or not), it is used by the patriarchy to promote the Good Mother myth and, moreover, normalize benevolent sexism (in which women are good when they are virgin mothers like Mary, but bad or less than a woman if they are not) and keep them from engaging in collective resistance (Gomez 2024). As a survival/liberative tool, she helps people to continue with their lives despite their ongoing struggle. But are these roles of advocate/intercessor, guide, teacher, source of wisdom and power, a help in times of suffering and weakness, expressed as maternal care, not the roles of the Holy Spirit? Yves Congar, in his classic theology of the Holy Spirit written in three volumes, notes that Mary is one of three other elements within

Christianity that have come to substitute the prominence and role of the Holy Spirit (Congar 1983). This replacement of the Holy Spirit thus robs the Christian community of a serious engagement with the Holy Spirit in their daily lives and in the world, the one who brings about in us the love of God, neighbour and self. The Holy Spirit is, as Congar describes, 'concerned with God as love, in other words, with God in [God's] communication of [Godself] and as grace' (Congar 1983, p. 68).

The Mary of History

The silence on many of Mary's experiences as mother, daughter, wife, as a Jew living under Roman occupation, and as a woman with her own interests, likes, dislikes, desires and fears are either untold, minimized and, for all we know, removed from her story. Instead, like other maternal goddesses/deities, the people who have turned to her and utilized her as a female and maternal figure have imposed their needs and ideas of maternity and femininity on to her via a symbol-figure they have constructed, even if initially founded in reality and in Christian text and tradition. When this symbol is turned into the model of womanhood and motherhood, as she had been for many centuries, societies communicate through this figure their expectations of all women to become the mothers that they want them to be – to demand consciously or unconsciously to be the 'good mother' who is safe and comforting in a world that can feel hostile, unstable and uninterested in individuals. Just as the materfamilias of ancient Rome or *Mater Ecclesia* of the first three centuries communicated stability, unity and continuity for ancient Rome or the early church respectively, so the eternal Mother Mary figure continues to be used by popes to communicate assurance, stability, unity, community and love, in a church currently replete with problems of abuse of power, divided into left and right wings, and which is often tempted to become more corporatized and less pastoral. God as maternal or feminine is usually far from the Christian imagination given the consistent emphasis on Mary's maternity and femininity and less emphasis or exploration of other formidable female figures of the Bible, such as Phoebe, the only woman to be explicitly named a deacon in the text, or Mary Magdalene who was proclaimed 'Apostle to the Apostles' by Pope Francis in 2016, in recognition of her role as the first to see the resurrected Jesus, replacing the unfortunate and untrue image of her as the repentant whore, popularized by another pope, Gregory I, in 1591.

While the Mary of theological dogma (who supports central teachings of the Catholic Church) and the Mary of Christian piety (the eternal maternal figure who has supported the faith and lives of the everyday faithful, giving them hope amid their difficulties) served their purposes in the church, in their own way helping to build the church and communicate God's reign on earth (and sometimes not!), it is the real Mary (one whom we will never know fully, if at all, because of the lack of historical records about her) and the imagination of her as a fully human mother, which remains elusive to us but can provide a way in which women as mothers may find greater connection with especially as she is reinterpreted by feminist biblical scholars. Such images include: Mary the refugee mother (Matthew 2.16–18), who flees the threat of Herod's violence and who with her family barely escapes the tragic killing of the Innocents; Mary of the Magnificat (Luke 1.46–55), the empowered pregnant woman who speaks of and witnesses to this divine justice, in which the powerful are unseated while the lowly are lifted; Mary, our sister and companion, who walks with us rather than above us, alongside the communion of the saints who continue their work of building peace from heaven and on earth (Johnson 2009); and Mary the Indigenous mother, whom Indigenous peoples had connected with – not as a single mother to an infant child, but instead as the mother situated within community – and not just a human community but also the community of the earth and all its living creatures. As already mentioned above, this enabled Indigenous peoples, such as those from Mexico, to be open to a Christian faith imposed by their colonizers even though there was no exchange of faith. Indigenous faith was more often demonized and dismantled by colonizers than taken seriously as a valid faith for the people.

Can one even contemplate a Mary of history and how she can be empowering for women? In *Mary, Maternal Philosophy, and Empowered Mothering*, I argue that, while in the past a universal image of motherhood painted an ideal picture that was oppressive for all women, maternal philosophy has challenged this patriarchal-maternal image and has suggested what an empowered mother image might look like (Gomez, forthcoming). Using the list of characteristics that make for empowered mothering, I suggest instances within the life of the historical Mary that show how her mothering can be reimagined, such that it connects with the range of realities of actual mothering. That is, that while single motherhood and intensive motherhood exists, there is also the type of mothering that involves the whole community mothering, mothering in which the mother is not the all-sacrificial mother but tends to her own needs too, mothering that involves both mother love and mother hate, and mothering that is not necessarily spoken about in public, taboo subjects regarding motherhood that fall very much within the difficult realities of many. I suggest that if Mary could be reimagined in the light of the characteristics of empowered mothering, it will not only help mothers today connect more easily with her but, moreover, address the use of Mary as a tool of perpetuation of gender essentialism (in which women's ultimate role is as mothers), gender binarism (in which there are only two genders, male and female), and male heteronormativity (in which maleness is normative, and against which all are measured) communicated through a patriarchal church.

Bibliography

Yves Congar, 1983, *I Believe in the Holy Spirit*, Vol. 1, *The Holy Spirit in the 'Economy': Revelation and Experience of the Spirit*, trans. David Smith, New York: Seabury Press.

Congregation for Divine Worship and the Discipline of the Sacraments, Prefect – Cardinal Sarah, 2018, *Decree in the Celebration of the Blessed Virgin Mary Mother of the Church in the General Roman Calendar*, 11 February, https://www.vatican.va/roman_curia/congregations/ccdds/documents/rc_con_ccdds_doc_20180211_decreto-mater-ecclesiae_en.html (accessed 27.3.24).

Francis, 2018, Homily at Santa Marta, Memorial of Mary, Mother of the Church, 21 May 2018, https://www.romereports.com/en/2018/05/21/pope-francis-at-santa-marta-without-the-woman-the-church-does-not-advance/ (accessed 6.8.24).

Cristina Lledo Gomez, 2015, 'From Infants to Mothers: Recovering the Call to the People of God to Become Mother Church in *Lumen Gentium*', *Ecclesiology* 11, pp. 32–62.

Cristina Lledo Gomez, 2018, *The Church as Woman and Mother: Historical and Theological Foundations*, New York: Paulist Press.

Cristina Lledo Gomez, 2024, 'Pinays Rise Up, Bangon na: Reclaiming Pinay Power Dismantled by a Christian Colonial Past and Present', in Cristina Lledo Gomez, Agnes Brazal and Marilou Ibita (eds), *500 Years of Christianity and the Global Filipino/a: Postcolonial Perspectives*, London: Palgrave Macmillan.

Cristina Lledo Gomez, forthcoming, 'Mariology, Maternal Philosophy and Empowered Mothering', in Cristina Lledo Gomez and Julia Brumbaugh (eds), *Mothering and Theology / God of Interruption: Essays in Feminist Maternal Theology*, Mahwah, NJ: Paulist Press.

Elizabeth A. Johnson, 2009, *Truly Our Sister: A Theology of Mary in the Communion of Saints*, New York: Continuum.

Ambrose Mong, 2018, 'Our Lady of Guadalupe: Model of Inculturation', *International Journal for the Study of the Christian Church* 18, pp. 67–83.

16

Post-Christian Feminism

MICHAEL W. BRIERLEY

'You took my baby away from me! I didn't see what you did to him!' With those words, a woman suddenly and unexpectedly rounded on me one evening in the pub, some weeks after I had baptized her infant son in the village church, at what seemed at the time to have been a happy service. Taken aback, I realized that her exclamation was entirely justified: the baptism party had stood just behind me at the font, so she would not have had a good view of the sprinkling of the water.[1]

Beyond the specifics of that particular occasion, the mother's post-baptismal reaction can be interpreted along 'post-Christian' feminist lines. The post-Christian feminists considered in this chapter argue that baptism is a patriarchal ritual. The first, natural birth through the waters of the mother is subliminally regarded as so malign as to require correction by means of a new birth or rebirth through water from (generally until recently) a male cleric (Hampson 2013b, p. 57; Daly 1973b, p. 195; 1978, p. 99). The woman is deficient; the man provides completion. The woman's part is fallen; the man's is salvific. Thus, in Christian terms, it would seem *necessary* to take children away from their mothers and do to them something that is mysterious and hidden. On this reading, infant baptism could even be regarded as a form of child abuse.

It might be thought that such an interpretation of an innocent and joyful family event is extreme; yet that would be to underestimate the power of symbol and the depth of patriarchal abuse, and the seriousness with which both need to be taken. I write this chapter neither as a post-Christian, nor (if it be held that feminists are necessarily women) as a feminist, but as a Christian who believes that the patriarchal record is an appalling abyss which has to be thoroughly plumbed and negotiated if the faith is to emerge with integrity.[2]

The word 'post-Christian' began to be used by 'second-wave' feminists after Mary Daly (1928–2010) used it in a paper given to the American Academy of Religion in 1973, reflecting the fact that she no longer regarded herself as Christian (Daly 1973a, pp. 33–8). It was taken up in Britain in the 1980s by Daphne Hampson (b. 1944), who likewise resolved to leave the Christian faith (Hampson 1990a, p. 42; 1996a, p. 57; 2010, pp. 988–9). Recently, it has been suggested that 'post'-theory refers to the deconstruction of unitary accounts of knowledge, so that 'post' is more akin to 'critical' and 'post-Christian' thereby denotes the plurality of Christianity (hence one writer describes herself as being both Christian and post-Christian at the same time) (Isherwood and McPhillips 2008, especially essays by Gray and McPhillips, Stuart, Yamaguchi). This chapter uses 'post' in the more broadly accepted sense of 'after', so that 'post-Christian' designates those who identify as having moved on from Christian faith, which is how the term has been employed by Daly and by Hampson.

Daly and Hampson, as the American originator and British proponent par excellence of 'post-Christian' feminism respectively, together represent a highly instructive pairing for explication of this aspect of feminist theology. Both had oppressive experiences which caused them to break from Christianity; both wrote key texts in the field; and both exercised long tenure on the teaching staff of historic universities. Moreover, both have maintained 'theistic' positions, and both, it could be claimed, have been primarily concerned with how the feminist self 'comes to itself' in relation to other selves. It will also be argued below that both exhibit a fundamentally similar ontology. At the same time, they display differences of emphasis, as will become evident. This chapter conducts an exposition of the work of each in turn and, attending especially to the doctrine of God (as foundational for theology), offers an element of critique; in this light, it will conclude by assessing the phenomenon of post-Christian feminism.

Mary Daly

Mary Daly, the only child of Irish American, Catholic parents, was born and brought up in Schenectady, New York (Hunt 2017; Daly 1992). She studied English as an undergraduate, because the College of St Rose at Albany, New York, did not major in her preferred subject of philosophy. Offered a scholarship at the Catholic University of America at Washington, DC, she took an MA in English and, offered a further scholarship at St Mary's College, Notre Dame, Indiana, she procured a PhD in religion, going on to teach for five years. The only Catholic academies at that time where a woman could obtain a doctorate in philosophy were state-run universities in Germany and Switzerland, so she then spent seven years at

Fribourg, obtaining a baccalaureate in theology, a licentiate in theology, a doctorate in theology and finally a doctorate in philosophy, tutoring part-time in order to help fund her research.

After completing her studies, Daly spent a month in 1965 at the Second Vatican Council, and, excited at the prospect of reform, wrote *The Church and the Second Sex* (1968). Her new employers, the Jesuits who ran Boston College in Massachusetts, were less than impressed and attempted to terminate her contract; but under the pressure of orchestrated protests that drew national press attention, they reversed their decision and offered Daly tenure. The experience, however, took its toll on Daly, rendering redundant a manuscript that she had begun to write on Catholicism (Daly 1992) and 'radicalizing' her further (Daly 1992, pp. 7, 101, 107, 117; 2006, p. 68). While, retrospectively, she characterized her departure from Christian faith as a gradual process, a critical moment came in November 1971, when she became the first woman to preach at the Memorial Church of Harvard University in Cambridge, Massachusetts (Daly 1968, p. xi). Wishing neither to treat the engagement conventionally nor to decline it, she invited the congregation at the end of the sermon to follow her out of the church, both literally and spiritually – and several hundred did so (Daly 1992, pp. 137–40). This 'exodus' became the symbolic beginning of post-Christian feminism, and Daly's next book, *Beyond God the Father*, is consequently distinct from the first, being a 'radical' post-Christian feminist manifesto, as opposed to the 'liberal' Christian feminist stance of the former.

Those who have had to fight for their livelihood on the grounds of conscience tend, understandably, tightly to grip the rights that they have won (cf. Brierley 2004). Daly taught at Boston for over 30 years. Turned down for a full professorship in 1975 and again in 1989, she agreed to retire in her early seventies, in a two-year legal dispute with the college over her practice of teaching female and male students separately.

Daly saw her two books *Gyn/Ecology* (1978) and *Pure Lust* (1984) as the first instalments of a trilogy that dealt with eight 'deadly sins of the fathers'. In the event, her enthusiasm for the project seems to have been superseded by a different discursive style. *Quintessence* (1998), claiming to deal with the last three sins, yet (with a literary technique of imagined conversations between time travellers) not treating them explicitly, reflects her increasing estrangement from scholarly convention and the academic community (or, as she named it, 'academentia') (Daly 1998, p. 17; cf. 1978, p. xviii; Telling 2012); it is more akin to her last book, *Amazon Grace* (2006), leaving *Beyond God the Father*, *Gyn/Ecology* and *Pure Lust* as the substantial loci of her post-Christian oeuvre.

What is the essence of that oeuvre? While oppressive behaviour takes many forms, including racism and colonialism, Daly claimed that rape is the root and paradigm of all oppression.[3] She regarded the torture, murder and dismemberment (both literal and metaphorical) of women by men as the source and model of all other types of subjugation. (Daly 1973b, pp. xv–xvi). It was also endemic: the world exhibits a 'planetary sexual caste system' (Daly 1973b, p. 2). The five central chapters of *Gyn/Ecology* methodically laid out a shocking historical testimony.

At its most basic level, Daly suggested, patriarchy affects language. Men have usurped the fundamental activity of naming phenomena (cf. Gen. 2.18–19). Hence an essential component of Daly's work was the reversal of this theft: the 'castration' of masculine meaning, and the retrieval and redefinition of such a repertoire of vocabulary as to necessitate the publication of her own explanatory dictionary (Daly with Caputi 1987). She saw herself, for example, as a 'positively revolting hag', in the sense of a constructive, revolutionary woman, a cackling 'spinster' who laughed in the face of patriarchy and spun new webs of meaning, a 'crafty pirate' who skilfully plundered men's treasures for use by the sisterhood of women. She regarded such speech as the indispensable link between thought and action.

Christianity is one of the conceptual systems infected by patriarchy, with concomitant damage having been inflicted by the church on women (Daly 1968, pp. 74–114). Men have not only made God in their own image, projecting on to the divine their most distorted fantasies, they have then taken that image as their legitimation for human behaviour (cf. Hampson 2003, p. 146: 'The construct of God as "omni-everything" is masculinist to the core'). They have acted servilely in relation to a dominant deity, and conversely assumed a domineering role in relation to women. For Daly, the processions of the Godhead are as hierarchical and obnoxious as the processions of church, academy and military beloved by men on earth (Daly 1978, pp. 30, 37–45). Daly styled the Trinity as a homoerotic love-in; the incarnation as rape; and the ritual recollection and sacramental re-enactment of the incarnation as gang rape (Daly 1978, pp. 38, 109–10; 1984, p. 75). She was forthright and uncompromising.

Daly was also profoundly prophetic, having an 'urgency of vision' and an 'unwelcome message' for an 'uncomprehending audience' (Weaver 1985, p. 175). While, in the manner of prophets, she had blind spots, being criticized in due course for not taking sufficient account of multiracial and transsexual experience,[4] she was one of the earliest and most strident proponents of 'second-wave' feminism as it applied to religion, and proved herself again and again remarkably prescient, on matters from the iniquity of Nestlé baby milk marketing to the moral dubiousness of Christmas trees and the invasion of outer space (Daly 1984, pp, 53, 97–8; 1978, p. 1). 'When Daly is right she is very very right' (Madsen 2000, p. 334). She was particularly insightful about the long reach of patriarchy, its recurring features, and the strategies which its perpetrators use to deny and simultaneously perpetuate violence. Increasingly her work envisioned harmony with the animal kingdom and the forces of nature (with implicit echoes of Isaiah 11), on account of which she came to class her position as radical 'elemental' feminism (a stronger label, she thought, than radical ecofeminism) (Daly 1998, p. 235; Waslin 1995, p. 55).

Daly's rejection of Christianity was by no means atheistic in intent or result. While theology has a patriarchal habit of hypostatizing transcendence, turning God into a being, the reality of God was not, for her, dependent on such anthropomorphization (Daly 1973b, pp. 19, 33). Deity needed to be de-reified and (thus) de-limited: it was an intransitive verb rather than a noun, Be-ing rather than 'a Being'. Be-ing, having no object, undercuts the need for separation, and is the dimension of depth in all verbs (Berry 1988). The natural world participates in its powers: 'the Good Who is self-communicating Be-ing, Who is the Verb from whom, in whom, and with whom all true movements move' (Daly 1973b, p. 198; cf. Acts 17.28). For a short while, Daly used the word 'God' for Be-ing, but by the time of *Gyn/Ecology* she had come to view this appellation as fatally mired in sexist imagery and was content to refer to 'Goddess'. She felt it possible to relate to the divine personally, and was herself deeply affected, for example, by spiritual interactions with clover blossom and a hedge (Daly 1992, pp. 25, 51–2; 2006, pp. 46–7). Not for nothing has a mystical strain been identified in Daly's corpus (Monagle 2019). Indeed, Daly reflected that her doctoral studies were her way of rationally working through her experiences of depth – bringing philosophy to bear on her perception of ecstatic existence (Daly 1992, p. 418 n. 3). In this way, Daly's conception of divinity combined the twin dimensions of ultimacy and intimacy (corresponding to the transcendence and immanence of other theological systems).

Commentators have noticed how closely this feminist ontology aligns with two key influences on Daly's work: the Thomistic milieu in which she wrote her second and third doctorates, and the theology of Paul Tillich. Daly audited live lectures of Tillich in the late 1950s, and while she abhorred Tillich's moral failings, revealed by his widow after his death, the emphasis in Daly's writing on living 'at the boundary', the 'courage to be' (or in Daly's terms, the courage to see and 'sin big'), and the participation of beings in Being or ultimate reality, clearly accord with primary themes of Tillich's theological schema.[5] This encounter with Tillich can only have confirmed the participationist ontology which Daly imbibed from her immersion in Thomism for seven years at Fribourg (notwithstanding her revulsion at Aquinas's material on women).[6] The 'speculative theology' of her theological doctorate was an analysis of the *analogia entis*, under which positive knowledge of God could be obtained by and through God's creatures. Jacques Maritain's 'intuition of being', which Daly studied for her philosophical doctorate, likewise signified the intrinsic ability of concrete things to point beyond themselves; God could be inferred from the world. Daly gave this participationist ontology a dynamic twist, utilizing motifs of change and becoming in place of *stasis*. Although she distanced herself from process theism, there are clear resonances between her ontology and the type of philosophy inspired by Whitehead and Hartshorne.[7] If Eric Mascall wrote *He Who Is*, John Robinson *Thou Who Art*, Elizabeth Johnson *She Who Is* and Carol Christ *She Who Changes*, Mary Daly, reminiscent of the 'lure' of process divinity, wrote of 'She Who Attracts' (Daly 2006, pp. 17–29).

Such parallels are significant, because each of these three theologies – Thomism, Tillichianism and process theism – are attempts to move away from the ontological dualism which Daly so deplored. Dualism inherently tends to hierarchy. In conceiving of one reality, Thomists, Tillich and process theists provide an ontology which is conducive to the non-hierarchical, ethical demands of the feminist theological framework that Daly was constructing. Daly seems to imply at one point that her metaphysics could be construed as pantheism (Daly 1984, p. 400); but that descriptor may not be the best fit (Rodkey 2015, pp. 71–2). Given her insistence on the retention of some form of transcendence, it is possible that a more suitable construal would be panentheism,[8] which is, after all, the doctrine ascribable to Tillich and process theism, and a doctrine which comes suggestively close to some participationary accounts of Thomism (Bullimore 2022).

Daphne Hampson

By extraordinary coincidence, Daphne Hampson was in Cambridge, Massachusetts, on the day when Daly delivered her famous 'exodus' sermon, as she was spending a year at Harvard for a master's degree in theology (she happened not to be present and learnt about the event later in the day) (Hampson 1995). Born in Croydon and educated at boarding school, Hampson wished, as a teenager, to be ordained in the small and liberal Presbyterian Church of England (Brierley 2007, pp. 282–7). The church required ordinands to have a general arts degree; hence she went to read history and politics as an undergraduate at Keele, so excelling that she proceeded to work for a doctorate at Oxford on the British response to the German church struggle against the Third Reich. This left her wishing to pursue theology, so after teaching history for a year in the University of North Carolina at Greensboro, she studied at Harvard, and having written up her Oxford doctorate, took a lectureship in the history of religious thought at the University of Stirling (1974–76) before returning to the United States to begin a doctorate in theology (duly conferred in 1983). In 1977, she became the first woman with a full-time permanent position on the faculty of divinity at the University of St Andrews, where she remained (being awarded a personal chair in post-Christian thought in 2002) until 2003, when she retired to Oxford.

As a doctoral student at Oxford, Hampson had been drawn back to the Anglicanism of her early youth, and at St Andrews, she founded and chaired the Group for the Ministry of Women in the Scottish Episcopal Church and was involved in the English campaign for the ordination of women. Having become, however, literally sick with the lack of progress, in 1980 Hampson decided to leave the church. By this time she had wanted to be ordained for 20 years. 'Within weeks I was healing' (Hampson 1988a). For over a decade, she attended Quaker meetings, finding Quaker spirituality to be congruent with feminist values, but resisted joining the Society of Friends as a member.

Hampson has published five books, all since her departure from Christian faith: a textbook outlining her post-Christian position, *Theology and Feminism*; an extended post-Christian manifesto, *After Christianity* (1996a); an edited collection of essays by several contributors, debating Christianity (1996c); a historical study of Lutheranism and Catholicism, *Christian Contradictions* (2001); and an introduction to Kierkegaard (2013a).

Hampson consistently gives two separate reasons for rejecting Christian faith. The first is that God cannot have been uniquely incarnated in Jesus, for whatever God is, God cannot be related to one person in a different way from everyone else: God must potentially be available to all people in the same way. The 'scandal of particularity' is aptly named: there can have been no particular revelation in Jesus as the Christ. The second reason is expressly feminist: Christianity is intrinsically patriarchal in its symbol structure and its scripture. Its symbol structure conceives of God as other, placing God in a heteronomous relation to the self; and scripture is publicly read out as authoritative, its sexism thereby being imported from the past into the present and elevated as sacred, against the equality that should prevail between human beings. In this way, Christianity is not consonant with humanity's highest ideals.

Atheism is not Hampson's alternative to Christianity: 'The only exit (other than atheism) is to change one's conception of God' (Hampson 1988b, p. 128). Hampson remains, no less than Daly, a theist in the western theological tradition. She demands a 'major shift of paradigm in our conceptualization of what God is' (Hampson 1996a, p. 214, cf. pp. 249, 253). 'I want a revolution in how we conceive God' (Hampson 1987, p. 11). Like Daly, her theological work, beginning with her doctorate, has been a way of working out this revolution, configuring how the self relates to God. Hampson takes from Lutheranism the notion that the self lives only insofar as it is grounded in God (though she objects to the associated 'breaking' of the self that this involves) (Hampson 1988a). She seems antipathetic towards Catholicism, partly because of its institutionalism, and partly perhaps because of a Protestant (or feminist) aversion to ritual (Hampson 2007); while realizing that, at least in its participationist expressions, Thomist Catholicism seems not so very far from the coming-to-be of the self as grounded-in-God which she finds both in Luther and in Kierkegaard (Hampson 2001, pp. 6, 223, 243–4). She also draws on Schleiermacher, as the first major post-Enlightenment figure to think of the self in intimate connection with a God who is more than the self (Hampson 1996a, pp. 212–18; 2001, pp. 288–9).[9]

Hampson seeks a doctrine of God that fits with this view of the self as not 'monadic, with rigid ego-boundaries', but open and porous (Hampson 2005, p. 44). Accordingly, God is not 'separate' from the cosmos; for such separatism is a peculiarly masculine trait, leading to heteronomy and domination (Hampson 1998a, p. 223; 1990, p. 378; 1996, pp. 123–9) – the stance involved in worship (Hampson 1996a, pp. 78, 251). Moreover, the resultant God would be obliged to be interventionist, which is unacceptable from the standpoint of theodicy (Hampson 1996a, p. 237). Rather, God is that 'on to which we open out', 'immediately connected' to ourselves (Hampson 1996a, p. xix). '[W]e must conceive God to have an essential interconnectedness with all else that is. God then cannot become an other' (Hampson 1998a, p. 224). 'A conception of God as not to be separated from ourselves is alone compatible with human maturity' (Hampson 1989, p. 38; cf. 1993a, p. 56). With hints of Daly, Hampson describes God as 'spinning' or sustaining the web of reality (Hampson 1986, p. 57; 1988b, p. 139). God is that which empowers us, that on which we draw – a sort of reservoir of strength and love (not far from Daly's allusion to a 'flow of healing energy') (Hampson 1996, p. 251; Daly 1973, p. 41). Hampson therefore finds 'the sense of God as spirit ... particularly suggestive' (Hampson 1985, p. 347), and avers that a shift towards conceiving God as Spirit 'would constitute the undoing, yet also the renewal, of Western culture' (Hampson 2007, p. 74; 2009, p. 176). She warmed to the advocacy of this notion by Geoffrey Lampe (whom she knew personally), while finding Lampe problematic because of his Christology (a Christology typifying a strand of Anglican thought that, as will be seen below, escapes her criticism) (Hampson 1996b, p. 584; cf. Lampe 1977).

God, while not transcendent is, for Hampson, still beyond the cosmos, and has transcendental 'function' (Hampson 1996, pp. 240, 244, 247). She was firm in rejecting pantheism (Hampson 1985, p. 349), and took exception to its non-realist expression (Hampson 1997). She also thought it unavoidable for humans to relate to God personally (for example in prayer), for relating to an 'other' is the only way in which humans know how to relate (Hampson 1985, p. 349; 1996, pp. 241–3; 1998b, p. 140 n. 21). Thus Hampson has a doctrine of God remarkably like that of Daly: God as a power integrally related to creation, yet more than creation, and relatable to in personal terms. The simultaneous motifs of integral connection and 'beyondness' are hallmarks of panentheism and, as with Daly's doctrine of God, it is difficult to avoid the categorization of Hampson's God as anything other than panentheistic (Papanikolaou 2003, p. 43).

Hampson's first objection to Christianity is not watertight. By insisting that Christians are those who claim 'uniqueness' for Jesus as the Christ, she states that she aims to give Christianity the 'widest possible definition' (1994, p. 210). This is 'the only definition of Christianity which there could be' (Hampson 1996, p. 21). But this is not the case. Christians can be more widely defined as those who self-identify as Christian, regarding themselves in some sense as followers of Christ. Hampson's understanding rules out by definition those Christians who, like her, consider God to be potentially available to all people, and interpret Christ's 'uniqueness' in the sense that all human beings are unique – a Christology 'of degree' rather than 'of kind' (Hampson 1993b, p. 30 n. 5). This is the reason why some critics have declared Hampson to be decrying (only) a conservative version of the faith, and why Hampson has not comprehended the charge (Hampson 1992, p. 141; 1993b, pp. 23–4; 1996, pp. xv–xvi; cf. Daggers 2002, pp. 139–40). Hampson's own original Christian faith was markedly liberal, which may explain why liberal interpretations of

Christianity are not, for her, now viable. She is driven to decreeing that (on her definition) 'degree christologians' are not Christian, which unenviably puts herself in the position of heteronomy towards others that she so associates with patriarchy and abjures as incommensurate with feminism (Hampson 1990a, pp. 8, 63, 158–9; 1996a, p. 43; 2017).[10] Admittedly, only liberal interpretations of Christianity escape such a critique via this route, but there are plenty of liberal Christians (indeed, arguably a veritable tradition of Anglican liberals) who do so (cf. Hampson 1996, pp. 38–42).

Hampson's feminist objection to Christianity is more penetrating (Soskice 1996, p. 125). While non-dualistic (including panentheistic) ontologies counter Hampson's argument (held in common with Daly) that Christianity has dichotomized the divine, nevertheless the charge remains (as Daly also held) that the values of such ontological dualism yet impinge on human conduct. Scripture is just one of a number of ecclesial constructions that has soaked up patriarchal dualism, and the subliminal imbibing of that patriarchy, through scripture's normative status, requires conscious strategies of resistance. The position (and experience) of those who hold that such resistance is not worth the effort, even if not all Christians reach the same verdict, is to be respected.

Conclusion

While there are differences between the post-Christianities explored here – Hampson situates her work within the Enlightenment tradition, Daly was more independent from what she called 'male-stream' theology; Hampson is forensic in style, Daly more poetic; Hampson is by training a historian, Daly was more of an ethicist – nonetheless, both unite in perceiving Christianity to be imbued with a sexist symbol system based on a separatist ontology, and thus as fundamentally patriarchal. It has been seen that Daly and Hampson's preferred ontology is panentheistic, and to that extent, it is reconcilable with panentheistic forms of Christianity: 'behind the exotic appearance of Daly's "revolutionary" spiritual path one can … discern a "grammar" of divinity that is fundamentally coextensive with that of Christian theism' (Waslin 1998, p. 158).

> Daly's post-Christian God is very familiar to feminists who remain within the Christian tradition … one can read Daly as an illustration of what can happen to the Christian interpretation of existence when a relational metaphysics is substituted for a substantive metaphysics

> ... like many another philosopher in the twentieth-century Christian tradition, she ... spins [the substance philosophy] into the more fluid forms of relational philosophy ... Daly illustrates a Christian feminist response to the notion of God in covert form. (Suckocki 1994, pp. 63–4)

It has also been seen that there are liberal interpretations of Christian faith which circumvent Hampson's objection to Christology, while her assertion about patriarchal ecclesial praxis remains a serious issue for Christian faith.

One feminist has posited that the word 'post-Christian' is 'provisional' (Waslin 1996, p. 192). More precisely, it could be said that the term is 'transitional', defined by what it is not, in the sense that 'post-Christians' (like, say, 'post-evangelicals') are those who have left one region of faith or theology and are reassessing where they reside theologically, possibly prior to taking up life in another 'country'. Daly herself had moved on from the word by 1978, because it 'focused attention on where I had been rather than on where I now had arrived', rather like a woman 'identifying as a "divorcée" long after the event had occurred' (Daly 1978, p. xxiii). Indeed, it is possible to transition back again. Beverley Clack, for instance, became post-Christian in 1999 (not least after reading Hampson), because of difficulties that she had with doctrine and the church (Clack 1999). She found the church resistant to change, neither acknowledging its prejudice nor registering the cost of its inertia, and the normativity of scripture did not give room for the detailed criticism which its recitation required. Clack felt that she needed integrity and freedom, and that these were best found outside a Christian fold. By 2016, she had found her way back to Christian faith: she came to a new appreciation of Christian doctrine, and thought that patriarchy could most effectively be tackled from within. 'I am not now convinced that this post-Christian move is necessary' (Clack 2016, p. 233). Interestingly, Clack had not envisaged the original transition as necessarily permanent (Clack 1999, pp. 97–8). Sometimes, adherents may simply need 'time out'.

Some post-Christians have found a new 'home' in 'Goddess' theology, or 'thealogy'. Carol Christ (1945–2021) is an example of one post-Christian Goddess theologian whose work could profitably be compared to that of Daly and of Hampson (Christ 1997, 2002, 2003, 2016). Nor are all thealogians post-Christian: a number of leading contributors to the movement (such as Naomi Goldenberg and Melissa Raphael) hark from a Jewish background. 'Post-traditional' feminist theology is diverse, as is its traditional counterpart.

However far human symbol systems affect human behaviour, the record of Christianity is grim (e.g. Brock and Parker 2012). However far the Bible has a subconscious impact on those who hear it, it cannot be denied that parts of it are profoundly patriarchal. These facts need to be faced in all their fullness, and the potential harm implicit in Christian faith must be actively confronted and reversed.[11] The past needs to be rectified, doctrines need to be wholesomely constructed, and hermeneutics of suspicion and resistance need to be applied to scripture. Christian feminists believe that the liberative capacity of the faith outweighs its oppressive elements; post-Christian feminists assess the balance as tipping in the other direction. Christian feminists believe that the faith is capable of reformation (and are sometimes as astounded by the faith's ability to renew itself as they are horrified by its past); post-Christian feminists regard the transformation as too piecemeal or too slow. Christian feminists believe that 'strategies of resistance' can be harnessed for reading scripture; post-Christian feminists regard the deployment of such strategies as the necessary and burdensome rule rather than the exception (Wootton 2008, pp. 76–7; Jobling 2008, p. 89). Christian feminists believe that it is possible to engage with the pivotal figure of Jesus in inclusive ways; post-Christian feminists believe that the centrality of Jesus cannot avoid making maleness normative. These are matters of personal judgement, invariably informed by individual circumstances and biography, and good company is to be found on both sides. Carefully weighed decisions of conscience in each direction merit respect, even as different perspectives strive for liberation alongside one another.

Indeed, the common endeavour for liberative forms of theological discourse and ethics can bring Christians and post-Christians together. Given that the theologies of Daly and Hampson can be characterized as panentheistic, and that panentheism not only has a respectable place within Christian faith but a morally promising one, it is possible that there are greater opportunities for exchange and rapprochement between Christians and post-Christians than a simple oppositional framing of them might imply (cf. Brierley 2004; 2006). If symbol systems indeed affect ethical behaviour (and in turn are themselves affected by ethical considerations, as the history of modern doctrine shows), then open dialogue is one fruit of praxis that will indicate healthy doctrine (and may render it healthier still). '[Women] insist that the ultimate judge of any philosophical thinking is not simply coherence and consistency, but the pragmatic criterion of the philosophy's impact on communities of inclusive wellbeing' (Suckocki 1994, p. 67). Or, as said one astute prophet, 'wisdom is vindicated by her deeds' (Matt. 11.19).

Notes

1 It was the first baptism that I conducted as a newly ordained priest: since then, my practice has been to invite parents to hold their child for baptism, so that they are tangibly involved in the rite and have the best sight of the sacrament as it is administered, allowing the officiant to focus on the words and elements of the liturgy.

2 The notion that 'men can be feminists' might be an instance of the patriarchal tactic that Mary Daly called 'erasure', namely, masculine attempts to take over and erase women's voices and experience.

3 Without anthropological evidence, this contention would seem rhetorical. Daly's claim that all the world's religions function to legitimate patriarchy (Daly 1975, p. 20) similarly is more rhetorical than evidential. For Daly's use of rhetoric (and language), see Griffin 1993 and Ratcliffe 1996.

4 For racial critique of Daly, see Katherine 1999, and Hedrick 2013. For transsexual critique of Daly, see Kubala 2020, and the literature listed in Rodkey 2018.

5 For Tillich's influence on Daly, see Schneider, 2000; Stenger and Stone 2002, pp. 98–134; and Rodkey 2015.

6 For Thomist influence on Daly, see Waslin 1998, pp. 11, 88–119. Mary Hunt jokes that Daly was a 'peeping Thomist' (Hunt 2014, p. 225). Cf. Daly 1968, pp. 23–4; 1973, pp. 37–9.

7 Daly 1973b, pp. 188–9. Cf. Weaver 1985, pp. 171–2, 177; Waslin 2018, pp. 116–17; and Suhonen 2000, pp. 113, 125. Also Daly 1977, pp. 84–98.

8 Rodkey himself proposes that Daly is best situated among 'death of God' theologians (Rodkey 2018, pp. 166–7); and if the 'death of God' is read as the demise of classical theism then, again, panentheism becomes Daly's natural home.

9 Hampson is not so drawn to process theism, viewing its di-polar conception of God as still too dichotomous (Hampson 1996a, p. 134; 1996b, p. 584; cf. Clague 1998, p. 53).

10 Rosemary Radford Ruether accuses Hampson of absolutizing her own experience and ignoring 'the plurality of contemporary Christianity' (Hampson and Ruether 1987, p. 14).

11 As Catherine Keller says (1996, p. 133), it is not that Daly needs rebaptism, but that Christian faith needs rather to be baptized by Daly, in the sense of taking her critique with the utmost seriousness.

Bibliography

Wanda W. Berry, 1988, 'Feminist Theology: The "Verbing" of Ultimate/Intimate Reality in Mary Daly', *Ultimate Reality and Meaning* 11, pp. 212–32.

Michael W. Brierley, 2004, 'Naming a Quiet Revolution: The Panentheistic Turn in Modern Theology', in Philip D. Clayton and Arthur R. Peacocke (eds), *In Whom We Live and Move and Have Our Being: Panentheistic Reflections on God's Presence in a Scientific World*, Grand Rapids, MI: Eerdmans, pp. 1–15.

Michael W. Brierley, 2006, 'The Potential of Panentheism for Dialogue between Science and Religion', in Philip D. Clayton and Zachary R. Simpson (eds), *The*

Oxford Handbook of Religion and Science, Oxford: Oxford University Press, pp. 635–51.

Michael W. Brierley, 2007, 'The Panentheist Revolution: Aspects of Change in the Doctrine of God in Twentieth-Century British Theology', unpublished PhD thesis, University of Birmingham.

Rita N. Brock and Rebecca A. Parker, 2012, *Saving Paradise: Recovering Christianity's Forgotten Love for this Earth*, London: Canterbury Press.

Matthew J. Bullimore, 2022, 'Panentheism and Radical Orthodoxies', *Modern Believing* 63 (2), pp. 148–54.

Carol P. Christ, 1997, *Rebirth of the Goddess: Finding Meaning in Feminist Spirituality*, Reading, MA: Addison-Wesley Publishing Co.

Carol P. Christ, 2002, 'Feminist Theology as Post-Traditional Thealogy', in Susan F. Parsons (ed.), *The Cambridge Companion to Feminist Theology*, Cambridge: Cambridge University Press, pp. 79–96.

Carol P. Christ, 2003, *She Who Changes: Re-Imagining the Divine in the World*, New York: Palgrave Macmillan.

Carol P. Christ and Judith E. Plaskow, 2016, *Goddess and God in the World: Conversations in Embodied Theology*, Minneapolis, MN: Fortress Press.

Beverley J. Clack, 1999, 'On Leaving the Church', in Clive Marsh and Jane V. Craske (eds), *Methodism and the Future: Facing the Challenge*, London and New York: Cassell, pp. 88–98.

Beverley J. Clack, 2010, '"Just Dare and Care": Mary Daly 16 October 1928 – 3 January 2010', *Feminist Theology* 18, pp. 254–6.

Beverley J. Clack, 2016, 'On Returning to the Church: Practising Religion in a Neoliberal Age', *Modern Believing* 57, pp. 229–40.

Julie P. Clague, 1998, 'BISFT Interview with Dr Daphne Hampson', *Feminist Theology* 17, pp. 39–57.

Jennifer A. Daggers, 2002, *The British Christian Women's Movement: A Rehabilitation of Eve*, Aldershot: Ashgate.

Mary Daly, 1968, *Church and the Second Sex*, 3rd edn (1985), Boston, MA: Beacon Press.

Mary Daly, 1972, 'The Women's Movement: An Exodus Community', *Religious Education* 67, pp. 327–35.

Mary Daly, 1973a, 'Post-Christian Theology: Some Connections between Idolatry and Methodolatry, between Deicide and Methodicide', in Joan A. Romero (ed.), *Women and Religion: 1973: Pre-Printed Papers for the Working Group on Women and Religion*, Tallahassee, FL: American Academy of Religion, Florida State University, pp. 33–8.

Mary Daly, 1973b, *Beyond God the Father: Toward a Philosophy of Women's Liberation*, 2nd edn (1986), London: Women's Press.

Mary Daly, 1975, 'The Qualitative Leap Beyond Patriarchal Religion', *Quest* 1 (4), pp. 20–40.

Mary Daly, 1977, 'The Courage to Leave: A Response to John Cobb's Theology', in David R. Griffin and Thomas J. J. Altizer (eds), *John Cobb's Theology in Process*, Philadelphia, PA: Westminster Press, pp. 84–98.

Mary Daly, 1978, *Gyn/Ecology: The Metaethics of Radical Feminism*, 2nd edn (1990), Boston, MA: Beacon Press.

Mary Daly, 1984, *Pure Lust: Elemental Feminist Philosophy*, London: Women's Press.
Mary Daly, 1992, *Outercourse: The Be-Dazzling Voyage*, New York: HarperCollins.
Mary Daly, 1998, *Quintessence ... Realizing the Archaic Future: A Radical Elemental Feminist Manifesto*, Boston, MA: Beacon Press.
Mary Daly, 2006, *Amazon Grace: Re-Calling the Courage to Sin Big*, New York and Basingstoke: Palgrave Macmillan.
Mary Daly, forthcoming, *Catholicism: The End or the Beginning?*, ed. Margaret M. Stapleton Smith, Cambridge: Cambridge University Press.
Mary Daly with Jane Caputi, 1987, *Websters' First New Intergalactic Wickedary of the English Language*, Boston, MA: Beacon Press.
Frances M. Gray and Kathleen McPhillips, 2008, 'A Third Way: Explicating the Post in Post-Christian Feminism', in Lisa Isherwood and Kathleen McPhillips (eds), *Post-Christian Feminisms: A Critical Approach*, Aldershot: Ashgate, pp. 167–77.
Cindy L. Griffin, 1993, 'Women as Communicators: Mary Daly's Hagography as Rhetoric', *Communications Monographs* 60, pp. 158–77.
M. Daphne Hampson, 1985, 'The Challenge of Feminism to Christianity', *Theology* 88, pp. 341–50.
M. Daphne Hampson, 1986, 'Reinhold Niebuhr on Sin: A Critique', in Richard D. Harries (ed.), *Reinhold Niebuhr and the Issues of Our Time*, Oxford: Mowbray, pp. 46–60.
M. Daphne Hampson, 1988a, 'Luther on the Self: A Feminist Critique', *Word and World* 7, pp. 334–42.
M. Daphne Hampson, 1988b, 'On Power and Gender', *Modern Theology* 4, pp. 234–50.
M. Daphne Hampson, 1989, 'The Theological Implications of a Feminist Ethic', *Modern Churchman* 31 (1), pp. 36–9.
M. Daphne Hampson, 1990a, *Theology and Feminism*, Oxford: Blackwell.
M. Daphne Hampson, 1990b, 'Where Do We Go From Here?', *Theology* 93, pp. 373–80.
M. Daphne Hampson, 1992, 'On Being All of a Piece / At Peace', in Teresa L. E. Elwes, *Women's Voices: Essays in Contemporary Feminist Theology*, London: Marshall Pickering, pp. 131–45.
M. Daphne Hampson, 1993a, 'Theological Integrity and Human Relationships', *Feminist Theology* 2, pp. 42–56.
M. Daphne Hampson, 1993b, 'Sources and the Relationship to Tradition: What Daphne Hampson is Supposed to Hold (and What She in Fact Holds)', *Feminist Theology* 3, pp. 23–37.
M. Daphne Hampson, 1994, 'After Christianity: The Transformation of Theology!', *Literature and Theology* 8, pp. 209–17.
M. Daphne Hampson, 1995, 'Exodus or Not?', in Angela Berlis, Julie M. Hopkins, Hedwig Meyer-Wilmes and Caroline V. Stichele (eds), *Women Churches: Networking and Reflection in the European Context*, Yearbook of the European Society of Women in Theological Research 3, Kampen: Kok Pharos, and Mainz: Matthias-Grünewald Verlag, pp. 73–85.
M. Daphne Hampson, 1996a, *After Christianity*, 2nd edn (2002), London: SCM Press.

M. Daphne Hampson, 1996b, 'Monotheism', in Paul A. B. Clarke and Andrew Linzey (eds), *Dictionary of Ethics, Theology and Society*, London and New York: Routledge, pp. 582–5.

M. Daphne Hampson (ed.), 1996c, *Swallowing a Fishbone? Feminist Theologians Debate Christianity*, London: SPCK.

M. Daphne Hampson, 1997, 'On Being a Non-Christian "Realist"', in Colin G. Crowder (ed.), *God and Reality: Essays on Christian Non-Realism*, London: Mowbray, pp. 85–99.

M. Daphne Hampson, 2001, *Christian Contradictions: The Structures of Lutheran and Catholic Thought*, Cambridge: Cambridge University Press.

M. Daphne Hampson, 2003, review of Grace M. Jantzen, *Becoming Divine*, *International Studies in Philosophy* 35 (1), pp. 146–7.

M. Daphne Hampson, 2005, 'Reply to Laurence Hemming', *New Blackfriars* 86, pp. 24–47.

M. Daphne Hampson, 2007, 'The Sacred, the Feminine and French Feminist Theory', in Griselda F. S. Pollock and Victoria E. Turvey Sauron (eds), *The Sacred and the Feminine: Imagination and Sexual Difference*, London: I. B. Tauris, pp. 61–74.

M. Daphne Hampson, 2009, 'That Which Is God', in Gillian O. Howie and J'annine A. Jobling (eds), *Women and the Divine: Touching Transcendence*, New York: Palgrave Macmillan, pp. 171–86.

M. Daphne Hampson, 2010, 'Post-Christian Thought', in Daniel M. Patte (ed.), *The Cambridge Dictionary of Christianity*, New York: Cambridge University Press, pp. 988–9.

M. Daphne Hampson, 2013a, *Kierkegaard: Exposition and Critique*, Oxford: Oxford University Press.

M. Daphne Hampson, 2013b, 'The Question of God: Ethical and Epistemological Criteria', in Richard J. Noake and Nicholas A. V. Buxton (eds), *Religion, Society and God: Public Theology in Action*, London: SCM Press, pp. 49–63.

M. Daphne Hampson, 2017, 'Luther, Lutheranism, and Post-Christianity', in Derek R. Nelson and Paul R. Hinlicky (eds), *The Oxford Encyclopedia of Martin Luther*, vol. 2, New York: Oxford University Press, pp. 396–416.

M. Daphne Hampson and Rosemary R. Ruether, 1987, 'Is There a Place for Feminists in a Christian Church?', *New Blackfriars* 68, pp. 7–24.

Elizabeth A. Hedrick, 2013, 'The Early Career of Mary Daly: A Retrospective', *Feminist Studies* 39, pp. 457–83.

Sarah L. Hoagland and Marilyn P. Frye (eds), 2000, *Feminist Interpretations of Mary Daly*, University Park, PA: Pennsylvania State University Press.

Mary E. Hunt, 2010, 'On Mary Daly', *Journal of Feminist Studies in Religion* 26, pp. 7–9.

Mary E. Hunt, 2014, 'Pure Complexity: Mary Daly's Catholic Legacy', *Feminist Theology* 22, pp. 219–28.

Mary E. Hunt, 2017, 'Biographical Sketch', in Mary Daly, *The Mary Daly Reader*, ed. Jennifer J. Rycenga and Linda L. Barufaldi, New York: New York University Press, pp. xv–xix.

Lisa Isherwood and Kathleen McPhillips, 2008, 'Introduction', in Lisa Isherwood and Kathleen McPhillips (eds), *Post-Christian Feminisms: A Critical Approach*, Aldershot: Ashgate, pp. 1–10.

J'annine A. Jobling, 2008, 'Post-Christian Hermeneutics: The Rise and Fall of Female Subjectivity in Theological Narrative', in Lisa Isherwood and Kathleen McPhillips (eds), *Post-Christian Feminisms: A Critical Approach*, Aldershot: Ashgate, pp. 89–103.

Stephanie J. Kapusta, 2021, 'Mary Daly's Philosophy: Some Bergsonian Themes', *Feminist Philosophy Quarterly* 7 (2), pp. 1–27.

Amber L. Katherine, 1999, '(Re)reading Mary Daly as a Sister Insider', in Claudia F. Card (ed.), *On Feminist Ethics and Politics*, Lawrence, KS: University Press of Kansas, pp. 116–39.

Amber L. Katherine, 2000, '"A Too Early Morning": Audre Lorde's "An Open Letter to Mary Daly" and Daly's Decision Not to Respond in Kind', in Sarah L. Hoagland and Marilyn P. Frye (eds), *Feminist Interpretations of Mary Daly*, University Park, PA: Pennsylvania State University Press, pp. 266–97.

Catherine E. Keller, 1996, 'Mary Daly: 1928–', in Donald W. Musser and Joseph L. Price (eds), *A New Handbook of Christian Theologians*, Nashville, TN: Abingdon Press, pp. 127–34.

Juliana M. Kubala, 2020, 'Teaching "Bad Feminism": Mary Daly and the Legacy of '70s Lesbian-Feminism', *Feminist Formations* 32, pp. 117–36.

Geoffrey W. H. Lampe, 1977, *God as Spirit* (Bampton lectures, 1976), Oxford: Clarendon Press.

Catherine Madsen, 2000, 'The Thin Thread of Conversation: An Interview with Mary Daly', *Cross Currents* 50, pp. 332–48.

Clare Monagle, 2019, 'Mary Daly's *Gyn/Ecology*: Mysticism, Difference and Feminist History', *Signs* 44, pp. 333–53.

Aristotle Papanikolaou, 2003, 'Person, *Kenosis*, and Abuse: Hans Urs von Balthasar and Feminist Theologies in Conversation', *Modern Theology* 19, pp. 41–65.

Krista L. Ratcliffe, 1996, *Anglo-American Feminist Challenges to the Rhetorical Traditions: Virginia Woolf, Mary Daly, Adrienne Rich*, Carbondale, IL: Southern Illinois University Press, pp. 65–106.

Christopher D. Rodkey, 2015, 'The Nemesis Hex: Mary Daly and the Pirated Proto-Patriarchal Paulus', in Russell Re Manning (ed.), *Retrieving the Radical Tillich: His Legacy and Contemporary Importance*, New York: Palgrave Macmillan, pp. 65–80.

Christopher D. Rodkey, 2018, 'Mary Daly (American, 1928–2010)', in Christopher D. Rodkey and Jordan E. Miller (eds), *The Palgrave Handbook of Radical Theology*, Cham, Switzerland: Palgrave Macmillan, pp. 155–69.

Rosemary Radford Ruether, 2008, 'Ecofeminist Thea/ologies and Ethics: A Post-Christian Movement?', in Lisa Isherwood and Kathleen McPhillips (eds), *Post-Christian Feminisms: A Critical Approach*, Aldershot, Ashgate, pp. 39–52.

Laurel C. Schneider, 2000, 'The Courage to See and to Sin: Mary Daly's Elemental Transformation of Paul Tillich's Ontology', in Sarah L. Hoagland and Marilyn P. Frye (eds), *Feminist Interpretations of Mary Daly*, University Park, PA: Pennsylvania University Press, pp. 55–75.

Janet M. Soskice, 1996, 'Response', in M. Daphne Hampson (ed.), *Swallowing a Fishbone? Feminist Theologians Debate Christianity*, London: SPCK, pp. 125–8.

Mary Ann Stenger and Ronald H. Stone, 2002, *Dialogues of Paul Tillich*, Macon, GA: Mercer University Press.

Elizabeth B. Stuart, 2008, 'The Return of the Living Dead', in Lisa Isherwood and Kathleen McPhillips (eds), *Post-Christian Feminisms: A Critical Approach*, Aldershot, Ashgate, pp. 211–22.

Marjorie H. Suchocki, 1994, 'The Idea of God in Feminist Philosophy', *Hypatia* 9 (4), pp. 57–68.

Marja Suhonen, 2000, 'Toward Biophilic Be-ing: Mary Daly's Feminist Metaethics and the Question of Essentialism', in Sarah L. Hoagland and Marilyn P. Frye (eds), *Feminist Interpretations of Mary Daly*, University Park, PA: Pennsylvania University Press, pp. 112–31.

Kathryn Telling, 2012, 'Quite Contrary: Mary Daly Within and Without Women's Studies', *Journal of International Women's Studies* 13, pp. 32–43.

Susan J. Waslin, 1996, 'The Significance of Mary Daly's Thought for Feminist Theology', in Alison E. Jasper and Alastair G. Hunter (eds), *Talking It Over: Perspectives on Women and Religion, 1993–5*, Glasgow: Trinity St Mungo Press, pp. 169–93.

Susan J. Waslin, 1998, 'The Theoretical Contexts of Mary Daly's Thought', unpublished PhD thesis, University of St Andrews.

Mary Jo Weaver, 1985, *New Catholic Women: A Contemporary Challenge to Traditional Religious Authority*, New York: Harper and Row.

Janet H. Wootton, 2008, 'Who's Been Reading MY Bible? Post-Structuralist Hermeneutics and Sacred Text', in Lisa Isherwood and Kathleen McPhillips (eds), *Post-Christian Feminisms: A Critical Approach*, Aldershot, Ashgate, pp. 71–88.

Sakoto Yamaguchi, 2008, 'Re-Membering Jesus: A Post-Colonial Feminist Remembering', in Lisa Isherwood and Kathleen McPhillips (eds), *Post-Christian Feminisms: A Critical Approach*, Aldershot, Ashgate, pp. 179–99.

PART 4

Rite

17

Art and the Theology of Difference

CLAIRE RENKIN

'Pachamama': Controversies over images of the female body in Western Christianity: *Our Lady of the Amazon* in 2019

In October 2019 a meeting of the Catholic Indigenous people of the Amazon took place in Rome. This Amazon Synod, as it was called, brought together a diverse representation of Indigenous peoples who lived in the vast river basin. Pope Francis intended the meeting to be an opportunity for him and clergy at large to listen to, and debate with, representatives of many communities whose way of life is coming under threat from degradation of the forest as well as from economic and political marginalization. Francis urged the delegates (including the bishops of the Amazon) to listen to one another and to consider how the church can best meet the pastoral needs of Amazonia. In much of the western world the Synod of the Amazon barely rated a passing mention in the media and press. All that changed as soon as the media seized on the *vandalization* of a small wooden sculpture of a pregnant woman. Its story exemplifies some of the unexpected ways in which visual images can destabilize discourse about gender difference within Christianity.

What the American writer Rita Ferrone dubbed the 'L'affaire Pachamama' erupted around a sculpture that was installed temporarily during a tree-planting ceremony in the Vatican Gardens (Ferrone 2019, p. 11). During the ceremony, an Amazonian woman introduced the sculpture under the title *Our Lady of the Amazon*, whereupon the Pope blessed it. It did not take long before polemicists hurled denunciations of paganism and charges of idolatry against both the Indigenous sculpture and those who had taken part in the simple ceremony. Together with other objects that had been assembled in the Vatican Gardens, Pachamama was carried in procession from there to the nearby Carmelite church of St Maria Transpontina. A prayer corner had been prepared to receive diverse objects including a canoe, two figures representing martyrs, and

Pachamama, alias Our Lady of the Amazon. Amazingly, the ire of the 'self-appointed guardians of orthodoxy' fanned by right-wing media appears to have prompted a devout young Austrian to an act of vandalism, when he seized the sculpture of the Pachamama from the church and tossed it into the Tiber (Ferrone 2019, p. 11). The sculpture had to be fished out of the Tiber and returned to the church along with an apology from Pope Francis to the Amazonian peoples.

This remarkable episode reminds us of the Western Church's long history of suspicion, denunciation and obsessive surveillance meted out to depictions of women, most prominently Mary the Mother of God (Malone 2000, pp. 144–72; Johnson 2003, pp. 3–70). The core of these suspicions regarded any overly fleshy image of the Virgin as being either pagan or derived from pagan images. Having enculturated the Hellenistic philosophy of the ancient world, particularly that of Plato's followers, the patristic writers embraced an anthropology based on a binary hierarchy. This androcentric model tended to view women as deficient males. As we all know, the dualisms that accompanied this ideology privileged the male as rational, that is, moved by things of the spirit, whereas the same assumptions dismissed the feminine as being ruled by the passions of the flesh. It was assumed that few women (except saints) could transcend their bodily limitations. Thus, much of the language and many of the symbols of western Christian culture developed out of a habit of binary thinking. These habits of thought forbade women to transmute male-focused language and male-centred symbols into others that might validate women's experience and assert their difference from men. Instead, the culture we have inherited still incorporates a language that tends to define and contain women as nothing other than 'not male'.

By reactivating these outdated conceptual foundations, 'L'affaire Pachamama' signals yet again the extent to which the patriarchal ideology of the Catholic Church remains too readily captive to the binary thinking about sexuality and gender. To explain this heritage, the feminist theologian Tina Beattie emphasizes how the patristic fathers wrestled with the perceived threat of pagan polytheism. In her view their dread of the spectre of sexual violence and moral depravity provided the context in which the Mary/Eve typology emerged. In order to rescue Mary from any taint of influence by pagan cultic sex, Mary had to assume the role of a pure, sexless ideal, while Eve took on the opposite abject face of female sexuality degraded by sin (Beattie 2002, pp. 61–3).

As recently as four years ago in 2019, the sculpture of *Our Lady of the Amazon* triggered a similar charge of paganism, involving nothing less than 'a grave sin, a crime against the divine law' (Ferrone 2019, p. 1).

Attacks based on misinformed and crude understandings of Amazonian culture fed the hysteria of such denunciations. Throughout the Amazon region, the figure of Pachamama evokes for the Indigenous people the female goddess both of fertility and of Mother Earth. The complex history of the ways in which the figure of Pachamama gradually became associated with the Virgin Mary suggests a multi-layered process that dates back as far as the beginnings of colonialism in the sixteenth century (Tola 2018). It is precisely within a richly layered and multivalent system of meaning-making that the symbolic meaning of *Our Lady of the Amazon* gives expression to the aspirations of the Amazonian woman who drew the Pope's attention to the sculpture. This unnamed woman in the presentation to the Pope named the figure of a young heavily pregnant woman as an image of Mary. Almost immediately, journalists dismissed this woman's voice together with her awareness of her own personal relationship with this particular portrayal of the Mother of God. To heighten the controversy, journalists and their supporters sought out male clerics who supposedly could explain or, as jargon has it, 'mansplain' the identity of the figure! It was as if the authority of an Amazonian woman's own knowledge of her creatureliness counted for nothing in her quest to explain the image. Her awareness of the fleshly markers that she shared with the sculpted figure carried no weight with right-wing polemicists or the press (Ferrone 2019; Dodd 2019).

This stunning tale of how stubbornly some voices in a patriarchal church continue to reject women's experience cries out to be exposed. In the present atmosphere, how might those women and men who continue to search for a more inclusive, generous and life-affirming space within the church find meaning in biblical narratives that so often exclude the perspective of women? Is the language of prayer and theology so dominated by abstraction and dialectic that the renewal of metaphor and symbol seems all but impossible? I argue that the resources of the Catholic imagination do in fact provide us with symbols and stories that women can use to articulate a new perspective.

Writing as an art historian, I present some examples of such rethinking, whereby the gospel story of Christ's liberating mission gets shifted on to women's experience. Unlike so much western theology that seeks to 'capture in systems and dogma', the language of visual art can engage our imaginations and intellect in more expansive and embodied ways (Isherwood 2011, p. 166). For women, the quest to find language through which to speak of the Christian God stumbles over the patriarchal construct of the male God-father. This image of a male generative power leaves too little space for women to imagine God as a symbol of female fertility and sexuality. As Tina Beattie argues, in Catholic theology woman has functioned as a symbol that helps the male subject to orientate himself in relation to God and to his own creatureliness. Ignoring the facts of gender difference, such male-centred manipulation of symbols lacks any meaningful relationship to the female body or to the needs of women (Beattie 2002, p. 164).

Contemporary Images of a Woman-centered Biblical Narrative: Jan Hynes

The figure of Mary, Mother of God occupies a problematic position for feminist theologians. However, if we are to envision a theological space where women's bodies fully reflect the mystery and redemptive promise of the incarnation, the narrative of Mary's role in salvation offers us the tools to reconstruct a liberating model of redemption. In this version a narrative that eschews binary solutions seeks reconciliation between flesh and spirit, male and female. Visual language inspires feminine retelling of Marian narratives that challenges us to find a different image of God that embraces female subjectivity (Johnson 2003; Maunder 2019).

The first three of my four contemporary images come from the Australian artist Jan Hynes. Her paintings evoke the culture and physical landscape of Townsville, a mid-sized regional city located on the northeast coast of Queensland. Hynes finds her inspiration in the life of this town, and her works evoke the subtropical colours and abundance of plant, animal and bird life that provide a sensual visual environment for the social mixture of Indigenous Australians, Anglo-Celts and more recent immigrants. The paintings I discuss are part of a series inspired by the infancy narrative in Luke's Gospel. Jan's interpretations of the familiar stories of the annunciation and the visitation reimagine the narratives to reveal fresh readings. There is a playfulness in the way Hynes subverts and adapts the traditional symbols of Marian iconography in these paintings. In her painting of the annunciation Hynes invents a provocative title: *The Annunciation in Townsville: It's Come Back Positive* signals our contemporary domestic world in which the biblical story unfolds.

To be sure, Mary appears dressed in her traditional blue, while her generous, curvaceous body reveals her pregnancy. While the architectural features of her home (the tin roof and veranda – a necessity in the height of summer) situates the biblical story in a world remote from first-century Palestine, Hynes contrives to discern offbeat meanings in the refashioned

Figure 1: Jan Hynes, The Annunciation in North Queensland: It's Come Back Positive, *2005*

symbols and metaphors that she takes from the narrative of salvation history.

Our artist populates the scene with a number of familiar Australian features: red-flowering bush, a garden hose and the very prominent ibis. Other anecdotal inclusions, like a child's lamb-on-wheels and the tiny star hanging over the front door, expand the symbolic repertoire. Hynes employs this contemporary Australian setting in order to redeploy familiar symbols from the western visual tradition of scenes of the annunciation. Gabriel enters into Hynes' world suspended from a hang-glider, the angel's wings wittily transformed into the sails of the glider. The lily's evocation of Mary's purity finds a place in Hynes' Marian nod to tradition. Instead of dominating the composition, as is the case in so many paintings of the annunciation, Hynes' lilies stand silhouetted in the middle distance. Water spouting from the sprinkler hose recalls the image of a fountain as a symbol of salvation, an attribute of the Virgin since the Middle Ages. In the painting's translation of traditional symbols, the white ibis replaces the dove as a symbol of the Holy Spirit. In both a literal and figurative sense Hynes challenges the viewer to find meaning in this defamiliarizing portrayal of Mary, the virgin mother. No longer does her bodily image evoke a perfect and indeed unattainable model for women. Formal features, such as the shape of the painting, allude to art historical conventions that suggest certain cultural values. In a novel manner Hynes deploys the triptych form familiar from late medieval paintings of the Virgin and Child. The upper section of the three-part structure features the familiar Gothic arch.

How does Hynes' reframing of the annunciation story invite the viewer to imagine a different vision of the presence of the divine? My experience of teaching undergraduate and graduate theology students has led me to make the following observation. In the classroom, students respond to Hynes' *Annunciation* with both positive and negative reactions that divide by gender. Most students understand the substitution of colloquial, domestic features for the traditional iconography. Often women express delight particularly at seeing Mary depicted in a state of exhaustion with swollen ankles. But other students, typically young men, disapprove of the everyday suburban ordinariness of the setting. To paraphrase their objections: 'The annunciation doesn't look *like this*!' Often further discussion pinpoints specifically what evokes discomfort from these students: the depiction of Mary. Typically, women students agree that Hynes' depiction of Mary departs from the idealized beauty of so many Renaissance Madonnas. However, these women comment on how refreshing and inspiring they find it to gaze upon a Mary who reclaims the fecundity, indeed the fleshiness, of her body as a site of divine encounter. In Hynes' Mary, the pendulous breasts and swollen belly evoke – especially for women – the physicality of pregnancy. The incarnation takes place inside Mary's body, envisioned here as a space of flesh that will stretch and respond to the life within. Such a rendering of theological mystery situates the promise of God's reconciliation with creation within the messy flesh of Mary's body. As early as the fourth century the great church father Gregory of Nazianzus used the prescient words 'the subtlety of God and the density of flesh' to characterize what Jan Hynes has dramatized many centuries later: the fragility of the flesh where human life and the promise of redemption meet (quoted in Beattie 2002, p. 125).

Hynes continues to explore the Lukan infancy narrative from a feminist perspective in a further two paintings, *Elizabeth Meets Mary at the C-Bar Over Skinny Decaf Cappuccino and Carrot Cake* (2002) and *Elizabeth and Mary Meet at the C-Bar Over Black Coffee and Mud Cake* (2002).

Together these images unpack the stories of the visitation in a radically down-to-earth way. The two women share their relationality without

Figure 2: Jan Hynes, Elizabeth meets Mary at the C-Bar Over Skinny Decaf Cappuccino and Carrot Cake, *2002*

reference to any vertical presence of higher authority. Most important, the two women dwell in the present, yet with visible premonitions of what lies ahead. Mary wears a crucifix at her neck, a subtle reminder to the viewer of the suffering her son will endure. Elizabeth and Mary model the grace of living in the midst of the moment, witnessing life as it enfolds. Tina Beattie develops the concept of the 'broken middle' (derived from Gillian Rose), as the place where we live our lives grappling with the consequences of the Fall, yet we also dwell in a space of hope, the gift of Christ's incarnation (Beattie 2002, pp. 2, 49, 105, 126). Hynes' painting evokes how the ongoing reality of human history must always rub up against the 'not-yet mystery of the resurrection'. Hynes' New Testament women savour their own companionship without encountering males who may not understand what the women understand (Beattie 2016, p. 338).

The visitation featured as a popular subject in western art from the thirteenth century. Iconographically, the introduction of several male-

Figure 3: Jan Hynes, Elizabeth and Mary Meet at the C-Bar Over Black Coffee and Mud Cake, 2002

focused details into the scene reveals how easily the narrative became reframed to reflect a male ideology. Many depictions of the scene introduce Zechariah and Joseph, the husbands respectively of Elizabeth and Mary: for example, Lievens, *The Visitation*, 1638–40; del Piombo, *The Visitation*, c. 1508. Luke's text clearly indicates that neither man was present at the encounter between the two women. By inserting the men into the dramatic meeting between Elizabeth and Mary, artists supply the necessary reassurance to the viewing community, that the presence of husbands guarantees the social norms of patriarchal authority and control of the women's behaviour.[1] Second, it was common, especially in Italy, to show Elizabeth kneeling or in the act of kneeling as she greets Mary. Such a posture signalled to the viewer Elizabeth's recognition of the Virgin's status as 'mother of the Lord'. Indeed, as scholars have noted in Elizabeth's words to Mary, the older woman is the first in Luke's Gospel to name Jesus as Lord (Reid 1996, p. 72). Elizabeth's posture of honouring Mary cast their relationship as one in which patriarchal symbols of status and hierarchy are evoked. By expressing her unworthiness before Mary, Elizabeth's act acknowledges the inequality between her son John the Baptist and Christ.

Hynes' portrayal of the story accentuates a different set of values, which are evoked in the encounter between two women. In the earlier painting, *Elizabeth meets Mary at the C-Bar over Skinny Decaf*, the two women appear before the viewer reaching out towards each other (Figure 2). Traditionally artists drew attention to the age difference between the women. Often Elizabeth appeared with sunken cheeks and a lined face. Here Hynes instead shows Elizabeth dressed in a way that suggests the older woman's sensible approach to life. Her maturity and kindness stand out as she reaches out to the younger woman with both hands. Her firm grasp of Mary's hand and the steady, inquiring gaze directed at her younger cousin denote tender solicitude. The viewer observes Mary's vulnerability: her sunburned arms and downward gaze remind us of the perils of Mary's journey from Nazareth to Elizabeth's home in the uplands of Judah. Awe radiates from these majestically fecund women. The viewer's sense of the immanence of the divine relies not on haloes or cherubs floating on puffy white clouds. Hynes communicates the profound mystery of incarnation in the mutuality of each woman's knowing of God through the bodiliness of her unexpected pregnancy (Reid 1996, p. 81). Hynes' painting evokes many women's experiences of finding support and affirmation of each other in the demanding circumstances of pregnancy. Elizabeth and Mary's solemn physical embrace unfolds before us like a mutual blessing they confer upon each other. As they reach out to each other they claim their part in salvation history, for each other and indeed for all humanity.

Hynes takes up the story of Elizabeth and Mary in her painting titled *Elizabeth and Mary meet at the C-bar over Black Coffee and Mud Cake*, 2004 (Figure 3). Several years have elapsed since the two women greeted each other and shared the news of their unexpected pregnancies. In the foreground their children John the Baptist and Jesus playfully anticipate the future moment of John's baptism of Jesus. Once again Elizabeth and Mary meet in the same cafe we saw in the earlier painting. Now their body language suggests a more introspective mood. Though none of the Gospels describe such a scene, Hynes explores the gaps in the textual narrative in order to probe beyond the silences of the text. The gestures and facial expressions of the two women make plain that they are caught up in reflection. The Gospels rarely describe moments in which a woman's subjectivity, her capacity to reflect on her situation, might be understood as theologizing. We are told after the annunciation to the shepherds (Luke 2.19) and after the finding in the temple (Luke 2.51) how Mary treasured up all these things and pondered over them in her heart. At both moments the narrator's characterization of Mary's inner response highlights her freedom not to rush to judgement. Instead, by 'keeping' these moments in her heart, she practises what we might identify as a discerning openness to God's promise. Hynes' painting of two women portrayed in a moment of tiredness, attentiveness to each other and reflective along-sidedness frames this scene through the image of Mary as disciple. Hynes' Mary listens, contemplates and thinks about how her life is shaped by God's Spirit. The painting invites the viewer to explore the uncertainty and challenge of occupying the space of the broken middle, where for women the messiness of our lives becomes the matter of everyday theological praxis.

A Transition from the Virgin Mother to the Holy Harlot

The final section of this chapter will configure differently certain elements of the praxis of difference that I have engaged so far. As I have suggested, visual images like Jan Hynes' infancy paintings or the work of Indigenous artists disrupt expectations based on the patriarchal artistic and theological canon. Now attention shifts to a polar opposite of the Virgin: Mary Magdalene. After the Virgin, the Magdalene for centuries occupied an honoured place in the devotional life of Catholics. And just as the Virgin accumulated devotional titles striving to capture in figurative language in art and hymnody the devotional and cultural role of the Virgin as not only virgin mother, but virgin, wife and widow, so we find that the figure traditionally identified as Mary Magdalene similarly unleashed the fervour of the devout. However, unlike the roles and expectations assigned to the Virgin, the Magdalene inspired devotion that extolled and venerated her in not one but many roles. She had been a penitent prostitute, an apostle to the apostles, a preacher, a desert mother and an exemplary intercessor for the most notorious sinners. This woman, who in John's Gospel first announces the resurrection of Christ to the disciples, challenged lots of the religious, social and gender categories of the western Christian tradition. Having never been a virgin or a wife or a mother, the Magdalene even today continues to subvert saintly and gender paradigms (Jansen 1999; Arnold 2018; Haskins 1994; Wijnia 2021).

Her cult arose from a complex interweaving of sources that include both scriptural and legendary material. In the West, the cult of the Magdalene found its origins in a sermon preached in September 591 by Pope Gregory the Great (590–604). In this homily, Pope Gregory proclaimed, 'We believe that this woman [Mary Magdalene] whom Luke calls a female sinner, whom John calls Mary is the same Mary from whom Mark says seven demons were cast out' (Jansen 1999, pp. 32–3). Gregory conflated no fewer than three distinct female figures from the New Testament: (1) Mary, the sister of Martha and Lazarus; (2) the unnamed woman who anoints Christ's feet (and also his head in Matthew's and Mark's Gospel); and (3) Mary of Magdala, whom Christ freed from the possession of demons. Owing to Gregory's authority, for almost a thousand years the Magdalene functioned in the church as a *conflation* of three distinct figures (Jansen 1999, pp. 32–5).

The triplicated female saint who emerges from Gregory's homily embodied many of the paradoxes of female identity in the Christian tradition. Medieval interpreters celebrated (1) her spiritual growth from public sinner to penitent contemplative; (2) her symbolic embodiment of the church; and (3) her initial role as apostle to the apostles. By the early sixteenth century, Gregory's conflation faced serious challenges. Protestant theology *replaced* the notion of a tripartite converted sinner/prostitute with the single figure of Mary of Magdala, from whom Christ expels seven demons (Luke 8.2–3). Protestants also emphasized John's account of the risen Christ's appearance to Mary Magdalene after the resurrection. In 1969, Pope Paul VI accepted Protestant and Eastern Orthodox practice when he declared that, 'as the result of scholarly re-evaluation of her biblical persona', Mary Magdalene's character was officially relieved of its sinful imputation (Haskins 1994, p. 388). Now shorn of her doubtful scriptural additions and legendary material, the Magdalene seems ready to face the modern world. But does she?

Whereas in past centuries visual images of the Magdalene mirrored a vast array of contradictory and even subversive roles, today images of the Magdalene tend to pare down the multiplicity of the traditional figure. The very complexity of her supposed roles subverts any attempt to confine women in a narrow or fixed role.[2] Here the concept of 'queering' or 'skewing' the traditional Magdalene may provide a more imaginative and expansive terminology for interpreting ways in which the Magdalene's imagery continues to speak to us (Cheng 2011). By eluding the constraints of fixed roles, her figure can function for us as the quintessence of anti-reductionism. The Magdalene can personify feminists' combat against reductive thinking about women's roles in the church and their emerging difference from traditional ones.

CLAIRE RENKIN

Donatello's *Penitent Magdalen*, a Work Dated *c.* 1450

Donatello's statue of the penitent Mary Magdalene remains one of the most powerful and moving images of this saint, or indeed of any saint.

Sculpted in wood and then gilded, the statue exudes an effect of visual opulence, particularly on the surface of the saint's hair. The *vita eremitica*, which appeared first in the ninth century, narrates the Magdalene's escape into the desert in pursuit of a life of penitence and prayer. In assimilating the Magdalene's legendary conversion to a life of asceticism with the life of another converted prostitute, St Mary of Egypt (fourth century), the Magdalene's path to holiness acquired features familiar from this ancient *vita*. In fact, the enduring image of the Magdalene clothed in nothing but her own hair had originated in the iconography of Mary of Egypt. By the late twelfth century the story of how

Figure 4: Donatello, The Penitent Magdalen, *c. 1450*

she had pursued a solitary life in the desert or, as some claimed, also in the wilderness around Sainte-Baume in south-eastern France, inspired visual imagery in churches, monasteries and illuminated books. Particularly in France, her existence as a 'desert mother' showed a female saint's power to *destabilize* or even to rebut a key church teaching that held that women's fallen, polluted bodiliness debarred them from exercising spiritual authority (Ward 1987, p. 10–26; Glover 2023, pp. 36–40).

More vividly than any other artist, Donatello dramatized how the differentness of her body exuded authority. Until the mid-twentieth century, Donatello's Magdalene stood in the Baptistery of Florence Cathedral (Dunkelman 2005–06, pp. 10–13). Today this eye-catching sculpture dominates a dimly lit gallery in the museum of the Duomo. Although she stands erect, her haggard face betrays the ravages of a harsh ascetic life. Her litheness, luxurious hair and ease of movement convey both strength and formidable spiritual power. In a manifestation of striking difference, her body looks not so much surprisingly robust as androgynous in its muscularity, its lack of body fat, and its all-round fitness.

Conclusion

The stunning 'queering' of Donatello's woman reminds us that contemporary discourse tends to diminish scriptural figures like the Magdalene, whereas the western visual tradition does just the opposite. Donatello maximizes the differentness of this woman. He shows yet again how visual art pushes boundaries. The controversies triggered by the 'Pachamama' Affair like the offbeat images of the Virgin by Jan Hynes take us into the same unheard kind of territory.

In my own classroom practice, I draw on the multiple interpretative possibilities that visual images of Mary Magdalene suggest. Few female figures of the Christian tradition evoke so relentlessly many sorts of ambiguity. If, as we know, symbolic language shuns fixed meaning, how for example does the ointment jar, one of the Magdalene's attributes, keep evoking multiple meanings?

Figure 5. Jan van Scorel, Mary Magdalene, *c. 1530.*
Used with permission, Rijksmuseum, Amsterdam.

Through a list of questions about the jar, let us enumerate some of the ways in which this symbol tends to unleash creative instability: is this the ointment jar of the prostitute? Or does it serve mainly to remind us about the Magdalene's ancient role of the bringer of myrrh (*myrrhophore*) to anoint Christ's body at the tomb? Or, rather, does it serve above all to recall Mary of Bethany's prophetic anointing of Christ's feet in John's Gospel? Looking further back in salvation history, we find an echo of the ointment jar which the bride in the Song of Songs carries as she searches for her beloved. Rather shockingly, all of these references allude to the sensual skin-on-skin encounter in which the Magdalene engages (Jolly 2014). Any act of anointing that a woman performs on a man's body affronts patriarchal narratives that construct women's fleshliness as an obstacle to male salvation. Teaching practices that upset assumptions about canonicity and authority open spaces for thinking and seeing in new ways. These practices help us to attend to previously overlooked details that challenge what has been a dominant narrative. In all the ways that I have mentioned, offbeat visual images can subvert or queer conventional theology concerning women.

Notes

1 In the late Middle Ages popular devotional texts like the *Meditations on the Life of Christ* write how Mary sets off from Nazareth with her spouse, travelling during the day in order to avoid being noticed by people. See Pseudo-Bonaventure 1961.

2 Both Jansen (1999, p. 336) and Arnold (2018, pp. 223–43) bring a more nuanced analysis to the role of hagiographical sources in the study of feminist history and theology. Tina Beattie (2016, pp. 335–8, 347–8) argues that too much of contemporary biblical and feminist scholarship dismisses or overlooks the rich 'layerings of interpretations' that texts by women and images of them disclose about the figure of the Magdalene.

Bibliography

Diane Apostolos-Cappadona (ed.), 2018, *Biblical Women and the Arts*, New York: T&T Clark.

Margaret Arnold, 2018, *The Magdalene in the Reformation*, Cambridge, MA: Belknap Press.

Tina Beattie, 2002, *God's Mother, Eve's Advocate: A Marian Narrative of Women's Salvation*, London: Continuum.

Tina Beattie, 2016, '"The Touch that Goes Beyond Touching": A Reflection on the Touching of Mary of Magdala in Theology and Art', in Reimund Bieringer, Barbara Baert and Karlijn Demasure (eds), *Noli me tangere in Interdisciplinary Perspective: Textual, Iconographic and Contemporary Interpretations*, Leuven: Peeters.

Frank Burch Brown (ed.), 2014, *Oxford Handbook of Religion and the Arts*, New York: Oxford University Press.

Patrick S. Cheng, 2011, *Radical Love: An Introduction to Queer Theology*, New York: Seabury Books.

Liz Dodd, 2019, 'The Dishonest Cruelty of the Thief Who Drowned Our Lady of the Amazon', *The Tablet*, 22 October, https://www.thetablet.co.uk/blogs/1/1313/the-dishonest-cruelty-of-the-thief-who-drowned-our-lady-of-the-amazon (accessed 27.3.24).

Martha Levine Dunkelman, 2005–06, 'Mary Magdalen: A Model of Courage and Survival', *Woman's Art Journal* 26 (2), pp. 10–13.

Rita Ferrone, 2019, 'A Hermeneutic of Suspicion: L'affaire Pachamama', *Commonweal* 146 (17), online: https://www.commonwealmagazine.org/hermeneutic-suspicion, (accessed 18.12.23).

Sarah Glover, 2023, 'Queering Early Monasticism, The Lives of Ascetic Women: A Preliminary Investigation', *Tjurunga* 98, pp. 36–40.

Susan Haskins, 1994, *Mary Magdalen: Myth and Metaphor*, New York: Harcourt, Brace and Co.

Lisa Isherwood, 2011, 'Dancing Theology on Earthquakes: Trends and Direction in Feminist Theologies', *Expository Times* 122 (4), pp. 157–66.

Katherine Jansen, 1999, *The Making of the Magdalen: Preaching and Popular Devotion in the Later Middle Ages*, Princeton, NJ: Princeton University Press.

Elizabeth A. Johnson, 2003, *Truly Our Sister: A Theology of Mary in the Communion of Saints*, New York: Continuum.

Penny Howell Jolly, 2014, *Picturing the 'Pregnant' Magdalene in Northern Art, 1430–1550*, Farnham: Ashgate.

Mary T. Malone, 2000–03, *Women and Christianity, The First Thousand Years*, 3 vols, Dublin: Columba Press.

Chris Maunder (ed.), 2019, *The Oxford Handbook of Mary*, Oxford: Oxford University Press.

Margaret Miles, 1989, *Carnal Knowing: Female Nakedness and Religious Meaning in the Christian West*, Boston, MA: Beacon Press.

Pseudo-Bonaventure, 1961, *Meditations on the Life of Christ: An Illustrated Manuscript of the Fourteenth Century, Paris, Bibliothèque Nationale, Ms. Ital. 115*, Isa Ragusa and Rosalie B. Green (eds), Isa Ragusa (trans.), Princeton, NJ: Princeton University Press.

Barbara E. Reid, 1996, *Choosing the Better Part? Women in the Gospel of Luke*, Collegeville, MN: The Liturgical Press.

Miriam Tola, 2018, 'Between Pachamama and Mother Earth: Gender, Political Ontology and the Rights of Nature in Contemporary Bolivia', *Feminist Review* 118, pp. 25–40.

Benedicta Ward SLG, 1987, *Harlots of the Desert: A Study of Repentance in Early Monastic Sources*, Oxford: A. R. Mowbray and Co.

Lieke Wijnia (ed.), 2021, *Mary Magdalene: Chief Witness, Sinner and Feminist*, Zwolle: Waanders Publishers; Utrecht Museum Catharijneconvent.

18

Feminist Preaching: A Proclamatory Movement to End Patriarchy for Full Humanity

HYERAN KIM-CRAGG

What is at Stake?

I wrote this chapter with a sense of urgency. Some people think that feminism is opaque or even outdated. But the issues that feminists have worked so hard on for decades are far from being resolved. In fact, misogyny is on the rise. As a reaction to the #MeToo movement, a counter-narrative of anti-feminism is being constructed and told. Gender-based violence and sex-trafficking are growing around the world. I approach feminist preaching in this dire context where women's bodies are sold and beaten up and women's leadership is threatened and squashed down. Most of all, blunt anti-feminist rhetoric and misogynist speech are spreading in public and gaining popularity, including but not limited to the forum of Christian preaching. Such homiletical speech is not unrelated to hate speech, because its goal is to promote hatred towards women and justify gender-based oppression and discrimination. Any discourse on praxis and method on feminist preaching must address this context with a keen awareness.

In this chapter, I will disclose the blunt opposition to women's preaching by showcasing a sermon that John MacArthur preached on 9 November 2019 at Grace Community Church where he has been the pastor since 1969 (Grace Church 2023). In a sermon titled 'Does the Bible Permit a Woman to Preach?', he explains his opposition based on 1 Corinthians 14.34–35. Analysing this representative sermon may help us reflect on what is at stake in advancing feminist preaching. Today there are too many preachers like MacArthur, unfortunately. He is arguably one of the most popular, at least in the US, because of his influence through his website radio programme called *Grace to You*. His sermon serves as an example of what feminist preachers come up against.

Second, I will lift up remarkable feminist and womanist homileticians and their scholarly contributions. This scholarship effectively contests and directly contradicts the arguments that preachers like MacArthur make. Furthermore, readers may be inspired by these contributions that go beyond simple oppositional or reactionary tracts but tap into deep wells of wisdom that are fundamental to preaching in general and feminist preaching in particular. A final observation will illuminate culminative homiletical insights in order to advance feminist preaching.

Interrogation of the Sermon 'Does the Bible Permit a Woman to Preach?'

Preaching Style and Sermon Pattern

MacArthur's sermon is quite authoritarian and argumentative in terms of style. This style seems to suit his purpose to persuade his audience 'why' women should not preach. His sermon is charged with energy. He preaches for 75 minutes! It is hard to know what motivated him to preach this sermon exactly, but he begins his sermon by saying that the issue of women preachers was raised on the Internet and he was somehow implicated in the discussion. One may guess that his position was challenged and became controversial.

MacArthur's sermon is expository in that a message is derived from scripture. The purpose of expository preaching is to promote 'the centrality and the authority of Scripture in the task of preaching' (McClure 2007, p. 30). It is also deductive in terms of how it unfolds. That is, a main message is already stated at the beginning and then reasons are provided for why that message is posited as correct and true. Even if the title is inquisitive – 'Does the Bible Permit a Woman to Preach?' – its main message is less open ended. In fact, its message is blunt: 'The Bible prohibits women from preaching.'

Homiletical Exegesis and the Treatment of the Bible

The sermon selects limited passages in the Bible and treats them as if they were representative of the entire Bible. As a matter of fact, the choices are very selective. There are no passages from the Gospels quoted and surprisingly there is absolutely no mention of Jesus, other than a single reference to Jesus Christ as the head of the church. The selected passages come from a few Epistles: 1 Corinthians 14 (used as the main text for the sermon); 1 Corinthians 11; 1 Corinthians 6; Ephesians 5; Titus 1; Titus 2; 1 Timothy 2; and Galatians 3. The sermon also makes some sweeping references to the Hebrew Bible (e.g. Genesis 3 and Isaiah 3). It is apparent that this sermon heavily relies on the Epistles. Notably, leaders such as Miriam and Deborah are not mentioned.

The sermon introduces Greek words, such as αἰσχρὸν (aischron) meaning 'improper' or 'shameful' or 'disgraceful' (1 Cor. 14.35) and how this word appears in such texts as 1 Corinthians 11.6; Ephesians 5.12; Titus 1.11 in an attempt to justify the silence of women in the church. This kind of cross-referencing tactic attempts to convince the audience that this biblical teaching about women preachers is universal and ubiquitous because the same word is used in different churches at different times.

Yet I suggest that this kind of selective reading and literalist (fundamentalist) approach to the Bible is unhelpful as it does not take account of the particular context from which various Epistles are written. It does not note how some of the pastoral Epistles (e.g. 1 and 2 Timothy and Titus) are pseudepigraphal, which, as most scholars agree, means that they were composed in the post-Pauline era in the late first and second century where gender hierarchy was being established.

Preaching Content: Over-reliance on Paul's Teaching at the Expense of the Teaching of Jesus

The sermon claims that Paul's teaching, namely, that women should be silent in the church, is crystal clear. Furthermore, at one point in the sermon it makes a bold claim that Paul's teaching is a divine doctrine because it is universal and ubiquitous. In other words, it argues, the lesson from Paul for the church in Corinth has been and should be applied, not just for that local church to follow at a particular time but for all believers everywhere and at all times.

The sermon continues to claim that Paul's teaching is unmistakable because his word is inspired by the Holy Spirit. It links Paul's word with the word of God, stressing how Paul's teaching is in line with a divine order, a hierarchical order, citing Ephesians 5.22–24 (NIV):

> Wives, submit yourselves to your own husbands as you do to the Lord. For the husband is the head of the wife as Christ is the head of the

church, his body, of which he is the Saviour. Now as the church submits to Christ, so also wives should submit to their husbands in everything.

Then, it states, 'What Paul wrote is the Lord's command',[1] suggesting that the word of Paul becomes the word of God.

I use the verb 'link' intentionally here to indicate that this argument of women's silence in the church, based on Paul's advice to the church in Corinth, is closely linked to the patriarchal reference of women's submission to men. To back up the argument as to why Paul's word is the word of God and why women's subordination to men and wives' submission to husbands is taken as a divine order, the congregation is directed to Genesis 3, particularly 3.16, where God is depicted as speaking to Eve: 'I will greatly increase your pangs in childbearing; in pain you shall bring forth children, yet your desire shall be for your husband, and he shall rule over you' (NRSV). Again, this sermon links the woman's experience of pain in childbirth to a universal experience, and so too the husband ruling over his wife. However, it is notable that the sermon never mentions Genesis 1 where God created both men and women equally in God's image. Rather, it refers only to how Eve came second to Adam as a helpmeet in Genesis 2. Instead of seeing both texts in Genesis in tension, or at least noting these differences, the sermon limits its understanding to select passages rather than the whole story in the book of Genesis, which is not seamless but ambiguous, and not monolithic but plural (Beavis and Kim-Cragg 2017, p. 22).

Sermon Illustrations and References to Anti-Communist and Colonialist Conquering Agenda

Without apparent awareness of decades of scholarship on victim blaming, the sermon even suggests that women have overpowering desires that must be controlled by men for the sake of the harmony of the world. What is implied in this preaching is that the desires women have are inherently dangerous, rebellious, and against God's will. Following this logic, strong women must be squashed because when we have strong women, we have weak men, and weak men lead to the destruction of the order of the world. The sermon appears to establish the submission of women to men as a divine order that necessitates women's silence in church, and to directly infer from this that women should not preach.

The sermon goes on to attack the feminist movement as rebellious, feminist issues as monstrous, associating it with what he calls 'cultural Marxism', a destructive force that ruins the world. The Christianity that this represents is tainted with the 'red-complex', an irrational ideological dualism that sees as negative anything associated with socialist ideas. Such sermons agitate their hearers with Cold War politics.

In order to maintain the notion of a gender hierarchy, the sermon argues that gender lines must be irreducibly drawn and regarded as divinely ordained, and this includes gender-confusion, crossing-gender or gender-blurring as a threat to the divine hierarchy. As part of this, the sermon ridicules men visiting women's clothing stores and men growing their hair long. It even suggests that it is the scientific fact that women's hair is supposed to grow faster than men's because God created them that way and that is how women with beautiful long hair glorify God. Comments such as these may well be interpreted as homophobic and transphobic.

The final remark exposes the sermon's hidden agenda. After making an appreciative comment about his church's female members, whom the preacher describes as tender, kind and sweet, he says, 'Men, we have our worlds to conquer.'[2]

Contributions of Womanist and Feminist Homileticians

Many sermons, such as the one examined above, are not only anti-feminist but pro-conquest. They posit that feminism is an enemy of men whose mission is to conquer the world, and women preachers are dangerous because they could become agents to stop men from conquering the world. MacArthur is not wrong here. Women preachers and many conscientious preachers of every gender identity do indeed feel called to preach against conquering the world by men, or by anyone. Preaching should be liberative because it seeks to save humans from such negative pursuits as conquest. David Buttrick captures this purpose of preaching succinctly:

> Preaching is liberation. We speak to set people free ... There can be no redemption of the self without a liberation of the social world, and no redemption of the social world without release from the self's inner bondage. All we are saying is that preaching, as it shares God's saving purpose, will be a liberating word. (Buttrick 1987, pp. 452–3)

If women's silence contributes to conquering the world, feminist preaching must contribute to breaking that silence. Violence should never be the agenda of Christianity. And Christian preaching should never be used as a means to condone and commit violence. Breaking that silence by sharing the good news of Jesus Christ is a primary goal of womanist and feminist preaching.

Literature Review

With this goal in mind, let us briefly review some, not all, monographs on womanist and feminist preaching published in North America. This review may help identify characteristics, theories and practices of womanist and feminist preaching. Drawing a firm line between womanist and feminist preaching publications may not be fruitful, albeit recognizing their distinctiveness. Thus, I will treat them in a more organic way by arranging them chronologically in ways to demonstrate how pivotal moments and central thoughts have emerged along with their points of convergence and divergence.

Around the same time that womanist thought emerged in 1985, there was an intellectual movement to make women preachers visible, which led to the publication of the series, *Those Preachin' Women* (Mitchell 1988, p. 13). This movement is remarkable when we consider how strong the opposition to women in the pulpit has been. Ella Pearson Mitchell called the growing interest in this publication 'a miracle' when there was a second printing required less than a year following its release. This excellent and successful publication multiplied to four volumes (1985–2008) and continues to flourish today.

The term 'womanist' was coined by Alice Walker in 1979 in her short essay, 'Coming Apart' (Johnson 2017, p. xvii). In Walker's 1983 essay collection, *In Search of Our Mothers' Gardens: Womanist Power*, she defined womanism as the approach of a 'black feminist or a feminist of color' that took seriously the experiences of African American women by simultaneously analysing the threefold oppression of racism, sexism and classism (1983, p. xi). By 'simultaneously' we mean without denying or subordinating any aspect of these triple forms of oppression but attending to them in interlocking ways. Womanist work began as a protest to both white feminists who neglected race and class issues and male (including Black) liberationists who failed to consider gender (Bridgeman 2014, p. 432). Womanist homiletics sheds light on these multidimensional realities of oppressions when preachers interpret the ancient text and engage the current realities, including sexist language and oppressive practices, by using emancipatory practices and embodied rhetorical praxis (Cannon 1993; Fry Brown 2003; Weems 2006; Flake 2007; Thompson 2018). Womanist homiletics has a mandate to name interlocking systems of oppression in preaching (Johnson 2017, p. 105). Its goal is to form an appreciation of the way in which the African American woman's experience has informed her sacred rhetoric. Its goal is also to expand the Black preaching tradition to include a concept of emancipatory wholeness (Allen 2013, pp. 82–3).

One of the first monographs on the topic of white feminist preaching was written by Christine M. Smith in 1989. She uses the metaphor of 'weaving' to speak of preaching from feminist perspectives and notes that this is an image that emerged in a theme: 'recent literature of feminist theology, women's published sermons, feminist spirituality, and women's psychology' (Smith 1989, p. 7). From this metaphor, four principles of sermon design – proportion, balance, emphasis and rhythm – can be teased out (pp. 140–50). These principles illuminate the following insights. First, measuring women's experience matters (proportion), yet simply including experiences as an example in a sermon is insufficient. Rather, balance is required when preaching exposes sexism and emphasizes resilience and resistance. A feminist pattern is essentially like listening to one's own heartbeat, or its rhythm of life. Here, rhythm is a fundamental part of our innermost selves, finding one's call, taking an eschatological journey, going through one life from birth to death (Kim-Cragg 2021b, ch. 4).

Three years later, in 1992, another monograph came out. Carol M. Norén probed the identity of women as preachers, and named the challenges and the sensitivities involved when women are in the pulpit (Norén 1992, p. 11). In search of this vocational identity, the call to preach, she traces the nineteenth-century pioneering women preachers in the US, including Antoinette Brown, Jarena Lee and Phoebe Palmer. She uses published sources to analyse sermons and examine the work of proclamation, its homiletical theology (language and metaphor) and its biblical interpretation. Norén also employs interview research methods to hear experiences of women preachers that are close to their hearts in terms of claiming and exercising authority in relation to worship leadership. She describes how women preachers negotiate their preaching authority in relation to their vulnerability in the role. She also talks about how self-disclosure is part of sermonizing, sharing first-hand life stories while tackling issues related to attire, facial expression against gender stereotypes.

Four years later in 1996, another consequential feminist work was written by Lee McGee: *Wrestling with the Patriarchs: Retrieving Women's Voices in Preaching*. Her book employs an interdisciplinary methodology drawing on developmental and behavioral psychology. McGee studied the impact of the culture that silences women and girls in general and women preachers in particular. With the goal of reclaiming women's voices for the church, McGee provides practical exercises and strategies as well as pedagogical models that recognize unique gifts and styles of women preachers. These helpful strategies are deeply rooted in past experiences but orientated towards the future. As the subtitle of the book indicates, McGee's contribution lies in 'retrieving women's voices' in preaching. It assumes that women have unique voices and yet they have been lost in history and current culture. Here the very process of preaching is understood as giving voice.

Almost 20 years after McGee's book was published, the attention to women's voices in preaching was still needed. Mary Donovan Turner and Mary Lin Hudson's scholarship exploring the relationship between voice and preaching helped to further this agenda. Juxtaposing silence with voice, they examine voice as an emerging metaphor for human experience that conjures theological meanings and is helpful for articulating a homiletical voice for women in preaching. Turner and Hudson masterfully illuminate 'polyvalent dimensions' of the voice as they highlight multiple voices of women preachers and manifold insights of current homileticians gathered from the intentional conversation of their two study groups (Turner and Hudson 2014, p. xii). The work of either retrieving or finding the voice of women in preaching is ultimately redemptive work, and moves us towards a proclamation of the liberating word of God.

Here we can extend our look at feminist homiletical theory towards homiletical Christology. If Christian preaching is in service of proclaiming Jesus as Christ and saviour, then the saving act of Jesus is part of the work of homiletics. The relationship between preaching, Christology (soteriology) and women is complex. To Susan Bond, this relationship has been 'troubling' largely, though not entirely, because of sacrificial atonement theology, with a visceral expression of the blood of Jesus that saves people who believe in him and cleanses their sins (Bond 1999). She notes that her soteriological investigation was encouraged by the work of feminist homiletician Christine Smith (1992) and womanist theologian Jacqueline Grant (1989). Bond adamantly argues that the work of homiletics must be delivered from captivity to both narrowly defined homiletical strategies and methods of sermon construction *and* heavy reliance on biblical exegesis. Homiletics must belong to a theological enterprise by probing theological biases and providing various options for the congregation to develop theological thinking. It is also important to deepen theological literacy and christological reflection linked to lived experiences and religious practices. It should be noted that her work is highly theoretical and deploys a sophisticated systematic theology approach that examines various christologies. However, Bond underscores the importance of communal practices including ritual practices and interfaith practices derived from the lived experiences of people. She advocates a lived theology that informs and advances preaching.

Attention to the importance of communal practice from a feminist perspective was proposed by Lucy A. Rose two years earlier. Even if her monograph did not explicitly name a feminist agenda, Rose proposes an understanding of preaching as 'conversational', informed by a methodology that is 'non-hierarchical, heuristic, and communal' (Rose 1997, p. 3). Lifting up the agency of people in the pew within the preaching event is not a new idea in the twentieth century – explorations of this theme can be found one century earlier. In 1888, for example, Frances Willard made a case for this approach. She was promoting women's leadership in the church and warned that selective interpretation created a 'stereoscopic' way of reading the text. Perhaps she had preachers like MacArthur in mind! She argued that proper interpretation required a broader reading and the participation of women and men together in the work of interpretation (Willard 1888, p. 21).

The feminist preaching voice is more subtle and versatile than any instrument in an orchestra. This is good because it must simultaneously recall the past, address the present, and usher in the future (Sittler 1966). This voice is not just audible and temporal but also embodied and spatial. The tradition of testimonials offers us an important way to understand this. There are many homiletical books on feminist preaching that feature pioneering women who have exemplified testimony as a preaching tradition. These women go all the way back to Mary Magdalene and the women at the resurrection of Jesus. They also include Hildegard of Bingen and more contemporary examples such as Louisa Mariah Layman Woosley and Beverly Wildung Harrison (Florence 2007; Kim 2004; Turner and Hudson 2014).

Testimony understood as telling one's own story in the light of the gospel has been a way for women to authorize their own preaching ministry for centuries. This was particularly critical when the official ecclesial authority failed to acknowledge women as preachers. Despite this barrier, women preachers throughout the centuries were not afraid to stand and speak of the gospel as it related to their lives (Kim-Cragg 2021a). This self-disclosure incurs vulnerability but preachers' vulnerability is not counted as weakness. In fact, this testimony issues from self-love, self-affirmation, and the claiming of dignity, vocational identity, and integrity as a person whom God has claimed as God's own. Paradoxically, the power of testimony as a rhetorical homiletical device creates a counter-narrative to the dominant narrative that fuels misogyny and degrades women's body and women's sexuality, while downplaying women's call to preach and dismissing women's leadership.

As far as women's testimony is concerned, feminist preaching has always faced the harsh wind of patriarchy and swum against the current of sexist culture. Preaching associated with the ordination of women has been 'an uphill calling' (Zikmund et al. 1998). Virginia Woolf describes facing the patriarchal 'Angel in the House' whispering to women about what they are 'supposed' to be and do, depicting a kind of demonic force keeping women down (Woolf 1931). The voice of the angel in the European tradition is echoed in Asian cultures that perpetuate the so-called wisdom: 'She who knows, doesn't speak. She who speaks, doesn't know.' Voicelessness marks the identity of womanhood. Feminist preachers have had to refuse to listen to the dominant voice that suggests the silent woman as the 'ideal of womanhood'.

Homiletical Observations for the Future of Feminist Preaching

Beyond Essentializing Women and the Gender Binary Norm in Preaching

It is unhelpful, even dangerous in some cases, to essentialize woman as if all women have the same experience and have an unchanging and fixed identity. It is equally critical to move beyond the gender binary and biological realms for those of us engaging feminist discourse. Yet, the feminist movement is not over yet and there is still a need to prioritize women's basic rights: rights to their body, rights to speak, and rights to equal leadership (Bouriser 2021). Feminist approaches to preaching are not immune from the powerful and ongoing cultural forces of sexism and gender-based violence. In this regard, an operative definition of feminist preaching drawn from this study is a *liberative proclamatory movement to end patriarchy and sexism, as well as other forms of oppression, towards a full humanity for all*. To put it in Rebecca Chopp's language, 'When a woman stands to preach, proclamation leaves its ecclesial prison' (Chopp 1991, p. 4). To engage in feminist preaching is to set the prisoner free. That is the first observation.

Beyond Biblical Literalist Preaching

An interrogation of John MacArthur's sermon has unmasked the danger of preachers who continue to publicly impose silence on women in the church and adamantly oppose women's call to preach. This problematic stance is directly related to biblical literalism. Biblical literalist preaching superimposes a cultural script on the text rather than allows the text to speak for itself. It dismisses or ignores dissident voices within the text and, like women, refuses to let them speak. Feminist preaching must continue to oppose Bible-literalist preaching. Instead, feminist preaching opts for rigorous wrestling with the text. With the audacity that is hope of liberation, feminist preaching boldly and carefully exposes and engages disturbing and difficult stories embedded in scripture. At the same time, it invites people to discover the ancestors' wisdom and detect the sounds of suffering to which God is calling them to minister – including, but not limited to, the suffering of women. Scripture in feminist preaching is both handled as a paradox and riddled with ambiguity. The task of feminist preaching is to empower the community to know and bring their own questions about the intricacies and tensions within the text. That is the second observation.

Beyond Solo Preaching

Feminist approaches to preaching aim to be collective and communitarian. The feminist preaching voice is symphonic in character (Turner and Hudson 2014, p. 134). It is not a lone voice but that of the people (Hannan 2021). Its voice is not the totalitarian and authoritarian singular voice but the heterogenous, porous, ample voices that enable dissent and even empower scandalous voices to speak. In fact, the feminist preaching voice encourages not just the speaking voice but also the listening ear that is attentive to the voice of others in the community. In this sense, feminist preaching is mutually acoustic, proclaiming a listening God who hears people into speech (Turner and Hudson 2014, p. 106). That is the third observation.

Beyond Colonial, Classist and Racist Preaching Towards Intersectional Feminist Preaching

The final remark of John MacArthur's sermon unveiled the conquest agenda of preaching that continues today in the postcolonial era. This blunt and alarming proclamation shakes our dormant bodies and wakes our naive minds, speaking loud and clear to say that feminist preaching cannot be fully achieved without postcolonial scrutiny and decolonizing muscle work. As womanist criticism and womanist theology seek to remove the blindfold that prevents white feminism and liberation theology from beholding the full range and depth of colonial injustice, postcolonial criticism and other emerging disciplines, including queer studies and disability studies, offer indispensable insights for the liberative proclamatory movement to end patriarchy and sexism as well as other forms of oppression for full humanity in creation (Kim-Cragg 2021b).

Notes

1 https://www.youtube.com/watch?v=n8ncOf82ZJo&t=8s (1:12:39-42) (accessed 27.3.24).
2 https://www.youtube.com/watch?v=n8ncOf82ZJo&t=8s (1:13:43-45) (accessed 27.3.24).

Bibliography

Donna E. Allen, 2013, *Toward Womanist Homiletic: Katie Cannon, Alice Walker, and Emancipatory Proclamation*, New York: Peter Lang.
Mary Ann Beavis and HyeRan Kim-Cragg, 2017, *What Does the Bible Say? A Critical Conversation with Popular Culture in a Biblically Illiterate World*, Eugene, OR: Cascade.
L. Susan Bond, 1999, *Trouble with Jesus: Women, Christology, and Preaching*, St Louis, MO: Chalice.
Helen Bouriser (ed.), 2021, *Rowman and Littlefield Handbook of Women's Studies in Religion*, Lanham, MD: Rowman and Littlefield.
Valerie Bridgeman, 2014, 'Womanist Criticism', in Julia M. O'Brien (ed.), *The Oxford Encyclopedia of the Bible and Gender Studies*, Vol. 2, New York: Oxford University Press, pp. 431–9.
Teresa Fry Brown, 2003, *Weary Throats and New Song: Black Women Proclaiming God's Word*, Nashville, TN: Abingdon Press.
David Buttrick, 1987, *Homiletic: Moves and Structures*, Philadelphia, PA: Fortress Press.
Katie Geneva Cannon, 1993, 'Womanist Interpretation and Preaching in the Black Church', in Elisabeth Schüssler Fiorenza (ed.), *Searching the Scriptures: A Feminist Introduction*, New York: Crossroad, pp. 326–37.
Rebecca Chopp, 1991, *The Power to Speak*, New York: Crossroad.
Elaine Flake, 2007, *God in Her Midst: Preaching Healing to Wounded Women*, Valley Forge, PA: Judson Press.

Anna Carter Florence, 2007, *Preaching as Testimony*, Louisville, KY: Westminster John Knox Press.
Grace Church, John MacArthur, https://www.gracechurch.org/Leader/MacArthur/John (accessed 1.5.23).
Jacqueline Grant, 1989, *White Women's Christ and Black Women's Jesus: Feminist Christology and Womanist Response*, New York: Oxford University Press.
Shauna Hannan, 2021, *The Peoples' Sermon: Preaching as a Ministry of the Whole Congregation*, Minneapolis, MN: Fortress Press.
Kimberly P. Johnson, 2017, *The Womanist Preacher: Proclaiming Womanist Rhetoric from the Pulpit*, Lanham, MD: Lexington Books.
Eunjoo Mary Kim, 2004, *Women Preaching: Theology and Practice throughout the Ages*, Cleveland, OH: Pilgrim Press.
HyeRan Kim-Cragg, 2021a, 'Homiletical Changes and Preaching Leadership of Women in the Christian Church', in Helen Bouriser (ed.), *Rowman and Littlefield Handbook of Women's Studies in Religion*, Lanham, MD: Rowman and Littlefield.
HyeRan Kim-Cragg, 2021b, *Postcolonial Preaching: Creating a Ripple Effect*, Lanham, MD: Lexington Books.
John M. McClure, 2007, *Preaching Words: 144 Key Terms in Homiletics*. Louisville, KY: Westminster John Knox Press.
Lee McGee, 1996, *Wrestling with the Patriarchs: Retrieving Women's Voices in Preaching*, Nashville, TN: Abingdon.
Ella Pearson Mitchell (ed.), 1988, *Those Preaching Women: More Sermons by Black Women Preachers*, Vol. 2, Valley Forge, PA: Judson.
Carol M. Norén, 1992, *The Woman in the Pulpit*, Nashville, TN: Abingdon.
Lucy Atkinson Rose, 1997, *Sharing the Word: Preaching in the Roundtable Church*, Louisville, KY: Westminster John Knox Press.
Joseph Sittler, 1966, *The Anguish of Preaching*, Philadelphia, PA: Fortress Press.
Christine Smith, 1989, *Weaving the Sermon: Preaching in a Feminist Perspective*, Louisville, KY: Westminster John Knox Press.
Christine Smith, 1992, *Preaching as Weeping, Confession, and Resistance: Radical Responses to Radical Evil*, Louisville, KY: Westminster John Knox Press.
Lisa Thompson, 2018, *Ingenuity: Preaching as an Outsider.* Nashville, TN: Abingdon.
Mary Donovan Turner and Mary Lin Hudson, 2014, *Saved from Silence: Finding Women's Voice in Preaching*, St Louis, KY: Lucas Park.
Alice Walker, 1983, *In Search of Our Mothers' Gardens: Womanist Power*, San Diego, CA: Harcourt Brace Jovanovich.
Renita Weems, 2006, 'How Will Our Preaching Be Remembered? A Challenge to See the Bible from a Woman's Perspective', *The African American Pulpit* 9 (3), pp. 26–9.
Frances Willard, 1888, *Woman in the Pulpit*, Boston, MI: D. Lathrop.
Virginia Woolf, 1931, 'Professions for Women', https://www.wheelersburg.net/Downloads/Woolf.pdf (accessed 27.3.24).
Barbara Brown Zikmund, Adair T. Lummis, Patricia MeiYin Chang, 1998, *Clergy Women: An Uphill Calling*, Louisville, KY: Westminster John Knox Press.

19

Vocation: Listening, Persistence and the Hard Work within the Church

KERRIE HANDASYDE

Glory Boughton came back home to Gilead, hill of testimony, not to preach but to wait on her dying father, her older brother and, with the kind of resignation that makes a reader weep, her brother's son. In Marilynne Robinson's novel, *Home*, Glory imagined that if she'd not been born a woman, she might have been ordained. As a child, her older sister had 'told her that clergy were only and always men, excepting Aimee Semple McPherson, who proved the rule. But she knew how things were before she was told.' The church and community mediated the voice of God, dispelling unreasonableness. Given her godly small-town surroundings, her own listening was not strictly necessary; Glory knew God's calling to ministry of the word would not come to her 'however pious, however beloved'. Instead, she would return to care for her father in his final years. Glory accepted the disconnect between her unacknowledged calling and the life she led. But, in her father's house, 'in the middle of the night, it was part of the loneliness she felt, as if the sense that everything could have been otherwise were a palpable darkness. Darkness visible' (Robinson 2008, p. 20). Voices from present and past centuries interceded against hope, and the 'darkness visible' of Milton's *Paradise Lost* captured her separation from the voice of God (Milton 1667, I.64).

Vocation as an occupation called into by God has always been socially scripted by gender, race, class and tradition. It has been situated too, dependent on the here-and-now of a particular place and a society's state of fixedness or flux. In effect, human expectations around vocation fill the air between God and community of faith, sometimes-often preventing listening in case God speaks out of the blue, as if hearing something unexpected might also be invitation into heresy, or indecency and scandal (as Pentecostal preacher Aimee Semple McPherson was accused). In most places and times, most habitations, acceptable vocations for women have been defined in terms of what is decent and that, in turn, has been defined in terms of what is natural or true – as if all else is distorted and false, as if women's vocations beyond the most habituated of expectations were shameful, monstrous even. In this stultifying decency, in the dusty clutter and claustrophobia of Glory's father's home, women's vocation is defined by gender. But with recognition of the cultural construction of womanhood came a shift out of essentialism, from being to becoming. And with becoming, all things are almost possible. In the flux, it is worth the listening.

This chapter examines theologies that variously limit and expand faithful vocation and, with it, proximity to God. It begins with the idea, so prevalent for so long, that simply being a woman narrowed vocation to one of two callings: marriage or religious orders. It examines how essentialism and evangelicalism combined to enlarge vocation within limits. It then looks at the shift in thinking that understood women might *become* rather than merely *be*; that tradition might be inscribed in ways that authorize hope. Writing and remembering women's vocations reinscribes the Christian story and shapes expectation. It touches on women's ordination literature – it is a genre all of its own – but, importantly if church is to be reimagined as it must be in a feminist ecclesiology and in the face of secularization, it explores responsiveness to vocation beyond ordination. Finally, it turns to consider (fret over, rail against) the move within the church that would see women's vocations revoked in favour of the repressive essentialist theology so benignly marketed as complementarianism and the move within society to commodify women, to market, sell and exploit. Vocation is entangled in tradition, theology, economy.

On Stasis

For centuries, women's vocations were narrowed to sex or no sex; childbearing or chastity; bride of man or bride of Christ. With gender as the determining characteristic of vocation came the notion that women shared one nature, one true womanhood that was pure and pious, subservient and domestic. Such essentialism overlooked the diverse realities of women's working lives in the home and beyond, as if women's workforce labour was not the majority experience (Fessenden 2002). It also failed to contain women's energies. In the nineteenth century, the vocation of motherhood expanded; women were authorized to extend moral maternalism into church women's organizations such as the Young Women's Christian Association and Woman's Christian Temperance Union. In evangelical associations, women took up temperance campaigning, working to temper men's alcohol consumption in the hope it might ameliorate men's violence and neglect towards women and children. They campaigned for legislative changes to protect women: for example, raising the age of consent and introducing women police officers (Warne 2017, p. 15). In Australia, where the suffrage debate was more focused on moral maternalism and less on rights as it was in the UK and US, women successfully campaigned for the vote on the grounds that they could be trusted at the polling booth to make more moral choices than men (Lake 1999, pp. 28–31). First-wave feminism built on the theology of true womanhood to extend women's domestic moral responsibility out into the wider world. Being a mother and 'help-meet' (Gen. 2.18 KJV) could be writ large; women could 'mother' a whole society. Maternalism opened the door to political existence, to being beyond the home while still in service to it.[1]

Maternalism was about individual and social morality, but it was also about the world of work. It made the raising of good citizens a civic duty and it strategically located goodness within the wider economic system but outside business. The feminization of the domestic sphere strategically sectioned off virtue, leaving the world of commerce and industry free to engage whatever vices were necessary for profit (Taylor 2016). In this reading, maternalism as an essentializing theology had vocational purpose for men as it contained religious morality to the home while men got on with business and its necessary evils. Moral formation took place at home, not at work, and women's motherly homely vocation was necessary for the religious justification of a capitalist industrialized economy.

Theologizing within the maternalist world view, American social gospel writer Vida Dutton Scudder reasoned that women's aptitude in domesticity and child-rearing had revolutionary possibilities within a new Christian socialist reality. Taking F. D. Maurice's sociality of the Trinity, she argued that the mutuality of the three-in-one God was reflected in the mutuality of women's domestic spaces. The 'cooperative method and spirit' that they modelled offered a pattern for a better society – one based on divine love rather than individualistic gain and personal advantage (Smith 1993, pp. 421–2). Supporting women textile workers in the 1912 Bread and Roses Strike in Lawrence, Massachusetts, and risking her own employment in the process, Scudder envisaged socio-economic restructure that would transform vocation for all (Scudder 1937). Sixty years later, her thought was echoed in Letty M. Russell's feminist ecclesiology of 'good housekeeping ... that responds to people's need for solidarity and care empowering them through a relationship of mutuality' (Russell 1987). Vocation, they hoped, might be realized in the context of a transformed society.

Russell and Scudder responded in part to the lack of a coherent Christian social reform agenda, and especially to evangelicalism's individualism and piecemeal activism. Evangelical pragmatism, urgency and zeal had enabled practical adjustments to the possibilities for women's vocations without significant attention to the restrictive theology of women. In the nineteenth century, evangelical missionary expansion, a lack of volunteer men and the assurance of women's 'essentially' maternal outlook combined to authorize women's missionary service at home and abroad. This brought significant new vocational opportunities for white Protestant women. Unmarried women could travel and work far from home, and the wives of male missionaries could participate in ministry beyond the scope of the local parish. But even as women entered professions in the early to mid twentieth century, white women missionaries lived within the church's essentialist gender theologies, and it was this vision they extended to Indigenous women. Women missionaries most often proselytized in their own westernized homes, inviting local women in to learn modern domestic science so that not only vocation but faith itself was gendered. Women missionaries effectively made pulpits out of domestic spaces and made women's domestic vocation sacred (Choi 2014). In the twentieth century, women missionaries in Pasifika nations, Australia and Aotearoa New Zealand assumed the only vocational education suited to Indigenous women was for the purposes of domestic science, mothercraft and, in racially stratified colonial encounter, mission to other Indigenous women (Raftery 2013, pp. 33–4).

The elevation of Christian motherhood had further consequences on the mission field. White women assumed that female expressions of faith would include conversion to western expressions of mothering as they often assumed Indigenous women were 'less feminine, less human and less spiritual' (Moreton-Robinson 2000, p. 24). In Australia and Canada, such assumptions justified women's support for the forcible removal of Indigenous girls from their mothers and their training in so-called feminine domestic skills (Jacobs 2009, p. 87). Even without child-removal practices, upskilling in scientific methods of housekeeping and modern ways of motherhood disrupted parental bonds and emphasized the subordination of wives to husbands while overlooking the important social role of sister in Polynesian and Melanesian societies (McDougall 2014).

Further, as Kwok Pui-lan writes, 'female missionaries often assumed a self-styled mothering role in their relationship with native Christians', even speaking of adults as their 'children' (Kwok 1996, p. 253). It was a long way from mutuality. Rarely, Indigenous women mothered the missionaries, as in the example of Emma Timbery and Retta Dixon. When Dixon, a young white faith missionary, was sent to the La Perouse mission south of Sydney in 1897, Timbery, a Dharawal-speaking woman, announced that she would be 'as a mother' to Dixon. It was a promise of 'affection, support and protection' and an assertion of 'seniority in age and status' consistent with Indigenous social norms (Cruickshank and Grimshaw 2019, p. 113). Eventually, ethnicity overtook 'age and status'. Dixon became Director of the Aborigines Inland Mission, and mother to all. When it came to the expansion of women's vocation, arguments from nature had racist consequences because racial discrimination was also authorized on the basis of 'nature'.

On Nature

The notion of spiritual motherhood, building on the older expression 'Mothers in Israel', which was heard in Quaker and Methodist circles, also aided the acceptance of women's preaching in the nineteenth century (Mack 1999, pp. 32, 35–6). Most nineteenth-century arguments for women's preaching chipped away at the limit, without challenging the fact, of natural womanhood, for undermining divinely ordered nature would leave a woman open to accusations of unnaturalness, and this was a transgression that would see her silenced. Women preachers instead subverted discourses of authority through the authority of scripture. Because evangelicalism insists the Bible must be plainly interpreted by every believer *and* is the inspired word, women asserted their equality through the authority of scripture, speaking in acts of pious duty to God the Father.

Evangelicalism provided an effective but 'paradoxical relationship ... to patriarchal discourse' (Krueger 1992, pp. 6–11). In 1837, Quaker abolitionist Sarah Grimke argued that women's inequality was a male distortion of God's intention in scripture but affirmed the domestic 'ordering of nature' (Grimke 1838, p. 49). In 1859, Catherine Booth reasoned that first-century customs regarding women were not synonymous with the nature of women:

> Many labour under a very great but common mistake, viz. that of confounding nature with custom. Use, or custom, makes things appear to us natural, which, in reality, are very unnatural; while, on the other

hand, novelty and rarity make very natural things appear strange and contrary to nature. (Booth 1859, p. 3)

Both these women used the Bible to enlarge the capacity of others to pursue preaching as vocation. In contrast, Elizabeth Cady Stanton's undermining of biblical authority in *The Woman's Bible* (1895) diminished her authority in the suffrage movement and saw her work silenced for decades (Mace 2009).

Owing to the internal contradictions of evangelicalism's discourse of authority, the 'very natural' preaching of women continued to be seen as a spectacularly 'strange' vocation. For another century after Booth, it was largely limited to working-class women and millennialist movements where the edges of decency were complicated by economics and urgency. In the twentieth century, as middle-class women responded to the call to preach, they found themselves asked to perform natural motherly womanhood in order to authorize the exceptionalism of being other or more than a mother, and stepping into the pulpit. For example, Winifred Kiek, ordained in 1927 as the first woman minister in a mainline Australian church, had to prove her credentials as a mother before she was accepted as a minister, inviting reporters into her tidy home in order that she speak with authority in the house of God (Handasyde 2021a, pp. 91–3).

Institutional governance, even in parts of the church where women were strong in number, also remained under the authority of men throughout this period. Given the proven skill of women in organizing and financial management of women's organizations in the nineteenth and twentieth centuries (Warne 2017, pp. 1–8), the male hold on church governance really speaks of theological commitment to women's oppression within the so-called divine order.

As women moved into theological education, essentialism continued to hold power. Georgia Harkness, having campaigned successfully for women's ordination in the Methodist Episcopal Church, and having taught at women's colleges for 15 years following her doctorate, was approached in 1940 to teach at Garrett Theological Seminary training men for ministry. A systematic theologian, she would replace the retiring professor of systematics. But, in deference to gender and that old dualism in which women were relegated to the practical and men elevated to the intellectual, a new title was created for her appointment: Professor of Applied Theology. She was the first woman appointed to teach at an American seminary, but systematic theology remained men's business (Handasyde 2021b, p. 47).

Harkness addressed the theological issues underlying injustice in her 1972, *Women in Church and Society*. Like Hatty Baker (1911), Elisabeth Schüssler Fiorenza (e.g., 1993) and Rosemary Radford Ruether (e.g., 1985) and a host of others writing on women's ordination throughout the twentieth century and beyond, Harkness outlined the biblical and historical precedents for women's ordination and a diversity of ministries, along with the current and particular obstacles to the fulfilment of vocation. They suggest where the narrative, if told differently, might lead to another ending in which women are liberated and transformation is possible. These patterns in ordination literature reveal where women see that authority lies. The evidence would suggest that retelling the story is important, but more is required.

Harkness notes that, apart from pastoral ministry, there are 'other forms of ministry open to women ... largely noncontroversial' but subordinate (Harkness 1972, p. 221). Schüssler Fiorenza resists advising women to pursue the 'lowest rung' of ministry and the ecclesiology of servanthood already internalized by women in a patriarchal society (1993, pp. 11, 23, 301). Oppression is evident in trivialization, vilification and silencing (p. 311), and these may be found within ordination as many women have discovered when sent to small parishes out of the way of power. Little wonder that many have called for faith communities just for women, where they can find their voice on the way (Ruether 1985; Slee 2004, p. 71).

Feminist vocational development, if it is to be more than training to keep up with the patriarchy, must match content with process. This applies whether vocation is in pastoral ministry, theological education, spiritual direction, leadership or countless other callings in the liminal space between human and divine. For this reason, space must be held, processes altered to be consistent with non-coercive ends, and women's formation valued not only for what it might offer an often graceless institution but for women's and God's own sake.

On Becoming

The lack of substantial and widespread movement in women's vocations while essentialism reigned confirms that arguments from nature – theologies of stasis – can only limit and contain. While first-wave feminism's organizing and missionary ventures brought change for some women, it served to bolster a theology of unchanging, true womanhood. This was practical, limited change in the service of theological and ontological stasis. However, the move from static 'being' towards responsive 'becoming' has been slow among women as they are conditioned to exist for men. As Simone de Beauvoir described in *The Second Sex* (1949), women are constructed within and for patriarchy.[2] This is why feminist theologies demand more than admission to previously male roles with all their patriarchal assumptions. Vocation – in all its forms, extending well beyond the pulpit – must be undertaken in ways that embody justice and solidarity and, resisting the institution of new barriers, responsiveness.

Responsive becoming, with all its vocational possibilities, has been actively resisted by the church. English theologian Kathleen Bliss, in work for the World Council of Churches on 'The Service and Status of Women in the Churches' (Bliss 1952), expressed frustration at the ongoing 'theoretical argument about what women can, may or ought to do. Such arguments quickly lead into the quagmire of discussing what woman is, as though she were a given and finalized collection of attributes and limitations.' In the quagmire, the very ground beneath our feet sinks away. The churches' preference for stasis, their insistence on women fulfilling their duties according to 'nature' for the sake of the preservation of a divinely ordered world, saw women leave the church in numbers. Theologians and sociologists call this exodus secularization, even though, beyond the church, many women continued to live within other expressions of spirituality, other forms of God-seeking and of vocation.

Christian vocation expands considerably with theologies of becoming, self-realization or journey. Developing in the twentieth century, the idea of becoming addresses human potentiality in change, transformational liberation in word and flesh. Women novelists were drawn to themes of vocation in the late nineteenth and early twentieth centuries, writing women's lives into possibility at a time when movement felt at last imaginable: Louisa May Alcott, Mary Anne Evans writing as George Eliot, Virginia Woolf, Stella Miles Franklin. It is no coincidence that these women authors write characters who write, who embody hope in word and flesh. Scudder, who wrote 16 books and over 150 articles, imagined women's vocation in *A Listener in Babel* (1903). Having found her own vocation in teaching, she hoped her students might have 'economic independence' and 'liberty to find untrammelled self-realization, such as I think women have never before found, in the arts and professions, in business life, even in marriage' (Scudder 1937, p. 388). The call to women's self-realization marked a wholly different way of thinking about women and vocation.

In *A Listener in Babel*, the young woman protagonist spends much of the novel in conversation, or overhearing on the edges as women must often do, around how to respond to the injustice that characterizes life in industrialized society; sacred vocation concerns justice. Then, having listened, she articulates how her vocation 'ministers to the common life of all' (Scudder 1903, p. 318). Vocational realization demands listening, naming, doing – and refusing those options that institute or perpetuate injustice. As Shelley Rambo notes in her discussion of theological writing as vocation:

> The process of writing becomes a way of incarnating words, of bridging words and Word, of refusing the 'wretched choices' often presented to us by our religious traditions. It is courageous work, in which the prohibitions and prescriptions about who can speak authoritatively about the Word are always present. (Rambo 2011, p. 51)

It seems a contradiction in terms, but living within tradition requires tenacious resistance to stasis. Resistance requires writing, speaking, theologically articulating.

Writing on a theology of becoming, Catherine Keller describes living courageously within movement:

> A theology of becoming negotiates its solidities, its solidarities, *within* the flux. It sketches not disorder but responsive, flexible and *therefore steadfast* forms of self-organization. We gain the courage of our connections. They might not hold. But in the grace of this rhythm and the *divining* of this love, the dark draws music. (Keller 2003, p. 216)

In this theology of becoming, we move towards God within 'the dark'. Living within the flux, binaries are destabilized. It is responsive, faithful connection that matters in this understanding of selfhood and, so, in the discerning of vocation. We divine courageously, listening for calling out of the blue and in the midst.

Vocation is heard and enacted in word-meets-flesh. We put aside, with Heather Walton, stories of vocation as otherworldly or of the heroic masculine soul who 'wrestles with his God, until he finally succumbs and agrees to speak' (Walton 2014, p. 19). These narratives of lonely withdrawals and battles make an idol of the self. This is not courage. Instead, stories of vocation need to be incarnational, and inscribed in 'material, communal, ecclesial, political contexts' (Walton 2014, p. 20).

On Courage

In the late twentieth century, as secularization took hold in western democracies, and women continued to leave the church, the institution ceded ground. Vocations within the church opened up for women in the wake of feminist theological persuasion and as the church recognized its need to change or die. Now, as western churches continue to decline in number, the ground women gained is inching back. Moving with the culture on gender (albeit tardily) did not advance the church's numbers and, in reaction to secularization, the institution is in retreat, no longer needing to perform its commitment to liberalism for the wider society. Large segments of the church are hunkering down in defence against the world: caring less now about who else might be lost in the process; losing courage for reform as the instinct for self-protection kicks in. Conservative strongholds are valorized.

Theologies of complementarianism seek to sacralize women's service to hegemonic masculinity in the church and the workplace.[3] They call on another notorious line from Milton: 'He for God only, she for God in him' (Milton 1667, IV.299). Despite many decades of feminist theology that makes the case for women's equality, complementarianism follows the ethos of the marketplace where women's labour is exploited and women's bodies are commodified like never before. Likewise, churches sell their spiritual wares, enculturated within an economy at odds with the *oikos* of God. The market is omnipotent, omniscient, omnipresent. It reaches its technologies into our homes and its assumptions into our minds. Darkness visible.

Staying within the church is hard work. Continuing to listen and persist with vocation within a tradition that has accorded women's subservience divine imprimatur is not for the faint-hearted; in the church's fixedness and its retreat, many have lost heart. Women's vocations have tested the limits of essentialist understandings, chipped away at the sacred roadblock of so-called natural womanhood, and written around the 'wretched choices' until calling is incarnated. Putting women's lives into words inscribes living tradition and that makes the exceptional more and more possible. It rewrites where and how we embody justice, solidarity and responsiveness; how we embody the sacred and its traditions. Theologies that resist stasis, reform strongholds, destabilize binaries, that find their solidarities 'within the flux', these bring us into divine proximity – and into hearing. Uncertainty breathes possibility even under louring skies; we listen in the dark and we 'pray with eyes wide open' (Slee 2004, p. 1).

Notes

1 During the writing of this paragraph, I hung out the household's washing. Like many women scholars, my research has been largely unpaid and I have had to fit vocation around contract or casual employment and home responsibilities.
2 During the writing of this paragraph, my husband found a tear in his work clothes and I caught myself offering to mend it before thinking better of it.
3 During the writing of this paragraph, I went out in the late afternoon to teach my teenage daughter to drive.

Bibliography

Hatty Baker, 1911, *Women in the Ministry*, London: C. W. Daniel.
Simon de Beauvoir, 1949, *The Second Sex*, Paris: Gallimard.
Kathleen Bliss, 1952, *The Service and Status of Women in the Churches*, London: SCM Press.
Catherine Booth, 1859, *Female Ministry, or Woman's Right to Preach the Gospel*, London: Morgan and Chase.
Hyaeweol Choi, 2014, 'The Missionary Home as a Pulpit: Domestic Paradoxes in Early Twentieth-Century Korea', in Hyaeweol Choi and Margaret Jolly (eds), *Divine Domesticities: Christian Paradoxes in Asia and the Pacific*, Canberra: Australian National University Press, ch. 1.
Joanna Cruickshank and Patricia Grimshaw, 2019, *White Women, Aboriginal Missions and Australian Settler Governments*, Leiden: Brill.
Tracy Fessenden, 2002, 'Gendering Religion', *Journal of Women's History* 14 (1), pp. 163–9.
Sarah Grimke, 1838, *Letters on the Equality of the Sexes and the Condition of Women*, Boston, MA: Isaac Knapp.
Kerrie Handasyde, 2021a, 'Mother, Preacher, Press: Women Ministers and the Negotiation of Authority, 1910–1933', in Kerrie Handasyde, Cathryn McKinney and Rebekah Pryor (eds), *Contemporary Feminist Theologies: Power, Authority, Love*, Abingdon: Routledge, pp. 88–99.
Kerrie Handasyde, 2021b, 'One Woman, Two Churches: Theologies of Women, 1920–1960', in Lisa Isherwood and Megan Clay (eds), *Women in Christianity in the Modern Age (1920–today)*, Abingdon: Routledge, pp. 32–52.
Georgia Harkness, 1972, *Women in Church and Society*, Nashville, TN: Abingdon.
Margaret D. Jacobs, 2009, *White Mother to a Dark Race: Settler Colonialism, Maternalism, and the Removal of Indigenous Children in the American West and Australia, 1880–1940*, Lincoln, NE: University of Nebraska Press.
Catherine Keller, 2003, *The Face of the Deep: A Theology of Becoming*, Florence, SC: Taylor & Francis.
Christine L. Krueger, 1992, *The Reader's Repentance: Women Preachers, Women Writers, and Nineteenth-Century Social Discourse*, Chicago, IL: University of Chicago Press.
Kwok Pui-Lan, 1996, 'The Image of the "White Lady": Gender and Race in Christian Mission', in Elisabeth Schüssler Fiorenza (ed.), *The Power of Naming:*

Concilium Reader in Feminist Liberation Theology, Maryknoll, NY: Orbis Books, pp. 250–8.

Marilyn Lake, 1999, *Getting Equal: A History of Australian Feminism*, St Leonards, New South Wales: Allen and Unwin.

Emily Mace, 2009, 'Feminist Forerunners and a Usable Past: A Historiography of Elizabeth Cady Stanton's *The Woman's Bible*', *Journal of Feminist Studies in Religion* 25 (2), pp. 5–23.

Phyllis Mack, 1999, 'Methodism and Motherhood', in Jane Shaw and Alan Kreider (eds), *Culture and the Nonconformist Tradition*, Cardiff: University of Wales Press.

Debra McDougall, 2014, '"Tired for nothing?": Women, Chiefs, and the Domestication of Customary Authority in Solomon Islands', in Hyaeweol Choi and Margaret Jolly (eds), *Divine Domesticities: Christian Paradoxes in Asia and the Pacific*, Canberra: Australian National University Press, ch. 7.

John Milton, [1667], 'Paradise Lost', in *The Poetical Works of John Milton*, ed. William Michael Rosetti, New York and Melbourne: Ward, Lock and Co., n.d.

Aileen Moreton-Robinson, 2000, *Talkin' Up to the White Woman: Indigenous Women and Feminism*, St Lucia, Queensland: University of Queensland Press.

Judith Raftery, 2013, *Evangelisation and Social Betterment: Four Decades of Churches of Christ Aborigines Mission in Western Australia*, Mulgrave, Victoria: Australian Churches of Christ Historical Society.

Shelley Rambo, 2011, '"A Wretched Choice"? Evangelical Women and the Word', in Emily A. Holmes and Wendy Farley (eds), *Women, Writing, Theology: Transforming a Tradition of Exclusion*, Waco, TX: Baylor University Press, pp. 33–52.

Marilynne Robinson, 2008, *Home*, London: Virago Press.

Rosemary Radford Ruether, 1985, *Women-Church: Theology and Practice of Feminist Liturgical Communities*, San Francisco, CA: Harper and Row.

Letty M. Russell, 1987, 'Good Housekeeping', excerpted in Ann Loades (ed.), *Feminist Theology: A Reader*, London: SPCK, 1990, pp. 225–37.

Elisabeth Schüssler Fiorenza, 1993, *Discipleship of Equals: A Critical Feminist Ekklesia-logy of Liberation*, London: SCM Press.

Vida D. Scudder, 1903, *A Listener in Babel*, Boston, MA: Houghton, Mifflin and Co.

Vida D. Scudder, 1937, *On Journey*, Boston, MA: Dutton and Co.

Nicola Slee, 2004, *Praying Like a Woman*, London: SPCK.

Gary Scott Smith, 1993, 'Creating a Cooperative Commonwealth: Vida Scudder's Quest to Reconcile Christianity and Socialism, 1890–1920', *Anglican and Episcopal History* 62 (3), pp. 397–428.

Elizabeth Cady Stanton, ed., 1895, *The Woman's Bible*, New York: European Publishing Company.

Barbara Taylor, 2016 [1983], *Eve and the New Jerusalem: Socialism and Feminism in the Nineteenth Century*, London: Virago Press.

Heather Walton, 2014, *Writing Methods in Theological Reflection*, London: SCM Press.

Ellen Warne, 2017, *Agitate, Educate, Organise, Legislate: Protestant Women's Social Action in Post-Suffrage Australia*, Melbourne: Melbourne University Publishing.

20

Wording Prayer: Method and Praxis in Feminist Theologies

GAIL RAMSHAW

Over the last 50 years, many English-speaking Christian churches, although not all, have made considerable changes in the wording of their prayers. The first such wave occurred when translations were made from prior languages, from Latin to the vernacular and from archaic to modern English. These efforts brought about various kinds of change, since translations can never be precisely accurate, given that in both the original and the current languages, words carry their own connotations, and syntax contributes to meaning. The search for theologically appropriate vocabulary and pastorally successful rhetoric is continuously open to devout debate. One ongoing issue is whether prayer is essentially conservative – it worked last solstice, so let's try it again – or prophetic, asking God to overturn the social order. And where are you, dear reader, on such a continuum?

This chapter addresses the second wave of such changes in English-language worship resources: those instituted or energized by feminist interests, focusing on the full equality of women and men. A massive bibliography of such amended and innovative prayer exists. Some prayers aim to assist private devotions; some serve separatist assemblies of women; some are denominationally authorized for use after extensive review; some gently invite all the baptized into new insights; others urge radically new Christian practice. Some prayers are published by individuals, while some are anonymous contributions to church publications. Some texts rely on an *essentialist* view of sexual differentiation, in which males and females are by nature – in their essence – wholly different from each other. These texts *maximize* sexual difference. Others are *constructionists*, judging that since societies make up – construct – most gendered distinctions, these can be discarded or amended. Such resources *minimize* sexual differences. Some collections are explicitly *ecofeminist*, connecting women closely with nature and its devaluation in much of society. Recently most authors have laid aside the classic category *feminine*, a term that designated characteristics and behaviours especially appropriate to females. Some collections celebrate *women's experience*, while others resist such global commonality. Because the term feminism has been identified with white western women, some African Americans use instead the term womanism, and Latinas Mujeristas. Not all women are feminists; not all feminists are women. Furthermore, recent criticism of binary categories challenges the validity of many of these distinctions. Thus, the sizable library of materials does not lead to a ready collaboration within the Christian sisterhood in resolving the issues of prayer. Rather, there is now a wide prayer highway available demarcating the route between the feminist and God.

One lane on this highway is characterized by radical change in religious speech, with feminists advocating revolutionary innovation in the understanding of God and in the purpose of religious practice. Christian language and symbols have been replaced with interfaith speech and inventive rituals, which intend to strengthen women in their search for justice regardless of classic religious boundaries. Decades of experimentation have resulted in collections of expertly crafted texts and creative rituals (e.g., Neu 2020). Appropriately labelled as feminist rituals, these texts and rites attend to the situation of women more than to any historic Christian tradition. It would be helpful to Christians who study feminist prayer to know how much and by whom these materials are adopted or adapted for small or large gatherings of worship, and then to discuss what it is that makes any prayer Christian.

However, this essay will focus on another lane of that wide roadway, prayers intended for use by the baptized assembly in communal worship. Over the last 40 years, many Christian feminists have participated in denominational worship reforms, serving as scholars, authors, editors, musicians, committee members, denominational personnel, bishops, presiders and weekly churchgoers, all using and examining communal public prayer. Current results of this worldwide discussion are apparent in the most recent denominational printed and online worship texts and hymn collections. To update these materials, I here add my own (1) continuous conversation with Christian women and men in positions of leadership whose ministry requires that they visit a variety of Sunday worshipping assemblies; (2) regular engagement with editors of liturgical materials, at this time five of the most prominent being women; and (3) participation at gatherings of liturgical scholars who evaluate past and present worship resources. Some prayers that I have composed are part of this treasury, and I am continually informed by worshippers' responses to my work (Ramshaw 2017).[1]

This chapter can now proceed to describe ten recent feminist-inspired changes in the wording of prayer within at least some Christian assemblies. The first change occurred widely in secular society, with the following nine changes addressing uniquely Christian concerns.

1 Prayer must reject use of androcentric terminology for humankind

The earliest of these second-wave changes corresponded to a contentious but now normally accepted alteration in the regular speech in American English away from androcentrism. Such an updating of the English language is widely practised both outside and inside the church, although more commonly in the United States than in Britain. This change is evident in the recent ecumenical translation of the Nicene Creed, in which 'For us and for our salvation' replaces the earlier 'for us men and for our salvation' (*Praying Together* 1988), since the word 'men' is seen as no longer acceptable as a term that includes women.

Although it has been argued that the intention of words such as 'mankind', 'men' and 'man' is inclusive, recent decades have shown that the reception of these androcentric categories is in many cases exclusively male, and thus they must be replaced with genuinely generic terms. In prayer, God cannot be asked to bless mankind. Jesus is not lauded for 'becoming man'. Prayers ought not to intercede for 'the men who lead the nations'. However, questions remain. Since in many places around the world it is only women who carry water from the well to the home, is it appropriate to pray for the 'women' who lug water daily? Any reference in prayer to 'brothers' is now regularly altered to 'brothers and sisters', although even this binary labelling is now being questioned. Would the 1991 New Revised Standard Version of Galatians 1.2, in which *adelphoi* is rendered as 'members of God's family', be useful for the current updating of prayer?

2 Prayer ought to reduce the use of male titles for God

Some theologians maintain that following the practice of Jesus, Father be honoured as the only faithful way to address God. As well, some Christians claim that calling God Father is a critique, not an endorsement, of cultural patriarchy. Not only the continuing address to 'Our

Father' but also the petition 'lead us not into temptation' characterize the conservative retention of an early twentieth-century version of the Lord's Prayer by a majority of Christian assemblies (*Praying Together* 1988, p. 11). Often this prayer is introduced with the words 'in the prayer that Jesus taught'. However, some assemblies have amended this Father, for example, by addressing the prayer to Father-Mother or to Abba-Amma. It ought to be no surprise that Christians do not agree about what to do with this most fundamental prayer.

Yet there is no question that over the last several decades many Christian prayer resources have reduced, sometimes radically, address to God as Father. Commonly, the replacement is the word God, often supported with an appropriate adjective such as 'loving'. Parent has not caught on. For several decades there has been considerable discussion of whether Mother can replace or complement Father, and while some church resources have occasionally invoked God as Mother, it has not become a standard substitution. More common than Mother is address to God as mother or as being motherly. In English, capitalizing the first letter of a word elevates that noun to a name and is thus significant, at least on the printed page, in the wording of communal prayer. What is gained or lost by addressing God as Mother? Who gets to decide?

Other male titles are also in decline. Since the Revolutionary War, Christian prayers in the United States refer to God as King far less than in Britain, and monarchial address is rare in newly composed prayer and hymnody. How ought the several dozen references in the Psalms to God as *melek* be rendered? Options include King, Queen, Majesty, Monarch, Sovereign, Ruler; one suggestion is to allow the verb 'reign' to carry the image. Or is monarchical imagery obsolete and ought best to be rejected in our time? Prayers that some decades ago addressed God as President are now recognized as afflicted by what we might call category confusion, in which the rendering is not an adequate translation but a questionable substitution.

The term Lord has current social meaning in some countries, but none in others, and perhaps this contributes to the decision of how often to replace it. Some womanists defend the address to God as Lord as a way to deny that the white man is their lord. Furthermore, as throughout Christian history, it is often the case that in prayer Lord is a title of address to Jesus, rather than to the triune God or to God the Father, and so this classic way to honour Jesus with divine honorific is still common. Yet current resources use the term Lord far less than did previous Christian prayer. Liturgical questions remain: in the classic phrase 'The Lord be with you', who is the Lord?

There has been considerable search for names and titles of God that carry no male connotation. Despite considerable biblically and theologically sophisticated arguments to replace male titles with Sophia, this naming of God has not caught on in mainstream Christian prayer, perhaps because the name has not enough of a Christian handle for worshippers to grasp. Wisdom as a stand-alone title is rare, perhaps because it is heard as simply a common abstract noun, although some prayers have been able to cast the noun successfully as a title of address. Because the Hebrew *ruach* is a feminine gendered noun, some Christians have composed texts that render Spirit as a female title, for example by linking it with explicitly female activities, such as childbirth. Some prayers link God with Mother Earth as a way to connect God to the things of this earth. Whether and how to introduce such innovation in divine address in public worship is much debated: how much can communal prayer be new, and thus formative, and how much ought it to be standard and thus participatory?

3 Prayer ought to reduce or eliminate masculine pronouns for God

Since most prayer texts are cast in the grammatical second person, by addressing God as you, the issue of gendered divine pronouns arises mostly in the use of psalms as prayer. Because the three-year lectionaries appoint sections of the Psalms for each Sunday and festival, churches must decide which psalm translation offers the best text for the people's prayer. Finding increasing usage among American mainstream Protestants is a 2006 liturgical translation of the 150 psalms in which there are no masculine pronouns for God.[2] The mastery of the effort has meant that many users are wholly unaware of this linguistic change. Ought this alteration and its significance be highlighted?

The classic eucharistic prayer invokes the Spirit on the elements and the assembly. Here is one place where God may be asked to send the Spirit so that *she* can transform all things. Such usage requires supportive mystagogy, as worshippers might wonder who this female is, and perhaps this is why such usage is rare. The neologism *Godself*, appearing in theological writings, is heard more in seminary worship than in regular parish contexts. Although *they* is now being used with singular referents, it is not advisable for God, since the spectre of tri-theism always haunts Christianity. Recalling some medieval mystics, can the Godhead be *It*?

4 Prayer ought to regularize alternative trinitarian language

For a thousand years women have emphasized prayer to the Trinity. Catherine of Siena and Julian of Norwich are two of the eminent Christian women who proposed alternative trinitarian language. In her *Revelations of Divine Love*, Julian wrote, 'For where Jesus appeareth, the Blessed Trinity is understood, as I see it' (Julian of Norwich 1961, p. 51). That is, the God these women worshipped, the Jesus they invoked, was the Trinity. In our time these women have been joined by an impressive number of influential female theologians who see in the Trinity an antidote to patriarchal religion, since the revelation of a triune deity stresses relatedness and reciprocity, rather than solitary authoritarianism. Although Catherine LaCugna did not propose alternative address to God for prayer, she did suggest that the western practice of naming God in Godself not be separated from a central matter of faith: that God is for us, an emphasis more common in eastern prayer (LaCugna 1991). It is God in Godself that teaches that the Trinity is to be named Father, Son and Spirit, because in God's own self, the Father is the Father of the Son, and the Son is the Son of the Father. However, for the worshipper, for whom God is for us, it is likely that Father is assumed to be my Father, Father for us, not the Son's Father. Would this difference in theological emphasis assist our expansion of language for the Trinity in prayer? Would it remain doctrinally faithful?

Although widely used, naming God as Creator, Redeemer and Sustainer has received considerable theological criticism, and recent worship resources have proposed other ways to name God that maintain classic trinitarian doctrine without resource to male categories. Yet it is curious that formulations proposed by respected theologians have not become mainstream: for example, Mother, Lover and Friend (McFague 1987); Abba, Servant and Paraclete (Ramshaw 1986, pp. 491–8); Spirit-Sophia, Jesus-Sophia and Mother-Sophia (Johnson 1992); Fountain, Offspring and Wellspring (Duck 1991, p. 185); Source, Wellspring and Living Water (Cunningham 1998, pp. 17, 121, 231). Leaders of worship need to inquire whether academic proposals for God-language ought to have far more effect on the communal wording of prayer. If not, why not? Do we need deeper lay catechesis?

What has become common in prayer and hymnody is for the Trinity to be named God, Jesus Christ, and the Spirit. Here the mystery of the Trinity has been diminished by the hope for gender inclusivity. This language does open the door to Arianism, in which Jesus and the Spirit are not addressed as fully divine. Ought this classic heresy be a concern in our time? Another common trinitarian technique is to cite God three times, each time applying distinctive verbs or gerunds: thus, for example, God who creates, God who saves, God who restores. Trinitarian Christians see in the Aaronic blessing of Numbers 6 just such a formulation: 'God bless you and guard you. God's light shine upon you and be gracious to you. God's presence be with you and give you peace' (cf. Num. 6.23–27). Here the Christian interpretive principle assists worshippers to recognize the Trinity in texts in which it was not originally intended. How much ought this historic hermeneutic be maintained among us?

Recently some prayers address the Trinity, rather than was the traditional western practice, that communal prayer be addressed 'to the Father, through the Son, in the Spirit'. That three sections of a prayer are addressed in succession to the first, the second and the third Person of the Trinity, or that the entire prayer invokes the triune God, diminishes the sense that the God who really matters, who listens to our prayer, is the Father.

5 Prayer ought to introduce more female-friendly models of salvation

Some Christians judge that the substitutionary theory of atonement has burdened their faith not only with a Father and Son, but also with a picture of male-identified violence. They see references in prayer to God's punishment of Jesus as an inadequate way to depict salvation, and in recent decades prayers have experimented with more female-identified expressions of the faith. Thus, believers have been born anew from the waters of baptism. Describing the church as the family of God and as the household of faith is common, and the baptized life is likened to a journey accompanied by God. In the Old Testament readings that are proclaimed in the slowly increasing phenomenon of holding an Easter Vigil, salvation celebrated at Easter is like the creation of a new world, safety from the flood, release from sacrifice, liberation from bondage, feasting with divine wisdom, return to the homeland, deliverance by the fish, and companionship in the furnace. With the preferred Easter Gospel reading being from John 20, the eleventh-century theory of divine punitive justice is replaced with a narrative of the woman encountering resurrection in a garden, a woman then sent out to spread the word. According to this biblical proclamation, salvation is freedom not from the terrors of hell but from the sexist legacy of the Garden of Eden. For many feminist Christians, Mary renewed has been salvific. Rather than a meek girl who is revered for her obedience and childbearing, Mary is celebrated as a woman of power and companion of the oppressed. That worshippers can join Mary in her robust song of the Magnificat expresses salvation as God's gift of mercy and strength to all in need.

6 Prayer ought to increase the use of diverse metaphors for God

There has been an extraordinary increase of non-male imagery for God in worship texts. A dominant momentum behind this lush growth of divine imagery was the feminist criticism of the historically overwhelming description of God as Father, in many churches reinforced by wall paintings of God (oddly?) as a grandfather. Some historic texts have wondrously diverse imagery: for example, the eighth-century hymn 'Be thou my vision' describes God as light, wisdom, word, shelter, tower, power, inheritance, treasure, light, sun, vision and ruler. Many Christians now welcome the biblical image of Christ as the mother hen. Given that in the scriptures Rachel is a shepherd and Deborah is a judge, nearly all occupational titles ought to be received as gender neutral. A recent study of new worship resource texts lists some 50 metaphors for the triune God found in new hymns (Ramshaw 2019, pp. 67–72). Some are biblical, such as Ancient of Days; some anthropomorphic, such as friend and healer; some objective, such as daystar and harbour; and others innovative, such as mother and water of life. In one hymn, God is 'Beauty, ever ancient, ever new'. Yet another several dozen images are applied to Christ, who is flower, gateway, liberator, lover, servant, tree of life, wisdom.

The idea is that no single image of the divine is sufficient, and that each metaphor both complements and corrects other images. Future will tell to what degree such a substantial corpus of expansive imagery, regularly spoken and sung by the assembly, will diminish in believers' imagination a male depiction of God that is still common in the culture and, sad to say, even in some children's catechetical materials (for correctives to uninspired children's catechetical materials, see Wood 1992; Sasso 1994; Wehrheim 1998). A question remains: are the divine descriptors common in our prayer excessively nice, easy to receive, and thus finally inadequate to envision God?

An additional technique found in some recent prayer is a meticulous pairing of the adjectives that accompany the address to God. Here the common use of synonyms, such as good and gracious God, is replaced with a surprising complexity: God is gracious and mysterious, or majestic and motherly, or merciful and just, a God of suffering and glory, a God beyond and within. In some prayers the traditional conclusion to prayer, naming Christ as Lord, is augmented into *through Jesus Christ, our Saviour and Lord*. The imagery is doubled: the name Jesus contrasts with the title Christ, with an endearing Saviour and an authoritative Lord enriching our prayer with divine complexity.

7 Prayer ought to include references to biblical and historical women

Thoughtful feminist critique of the *Common Lectionary* (1984) urged that more biblical stories of women should be included in the Sunday readings. This did occur in the *Revised Common Lectionary* (1992),[3] which proclaims many more women than was historically the case. In some cases, the replacement reflects recent biblical studies. For example, at the Easter Vigil, the song of Moses (Ex. 15.1), which served to conclude the narrative of the crossing of the Red Sea, has been replaced with the more ancient song of Miriam, leading the women's dance (Ex. 15.20–21). Narratives about women in the early church are now read from Acts during the Sundays of Easter. As a result of these biblical readings, the names of women are heard also in communal prayer, with phrases such as God of Sarah or God of Dorcas, setting women into worshippers' imaginations. Many new hymns include references to biblical women. During this period, Mary Magdalene, who had been honoured in the early church as the apostle to the apostles, was decriminalized: the practice of describing her as a reformed prostitute was recognized as a catechetical device perpetrated by Pope Gregory I that ought now to be relegated to ecclesiastical museums, the result being current references in prayer to her as a faithful follower of Christ and an apostle of the resurrection.

The interest among Protestants in a restored or wholly new commemoration of post-biblical saints also led to more women's names being spoken in worship, with women of all ages, nationalities, occupations and talents included. The voluminous library of women's biographies ended a historic pattern of identifying women with either giving birth or remaining virgin. Current lists of holy women who are remembered in prayer raise up every kind of baptized female, in hopes of deepening Christian imagination about the options of faithful living.

8 The inherited corpus of prayer texts and hymns must be edited and retranslated to ensure inclusivity

If items 1–7 on this list haven't given Christians enough topics for debate, there remains the issue of continued use of beloved texts that are now viewed as sexist. How often ought even Christmas carols be recast, so that it is not 'Christian men', but 'Christian friends' who are rejoicing? When is memory more important than inclusive speech? How can we serve both the elderly and the children? Many beloved hymns describe God as King, solely because, in English, king rhymes with sing, the most egregious example of this being St Francis's Canticle of the Sun, the original of which never likened God to a king.[4] Editorial committees preparing updated collections of hymns have struggled valiantly when making these decisions, and not all committees come to similar conclusions. Some hymns that were composed in a language other than English are wholly retranslated, thus replacing usage that sounds archaic. Charles Wesley's original line to our 'Hark! the herald angels sing' was 'Hark! How all the welkin rings, Glory to the King of kings'. Over the centuries, many classic texts have been emended to provide more appropriate Christian prayers and praises, although worshippers may balk at emending lines that are now familiar or even beloved to them.

9 Churches must develop prayer texts for lament

Over the centuries, Christians spent considerable time lamenting, with most of their focus on personal sinfulness, and often not during Sunday worship. Even when social distress or ecological disaster was lamented, generally the scourge was viewed as divine punishment for sin, thus offering more occasion for confession of sin. But in recent decades many Christians have called for broader texts of lament, indeed after 9/11 asking why such laments were not readily available.

From their start, Christian feminists have engaged in lament. Early feminist lament texts grieved that males ignored most of the women cited in scripture and discounted the presence of the females gathered in worship. Feminist Christians held up before God the unending suffering of the world's women, not only those in the pews but also those housebound by their very bodies, those homeless across town, or trafficked across borders, or oppressed by totalitarian regimes, all those in misery across the oceans. With feminists modelling prayer for justice for those who are absent, those with conditions not usually cited publicly, and those with sorrows beyond the experience of the gathered group of the baptized, such prayers have inspired mainstream Christian resources to provide texts of lament for assembly use. How is such lament framed so that it functions as genuinely participatory prayer, even for those believers who do not share a passion for the issues?

In facing the lot of countless of the world's women, feminist prayer has challenged the practice of readily praising God as good and omnipotent. Genuine lament requires an altered vocabulary when addressing the God whose seeming lack of power over injustice challenges the faith of the baptized. Is God perhaps of infinite mystery, or of only faithful comfort? Should we more often join with Job to shout to God our discontent and misery?

10 Prayers traditionally spoken by a solo minister ought to include the voices of the assembly

In an American worship resource, the 1941 *Lutheran Hymnal*, the General Prayer, intended for all assemblies every Sunday and spoken aloud by the male pastor, was 565 words long, besides including a rubric for adding 'special supplications' (pp. 23–4). This comprehensive prayer was in many ways excellent, but no current worship resources propose that such a lengthy prayer be spoken by a single male voice. Feminists have from their beginnings modelled shared prayer around the circle or texts with interspersed responses by all those present. Giving many participants a voice embodied the hope for shared leadership and cooperative endeavours.

A simple way to provide for shared voices, common now in many denominations, is the use of the litany, in which a cue line prompts the assembly to repeat a phrase. Sometimes the length of the phrase requires a printed text. However, given that now presiders face the people, it may be that the tone of voice of the minister or the minister's welcoming hand gesture invites the assembly to repeat a line. Another technique to welcome diverse voices is for assemblies to train lay worshippers to compose the Sunday intercessions. In this practice, the prayers cannot be intensifications of the sermon, but instead offer to the assembly a different view of the world's needs from that of the preacher. Yet more: when is the use of communally improvised prayer liturgically wise? When, on the other hand, does it result in petitions that cannot unite the assembly?

It can be argued that many of the reforms advocated by the ecumenical liturgical movement are in fact responses to feminism. For example, worshippers and their chair arrangement replicate a circle, rather than long straight lines; prayer welcomes a multiplicity of voices of the assembly; silence is valued; worshippers, including the presider, face one another; texts reflect local realities and are composed locally; the church's calendar attends also to the natural cycles of the earth: all these can be seen as responding positively to the values of feminist Christianity. Thus, the changes in the wording of prayer ought not to surprise us, but rather confirm a general tendency in global Christianity that, all things being considered, at least to some extent women have arisen.

> O God,
> Author of our way,
> Word of our truth,
> Breath of our life,
> you create speech, you treasure silence.
> We lament with Hagar,
> we rejoice with Mary,
> and yet we stammer and stutter.
> O sweet Thesaurus of mercy,
> teach us to pray. (Ramshaw 2022)

Notes

1 In some denominational worship resources, the original author is not identified.

2 *Evangelical Lutheran Worship* (2006) and the Presbyterian *Book of Common Worship* (2018) include the same inclusive-language liturgical psalter, now being used also by some members of The Episcopal Church.

3 Consultation on Common Texts, *The Revised Common Lectionary*, 20th Anniversary Annotated Edition, Minneapolis, MN: Fortress Press, 2012.

4 For a better translation, see 'All Creatures, Worship God Most High', *Evangelical Lutheran Worship* #835.

Bibliography

Teresa Berger, 1999, *Women's Ways of Worship*, Collegeville, MN: Pueblo Press.
Book of Common Worship, 2018, Louisville, KY: Westminster John Knox Press.
Consultation on Common Texts, 1992, *The Revised Common Lectionary*, Minneapolis, MN: Fortress Press.
David S. Cunningham, 1998, *These Three are One: The Practice of Trinitarian Theology*, Malden, MA: Blackwell.
Ruth C. Duck, 1991, *Gender and the Name of God: The Trinitarian Baptismal Formula*, New York: Pilgrim Press.
Ruth Duck and Patricia Kastner, 1999, *Praising God: The Trinity in Christian Worship*, Louisville, KY: Westminster John Knox Press.
Evangelical Lutheran Worship, 2006, Minneapolis, MN: Augsburg Fortress.
Elizabeth A. Johnson, 1992, *She Who Is: The Mystery of God in Feminist Theological Discourse*, New York: Crossroad.
Julian of Norwich, 1961, *The Revelations of Divine Love of Julian of Norwich*, trans. James Walsh SJ, Trabuco Canyon, CA: Source Books.

The Lutheran Hymnal, 1941, Saint Louis, MO: Concordia Publishing House.
Catherine Mowry LaCugna, 1991, *God for Us: The Trinity and Christian Life*, San Francisco, CA: HarperCollins.
Sallie McFague, 1987, *Models of God: Theology for an Ecological, Nuclear Age*, Philadelphia, PA: Fortress Press.
Casey Miller and Kate Swift, 1976, *Words and Women: New Language in New Times*, New York: Harper Collins.
Janet Morley, 1988, *All Desires Known*, London: SPCK.
Diann L. Neu, 2020, *Stirring Waters: Feminist Liturgies for Justice*, Collegeville, MN: Liturgical Press.
Suzanne Noffke OP (ed.), 1983, *The Prayers of Catherine of Siena*, New York: Paulist Press.
Praying Together, 1988, English Language Liturgical Consultation.
Marjorie Procter-Smith, 1995, *Praying with Our Eyes Open: Engendering Feminist Liturgical Prayer*, Nashville, TN: Abingdon.
Gail Ramshaw, 1986, 'Naming the Trinity: Orthodoxy and Inclusivity', *Worship* 60 (November), pp. 491–8.
Gail Ramshaw, 1995, *God Beyond Gender: Feminist Christian God-Language*, Minneapolis, MN: Fortress Press.
Gail Ramshaw, 1996, *Liturgical Language: Keeping It Metaphoric, Making It Inclusive*. Collegeville, MN: Liturgical Press.
Gail Ramshaw, 2016, *Praying for the Whole World: A Handbook for Intercessors*, Minneapolis, MN: Augsburg Fortress.
Gail Ramshaw, 2017, *Pray, Praise, and Give Thanks: A Collection of Litanies, Laments, and Thanksgivings at Font and Table*, Minneapolis, MN: Augsburg Fortress.
Gail Ramshaw, 2019, 'Worshiping with Figures of Speech', in Stephen Burns and Bryan Cones (eds), *Fully Conscious, Fully Active: Essays in Honor of Gabe Huck*, Chicago, IL: Liturgy Training Publications, pp. 67–72.
Gail Ramshaw, 2022, *Blessing and Beseeching: Seventy Prayers Inspired by Scripture*, Minneapolis MN: Fortress Press.
Debra Rienstra and Ron Rienstra, 2009, *Worship Words: Discipling Language and Faithful Ministry*, Grand Rapids, MI: Baker Academic.
Rosemary Radford Ruether, 1983, *Sexism and God-Talk: Toward a Feminist Theology*, Boston, MA: Beacon Press.
Sandy Eisenberg Sasso, 1994, *In God's Name*, Woodstock, VT: Jewish Lights Publishing.
Mary Kathleen Speegle Schmitt, 1993, *Seasons of the Feminine Divine: Christian Feminist Prayers for the Liturgical Cycle*, New York: Crossroad.
Carol Wehrheim, 1998, *God Is Our Home*, Cleveland, OH: United Church Press.
Delores S. Williams, 1993, *Sisters in the Wilderness: The Challenge of Womanist God-Talk*, Maryknoll, NY: Orbis Books.
Douglas Wood, 1992, *Old Turtle*, Duluth, MN: Pfeifer-Hamilton Publishers.
Brian Wren, 1989, *What Language Shall I Borrow? God-Talk in Worship: A Male Response to Feminist Theology*, New York: Crossroad.

21

From a Thursday to a Sunday

ANNE ELVEY

When Holy Week in the Roman Catholic liturgical calendar came around in 2023, I felt grief for a lost church. My loss of church came in stages, first as a consequence of the actions of my partner, two friends and I as whistleblowers on a priest abusing children in our parish in the 1990s and later in the wake of the Royal Commission Report into Institutional Responses to Child Sexual Abuse published in 2017. Where survivors, their families, advocates and whistleblowers might have expected a public expression of repentance, compassion and support from Roman Catholic church leaders, after the report their response was on the whole defensive or muted. The poverty of ecclesial response coincides with what Dorothy Lee (2019) calls in this context 'the idolatry of maleness' which accompanies a Roman Catholic failure to recognize baptized women as potential candidates for ordination. The recurring impetus to avoid 'scandal' and a strange ecclesial legitimation of silence, moreover, feed into the misuse of the important concept of sacrament so that its power to affirm the connection between matter and spirit functions instead to hide real suffering.[1]

As a whistleblower, I regretted the length of time we took to act. But we did act and our actions meant we lost a community to which we were committed in a way that for me at least was irreplaceable. Alongside the experience of loss, and the exercises of power that surround it, is my understanding of my own embeddedness in wider abuses of power and privilege, especially in relation to Indigenous peoples and my inheritance as a descendant of the colonizers in what is an ongoing invasion of Country. Country is an Aboriginal English term for the lands on which Indigenous peoples have lived for well over 60,000 years; for example, where I live is Boonwurrung Country. Together with this recognition, I hold a commitment to ecological integrity, in large part learned from Aboriginal people and dovetailing with ecological feminist thinking and practice.

Further, my love of the ceremonies of the Easter Triduum, their heightened use of symbol and a liturgy that extends across days, feed my sense of a kind of 'material sacred' that informs poetic speech among other things (Elvey 2022b, pp. 45–50). But as the idolatry of maleness and threads of supercessionism and triumphalism continue in the practice of these ceremonies in mainstream Roman Catholic parishes, I cannot participate. Feeling the sorrow of this spiritual strike in Holy Week 2023, I drafted a series of poetic meditations that draw on the stories and symbols of the Easter Triduum (including the sometimes-forgotten Saturday). My purpose is to reinterpret this rite from the perspective of a settler continuing to live on stolen land and in resistance to institutional failures in relation to child sexual abuse. I keep an ear to Earth as our planetary context, a source of grace in a time of ecclesial failures to mediate the sacred.

In these poetic meditations, I have chosen to use mostly lower case, especially for the first person singular pronoun, in order to step away from a colonizing 'I'. I have used capitals for just a few words including the names of days. In one place 'on a Thursday' refers to 'soul murder', a term recognizing that sexual abuse of children by clergy is also a form of spiritual abuse (Tom Doyle to Royal Commission, 'Case Study 50'; see McPhillips 2018, p. 235). The section 'on a Saturday' responds to the reality that, as colonizers themselves, white feminists are not yet sisters to many other women, including Indigenous women (Pattel-Gray 1995). The final section, 'on a Sunday', asks about resurrection from a post-church, Earth-centred perspective where the Earth itself suffers abuse, in particular from human elites, including the 'double death' of species extinction (Rose 2022, pp. 150–1).

From a Thursday to a Sunday

Easter Triduum 2023

1 on a Thursday

   this is what happened
   i don't know the whole story
   this happened
   they go on as if nothing happened

          this is what happened

          you enter
          a garden awaits
          you can meditate here & forget
          your complicity
          the way you betrayed
          Spirit & people & Country
          over & over

          do not forget

   i don't know the whole story
   this happened
   they go on as if nothing happened
   this is what happened

          i don't know the whole story

          someone took bread
          broken blessed bodied
          it beckons
          an old tale
          written in a child's becoming
          enticing

          remember

FROM A THURSDAY TO A SUNDAY

this happened
they go on as if nothing happened
this is what happened
i don't know the whole story

    this happened

    every day was Thursday
    every table was a rite
    every people gathered in hospitality
    was sacred muster
    repeated
    making it matter
    every campfire with damper & billy
    gum leaves smouldering

    do not forget

they go on as if nothing happened
this is what happened
i don't know the whole story
this happened

    they go on as if nothing happened

    who is hungry & who is fed
    reside
    in the sacrament
    every day
    the child's flesh held & trespassed
    soul murder
    communities undone
    under sign of the cross

    remember

this is what happened
i don't know the whole story
this happened
they go on as if nothing happened

who are they

    these men in white collars
    men wearing magenta caps
    men who celebrate the sacred rites
    including to exclude
    they settle for settling
    they sleep in blue stone
    after the meal
    a garden awaits them
    there is blood on the ground
    they are perhaps us

do not forget

they go on as if nothing happened
this happened
i don't know the whole story
this is what happened

    remember

2 on a Friday

this one Friday
solemns me
at the stations & the 3 o'clock
my body tied to story

the story is not just one man
executed by imperial state
but many persons they are
not only human persons

the walk through the last days
four tellings of the story
flow in my blood
long after faith has shifted

FROM A THURSDAY TO A SUNDAY

i am inside this day
this day is inside me
even in the stretched day
after a betraying church

i tire of jesus this
& jesus that
calvary is empty
if there is g-d with us now

they (g-d) have crawled
into a burrow
with a last furred
family of its kind

they are moments
too late for the
adult child whose
betrayal was unliveable

they are gone when
bystanders become
whistle-blowers
they let their old

names drip from
tongues protecting
perpetrators signing
on with empires

there is not one
place in this story
for me on a Friday
i find not to be

a day of play
while solemn
rites are steeped
with supersession

the moon hangs
bold & bright
Earth cries out
with all the living

& the dead
say the names
over & over
the ones you know

extinct hooded
imprisoned at ten-
years-old murdered
by a stolen call

    i am even yet
    the imperial daughter
    descended from a colonized
    people who became

    invaders too
    i am a distress
    of patriarchal denials
    i am a cloth

    in a woman's hand
    touching a bloodied
    face unable to
    unlive this day

    so i will go at 3pm
    to watch the solemn
    service with my
    mother on channel 31

    in mourning & in love
    my skin prickling
    with the wrongness
    of it all

FROM A THURSDAY TO A SUNDAY

3 on a Saturday

dear sister

i understand i have not
acted like a sister

i was in the crowd yesterday
& saw your son die

one of my grandfathers
was a roman

my grandmother
a spoil of war

i live in that minor villa over there
by chance i am

of the household
acknowledged daughter of the head

among the slaves we keep
are kin i do not own as mine

i have heard them talk
in whispers of your son

the father of the house
was generous & let them fill the crowd

they were tutored
in what they were to say

i noticed there were other women
with you

independent of their men
what's the story there

i do not mean to be impertinent
or disrespectful

but no doubt i am
i wanted to say i am sorry

i could have kept the people of the house
away not added to the voices

raised against your son
tomorrow there will be stranger tales

today it is silent
under the torn curtain of your temple

with ghosts rumbling in their graves
& the stone in place

to seal the tomb
i am sorry

what could a woman with slaves
do for your son

i am not free though i am free
can i acknowledge the kin

of my household
all of them

let them speak in their own voices
i am sorry

for your loss
i recognize my part in it

FROM A THURSDAY TO A SUNDAY

4 on a Sunday

an ocean is feeding plastic to fish & birds
finding its ways in surge & multiplicity
in answer to its own laws
the calamity for us of breaching ours

> i have been inside this night
> listening to the breath of wing & fur rustling
> outside in garden's dark

in the chaos of leaf & branch
the entwining tangle of
becoming i do not know

if being's yes
will be enough
of if beyond the end of Earth

the universe will also die
if it does
will another creativity be born

> if resurrection is a part of Earth
> it is not singular

for now the slow decay of flesh
& stone
becomes the stuff of ground

> in waste & wreck
> from coal & oil & refuse
> the doubling death of kind
>
> what gives us grace
> to listen for the yes
> that slants the story true

Note

1 The word 'scandal' and the expression of a desire to avoid scandal recur with disturbing frequency in the testimony of officials of the Roman Catholic church in Australia to the Royal Commission. On the problem of sacrament as I experience it, and how this might be reimagined, see, Anne Elvey (2022a).

Bibliography

Anne Elvey, 2022a, '"If I Say ...": Poetry "after God" in Times of Eco-social and Ecclesial Trauma', in Jason Goroncy and Rod Pattenden (eds), *Imagination in an Age of Crisis: Soundings from the Arts and Theology*, Eugene, OR: Pickwick, pp. 85–106.

Anne Elvey, 2022b, *Reading with Earth: Contributions of the New Materialism to an Ecological Feminist Hermeneutics*, London: Bloomsbury T&T Clark.

Final Report of the Royal Commission into Child Sexual Abuse, 2017, Vol. 16, Bk 2, Barton, ACT: Commonwealth of Australia, https://www.childabuseroyalcommission.gov.au/sites/default/files/final_report__volume_16_religious_institutions_book_2.pdf (accessed 27.5.23).

Dorothy Lee, 2019, 'Women priests could help the Catholic Church restore its integrity. It's time to embrace them', *Vox*, 11 June, https://vox.divinity.edu.au/opinion/women-priests-could-help-the-catholic-church-restore-its-integrity-its-time-to-embrace-them/ (accessed 2.6.23).

Kathleen McPhillips, 2018, '"Soul Murder": Investigating Spiritual Trauma at the Royal Commission', *Journal of Australian Studies* 42 (2), pp. 231–42.

Anne Pattel-Gray, 1995, 'Not Yet Tiddas: An Aboriginal Womanist Critique of Australian Church Feminism', in Maryanne Confoy, Dorothy A. Lee and Joan Nowotny (eds), *Freedom and Entrapment: Women Thinking Theology*, North Blackburn, Victoria: Collins Dove, pp. 165–92.

Deborah Bird Rose, 2022, *Shimmer: Flying Fox Exuberance in Worlds of Peril*, Edinburgh: Edinburgh University Press.

Royal Commission into Institutional Responses to Child Sexual Abuse, 'Case Study 50 Transcripts', 7 February 2017, Day 243, 24826, http://www.childabuseroyalcommission.gov.au/case-study/261be84b-bec0-4440-b294-57d3e7de1234/casestudy-50,-february-2017,-sydney (accessed 5.6.23).

Index of Names and Subjects

Abba 177, 260, 262
Aboriginal 270, *see also* Country, First Nations, and Indigenous
abuse xiii, xix, 81, 116, 122, 135–48, 192, 194, 197, 270–1
academia 19, 165, 170
 academentia 199
Althaus-Reid, M. xiv, xv, 47, 101, 105, 116, 117, 119, 123, 179, 188
animal rights 74, 82
ankles 222
Aotearoa New Zealand 248
Aquino, M. P. 18, 22, 24
armpits 101
assimilation 61
Australia xii, 9, 41, 169, 221, 247, 250
autonomy 44, 81, 89, 155–6

baptism 197, 225, 263
BDSM 122–34
Beattie, T. xiv, 167, 218, 220, 223
beauty xvii, 34–5, 78, 84, 101, 222, 264
bedroom xix, 132
betrayal xix, 139, 225
binary xx, 16, 21, 23, 36, 65, 97, 105, 119, 157, 179, 218, 220, 241, 258, 259

birthing 44, 120, 157, 184, 187, 188, 197, 235, 261, 265
Bliss, K. 252
Black xvii, 9, 10, 16, 20, 23, 46, 58–9, 61, 65, 93, 114, 163, 167, 172, 237
blood xxii, 31, 44, 47, 239, 274, 276
body xci, xciii, 88, 101–12, 120, 127, 128, 130, 157, 158, 178, 180, 185, 217–22, 228, 241, 274
 body of Christ x, xvii, xix, 37, 123, 137, 142
Brazil 7, 8, 70, 103
bread 97, 115, 178, 180, 272
breasts 222
Brock, R. N. 104, 108, 113, 119, 120, 176–7
brown 16, 19
Brown Douglas, K. 177
Buddhist/Buddhism 16, 73, 80, 115

Cady Stanton, E. 250
calendar xvii, 185, 267, 270
Canada 248
Catherine of Siena 262
children 3, 26, 38, 44, 77, 97, 116, 135, 142, 157, 189, 192, 197, 235, 247, 264, 266, 270, 271

China 7
chores 6
Chung, H. K. 30, 105, 177
Circle of Concerned African
   Women Theologians 12
cisgender xvii, 11
class 33, 57–61, 63, 66, 73, 87,
   90, 102, 120, 125, 154, 168,
   177, 237, 242–3, 245
  middle-class 10, 22, 106, 153,
   163, 166, 171, 250
  working-class 24, 250
Coakley, S. xv, 167–8
collaboration xvi, xviii, 43–53
colonization xxii, 13, 16, 30, 34,
   46, 93, 118, 195, 270–1
compost 90
consent xvi, xix, 16, 122–34,
   192, 247
conversation xvi, 18, 22, 31, 87,
   116, 138, 141, 157, 163, 183,
   239, 240, 258
Copeland, S. 47, 103, 105
country 270, 272
courage xvii
cross-cultural, xv, 73, 106
crucifixion 136, 178, 179
cyberspace 31, 33, 39
cyborg 37

Dalit 32
Daly, M. xii, xx, 88, 103, 113,
   165–6, 170, 178, 197–202,
   206–8
dangerous memories 161
dark xxii, 102, 245, 253, 254
decolonial 30, 107, 243, see also
   postcolonial
Democratic Republic of Congo 8
diaspora 18
dignity 43, 93, 96, 130, 156, 240

disability 34, 75, 93, 102, 106,
   107, 154, 172, 243
divorce 10, 185
doctrine xix, xx, xxi, 75, 78,
   113, 120, 152, 159, 163–5,
   175, 185, 198, 204–5, 208, 262

earth-centred 73, 271
Easter xxii, 123, 179, 263, 265,
   271
ecology xviii, 70–86, 94
Eden 263
Egypt 25, 228
enlarged feminism xv
essentialism xx, 22, 30, 63, 73,
   104, 196, 246, 250, 254, 267
Ethiopia 8
ethnicity 7, 10, 15, 58, 63, 73,
   75, 102, 105, 155, 249, see also
   race
eucharist 37, 123, 177, 180, 185,
   186, 188
 eucharistic prayer 261
expansive language xxi

face 109, 158, 172, 175, 218,
   225, 267, 276
fat 101–2, 106–8
father 35, 118, 180, 199
 God the Father 199, 259–61,
   263
First Nations 47, see also
   Aboriginal, country, indigenous
flourishing xvi, 13, 44, 47, 90,
   130, 178
fountain 221, 262
France 43, 228
Friend, God as 262
friendship 107, 108
fundamentalism xix, 78, 118

INDEX OF NAMES AND SUBJECTS

gaze 88, 95, 124, 144, 156, 191, 222, 225
Gebara, I. 47, 74, 102, 178
gender-fluid 16, 36
Germany 198, 203
glory 115, 264, 266
Gnanadason, A. 74, 177
goddess 21, 73, 80, 166, 194, 201, 219
grace 107, 124, 151, 194, 256, 271, 279
Grant, J. 167, 239
greenwashing xviii, 80
gun violence 77

Hampson, D. xv, 166, 202–6
healing 137, 139, 143–5, 203
health xiv, 4, 45, 63, 140
  World Health Organization 81, 135
help-meet 247
hermeneutic of suspicion xvii
heteronormativity xx, 106, 117, 170, 196
hierarchy 57, 132, 143, 167, 202, 224, 234, 236
Hindu/Hinduism 73, 80
Holy Saturday xx, 179, 271, 277
household 6, 38, 255, 277, 278
housing xiv, 62, 66

imago 119, 120, 130
incarnation xvii, xix, 101, 103–4, 108, 113, 114, 118, 176, 177, 180, 186, 188
indecent 31, 32–3, 39, 116
India 8, 11, 32
indigenous 15, 16, 20, 31, 172, 190, 195, 217, 219, 220, 226, 248, 270

inequality xvii, 4–7, 57–69, 115, 136, 249
instability 154, 230
intersectionality 12, 58, 63, 80, 154, *see also* class, ethnicity
intertextuality xix, 154
intimacy 42, 49, 51, 125, 130, 192, 201
Iran 81
Isasi-Diaz, A. M. 12, 22–4
Isherwood, L. xiv, xix, 47, 102, 105, 107–8, 177, 179
Italy 70

Japan 61
Jewish/Judaism 73, 80, 123, 177, 188, 207
Julian of Norwich 262

killing xiii, 176, 195
Korea 11, 31
Kwok, P.-L. 12, 30, 124, 177, 248
kyriarchy 127

labour 42, 47, 51, 72, 156, 246, 254
LaCugna, C. 166, 262
lament 137, 266–7
land 6, 15, 64, 88, 178, 270
  stolen land 271
Latina/x 15–29, 66, 258
lectionary 265
LGBTQIA+ 70, 77, 81, 139, *see also* queer
liberation xxi, xxii, 12, 22, 32, 33–4, 39, 72, 113, 124, 153, 156, 160, 183, 236, 242
liberation theology xvii, 11, 17, 24, 30, 46, 116, 165, 167, 177, 237, 243

Loades, A. xiv
lover, God as 262

machismo 20
marriage 120, 165, 185, 186, 192, 246, 252
Mary, mother of Jesus (Virgin Mary/Mother of God) xvi, 25, 101, 124, 183–96, 218, 219, 220–6, 227, 263–4, 268
Mary Magdalene 194, 226–7, 228, 229–30, 240, 263
masculinity xviii, 21, 87–101, 168, 254
master's house xx, 163, 168, 170, 172
mastery 88–93, 96, 168
McFague, S. 164, 262
menstruation 117, 180, 188
mercy xxi, 35, 264
  Thesaurus of Mercy, 268
metaphor 37, 39, 58, 137, 154, 158, 180, 189, 219, 221, 238, 264–5
Mexico 15, 18, 24, 190, 195
migration 15, 17, 31, 70, 105
Minjung 11
misogyny 73, 74, 103, 130, 159, 232, 241
Mother, God as 262
Mother Earth 219, 261, *see also* Pachamama
motherhood xx, 184, 186, 195, 246, 248, 249
Mujerista xvi, 1, 22–4, 166, 258

nationalism 62, 70–86
neoliberalism 57, 105, 127
Nigeria 8, 151

ocean 82, 266, 279

Oduyoye, M. 12, 105, 110

Pachamama xxi, 25, 217–19, 229, *see also* Mother Earth
pain xvii, 106, 123, 125, 136, 139, 142, 144, 155, 158, 179, 188, 235
Pakistan 81
Palestine 220
panentheism 202, 205, 208
paschal mystery xvi, xxi, *see also* crucifixion, Easter, Holy Saturday, and resurrection
Pasifika (Pacific Islands) 10, 12
patriarchy xx, xxii, 10, 74, 78, 91, 106, 127, 155, 163, 165, 170, 193, 200, 206, 232, 243, 251, 259
pay-gap xiii
Philippines xvii, 7, 32, 38
Phiri, I. A. 12
Poland 81
pornography 119
post-Christian 197–214
postcolonial 30–41, 73, 93, 160, 166, 242, *see also* decolonial
poverty xvii, 6, 12, 31, 46, 57–69, 73, 82, 108
power xviii, 11, 13, 21, 31, 35, 42, 44, 48, 50, 58, 59–61, 104, 106, 118–19, 124–5, 136, 153, 177, 194, 228, 264, 270
property 6, 10, 95
psychoanalysis 158
purity 126, 136, 221

queer xv, 11, 21, 31, 32–3, 47, 103, 113–21, 168, 179, 189, 227, 227, 229–30

INDEX OF NAMES AND SUBJECTS

race xx, 10, 15, 16, 57, 59, 61, 63, 65, 71, 75, 88, 102, 120, 125, 153, 169, 177, 237, 245, *see also* ethnicity
racism 20, 59, 63, 65, 67, 130, 139, 167, 172, 237
Ramshaw, G. xxi, 175
rape 10, 32, 122, 200
redemption 74, 114, 160, 178, 220, 236
repentance 137, 270
resurrection xx, 26, 44, 90, 96, 101, 137, 178–9, 223, 226, 240, 263, 265, 271, 279
Royal Commission 141, 270
Ruether, R. R. 72, 74, 104, 113, 166, 178, 251
Russia 7

sabbath 109
sacrament 37, 101, 151, 187, 200, 270, 273
salvation 25, 74, 107, 109, 114, 178, 186, 220, 221, 230, 259, 263–4
scandal 245, 270
seminary xiii, 250, 261
silence 12, 136, 142, 143, 156, 191, 194, 225, 234, 235, 236–7, 242, 267, 268, 276
Slee, N. xv, xvi, 176, 177–8, 180
slimming 108
Soelle, D. 165
Sophia xvii, 35, 37, 75, 261, 262
Soskice, J. M. xiii
soul murder, 271
Source, Wellspring, Living Water, God as 262
Spain 15, 24, 34, 70
spinning 204

Spirit (Holy Spirit) xxi, 26, 35, 37, 118, 168, 190, 193–4, 205, 221, 226, 234, 261, 262, 272
struggle xxi, 17, 20, 23, 96, 101, 153, 155–6, 172
supremacy 46, 77, 80
surgery, cosmetic 103, 105; transgender 119
symbiogenesis 51

tenderness 21, 178, 190, 191, 192
Teresa of Avila 123
terrorism 83
theological education xv, 3, 12, 250, 251
Theotokos 184, *see also* Mary, mother of Jesus
toilets 6
Tonstad, L. 168–9
toxicity 132
transgender 32, 105, 118, 126, 180
trauma xix, 90. 122, 135–6
Triduum xxii, 271, *see also* paschal mystery
Trinity 165, 166, 168, 184, 189, 200, 247, 262–3

ubuntu 11
Uganda 70
Ukraine 71
unholy trinity 177

vagina 188
Vatican II 188, 191
Verb, God as 201
virginity 182–6

war 15, 71, 142, 186, 236, 260, 277

water 6, 82, 104, 197, 221, 239, 262, 263
whistle-blowing 270, 275
whole story xxii, 180, 235, 272–3, 274
Williams, D. 166
womb 185, 187
workforce 5, 19, 246

World Council of Churches 252
wound 21, 94, 137, 145, 178
writing xvi, 151,
Writing the Body, xvi

ying-yang 36

Zimbabwe 160

www.ingramcontent.com/pod-product-compliance
Lightning Source LLC
Chambersburg PA
CBHW022034290426
44109CB00014B/857